Statistical Methods for
Quality Improvement

Statistical Methods for Quality Improvement

THOMAS P. RYAN

Department of Statistics
Temple University
Philadelphia, PA

WILEY

JOHN WILEY & SONS

New York • Chichester • Brisbane • Toronto • Singapore

Library of Congress Cataloging-in-Publication Data:

Ryan, Thomas P.
  Statistical methods for quality improvement/by Thomas P. Ryan.
    p.   cm.—(Wiley series in probability and mathematical
statistics)
  Bibliography: p.
  Includes index.
  ISBN 0-471-84337-7
  1. Quality control—Statistical methods.   2. Process control—
Statistical methods.   I. Title.   II. Series.
TS156.R9 1988   88-14230
658.5′62—dc19   CIP

Printed in the United States of America

10 9 8 7 6 5 4 3

To my parents

Preface

A moderate number of books have been written on the subject of statistical quality control, which in recent years has also been referred to as *statistical process control* (SPC). These range from books that contain only the basic control charts to books that also contain material on acceptance sampling and selected statistical methods such as regression and analysis of variance.

Statistical Methods for Quality Improvement was written in recognition of the fact that quality improvement requires the use of more than just control charts. In particular, it would be difficult to keep a particular process characteristic "in control" without some knowledge of the factors affecting that characteristic. Consequently, chapters 13–16 were written to provide insight into statistically designed experiments and related topics.

The first two chapters provide an overview of the use of statistics in quality improvement in the United States and Japan. Chapter 3 presents statistical distributions that are needed for the rest of the book, and also reviews basic concepts in probability and statistics. Basic control chart principles are discussed in Chapter 4, and Chapters 5, 6, 8, and 9 contain the material on the various control charts. This material has several unique features. In particular, there is some emphasis on cumulative sum (CUSUM) procedures, and an entire chapter (Chapter 9) is devoted to multivariate charts. Chapter 7 discusses the commonly used process capability indices and compares them. The bibliography of control chart applications at the end of Chapter 10 is another unique feature of the book.

Quality improvement practitioners are beginning to recognize what can be accomplished using statistical design of experiments, but progress has been slow. With this in mind, Chapter 13 was written to show what can be accomplished using experimental design principles.

In recent years there has been much interest and discussion regarding a set of statistical and nonstatistical tools referred to as *Taguchi methods*. These are critically examined in Chapter 14. Evolutionary Operation is presented in Chapter 15; Chapter 16 is an updated treatment of Analysis of Means. The latter is a valuable tool that allows nonstatisticians, in particular, to analyze data from designed experiments.

In general, there has been a conscious attempt to bring the reader up to date in regard to the various topics that are presented in each chapter. There was also a concerted effort to use simple heuristics and intuitive reasoning, rather than relying heavily upon mathematical and statistical formalism and symbolism. The control chart material, in particular, has also been written under the assumption that a sizable percentage of readers will have access to a computer for control charting.

Chapters 4–10 could be used for a one-semester course devoted exclusively to control charts, and Chapters 13–16 could form the core for a course on design of experiments. Short-course instructors will also find ample material from which to pick and choose.

A book of this type is the end product of the combined efforts of many people, even though the book has only one author. The architects of many of the statistical tools presented herein have indirectly contributed greatly to the quality of the book. In particular, Jim Lucas's work on cumulative sum procedures is presented in detail for the first time in a statistics book, and the same can be said for Frank Alt's work on multivariate charts. I have also contributed some new control chart procedures, which hopefully will be viewed as improvements on the standard procedures.

Much of the material in the book has been presented in industrial short courses and college courses; the feedback from some of the participants has been valuable. There are also a number of colleagues who have read parts of the manuscript and have made helpful suggestions. Those deserving particular mention are Johannes Ledolter, Frank Alt, Jon Cryer, and Jim Lucas. The contributions of the editorial reviewers are also appreciated, as is the work of Joy Klammer who typed most of the manuscript. Permission from MINITAB, INC. to use MINITAB for generating certain tables is also gratefully acknowledged, as is permission from SQC SYSTEMS, INC. to use SQCS in producing many of the control charts and CUSUM tabulations that are contained in the book. Permission from various publications to reproduce certain materials is also appreciated, as are the efforts of the editorial and production people at Wiley, especially Isabel Stein and Shirley Thomas. Lastly, I am very much indebted to my editor, Bea Shube, whose patience and steadfast support made writing the book a less arduous task than it could have been, particularly during trying times.

THOMAS P. RYAN

Iowa City, Iowa
October, 1988

Contents

PART II   CONTROL CHARTS AND PROCESS CAPABILITY

PART I

Fundamental Quality Control and Statistical Concepts

CHAPTER 1

Introduction

Before examining the ways in which statistical methods can be used in quality improvement work, it seems pertinent to determine whether the use of statistical methods is really necessary. But first we need to address the question "What is quality?" How do we know when we have it? Can we have too much quality? The "fitness for use" criterion is usually given in defining quality. Specifically, a quality product is defined as a product that meets the needs of the marketplace. Those needs are not likely to be static, however, and will certainly be a function of product quality. For example, if automakers build cars that are free from major repairs for 5 years, the marketplace is likely to accept this as a quality standard. However, if another automaker builds its cars in such a way that they will probably be trouble free for 7 years, the quality standard is likely to shift upward. This is what happened in the Western world as the marketplace discovered that Japanese products, in particular, are of high quality.

A company will know that it is producing high-quality products if those products satisfy the demands of the marketplace.

We could possibly have too much quality. What if we could build a car that would last for 50 years. Would anyone want to drive the same car for 50 years even if he or she lived long enough to do so? Obviously styles and tastes change. This is particularly true for high technology products that might be obsolete after a year or two. How long should a personal computer be built to last?

1.1 QUALITY COSTS

The answers to the questions above are related to the matter of quality costs. It is often stated that "quality doesn't cost, it pays." Much has been

3

written about quality costs; see, for example, Lundvall and Juran (1974) and Society of Automotive Engineers working paper #SP-512, "Effective Quality Cost Analysis System for Increased Profit and Productivity" (February 1982).

What is the real cost of a quality improvement program? That cost is impossible to determine precisely, since it would depend on the quality costs for a given time period without such a program as well as the costs of the program for the same time period. Obviously we cannot both have a program and not have a program at the same point in time, so the quality costs that would be present if the program were not in effect would have to be estimated from past data.

Such a comparison would not give the complete picture, however. Any view of quality costs that does not include the effect that a quality improvement program will have on sales is a myopic view of the subject. Should a supplier consider the cost of a statistical quality control program before deciding whether or not to institute such a program? The supplier may not have much choice if it is to remain a suplier. As a less extreme example, consider an industry that consists of 10 companies. If 2 of these companies implement a statistical quality control program and, as a result, the public soon perceives their products to be of higher quality than their competitors' products, should their competitors consider the cost of such a program before following suit? Definitely not, unless they can adequately predict the amount of lost sales and weigh that against the cost of the program.

Lost sales as a part of quality costs has received very little attention in the literature. It is based upon a highly subjective estimate as Schmidt and Jackson (1982) indicate, but it is a factor that must be considered. Bajaria (1982) considers the cost of quality from the consumer's perspective and concludes that "consumers are forcing industry to look at quality costs from different perspectives. Industries can benefit from well-developed statistical methods that can address this issue most effectively." Genichi Taguchi (see Chapter 14) has defined quality as the "cost to society."

Schmidt and Jackson (1982) define the cost of quality (COQ) as the cost of producing, finding, correcting, and preventing defects, and state that "the cost of product quality in American industry is typically 10 to 20 percent of the cost of sales," whereas the cost of quality in the Japanese automobile industry has been in the 2.5 to 4.0 percent range.

The following excerpt from Schmidt and Jackson (1982) deserves much thought.

> Given that COQ is 10 to 20 percent of sales rather than 2.5 to 4.0 percent and that it is a cost of having done something wrong, U.S. industry's cost

reduction/profit improvement programs have certainly been suboptimal in the near term. The long-term implications of this laxity have now manifested themselves as U.S. reputation for poor quality and relatively low product value, resulting in a reduced share of markets once totally dominated.

The reason for this misdirection can be understood within the framework of traditional American management. The cost of direct labor was easy to identify, easy to measure, and large. Therefore, labor cost reduction programs and goals were easy to establish and sell. Progress toward those goals was easy to monitor, and reporting success in this area was very rewarding for a manager. COQ, on the other hand, was not easy to define in total nor to measure. Since traditional methods identified only a small portion of the total, COQ was thought to be very small. These two ideas, that COQ was small and was not measurable, relegated active pursuit of COQ reduction programs and quality improvement programs to secondary status. The errors of our past strategy are now painfully clear.*

What more need be said? Travis (1983) indicates that the cost of quality must be faced and emphasized by American industry, but he is referring to the added cost of a statistical quality control program, not the cost of having poor quality. It is the latter with which we must be concerned.

1.2 QUALITY AND PRODUCTIVITY

What about other impediments to achieving high quality? One problem is the misconception of some managers that there is an inverse relationship between productivity and quality. Specifically, it is believed (by some) that steps taken to improve quality will simultaneously cause a reduction in productivity.

This issue has been addressed by a number of authors including Fuller (1986) who relates that managers at Hewlett–Packard began to realize several years ago that productivity rose measurably when nonconformities (i.e., product defects) were reduced. This increase was partly attributable to a reduction in rework that resulted from the reduction of nonconformities. Other significant gains resulted from the elimination of problems such as the late delivery of materials. These various problems contribute to what the author terms "complexity" in the workplace, and he discusses ways to eliminate complexity so as to free the worker for productive tasks. Other examples of increased productivity resulting from improved quality can be found in Chapter 1 of Deming (1982).

*Reprinted with permission © 1982 Society of Automotive Engineers, Inc.

1.3   THE NEED FOR STATISTICS

Although American firms have been run profitably without the aid of statistical methods, their products have not always been of the highest quality. (In this section and throughout the book the word "statistics" refers to methods for analyzing data, not just to data as would be found in financial records or accounting ledgers. These "statistics" have always been a part of business.)

When a particular make of automobile has a defect in workmanship that could render a car unsafe, a recall is initiated and is widely publicized. Therefore, serious quality problems in the automotive industry are often known by the general public, whereas defects in workmanship of a less serious nature are generally known only by individuals who either purchase that make of car or read consumer reports.

In other less visible industries the cost of poor quality products may be known (perhaps only vaguely) by middle and top management in each corporation, and might not be generally known by consumers. Warranty costs and costs due to waste can provide tangible evidence of the cost of poor quality, and in many companies these costs as a percentage of gross sales are sizable. Nevertheless, these costs have essentially been tolerated and accepted as part of the costs of doing business. There is now an intangible cost of poor quality that is facing many American businessmen: namely, the cost of losing a majority of its sales to foreign competitors, including Japan. The Japanese have used statistical methods extensively in quality improvement work for three decades, and this emphasis has given new meaning to the words "MADE IN JAPAN." Japan's transition from a country whose products were once considered to be of poor quality to a country that now has a reputation for producing products of very high quality is traced in Chapter 2.

It is unfortunate that American firms have begun to use statistics as a direct result of the threat from foreign competition instead of recognizing many years ago that statistics is an important business tool. Why has such recognition been so slow in coming? As one chief executive officer stated several years ago (Conway, 1981) "everything we have been taught...about running our businesses is wrong."

These thoughts have also been expressed by Dr. W. Edwards Deming, the noted American consultant who is as responsible as Japan for American firms turning to statistics. Dr. Deming, who served as Professor of Statistics at the Graduate School of Business Administration of New York University for several decades, has for many years claimed that American management needs to "adopt the new philosophy." Specifically, attention should be focused on quality and service rather than looking only at profits. See

Deming's fourteen points (Deming, 1986) and, in general, Chapters 2 and 3 of that book.

Tribus (1986) argues that since financial figures are measures of past performance, using them to run a company is similar to driving a car by relying upon the white (or yellow) line seen in the rear-view mirror.

1.4 THE USE OF STATISTICS IN VARIOUS COMPANIES

Of the 62 U.S. companies included in a survey reported by Peters and Waterman (1982), 42 were rated "excellent." These 42 companies stress statistics to widely varying degrees. The statistics group at Du Pont consists of more than 40 people, roughly one-third of whom possess a Ph.D.; some of their statisticians are among the best in the world. This statistics group plays a vital role in policy-making at Du Pont. It is important that statistics departments in industry be involved in the mainstream of the company's activities, rather than serving as just a support group that answers questions concerning the analysis of data whenever called upon to do so.

The statistics group at Eastman Kodak is also well known and consists of a number of highly renowned statisticians.

Although not included in the Peters and Waterman survey, Bell Labs also has top-notch statisticians, and during the 1920s had an employee who is considered to be the father of statistical quality control—Dr. Walter A. Shewhart.

The other companies that were rated "excellent" have used statistics to a lesser degree, and some have probably used statistics only in a very routine manner. In many companies this is rapidly changing, however. For example, Hewlett–Packard increased its number of statisticians from a few in 1982 to about 50 in 1988, and is now using statistics extensively.

Hundreds of smaller companies have begun using statistical methods in their manufacturing operations, but many have not done so voluntarily. They have made the transition because the companies they supply have forced them to do so.

It does very little good for a company to begin using statistical methods unless its suppliers do the same. The use of statistical methods will not help very much if a company receives materials of poor quality from its suppliers. Accordingly, Ford Motor Company has implemented a vendor certification program, and other companies are using similar programs. The basic idea is for suppliers to become "self-certifying" by developing a history of producing materials of high quality.

One company that has voluntarily embraced statistics is Nashua Corporation, a Fortune 500 company that is located in Nashua, New Hampshire.

Nashua began a company-wide statistics program after meeting with Dr. Deming in 1979. The following year Dr. Lloyd S. Nelson was hired to fill the newly created position of Director of Statistical Methods, and a training program to educate all of their workers in statistics was started shortly thereafter.

It is worth noting that Nashua's statistical training program differs greatly from the numerous short courses on statistical quality control that have recently been offered. These short courses typically last 2–5 days and are intended simply to introduce people to statistical concepts and statistical thinking. Such courses should not be thought of as substitutes for in-house courses that are generally less intense and that afford the worker a greater opportunity to see how statistics can be used in his or her particular job.

When Nashua began its training program in the fall of 1980, it offered a 10-session course in elementary statistics that consisted of a 1-hour weekly lecture and homework assignments. This is certainly preferable to offering 10 hours of instruction in a 2-day course. Nevertheless, short courses on statistics certainly have their place as many smaller companies do not have people who are qualified to teach statistics courses in-house.

It is important that industrial training programs in statistics be thoughtfully conceived and taught by competent personnel. Unfortunately, this has not always happened in the past. [See Deming (1986, p. 131) for an interesting commentary.]

1.5 EARLY USE OF STATISTICS FOR QUALITY IMPROVEMENT

It should thus be apparent that a large number of American firms have begun to recognize that statistics is indeed necessary. We must realize, however, that many industrial firms have used statistical methods in manufacturing for decades. The American Society for Quality Control (ASQC) was formed in 1946; it published the journal *Industrial Quality Control*, the first issue of which had appeared in July 1944. In 1969 the journal was essentially split into two publications—the *Journal of Quality Technology* and *Quality Progress*. The former contains technical articles whereas the latter contains less technical articles and also has news items. The early issues of *Industrial Quality Control* contained many interesting articles on how statistical procedures were being used in firms in various industries, whereas articles in the *Journal of Quality Technology* are oriented more toward the proper use of existing procedures as well as the introduction of new procedures. The Annual Quality Congress has been held every year since the inception of ASQC, and the proceedings of the meeting are published as the *ASQC Annual Quality Transactions*.

Other excellent sources of information include the Fall Technical Conference, which is jointly sponsored by ASQC and the American Statistical Association (ASA), the Ellis R. Ott conference, and the Annual Meetings of ASA.

There are also various "applied" statistics journals, which contain important articles relevant to industry, including *Technometrics*, published jointly by ASQC and ASA, and *Applied Statistics*, a British publication. [Readers interested in the historical development of statistical quality control in Great Britain are referred to Pearson (1973).]

1.6 STATISTICAL METHODS VERSUS INSPECTION

We have now established that some firms (although still a very small percentage) were using statistical methods during the 1940s, and that the percentage of such firms has increased greatly during the 1980s. However, we have not as yet addressed the question "Why use statistics?" Consider the two manufacturing processes illustrated in Figure 1.1.

The first manufacturing process essentially represents the way many companies have operated. There has been no attempt to control the quality of a product at each stage of production, nor has there been any attempt to determine what factors influence product quality. As the prominent industrial statistician Harold F. Dodge (1893–1976) once stated, "You cannot inspect quality into a product." The quality of an item has been determined by the time it reaches the final inspection stage. Thus, 100% final inspection, as has been routinely practiced in many companies both large and small, will not ensure good quality. Studies have shown that only about 80% of nonconforming units are detected during 100% final inspection, so not only is such inspection rather expensive, it is also not effective in preventing nonconforming units from reaching customers.

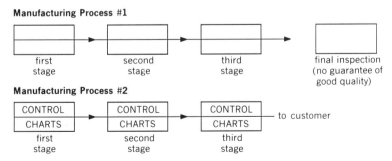

Figure 1.1 Two manufacturing processes.

What about using inspection at each stage of a manufacturing process? This would have the same weaknesses of 100% final inspection: nonconforming units would be undetected at each stage and the inspection would be too expensive. W. Edwards Deming has indicated that a company should use either 100% final inspection or no inspection, and that the former will generally be too expensive, although probably desirable for critical parts. Papadakis (1985) examines what he terms the "Deming Inspection Criterion." [See also Chapter 15 of Deming (1986).]

It is desirable to collect data at every stage of a production process and to analyze those data, as is shown for the second manufacturing process diagrammed in Figure 1.1. Here control charts are used at each stage of production, and other statistical techniques are used outside of and during production. If a process has been maintained in a state of statistical control at each stage of the process, there will theoretically be no need for final inspection. Granted, this is somewhat of an oversimplification, but the general idea is to "let the process do the talking," and use data obtained from the process to keep the process in a state of statistical control. Control charts are discussed in detail in Part II of this book, but it is important to understand that control charts alone are not sufficient to guarantee good quality. These are "listening" tools, which need to be supplemented with "conversational" statistical tools such as those presented in Part III. Included in "conversational tools" is the statistical design of experiments that can aid in designing a product that will be relatively insensitive to manufacturing variations, and variations in product usage (see Chapters 13 and 14).

In general, some statistical procedures are needed to control the variation in whatever is being measured. The use of robots in plants is reducing much of the variation that results from the use of human operators, but such usage can never be expected to completely eliminate variation at all stages of a production process.

There is also the matter of using statistics in all phases of a company's work, not just in plants. We live in a world in which the present generation of computer hardware and software allows us to collect and store vast amounts of data. It is important, however, that data be collected and stored in a manner that facilitates meaningful analysis of the data. Invoices, clerical errors, time lost due to illness, sales figures, and many other factors can be analyzed by statistical methods if good records are kept.

Administrative applications of control charts are discussed in Chapter 10. Such applications have been used extensively in Japan where company-wide quality control (CWQC) is practiced.

To the question "Why use statistics?" we can answer that virtually all human activity results in the production of data, and that unless such data are analyzed properly it is difficult to determine if such activity has been successful, and to determine what future actions should be taken. If a college basketball team hits only 36% of its field goals in a particular game, corrective action for future games might involve improving shot selection. Similarly, if nonconforming units can be traced primarily to a specific machine–operator combination, corrective action might consist of adjusting the machine, providing the operator with additional training, or perhaps assigning the operator to a different machine.

1.7 ACCEPTANCE SAMPLING

The reason inspection cannot be relied upon to ensure product quality was mentioned earlier in this chapter. Accordingly, we might now pose the question "Why use acceptance sampling?" since acceptance sampling plans are for inspection of part of an incoming or outgoing shipment with the intention of either accepting or rejecting an entire lot. Such plans are, in fact, based upon statistics and have indeed been used extensively in industry. Their use is declining, however, as firms are beginning to realize that control charts and other statistical methods should be used for *quality improvement*.

If a company is using acceptance sampling plans it should do so only temporarily, as acceptance sampling is simply a defensive measure for preventing product quality from deteriorating any further. It might thus be used for *quality control*, but not for *quality improvement*. The same message can be found in the acknowledged best reference on acceptance sampling, Schilling (1982, p. 5).

> Simultaneous use of acceptance quality control and process quality control should eventually lead to improvement in quality levels to the point that regular application of acceptance sampling is no longer needed.*

A somewhat stronger message is contained in Schilling (1983).

> Since we cannot "inspect quality into a product," acceptance sampling plans should always be set up to self-destruct in favor of such procedures as soon as conditions warrant.**

("Such procedures" refers to statistical process control procedures.) [See also Deming (1986, p. 133).] Thus, since acceptance sampling is temporal at

---

*© 1982 Marcel Dekker, Inc. Reprinted by permission.
**© 1983 American Society for Quality Control. Reprinted by permission.

best, space in this book that might have been used for acceptance sampling is devoted instead to statistical procedures that can and should be used on a continuing basis. Readers interested in acceptance sampling are referred to Schilling (1982).

SUMMARY

Statistical methods should be used to identify unusual variation and to pinpoint the causes of such variation, whether it be for a manufacturing process or for general business. The use of statistical methods should produce improvements in quality which, in turn, should result in increased productivity. The tools for accomplishing this are presented in Parts II and III.

REFERENCES*

Bajaria, H. J. (1982). The cost of quality—The consumer's perspective. In *Effective Quality Cost Analysis for Increased Profit and Productivity/SP-512*. Warrenton, PA: Society of Automotive Engineers, Inc.

Conway, W. E. (1981). Presentation to Ford Managers, May 15, 1981. (Videotape is designated as the "Nashua tape" and is available from Ford Motor Company.)

Deming, W. E. (1982). *Quality, Productivity, and Competitive Position*. Cambridge, MA: Massachusetts Institute of Technology, Center for Advanced Engineering Study.

Deming, W. E. (1986). *Out of the Crisis*. Cambridge, MA: Massachusetts Institute of Technology, Center for Advanced Engineering Study.

Fuller, F. T. (1986). Eliminating complexity from work: Improving productivity by enhancing quality. Report No. 17, Center for Quality and Productivity Improvement, University of Wisconsin–Madison.

Lundvall, D. M., and J. M. Juran (1974). Quality costs. In J. M. Juran, ed. *Quality Control Handbook*, 3rd ed. New York: McGraw-Hill.

Papadakis, E. P. (1985). The Deming inspection criterion for choosing zero or 100 percent inspection. *Journal of Quality Technology 17*(3): 121–127 (July).

Pearson, E. S. (1973). Some historical reflections on the introduction of statistical methods in industry. *The Statistician 22*(3): 165–179 (September).

Peters, T. J., and R. H. Waterman (1982). *In Search of Excellence*. New York: Harper & Row.

*The style of journal entries in this book is volume number (in italics), issue number (in parentheses), followed by page numbers.

Schilling, E. G. (1982). *Acceptance Sampling in Quality Control.* New York: Marcel Dekker.

Schilling, E. G. (1983). Two new ASQC acceptance sampling standards. *Quality Progress, 16*(3): 14–17 (March).

Schmidt, J. W., and J. F. Jackson (1982). Measuring the cost of product quality. In *Effective Quality Cost Analysis for Increased Profit and Productivity/SP-512.* Warrenton, PA: Society of Automotive Engineers, Inc.

Travis, L. L. (1983). Letter to the editor. *Quality Progress 16*(6): 5–6 (June).

Tribus, M. (1986). Testimony before the U.S. House of Representatives, Committee on Science and Technology, June 24, 1986.

CHAPTER 2

Japan's Approach to Quality Control

Several decades ago the words "MADE IN JAPAN" invariably meant that the merchandise on which they were imprinted was of poor quality; today products manufactured in Japan are considered to be of superior quality. How and when did this transition take place? What was the catalyst? What were the "tools" that were used?

2.1 DEMING'S VIEWS AND INFLUENCE

These questions can be answered as follows: the transitional period began in 1950; the catalyst was a series of lectures given by W. Edwards Deming; and the principal tool was statistics.

In 1949 Dr. Deming was invited to go to Japan to teach the Japanese something about statistical methods. (He previously visited Japan to help with their census and other matters in 1947 and 1948.) His first 8-day course in some fundamentals of the statistical control of quality began on July 10, 1950 in Tokyo with 220 engineers in attendance (600 had applied).

Several meetings with top management followed later that summer, and Japanese companies soon became committed to the goal of achieving high quality of manufactured products through the use of statistical methods. The Japanese were receptive to Deming's lectures since their companies were more or less "at the bottom looking up," with a strong need to improve product quality. On the other hand, American companies had been financially successful without the use of statistical methods, although not always "quality successful."

America has begun to listen (and hear), but American executives must realize that they must provide the impetus and continued support for a

14

statistical quality improvement program. It is naive to think that statistics can be used extensively and effectively in a company without the strong daily support of top management. Experience has indicated that such support is absolutely essential.

We should recognize, however, that statistics is not a panacea that can cure all the problems caused by poor management. There is growing acceptance of the statement made many years ago by Dr. Joseph M. Juran, the noted quality control consultant, that 85% of quality problems are caused by faulty systems (which are the responsibility of management), with the other 15% attributable to production workers. Workers certainly cannot be expected to produce high-quality products if machines are constantly in a state of disrepair.

In general, management must adhere to sound policies and procedures if the full value of a company-wide statistics program is to be realized. It is surprising that so many manufacturing companies (in the United States) are remiss in not providing training programs to enable workers to understand their jobs, and to understand how their jobs fit into the entire process.

Deming's views on the shortcomings of American management can be found in many places, including Chapter 2 of Deming (1986). In general, Deming claims that management (1) emphasizes short-term thinking and quarterly profits rather than long-term strategies, (2) is inadequately trained and does not possess an in-depth knowledge of the company, and (3) is looking for quick results.

Deming's view of Japanese management, however, was quite different when he addressed a group of leading Japanese executives on July 26, 1950. In reference to that talk Deming noted in the February 1981 issue of *Nation's Business*:

> I told them Japanese quality could be the best in the world instead of the worst. I was the only man in Japan then who believed that Japanese industry, with its magnificent work force, engineers and statisticians, and its unexcelled management, could do that. Many of them totally disagreed with me.*

Thus, management in Japan was ready for statistical training, whereas Deming believed that American management must be "transformed" to overcome its other (nonstatistical) shortcomings before statistical training programs could be initiated. See also Joiner (1985) for a similar view.

---

*Reprinted by permission from *Nation's Business*, February, 1981. Copyright 1981, U.S. Chamber of Commerce.

2.2   THE DEMING AWARD

Motivation is also an important factor. In 1950 Japanese industrialists knew that they had to improve product quality if they were to be successful in world markets. In the 1980s U.S. industrialists knew that they had to improve product quality to compete with the Japanese. What motivates the Japanese today? One answer is the Deming Prizes. The idea of awarding a prize to individuals and companies in recognition of their achievements in attaining high quality was first proposed by the late Ken-ichi Koyanagi in 1951 during his term as Executive Director of the Union of Japanese Scientists and Engineers (JUSE). There are actually two prizes, the Deming Prize and the Application Prize. The former is awarded to individuals who have made outstanding contributions to the theory or application of statistical quality control, or who have helped increase the use of statistical methods. The Application Prize actually consists of four prizes. The Application Prize is awarded to a large company; there is also the Small Enterprise Prize, the Division Prize, and the Factory Award. These prizes are awarded annually in recognition of great strides achieved toward attaining high quality. Firms that receive one of the four categories of the Application Prize automatically become eligible for the Japan QC Prize. This is awarded to firms that have continued to make great strides 5 years after receiving the Application Prize. (A National Quality Award was established in the United States in August 1987, with the award program to be handled by the Secretary of Commerce and the National Bureau of Standards.)

One would certainly expect that a Japanese company that works hard to win a coveted award would be more likely to have good quality than a company in any other country that does not have such a motivating factor. But has the Deming Prize and the other prizes really had *that* much effect on the Japanese quality of work? The best answer may be found in the words of Tatsua Itoh, a middle manager at Fuji Xerox: "Quality has become a religion, an obsession" (*The Wall Street Journal*, September 24, 1980, p. 44.) The following quote from the same article indicates that the competition is not restricted to the factory.

> Product quality has always been the main focus of the competition, but over time the concept has broadened to all aspects of a company's operations—products, sales, service, planning, even internal billing procedures.*

Most of the candidates for the awards now use company-wide quality control rather than limiting its use to the factory. It is also worth noting that the candidates put considerable effort into practicing for the competition.

The importance of company-wide quality control cannot be overemphasized. There is no reason why statistical and nonstatistical quality improvement techniques should be confined to the factory floor. (The use of statistical quality improvement procedures for administrative purposes is covered in Chapter 10.)

2.3 QUALITY CIRCLES

Another important Japanese innovation is the concept of quality circles. A quality circle is a group of employees, usually four to eight, who work together to solve quality problems. Quality circles became formalized in Japan in 1960 under the leadership of Dr. Kaoru Ishikawa, and have been used to some extent in the United States. Imitation may be the sincerest form of flattery, but the imitator is not always as successful as the originator. Such has been the case with quality circles. When people visit Japan to see how the Japanese operate, they invariably focus attention on what they can easily see—the size of a plant, the number of employees, the modernity of machines, the extent to which the workers appear industrious, etc. But the use of statistics in a plant may not be clearly visible on casual inspection. Consequently, company executives who have visited Japan have often overlooked the use of statistics. The omission of statistics from quality circles in the United States is the primary reason that many such circles have not been successful. Picture if you will a group of people sitting around a table discussing quality problems, but not having any data to indicate how serious the problems might be, when they began, or where they are occurring. It is difficult to imagine how such a scenario would result in the solution of very many problems.

Not only is the use of statistics in quality circles very important, but it is also quite important that quality circles be initiated by the workers who are to comprise the circles, not by management (unless the circle consists of management people). If circles for workers are formed by management, the workers are apt to receive the impression that management is blaming them for the problems, and it is thus the workers' responsibility to "get together and solve their problems." Quality circles must be spontaneously created by workers who see the need for group discussions, not formalized by management.

Just as the use of statistics should not be confined to the factory floor, quality circles should not be confined to workers on the factory floor. They can be profitably used at all levels of a company. It is particularly important for a company to have some quality circles that are composed of managerial people, since most quality problems are attributable to management.

2.4   JAPANESE COMPANIES IN AMERICA

It is easier to observe the industrial methods of the Japanese when they are nearby, rather than making such observations while in Japan. There are a number of Japanese companies in the United States, and one of the best known is Nissan Motor Manufacturing Corporation USA in Smyrna, Tennessee.

There are quite a few lessons that can be learned from the way Nissan operates. Although the vast majority of workers are American and the CEO is American, many of the company's operations are decidedly Japanese. These include a daily exercise program and the extensive use of robots in place of human labor in performing menial and boring jobs. Hundreds of robots have been used at Nissan.

Much has been written about the fact that Japanese workers receive relatively low wages. Although technicians at Nissan have averaged about 2–3 dollars less per hour than their UAW counterparts, they receive benefits (including bonuses twice a year) that at least partially offset the difference.

How do the workers feel about working for Nissan after having worked for some of Nissan's competitors? The following is a sampling of responses.

I took a $100-a-week pay cut to come here, but I think there is more of a future here. They gave me a lot of static when I left ... but I have no regrets. There were a lot of days that I'd hate to go to work there. The money was good but working there was no fun. It's a joy to come to work here.

. . .

I took the job here because I got tired of the humdrum attitude at .... It was like they were saying 'this is the way we've always done things, and this is the way we're going to do it.' There were a lot of good people at ..., but the way the system was set up hindered flexibility. I think we started on the right foot here in that we told people that our survival depends on all people working together.*

Their only objective is to build the best light truck in North America. As in a number of other Japanese and American companies, they use a demerit

*Reprinted with permission from *The Atlanta Journal* and *The Atlanta Constitution*, December 11, 1983.

system for nonconformities in which nonconformities of different degrees of seriousness are given differing numbers of demerits. Their goal has been to average fewer than 22 demerits per truck, which is the average of Nissan's sister plant in Kyushu, Japan. (Control charts for a demerit system are covered in Chapter 8.)

2.5   STATISTICAL TECHNIQUES

Since the Japanese have been so successful at achieving product quality and overall business quality, it might be tempting to simply adopt the statistical methods that they have used. We should resist that temptation, however, as there are a number of important statistical and computational tools that have not been used to any extent in Japan.

For example, control charts have been primarily maintained by hand rather than by computer, and multivariate charts (see Chapter 9) have not been generally used. I am not aware of any formal study to determine the statistical methods that have been used in Japanese industry, and the frequency of usage of each, but some indication is given by Kusaba (1981). He constructed a table that showed the number of times each of many statistical techniques appeared in presentations at QC Annual and Spring Conferences in Japan during 1970–1979. That table is reproduced here, with kind permission, as Table 2.1.

It is apparent from Table 2.1 that cause and effect diagrams, graphs, experimental designs, and Pareto diagrams are the statistical techniques that have been mentioned most frequently. All of these are covered in the present book, in addition to most of the other techniques listed in the table.

2.6   CAUSE AND EFFECT DIAGRAM

The cause and effect diagram was introduced in Japan by Professor Kaoru Ishikawa of the University of Tokyo in 1943. For that reason it is sometimes called an Ishikawa diagram; it has also been called a fishbone chart. The reason for the latter name should be apparent from Figure 2.1.

In Figure 2.1, vibration is the effect that is to be reduced, and there are four possible causes that are to be investigated. This is an example of a "dispersion analysis type" of cause and effect diagram. The other two major types are production process classification type, and cause enumeration type. The production process classification type is set up in accordance with the flow of the production process, whereas the cause enumeration type is

Table 2.1 Statistical Techniques Used in Presentations at Japanese QC Annual and Spring Conferences, 1970–1979

Technique	1970	1971	1972	1973	1974	1975	1976	1977	1978	1979	Total
Elementary											
Cause and effect diagram	28	16	15	18	19	16	23	36	30	73	236
Graph	29	16	19	18	19	15	26	36	26	20	224
Pareto diagram	6	7	10	9	12	2	10	22	17	21	116
Histogram	5	—	2	5	4	5	16	12	14	15	78
Control chart	7	4	1	8	5	5	8	12	8	15	73
Scatter diagram	3	—	—	7	—	3	4	12	15	13	57
Nomogram	—	—	—	—	1	2	4	—	—	—	4
Process capability chart	—	—	—	—	—	1	—	—	2	—	3
Certain Degree											
Design experiment	18	8	14	13	15	14	14	27	12	14	149
Single correlation, regression	10	5	—	9	4	3	13	6	9	9	68
Statistical test, estimation	1	1	—	—	3	3	6	3	6	2	25
Analysis of variance	2	3	—	3	1	1	—	2	9	4	25
Optimizing method	1		1				1	—	—	—	3
Cumulative method	—	—	—	1	—	1	1	—	—	—	3
Time series	—	—	—	—	1	2	—	—	—	—	3
High Degree											
Multiple regression	3	2	3	3	5	2	4	3	5	12	42
Principal component analysis	—	—	—	1	1	—	1	6	1	6	16
Discriminant analysis	—	—	—	—	1	2	—	1	—	2	6
Other multivariable analysis	—	—	—	—	—	—	—	1	1	—	2
Miscellaneous											
Distribution function	3	5	1	4	5	3	5	7	1	4	38
Tree analysis	—	—	1	—	—	1	3	—	6	6	17
Sensory measurement	—	—	4	2	1	4	2	4	—	—	17
Weibull probability paper	3	—	1	—	1	3	—	2	4	3	17
FMEA	—	—	—	—	—	2	1	—	6	5	14
Simulation	1	1	1	3	—	—	—	—	2	1	9
Relation chart	—	—	—	—	—	—	—	—	4	4	8
PERT	—	—	—	—	—	—	—	—	2	2	4
Others	5	1	1	4	2	1	1	—	2	4	21

From I. Kusaba, In-plant training—Applying statistical techniques. *ASQC Annual Quality Congress Transactions*, 1981, pp. 132–137. Reprinted with permission of the American Society for Quality Control.

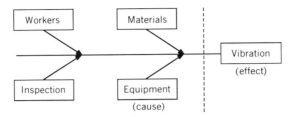

Figure 2.1 Cause and effect diagram.

simply a listing of all of the possible causes without trying to establish any structure relative to the process.

The diagram in Figure 2.1 is quite simplified and is meant to serve only as an illustration. Useful diagrams in practice will generally have more branches. There will always be a single "effect" (i.e., a quality characteristic) that we wish to improve, control, or eliminate. (In this example we would probably like to be able to eliminate vibration, but perhaps the best we can do is to control it at a reasonable level.) We should list as many possible or probable causes as we can think of without making the diagram too cluttered, maintaining the correct relationship between the causes. When a relationship between the quality characteristic and a cause can be shown quantitatively using numerical information, the cause should be enclosed in a box (as in Figure 2.1). When it is known that a relationship between a cause and an effect does exist, but the relationship cannot be supported with data, the cause should be underlined. Thus, in a typical diagram there will be some causes that will be enclosed in a box, some that will be underlined, and some that will be only labeled.

Cause and effect diagrams that are carefully and thoughtfully constructed should enable the cause of a quality problem to be quickly detected, so that corrective action can be taken. See Chapter 3 of Ishikawa (1976) for a detailed discussion of cause and effect diagrams.

2.7 PARETO DIAGRAMS

A Pareto diagram draws its name from an Italian economist, but J. M. Juran is credited with being the first to apply it to industrial problems. The idea is quite simple. The causes of whatever is being investigated (e.g., nonconforming items) are listed and percentages assigned to each one so that the total is 100%. The percentages are then used to construct the diagram that is essentially a bar chart. An example is given in Figure 2.2.

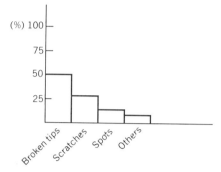

Figure 2.2 Pareto diagram (percentages). Item, condenser AG1; number inspected, 15,000; number of nonconforming units, 958.

In this illustration the percentage of nonconforming condensers of a certain type is 6.39. Since this is quite high, in general, it would obviously be desirable to determine the causes of the nonconforming condensers, and to display the percentage (or frequency) for each cause. In essence, we can think of a Pareto diagram as an extension of a cause and effect diagram, in that the causes are not only identified, but also listed in order of their frequency of occurrence. It is generally found that there are a "vital few"

Table 2.2 Nonconformities and Associated Monetary Losses

Lot number	Date (March)	NI[a]	Scratches	ML[a]	Broken tips	ML	Spots	ML	Others	ML
2014	1	1000	22	$86	36	$160	6	$20	3	$6
2026	2	1000	23	88	39	170	3	10	2	3
2013	3	1000	30	100	41	178	8	24	4	7
2032	4	1000	18	79	37	164	14	35	5	9
2030	5	1000	20	81	28	146	15	38	3	6
2028	6	1000	21	83	39	170	10	28	6	10
2040	7	1000	19	80	33	152	9	25	2	3
2011	8	1000	12	66	29	150	5	18	7	12
2010	9	1000	14	69	31	149	8	24	6	10
2015	10	1000	16	74	30	148	7	22	9	16
2022	11	1000	12	66	22	136	4	16	5	9
2021	12	1000	13	68	27	145	11	27	2	3
2024	13	1000	21	83	35	158	13	31	1	1
2023	14	1000	22	86	29	150	10	26	6	10
2018	15	1000	19	80	23	138	6	20	7	12
		15,000	282	1189	479	2314	129	364	68	117

[a] NI, number inspected; ML, money lost.

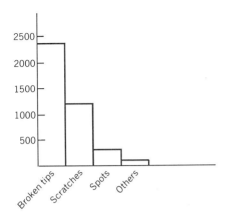

Figure 2.3 Pareto diagram (monetary losses). Item, condenser AG1; number inspected, 15,000; total dollar loss, $3984.

causes and a "trivial many," as was first claimed many years ago by J. M. Juran.

When Pareto diagrams are to be shown to management, it is desirable to use "money lost" (or something similar) as the label for the vertical axis, assuming that the losses can be determined, or at least estimated. Thus, the data might be collected and arranged as in Table 2.2.

When the data are collected and tabulated in this manner, it is easy to construct either type of diagram. The companion diagram to Figure 2.2 that shows the monetary losses is given in Figure 2.3.

Although the order of nonconformities is the same in both diagrams, that will not always be the case. A unit that is considered nonconforming (i.e., unfit for distribution) because of one type of nonconformity could perhaps be reworked, whereas a unit with another type of nonconformity might have to be scrapped. The severity of the nonconformity would also be a factor: how deep is the scratch, how big is the spot, etc. Although the order of nonconformities is the same, it is apparent that "broken tips" is even more of a problem from a monetary standpoint than from a percentage standpoint, but "spots" is less of a problem monetarily.

See Pitt (1974) for more discussion of Pareto diagrams with monetary values, including an example in which the order of nonconformities is different between the two types of diagrams.

There are obviously other modifications that could be used. The frequencies could have been used in Figure 2.2 instead of the percentages, but the configuration would be exactly the same. Similarly, percentages of the total dollar loss could have been displayed in Figure 2.3 instead of the individual dollar losses, but, again, the configuration would be the same.

We should realize that the usefulness of a Pareto diagram is not limited to data on nonconformities and nonconforming units. It can be used to

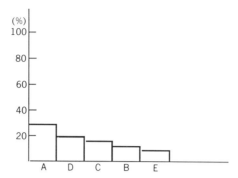

Figure 2.4 Pareto diagram for survey data. (A) Data lost in transcribing; (B) data not turned in by surveyor; (C) unable to contact customer; (D) customer refuses to answer certain questions; (E) other.

summarize all types of data. To illustrate, assume that the management of a company wishes to investigate the considerable amount of missing data in surveys that have been conducted to assess customers' views of the quality of their products. The results of the study are given in Figure 2.4.

In this example there is no evidence of a "vital few" and "trivial many," nor would we expect there to be from the nature of the categories A, B, C, D, and E. Nevertheless, such a diagram could be of considerable value to management.

See Chapter 5 and pp. 162–174 of Ishikawa (1976) for further reading on Pareto diagrams.

2.8   GRAPHS

Graphs had the second highest frequency of usage in Kusaba's table (Table 2.1). They are treated briefly here and covered in more detail in Chapter 11, in which both simple and advanced graphical methods are presented.

A Pareto diagram is a graph and it is somewhat similar to a *histogram*. The latter is also in the form of a bar chart, with the heights of the bars (rectangles) representing frequencies, although the frequencies are not arranged in descending order.

Figure 2.5 is a histogram that might represent quality control data that have been grouped into seven classes, such as values of a process characteristic that have been obtained over time. A histogram is thus a pictorial display of the way the data are distributed over the various classes. As such, it can indicate, in particular, whether the data are distributed symmetrically

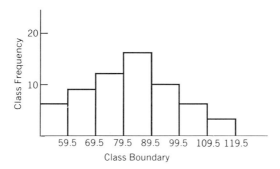

Figure 2.5 Histogram.

or asymmetrically over the classes. This can be very useful information, as many control charts are based upon the implicit assumption of a particular symmetric distribution, a normal distribution, for whatever is being charted. (A normal distribution is covered, along with other distributions, in Chapter 3.)

A *scatter plot* is another simple graphical device. The simplest type is a bivariate scatter plot, in which two quantities are plotted. For example, we might want to plot the number of nonconforming units of a particular product against the total production for each month, so as to see the relationship between the two. Figure 2.6 indicates that the relationship is curvilinear.

A *probability plot* is similar to a scatter plot, but differs in that the vertical axis designates the expected values for a specific probability distribution. Thus, if a set of data might reasonably have come from a particular distribution, the plot should form approximately a straight line. In particular, a normal probability plot is used for determining if sample data might

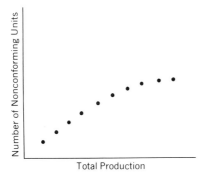

Figure 2.6 Scatter plot.

have come from a normal distribution. Probability plots are best constructed by a computer.

These graphs, along with plots of data over time, are simple but important graphical tools for quality improvement. They are discussed in detail in Chapter 11.

SUMMARY

Japan's ascension in regard to the quality of manufactured products is the result of their use of statistical methods as well as other factors. A major motivating factor is the Deming Award.

The Japanese have relied heavily upon simple graphical tools such as cause and effect diagrams and Pareto diagrams, and also run a very large number of statistically designed experiments each year. (Experimental designs are covered in Chapters 13 and 14.)

The Japanese managerial climate is also distinctive, and has contributed significantly to their success.

REFERENCES

Deming, W. E. (1986). *Out of the Crisis*. Cambridge, MA: Massachusetts Institute of Technology, Center for Advanced Engineering Study.

Ishikawa, K. (1976). *Guide to Quality Control*. Nordica International Limited, Hong Kong: Asian Productivity Organization. (Available in the United States from UNIPUB, New York, New York.)

Joiner, B. L. (1985). The key role of statisticians in the transformation of North American industry. *The American Statistician 39*(3): 224–227; Discussion: pp. 228–234 (August).

Kusaba, I. (1981). In-plant training—Applying statistical techniques. *ASQC Annual Quality Congress Transactions*, pp. 132–137.

Pitt, H. (1974). Pareto revisited. *Quality Progress 7*(3): 29–30 (March).

CHAPTER 3

Basic Concepts in Statistics and Probability

In this chapter we present the tools that form the foundation for the control charts that are covered in Part II and the other statistical procedures that are presented in Part III.

Almost all of the material in this chapter is typically found in introductory statistics texts. Exceptions include Bonferroni intervals and truncated normal distributions. These are needed for some of the newer methods that are presented in later chapters.

3.1 PROBABILITY

During a typical day many of us will hear statements that are probability-type statements although the word "probability" might not be used. One example (Statement 1) is a weather forecast in which a meteorologist states, "There is a 10% chance of rain tomorrow." What does such a statement actually mean? For one thing, it means that, in the opinion of the meteorologist, it is very unlikely that rain will fall tomorrow. Contrast that with the following statement (Statement 2): "If a balanced coin is tossed, there is a 50% chance that a head will be observed." Disregarding for the moment that the coin could land on its edge (an unlikely possibility), there are two possible outcomes, a head or a tail, and they are equally likely to occur. Finally, consider the following statement (Statement 3): "I found a slightly bent coin in the street. I am going to toss this coin 1000 times and use the results of this experiment to determine an estimate of the likelihood of obtaining a head when the coin is tossed once. Thus, if I observe 522 heads during the 1000 tosses, I estimate there is a 52.2% ($= 522/1000$) chance of observing a head when the coin is tossed once."

There are some important differences between these three statements. Statement 1 has to be at least somewhat subjective since it is not possible to repeat tomorrow 1000 times and observe how many times it rains, nor is it possible to know the exact likelihood of rain as in the case of the balanced coin. The second and third statements are illustrative examples of the two approaches that will be followed in this book: (i) acting as if the assumption is valid (i.e., the coin is balanced), and (ii) not making any assumption but rather collecting data and then drawing some conclusion from the analysis of that data (e.g., from the 1000 tosses of the coin). The latter approach is obviously preferable if there is any question as to whether or not the assumption is valid, and if the consequences of making a false assumption are considerable.

The word *probability* has not as yet been used in the section; instead *percent chance* has been used. The two terms can be thought of as being virtually synonymous, however. The first statement that was given (the weather forecast) is essentially a subjective probability statement. Statement 2 could be expressed concisely as

$$P(\text{Head}) = \tfrac{1}{2}$$

which is read as "the probability of a head equals $1/2$" on a single toss of the balanced coin. Thus, a 50% chance is equivalent to a probability of one-half.

Just as percentages must range from 0 to 100, the probability of some arbitrary "event" (such as observing a head) must be between 0 and 1. An "impossible event" (such as rolling a seven on a single die) would be assigned a probability of zero. The converse is not true, however: if an event is assigned a probability of zero it does not mean that the event is an impossible event. As mentioned previously, a coin *could* land on its edge (and most assuredly will if it is tossed enough times), but we customarily assign a probability of zero to that possible event.

With Statement 3, no probability was assumed, instead it was "estimated." In practice, this is customary since practical applications of probability go far beyond tossing a balanced coin or rolling a single die. In this instance the probability of observing a head on a single toss of the misshapen coin was estimated by tossing the coin a large number of times and counting the number of heads that was observed. Is 1000 tosses adequate? That depends upon the degree of accuracy that is required in estimating the true probability. The idea of determining the number of trials in an experiment from a stated error of estimation will not be pursued here. In general, however

$$\frac{x}{n} \to p \quad \text{as } n \to \infty$$

where x denotes the number of times that the event in question occurs, n denotes the number of trials, and "p" is the true probability that the particular event will occur on a single trial. The symbol $\to$ should be read as "approaches" and $n \to \infty$ designates the number of trials becoming large without bound.

How can these concepts be applied in a manufacturing environment? Assume that a particular plant has just opened and we want to estimate the percentage of nonconforming units of a particular product that the process is producing. How many items should we inspect? We would certainly hope that the percentage of nonconforming units is quite small. If it is, and if we were to inspect only a very small number of units we might not observe any nonconforming units. In that case our estimate of the percentage of nonconforming units produced would be zero (i.e., $x/n = 0$), which could certainly be very misleading. At the other extreme, we could inspect every unit that is produced for a particular week. This would be rather impractical, however, if the production item happened to be steel balls and thousands of them were produced every week. Consequently, a compromise would have to be struck so that a practical number of items would be inspected. (See Section 8.1.6 for a further discussion of this problem in the context of attribute control charts.) For a reasonable number of items to be inspected, the percentage of nonconforming items that the process is producing could then be *estimated* by dividing the number of nonconforming units observed by the total number of items that was inspected (i.e., x/n).

3.2 SAMPLE VERSUS POPULATION

For the example just given, the "reasonable number" of units that is inspected would constitute a *sample* from some *population*. The word *population* in statistics need not refer to people. A statistical population can consist of virtually anything. For the manufacturing scenario presented in the preceding section, the population could be all of the items of a particular type produced by the manufacturing process—past, present, and future. A sample is simply part of the population. There are various types of samples that can be obtained. One of the most common is a *random sample*. A random sample of size n is one in which every possible sample of size n has the same probability of being selected.

An example will be given to illustrate this concept. Suppose a population is defined to consist of the numbers 1, 2, 3, 4, 5, and 6, and you wish to obtain a random sample of size two from this population. How might this be accomplished? What about listing all of the possible samples of size two and then randomly selecting one? There are 15 such samples and they are given below.

12	15	24	34	45
13	16	25	35	46
14	23	26	36	56

In practice, a population is apt to be much larger than this, however, so this would be a rather cumbersome procedure, even if carried out on a computer.

Another approach would be to use a *random number table* such as Table A at the end of the book. That table could be used as follows. In general, the elements in the population would have to be numbered in some way. In this example the elements are numbers, and since the numbers are single-digit numbers, only one column of Table A need be used. If we arbitrarily select the first column in the first set of four columns, we could proceed down that column; the first number observed is 1 and the second is 5. Thus, our sample of size two would consist of those two numbers.

One fact that should be apparent for each of these procedures is that the elements of the population must be enumerated, and if these elements are not numbers they must be assigned numbers.

Can this be accomplished if a population is defined to consist of all of the units of a product that will be produced by a particular company? Certainly not. Therefore, in practice it is often impossible to obtain a random sample. Consequently, a *convenience sample* is frequently used instead of a random sample. For example, if samples of five units are obtained from an assembly line every 30 minutes, every item produced will not have the same probability of being included in any one of the samples.

The objective, however, should be to obtain samples that are *representative* of the population from which they are drawn. (We should keep in mind, however, that populations generally change over time, and the change might be considerable relative to what we are trying to estimate. Hence, a sample that is representative today may not be representative 6 months later.) How can we tell whether or not convenience samples are likely to give us a true picture of a particular population? We cannot unless we have some idea as to whether there are any patterns or trends in regard to the units that are produced. Consider the following example. Assume that every twenty-first unit of a particular product is nonconforming. If samples of size three happen to be selected in such a way (perhaps every 15 minutes) that one nonconforming unit is included in each sample, the logical conclusion would be that one out of every three units produced is nonconforming, instead of one out of twenty-one.

Consequently, it is highly desirable to acquire a good understanding of the processes with which you will be working before using any "routine" sampling procedure.

3.3   LOCATION

In statistics, various measures are used in "describing" a set of data. For example, assume that you have obtained a sample that consists of the following numbers:

$$15 \quad 13 \quad 11 \quad 17 \quad 19$$

How might you describe or summarize this set of data relative to what would seem to be a typical value?

One possibility would be to use the *median*, which is the middle value (after the numbers have been arranged in ascending order) if the sample consists of an odd number of observations, as it does in this case. Thus, the median is 15. If the sample had consisted of these five numbers plus the number 21, there would then not be a single middle number, but rather two middle numbers. The median would then be defined as the average of the two middle values, which in that case would be 16. Thus, when there is an even number of observations the median will always be a number that is not observed unless the two middle numbers happen to be the same. That might seem strange but it should be remembered that the objective is to *estimate* the middle value of the population from which the sample was drawn.

Another measure that is often used to estimate a typical value in the population is the (sample) *average*, which is simply the sum of the values divided by n. For this example the average is also 15 so the average and median have the same value. This will usually not be the case, however. In fact, the average might not even be close to the center of the sample when the values are ordered from smallest to largest. For the sample

$$28 \quad 39 \quad 40 \quad 50 \quad 97$$

the average (50.8) is between the fourth and fifth numbers so it is not particularly close to the middle value. This is the result of the fact that one observation, 97, is considerably larger than the others. Thus, although the average is often referred to as a *measure of center* or *measure of central tendency*, it often will not be very close to the middle of the data. Consequently, during the past 10 years, in particular, there has been considerable interest in the statistical community in developing estimators that are insensitive to extreme observations (numerical values that differ considerably from the others in the sample). These *robust estimators* have not been used to any extent in practice, however, and this is undoubtedly due to the fact that they are not particularly well known by practitioners. So are robust estimators really necessary? The answer is "yes," and the reader is referred to a (nonmathematical) paper with that title by Rocke, Downs, and Rocke (1982) and the references contained therein. The paper is oriented toward chemistry, but robust estimators can be used in all fields.

A *trimmed average* is one type of robust estimator. If, for example, 10% of the observations in a sample are trimmed from each end (where the observations are ordered), extreme observations, which could have considerable effect on the average of all of the observations, would thus be deleted. If there are no extreme observations, such "trimming" should have very little effect on the average. For example, if the smallest and largest values are deleted from the sample

$$11 \quad 13 \quad 15 \quad 17 \quad 19$$

the average remains unchanged, but if the same trimming is done for the sample

$$28 \quad 39 \quad 40 \quad 50 \quad 97$$

the average changes from 50.8 to 43.0.

Extreme observations might very well be values that have been recorded incorrectly. In any event, they are not typical observations. If the trimming is not done haphazardly, but rather some trimming procedure is consistently applied, a better estimate of the center of the corresponding population is apt to result. Nevertheless, trimmed averages will not be used for the control charts and other statistical procedures presented in this book. Instead, the conventional procedure of using all of the observations will be used, assuming that the data do not contain any errors. The need to be watchful for errors should be kept in mind, however, since errors do occur quite often in data collection and tabulation.

3.4 VARIATION

There is "natural" variation in everything. Is your driving time to work precisely the same every day? Of course not. It will depend upon factors such as weather conditions and traffic conditions. Assume that your time varies slightly for a particular week, but at the beginning of the second week an accident on the expressway causes you to be 30 minutes late for work. Your travel time for that day is not due to natural, random variation, but rather to an "assignable cause"—the accident.

With statistical procedures, in general, and control charts, in particular, a primary objective is to analyze components of variability so that variability due to assignable causes can be detected. If you are the "unit" that is being "measured" for travel time, you know why you were late for work and can thus explain the cause. A ball bearing, however, cannot explain why its diameter is considerably larger than the diameter of the preceding 500 ball bearings that have rolled off the assembly line. Thus, statistical procedures are needed to spotlight the abnormal variation, and, we hope, to pinpoint the contributing factor(s).

Before we can speak of normal and abnormal variation, however, we must have one or more objective measures of variation. The simplest such measure is the sample *range*, which is defined to be the largest observation in a sample minus the smallest observation. For the sample

$$11 \quad 13 \quad 15 \quad 17 \quad 19$$

the range is 8. It should be observed that only two of the five values are used in obtaining this number; the other three are essentially "thrown away." Because of its simplicity and ease of calculation by hand, the range has been used extensively in quality control work. Nevertheless, it is wasteful of information and will be inferior to good measures of variability that use all of the observations.

I stated in the preface that this book is written under the assumption that many if not most of its readers will be using a computer for constructing and maintaining control charts, in particular, as well as for the other statistical procedures presented herein. Therefore, simple and easy-to-use procedures will not be recommended over more efficient, but involved, procedures when they can both be handled with approximately equal ease on a computer.

If we were to start from scratch and devise a measure of variability that uses all of the sample observations, it would seem logical that what we construct should measure how the data vary from the average.

At this point we need to introduce some symbols. The sample average is a statistic and will henceforth be denoted by $\overline{X}$ which is read "x-bar." Its calculation could be expressed as

$$\overline{X} = \frac{\sum_{i=1}^{n} X_i}{n} \tag{3.1}$$

where the Greek letter Σ is read as (capital) **sigma** and is used to indicate summation. Specifically, what lies to the right of Σ is to be summed. The letter i in X_i is a subscript, which in this case varies from 1 to n. The number at the bottom of Σ indicates where the summation is to start, and the number (or symbol) at the top indicates where it is to end.

Thus, the average for the sample

$$11 \quad 13 \quad 15 \quad 17 \quad 19$$

could be expressed as

$$\overline{X} = \frac{\sum_{i=1}^{n} X_i}{n}$$

$$= \frac{\sum_{i=1}^{5} X_i}{5}$$

$$= \frac{X_1 + X_2 + X_3 + X_4 + X_5}{5}$$

$$= \frac{11 + 13 + 15 + 17 + 19}{5}$$

$$= 15.0$$

If we wanted to construct a measure of variability we might *attempt* to use $\sum_{i=1}^{n}(X_i - \overline{X})$. However, it can be shown that this sum will equal zero for any sample. This is due to the fact that some of the deviations $(X_i - \overline{X})$ will be positive whereas others will be negative and the positive and negative values add to zero. For the present sample of five numbers,

$$\sum_{i=1}^{5}\left(X_i - \overline{X}\right)$$

$$= -4 - 2 + 0 + 2 + 4$$

$$= 0$$

One obvious way to eliminate the negative deviations would be to square all of the deviations. The *sample variance*, S^2, is usually defined as

$$S^2 = \frac{\sum_{i=1}^{n}\left(X_i - \overline{X}\right)^2}{n - 1} \tag{3.2}$$

although a few authors have chosen to divide by n instead of $n - 1$. Arguments can be given in support of each choice, but a discussion of the merits of each will be delayed until the S^2 chart is presented in Chapter 5. Definition (3.2) will be used for all values of S^2 that are presented in this book.

It could be shown that S^2 can also be calculated as

$$S^2 = \frac{\Sigma X^2 - (\Sigma X)^2/n}{n - 1}$$

For the same sample of five numbers

$$S^2 = \frac{\Sigma_{i=1}^n (X_i - \overline{X})^2}{n - 1}$$

$$= \frac{\Sigma_{i=1}^5 (X_i - 15)^2}{4}$$

$$= \frac{(-4)^2 + (-2)^2 + (0)^2 + (2)^2 + (4)^2}{4}$$

$$= \frac{40}{4}$$

$$= 10$$

The sample variance is not as intuitive as the sample range, nor is it in the same unit of measurement. If the unit of measurement is inches, the range will be in inches but the variance will be in inches squared. This is not sufficient cause for discarding the variance in favor of the range, however.

Another measure of variability that is in terms of the original units is the *sample standard deviation*, which is simply the square root of the sample variance. Therefore,

$$S = \sqrt{\frac{\Sigma_{i=1}^n (X_i - \overline{X})^2}{n - 1}} .$$

is the sample standard deviation. For this example $S = \sqrt{10} = 3.16$. The standard deviation is also not as intuitive as the range, but will generally be of the same order of magnitude as the average deviation between the numbers. Thus, with the (ordered) numbers

$$11 \quad 13 \quad 15 \quad 17 \quad 19$$

the deviation between each pair of adjacent numbers is 2, so the average deviation is also 2. Therefore, a standard deviation of 3.16 is well within reason; a value of, say, 31.6 or 0.316 should lead us to check our calculations. This can be helpful as a rough check, regardless of the calculating device that is used to obtain the answer.

There are a few other measures of variability that are occasionally used, but the range, variance, and standard deviation are the ones that have been used most frequently, and these are the ones that will be used in this book.

3.5   DISCRETE DISTRIBUTIONS

In addition to the concepts of location and variability, it is important to understand what is meant by the word *distribution* in statistics. The word implies (even in a nonstatistical context) that something is distributed in a certain way. In statistics, that "something" is called a *random variable*. In keeping with my intention to explain concepts in a simple manner whenever possible, the mathematically formal definition of a random variable that is usually found in introductory statistics books will be eschewed in favor of a simpler definition. A random variable is literally "something that varies in a random manner."

The following example will be used for illustration. Assume that an experiment is defined to consist of tossing a single coin twice and recording the number of heads that is observed. The experiment is to be performed 16 times. The "something" that varies is the number of heads and this is our random variable. It is customary to have a random variable represented by an alphabetical (capital) letter. Thus, we could define

X = the number of heads observed in each experiment

Assume that the 16 experiments produce the following values of X:

$$0 \quad 2 \quad 1 \quad 1 \quad 2 \quad 0 \quad 0 \quad 1 \quad 2 \quad 1 \quad 1 \quad 0 \quad 1 \quad 1 \quad 2 \quad 0$$

There is no apparent pattern in the sequence of numbers so it can be stated that X *varies* in a *random* manner, and is thus a random variable.

A *line diagram* could then be used to portray the *empirical distribution* of X for these 16 experiments. The line diagram is given in Figure 3.1. The

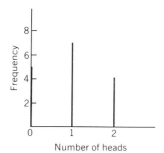

Figure 3.1 Empirical distribution.

height of each line represents the number of occurrences of each of the three numbers 0, 1, and 2. Thus, there were 5 zeros, 7 ones, and 4 twos.

An empirical distribution (such as this one) should not be confused with the theoretical distributions that are presented in the remainder of this chapter. A theoretical distribution is, roughly speaking, what the corresponding empirical distribution could be expected to resemble if there were a very large number of observations (e.g., millions). What should this particular empirical distribution resemble? The answer is the theoretical distribution that is presented in the next section.

3.5.1 Binomial Distribution

This is one of several distributions that will be presented. There is actually a very large number of statistical distributions (hundreds, at least) and the selection of these few distributions for presentation is based upon their wide applicability, and also because most of them relate to the control charts and other statistical procedures to be presented later.

The binomial distribution can be used when the following conditions are met.

1. When there are two possible outcomes (e.g., heads and tails). These outcomes are arbitrarily labeled *success* and *failure*, with the outcome that is labeled "success" being the one for which one or more probabilities are to be calculated. There is no intended connotation of good vs. bad. For example, if probabilities for various numbers of nonconforming items are to be computed, "nonconforming" is labeled "success."

2. There are *n* trials (such as *n* tosses of a coin) and the trials are independent. This means that the probability of a success on a single trial does not vary from trial-to-trial, and the outcome for a particular trial is not influenced by the outcome of any preceding trials.

Clearly the coin-tossing experiment given in the preceding section meets these requirements. The probabilities of observing 0, 1, and 2 heads will now be obtained in a somewhat heuristic manner. It should be apparent that whatever happens on the second toss of the coin is independent of the outcome on the first toss. When two events are independent, the probability of both of them occurring is equal to the product of their separate probabilities of occurrence. Thus, if H_1 represents a head on the first toss and H_2 represents a head on the second toss, then

$$P(H_1 \text{ and } H_2) = P(H_1)P(H_2)$$

$$= \left(\frac{1}{2}\right)\left(\frac{1}{2}\right)$$

$$= \frac{1}{4}$$

Similarly, it could be shown that the probability of two tails (zero heads) equals 1/4. One head could be observed in one of two ways, either on the first toss (followed by a tail) or on the second toss (preceded by a tail). Since the probability for each sequence is 1/4, the probability of observing one head is equal to the sum of those two probabilities which is 1/2.

If we define the random variable X as

$$X = \text{number of heads observed}$$

we can put together these probabilities to form the probability distribution of X. If we let $P(X)$ represent "the probability of X" (with X assuming the three different values), we then have the following:

X	$P(X)$
0	$\frac{1}{4}$
1	$\frac{1}{2}$
2	$\frac{1}{4}$

Thus, if this experiment was repeated a large number of times, we would theoretically expect that 1 head would occur 50% of the time, 2 heads would occur 25% of the time, and 0 heads would also occur 25% of the time.

Compare this theoretical expectation with the results of the 16 experiments depicted in Figure 3.1. The theoretical frequencies are 4, 8, and 4, which are very close to the observed frequencies of 5, 7, and 4. Although the theoretical frequencies of 4, 8, and 4 constitute our "best guess" of what should occur, we should not be surprised if the observed frequencies differ somewhat from the theoretical frequencies. In fact, it may be apparent that the observed frequencies could never equal the theoretical frequencies unless the number of experiments was a multiple of 4. (If the number of experiments is not a multiple of 4, the theoretical frequencies for 0 heads and 2 heads would not be an integer.) The important point is that the difference between the observed and theoretical frequencies should become very small as the number of experiments becomes very large.

The way that the probabilities were found for the coin-tossing experiment would certainly be impractical if the number of tosses, n, was much larger than two. In virtually any practical application n will be much larger than two so there is clearly a need for a general formula that can be used in obtaining binomial probabilities. The following symbols will be used.

$$p = \text{the probability of observing a success on a single trial}$$
$$1 - p = \text{the probability of } not \text{ observing a success on a single trial (i.e., a failure)}$$
$$n = \text{the number of trials}$$
$$x = \text{the number of successes for which the probability is to be calculated}$$

Regardless of the size of n, it is easy to find $P(x)$ when $x = 0$ or $x = n$. There is only one way to observe either no successes or all successes. Therefore, since the trials are independent, $P(n)$ is simply p multiplied times itself n times, i.e., p^n. Similarly, $P(0) = (1 - p)^n$. It is by no means obvious, however, what $P(x)$ equals when x is neither 0 nor n.

If we wanted the probability of x successes followed by $n - x$ failures, that would clearly be

$$p^x(1 - p)^{n-x} \tag{3.3}$$

If, instead, we just wanted the probability of x successes without regard to order, the answer would obviously be larger than what would be produced by Eq. (3.3). For example, if you tossed a coin 10 times there are many different ways that you could observe 4 heads and 6 tails, one of which would be 4 heads followed by 6 tails.

In general, the number of ways that x successes can be observed in n trials is $\binom{n}{x}$, which is defined as

$$\binom{n}{x} = \frac{n!}{x!(n - x)!} \tag{3.4}$$

where $n! = 1 \cdot 2 \cdot 3 \cdot 4, \ldots, n$. For example, if $n = 5$ and $x = 3$ then

$$\binom{5}{3} = \frac{5!}{3!2!}$$

$$= \frac{120}{(6)(2)}$$

$$= 10$$

If such computation is to be done by hand, it is easier to first simplify the quotient by dividing the larger of the two numbers in the denominator into the numerator. Thus,

$$\frac{5!}{3!} = \frac{1 \cdot 2 \cdot 3 \cdot 4 \cdot 5}{1 \cdot 2 \cdot 3} = 4 \cdot 5 = 20$$

so that

$$\frac{5!}{3!2!} = \frac{20}{2} = 10$$

By putting Eq. (3.4) together with Eq. (3.3) we have the following general expression for the probability of x successes in n trials.

$$P(x) = \binom{n}{x} p^x (1 - p)^{n-x} \qquad (3.5)$$

Although it was easy to find the probabilities of observing 0, 1, and 2 heads without using Eq. (3.5), the direct approach would be to use Eq. (3.5). Thus, we could have found the probability of observing one head as follows.

$$P(1) = \binom{2}{1}(.5)^1(.5)^1$$

$$= 2(.5)(.5)$$

$$= .5$$

Notice that if we were to attempt to determine the probability of 2 heads as

$$P(2) = \binom{2}{2}(.5)^2(.5)^0$$

$$= \frac{2!}{2!0!}(.25)(1)$$

we would have to know what to do with 0!. It is defined to be equal to one, and it should be apparent that if it were defined in any other way we would obtain an incorrect answer for this example. Specifically, we *know* that $P(2) = (.5)(.5) = .25$; therefore, we must have

$$P(2) = \frac{2!}{2!0!}(.25)(1)$$

$$= 1(.25)(1)$$

$$= .25$$

which will result only if 0! is defined to be equal to one.

A practical problem might be to determine the probability that a lot of 1000 capacitors contains no more than one nonconforming capacitor, if 1 out of every 100 capacitors produced is nonconforming. There are clearly two possible outcomes (conforming or nonconforming), but are the "trials" independent so that the probability of any particular capacitor being nonconforming does not depend upon whether or not any of the previously produced capacitors were nonconforming? This is the type of question that must be addressed for any manufacturing application, and applications of the binomial distribution, in general.

If this assumption is not valid, the binomial distribution would be of questionable value as a model for solving this problem. For this example we shall assume that the assumption is valid. The words *no more than one* indicate that we should focus attention upon 0 nonconforming units and 1 nonconforming unit, and add the two probabilities together. Thus,

$$P(0) = \binom{1000}{0}(.01)^0(.99)^{1000}$$

$$= (.99)^{1000}$$

$$= .000043$$

and

$$P(1) = \binom{1000}{1}(.01)^1(.99)^{999}$$

$$= .000436$$

Therefore, the probability of no more than one nonconforming unit in a lot of 1000 capacitors is $.000043 + .000436 = .000479$.

Both of these individual probabilities are quite small, but that is due primarily to the fact that X $(=$ the number of nonconforming capacitors) could be any one of 1001 numbers (0–1000). Therefore, we should not expect any one probability to be particularly high.

If the binomial distribution is a probability distribution (as it is), all of the probabilities will add up to one. It can be shown with some algebraic manipulation that

$$\sum_{x=0}^{n} \binom{n}{x} p^x (1 - p)^{n-x} = 1$$

for any combination of n and p, but that will not be demonstrated here. (You should recall that for the coin-tossing experiment with $n = 2$ and $p = 1/2$ the probabilities were $1/4$, $1/2$, and $1/4$, which obviously do add up to one.) It should also be noted that the binomial distribution is a *discrete* probability distribution, that is, the random variable X can assume only integer values.

We might ask the following question that relates to both the coin-tossing experiment and the nonconforming capacitor example. What would be our "best guess" for the value of X in a binomial experiment. In other words, how many heads would we expect to observe if we toss a balanced coin twice? How many nonconforming capacitors should we expect to observe in a lot of 1000 capacitors if 1 out of every 100 capacitors was nonconforming in the past? We should be able to answer these questions without any knowledge of the binomial distribution. We would certainly expect to observe 1 head in 2 tosses of the coin, and 10 nonconforming capacitors in the lot of 1000 capacitors. But what if we wanted to know how many nonconforming capacitors we should expect to find in a lot of 500 capacitors if 1 out of every 75 capacitors has been nonconforming in the past? Now the answer is not quite so obvious. Therefore, we need a way of formally determining the *expected value* of X [which is written $E(x)$] for the binomial distribution. It can be shown that

$$E(x) = np$$

For the coin-tossing experiment $n = 2$ and $p = 1/2$ so $np = 1$, and for the first capacitor example $n = 1000$ and $p = .01$ so $np = 10$. Thus, the theoretical results coincide with what common sense would tell us. For the second capacitor example $n = 500$ and $p = .0133$ (one divided by 75) so $np = 6.67$. This last result was probably not obvious. Notice that $E(x)$ for the binomial distribution will not always be an integer, although x itself must always be an integer.

This should not seem incongruous, however, because $E(x)$ is simply the theoretical "average" value of x, and should be very close to the actual average value of x if a binomial experiment is repeated a very large number of times.

The concept of the *variance* of a random variable is very important in statistics, in general, and particularly so for the control charts that will be presented in later chapters. You will recall that the sample variance, S^2, was introduced in Section 3.4 of this chapter. It was calculated from the data in a sample and is a *sample statistic*. *If* a person had an entire statistical population, he could then compute the population variance, σ^2, which is defined as

$$\sigma^2 = \sum_{i=1}^{N} \frac{(x_i - \mu)^2}{N}$$

where μ represents the average value (mean) of the population, and N represents the number of units in the population. However, since we should not expect to ever have an entire population before us, the *sample statistic*, S^2, can be used to estimate the *population parameter*, σ^2. The use of sample statistics to estimate population parameters is one of the primary uses of statistics. Such estimation will be done extensively in constructing control charts in later chapters as well as in the other statistical procedures to be presented. (See Section 3.7 for additional information on estimation.)

The variance for a probability distribution is somewhat different, however, in that it is not calculated from data. Such a variance will henceforth be denoted by Var(x). If X is a binomial random variable, it can be shown that

$$\text{Var}(x) = np(1 - p)$$

Notice that this does not depend upon any sample data, only upon the sample size. It was shown previously that the $E(x)$ for the binomial distribution is quite intuitive, but the Var(x) cannot be explained in a similar manner. The square root of the Var(x) can, however, be explained in the following manner. If p is close to $1/2$ and n is at least 15 or 20, then

$$P\left[E(x) - 3\sqrt{\text{Var}(x)} \le x \le E(x) + 3\sqrt{\text{Var}(x)}\right] \doteq 0.99$$

In words, we would expect the value of x to fall between the two endpoints of the interval almost all of the time. Thus, the square root of the variance (i.e., the standard deviation) can be combined with the mean to determine an interval that should contain x with a high probability. The standard deviation for a probability distribution thus measures the spread of the *possible* values of a random variable, whereas the sample standard deviation, S, is a measure of the spread of the *actual* values of a random variable that is observed in a sample.

The binomial distribution has been used extensively in quality improvement work. For example, it is used in constructing p charts and np charts that are presented in Chapter 8.

Binomial tables have been prepared for a number of different combinations of n and p. They are not provided in this book because they are not needed for the methods that are presented. They are needed for acceptance sampling and other applications, however. The reader with a need for such tables is referred to the extensive tables prepared by Weintraub (1963), Harvard Computation Laboratory (1955), and the U.S. Army Materiel Command (1972). Weintraub (1963) is recommended for $p < .01$.

3.5.2   Poisson Distribution

This distribution can be used when dealing with rare events. It has been used in quality improvement work to construct control charts for "nonconformities." (A product can have one or more nonconformities without being proclaimed a "nonconforming unit," so the terms are not synonymous.) It is similar to the binomial distribution in that it is also a discrete distribution. In fact, it can be used to approximate binomial probabilities when n is large and p is small.

Specifically, if we again consider the binomial distribution

$$P(x) = \binom{n}{x} p^x (1 - p)^{n - x}$$

and let $n \to \infty$ and $p \to 0$ in such a way that np remains constant ($= \lambda$, say), it can be shown that

$$\lim_{n \to \infty} P(x) = \frac{e^{-\lambda} \lambda^x}{x!} \qquad x = 0, 1, 2, \ldots \qquad (3.6)$$

where "lim" is short for "limit." The letter e represents the nonrepeating and nonterminating mathematical constant $2.71828\ldots$, and the right-hand side of Eq. (3.6) is the Poisson distribution, with λ representing the mean of X. Since this distribution can be obtained as a limiting form of the binomial distribution as $n \to \infty$ and $p \to 0$, it stands to reason that it should be possible to use the Poisson distribution to approximate binomial probabilities when n is large and p is small, and obtain a reasonably good approximation (if a computer is not available to produce the exact answer).

The Poisson distribution is a valuable distribution in its own right; it is not just for approximating binomial probabilities. The distribution is named for Simeon Poisson (1781–1840) who presented it as a limit of the binomial distribution in 1837. It was stated earlier that the Poisson distribution is used as a basis for constructing control charts for nonconformities. Before the distribution can be applied in a physical setting, however, it must be determined whether or not the assumptions for the distribution are at least approximately met. These assumptions will be illustrated with the following example.

Assume that sheets of steel are being produced in a manufacturing process and the random variable X is the number of surface scratches per square yard. Before it can be claimed that X is a Poisson random variable, the following questions must be addressed. (1) Do the scratches occur randomly and independently of each other? (2) Is the possible number of scratches per square yard quite large (theoretically it should be infinite)? The second question might be answered in the affirmative, but perhaps not the first one. If there are quite a few surface scratches on one section of steel, we might expect to observe a sizable number of scratches on adjacent sections. Or perhaps not. In any event, for this problem and for other practical problems our objective should be to determine whether or not a particular distribution can logically serve as a *model* (and nothing more) for physical phenomena under investigation. We can rarely expect all of the assumptions to be met exactly; we can only hope that they are approximately satisfied. We should be concerned, however, if there is evidence of a radical departure from the assumptions, and our concern should lead us to seek alternative approaches to the problem.

3.5.3 Hypergeometric Distribution

The last discrete distribution to be presented is the *hypergeometric distribution*. This distribution, like the binomial, has also been used extensively in sampling inspection work. The two distributions are similar in that both assume two possible outcomes. They differ, however, in that the hypergeometric distribution is applicable when sampling is performed without replacement. The following example is used for illustration. Assume it is known that a lot of 1000 condensers contains 12 nonconforming condensers. What is the probability of observing at most one nonconforming condenser when a random sample of 50 is obtained from this lot.

Why can't the binomial distribution be used to solve this problem using $p = 12/1000 = .012$, $n = 50$, and $x \leq 1$? Notice a subtle difference between this example and the example with the 1000 capacitors that was used to illustrate the binomial distribution. For the latter there was no sampling from a stated finite population; it was simply a matter of determining the probability of observing at most one nonconforming unit in 1000 when it is known that $p = .01$. For the current problem, however, we cannot say that the probability is .012 that any condenser in the random sample of 50 condensers is nonconforming. This is due to the fact that the probability of any particular condenser being nonconforming depends upon whether or not the previously selected condensers were nonconforming. For example, the probability that the second condenser selected is nonconforming is $12/999$ if the first condenser selected is conforming and $11/999$ if the first condenser is nonconforming.

Therefore, the binomial distribution cannot be used since p is not constant. We can, however, deduce the answer using the same type of heuristic reasoning as was used for the coin-tossing problem in the section on the binomial distribution. First, how many different samples of 50 are possible out of 1000? Of that number how many will contain at most one nonconforming unit? The answer to the first question is

$$\binom{1000}{50} = \frac{1000!}{50!950!}$$

This is analogous to the earlier example concerning the number of possible ways of obtaining one head in two tosses of a balanced coin which was

$$\binom{2}{1} = \frac{2!}{1!1!}$$

Thus, the two tosses were, in essence, partitioned into one for a head and one for a tail. For the current problem the 1000 condensers are partitioned into 50 that will be in the sample and 950 that will not be in the sample. How many of these $\binom{1000}{50}$ samples will contain at most one nonconforming unit? There are $\binom{12}{0}\binom{988}{50}$ ways of obtaining zero nonconforming units and $\binom{12}{1}\binom{988}{49}$ ways of obtaining exactly one nonconforming unit. Therefore, the probability of having at most one nonconforming condenser in the sample of 50 is

$$\frac{\binom{12}{0}\binom{988}{50} + \binom{12}{1}\binom{988}{49}}{\binom{1000}{50}} = 0.88254$$

The combinatorics in the numerator [such as $\binom{12}{0}$ and $\binom{988}{50}$] are multiplied together because of a counting rule that states that if one stage of a procedure can be performed in M ways, and another stage can be performed in N ways, the two-stage procedure can be performed in MN ways. For this example we can think of the number of ways of obtaining 0 nonconforming units out of 12 as constituting one stage, and the number of ways of obtaining 50 good items out of 988 as the other stage. Of course, the sample is not collected in two stages, but the sample can be viewed in this manner so as to determine the number of ways that zero nonconforming units can be obtained.

The general form for the hypergeometric distribution is as follows:

$$P(x) = \frac{\binom{D}{x}\binom{N-D}{n-x}}{\binom{N}{n}} \qquad x = 0, 1, 2, \ldots \min(n, D)$$

where N represents the number of items in the finite population of interest, with D representing the number of items in the population of the type for which a probability is to be calculated (nonconforming units in the previous example), and $N - D$ represents the number of items of the other type (e.g., conforming units) that are in the population. The sample size is represented by n, of which x are of the type for which the probability is to be calculated, and $n - x$ are of the other type. D must be at least as large as x, otherwise $\binom{D}{x}$ would be undefined, and, obviously, x cannot exceed n. Thus, x cannot exceed the minimum of n and D [i.e., $\min(n, D)$].

3.6 CONTINUOUS DISTRIBUTIONS

3.6.1 Normal Distribution

It is somewhat unfortunate that any statistical distribution is called "normal," since this could easily create the false impression that this distribution is "typical," and the other hundreds of distributions are "atypical."

The normal distribution (also sometimes called the Gaussian distribution) is the first *continuous* distribution presented in this chapter. A continuous distribution is such that the random variable can assume any value along a continuum. For example, if X = height of an adult human being then X can assume any value between, say, 24 inches and 108 inches (Goliath's estimated height). Although a person might actually be 68.1374136 inches tall, that person is not likely to ever have his or her height recorded as such. Thus, random variables that are continuous are, in essence, "discretized" by the use of measuring instruments. Height, for

Figure 3.2 Two normal distributions with different means but with the same standard deviations ($\sigma_1 = \sigma_2$).

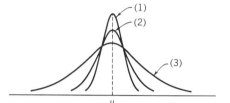

Figure 3.3 Three normal distributions with $\sigma_1 < \sigma_2 < \sigma_3$ and with the same mean.

example, is usually not recorded to an accuracy greater than one-fourth of an inch. Nevertheless, a normal distribution is often used to approximate the *actual* (unknown) distribution of many random variables.

The equation for the distribution is given by

$$f(x) = \frac{1}{\sigma\sqrt{2\pi}} e^{-(x-\mu)^2/2\sigma^2} \qquad -\infty < x < \infty$$

where μ represents the mean of the distribution, σ represents the standard deviation, π is the mathematical constant $3.14159\ldots$, and $-\infty < x < \infty$ indicates that the random variable X can assume any real number. There is actually not just *one* normal distribution since there are different normal distributions for different combinations of μ and σ. The value of σ determines the shape of the distribution, and the value of μ determines the location. This is illustrated in Figures 3.2 and 3.3. [The height of the curve at any point x is given by $f(x)$, but that is usually not of any practical interest.]

In practice, μ and σ are seldom known and must be estimated. This is particularly true when data are to be used in constructing control charts for measurement data.

A normal distribution has an important property that is illustrated in Figure 3.4. The number in each section of the curve denotes the area under the curve in that section. For example, 0.34134 represents the area under the curve between μ and $\mu + \sigma$, which is also the area between μ and $\mu - \sigma$

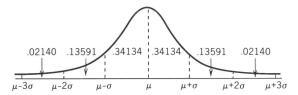

Figure 3.4 Areas under a normal curve.

since the curve is symmetric with respect to μ. The total area under the curve equals one, which corresponds to a total probability of one, with 0.5 on each side of μ.

The reader should make note of the fact that the area between $\mu - 3\sigma$ and $\mu + 3\sigma$ is 0.9973 [$= 2(0.34134 + 0.13591 + 0.02140)$]. Thus, the probability is only $1 - 0.9973 = 0.0027$ that a value of the random variable will lie outside this interval. This relates to the "3-sigma limits" on control charts, which are discussed in the following chapters.

The areas given in Figure 3.4 can be determined from Table B in the appendix of Statistical Tables. That table is for a *particular* normal distribution, specifically, the distribution with $\mu = 0$ and $\sigma = 1$. This distribution results when the transformation

$$Z = \frac{X - \mu}{\sigma}$$

is used for any normal distribution. This transformation produces the *standard normal distribution* with $\mu = 0$ and $\sigma = 1$. The transformation must be used before probabilities for any normal distribution can be determined (without the aid of some computing device).

To illustrate, suppose that a shaft diameter has (approximately) a normal distribution with $\mu = 0.625$ and $\sigma = 0.01$. If the diameter has an upper specification limit of 0.65, we might wish to estimate the percentage of shafts whose diameter will exceed 0.65, in which case a nonconformity will result. Since $0.65 = \mu + 2.5\sigma$, we can see from Figure 3.4 that the percentage will be less than 2.275%, since this would be the percentage for the area under the curve beyond $\mu + 2\sigma$. Specifically, we need to determine the shaded area given in Figure 3.5.

By using the transformation

$$Z = \frac{X - \mu}{\sigma}$$

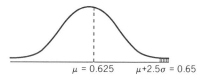

Figure 3.5 Distribution of shaft diameter.

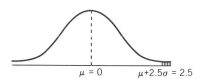

Figure 3.6 Standard normal distribution.

we obtain

$$z = \frac{0.65 - 0.625}{0.01} = 2.5$$

Notice that this z-value is the number of standard deviations that the value of x is from μ. This will always be the case.

We can now say that the probability of observing a z-value greater than 2.5 is the same as the probability of observing a shaft diameter in excess of 0.65. Thus, we need only determine the shaded area in Figure 3.6.

Since this shaded area does not cover $\mu = 0$, we must look up the area for $z = 2.5$ in Table B (at the end of the book), and subtract it from 0.5000. We thus obtain $0.50000 - 0.49379 = 0.00621$. Putting all of this together we obtain

$$P(X > 0.65) = P(Z > 2.5) = 0.00621$$

Thus, we expect approximately 0.621% of the shafts to not be in conformance with the diameter specification. (The probability is approximate rather than exact since a distribution was assumed that was approximately normal. We are not likely to encounter a random variable that has exactly a normal distribution.)

If there had been a lower specification limit, another z-value would have been calculated and the area obtained from that value would be added to 0.00621 to produce the total percentage of nonconforming shaft diameters. For example, if the lower specification limit was 0.61, this would lead to a z-value of -1.5 and an area of 0.06681. The total percentage would then be $6.681\% + 0.621\% = 7.302\%$.

In determining areas under the z curve it is generally desirable to shade in the appropriate region(s) before going to Table B. This will lessen the chances of making an error such as *subtracting* a number from 0.5000 for a problem in which the number should instead be *added* to 0.5000.

The determination of probabilities using the normal distribution should be accomplished in accordance with the following step-by-step procedure:

1. Transform the probability statement on X to the equivalent statement in terms of Z by using the transformation

$$Z = \frac{X - \mu}{\sigma}$$

2. Shade in the appropriate region(s) under the z curve as determined from the probability statement on Z.
3. Find the area(s) in Table B and obtain the answer in accordance with the following.

General Form of the Probability Statement		Action to Be Taken
1. $P(a < z < b)$	$(a < 0, b > 0)$	Look up the area in the table for $z = -a$ and $z = b$ and add the two areas together to obtain the answer.
2. $P(a < z < b)$	$(0 < a < b)$	Look up the area for $z = a$ and subtract it from the area for $z = b$.
3. $P(a < z < b)$	$(a < b < 0)$	Look up the area for $z = -b$ and subtract it from the area for $z = -a$.
4. $P(z > a)$	$(a > 0)$	Look up the area for $z = a$ and subtract it from 0.5.
5. $P(z > a)$	$(a < 0)$	Look up the area for $z = -a$ and add it to 0.5.
6. $P(z < a)$	$(a > 0)$	Look up the area for $z = a$ and add it to 0.5.
7. $P(z < a)$	$(a < 0)$	Look up the area for $z = -a$ and subtract it from 0.5.
8. $P(z > a$ or $z < b)$	$(a > 0, b < 0)$	Look up the area for $z = a$ and $z = -b$, add the two areas together and subtract the sum from 1.0.

It should also be noted that $P(z = a) = 0$ for any value of a. Thus, it is not possible to determine the probability that a shaft will have a diameter of, say, 0.640 feet; a probability can be determined only for an interval. *This is true for any continuous distribution.*

In summary, a normal distribution can often be used to approximate the actual (unknown) distribution of a random variable. The choice of which distribution to select for the purpose of determining probabilities such as those given in this section depends to a great extent upon how much accuracy is required as well as the availability of tables and/or software. All of the control charts presented in later chapters have an implicit assumption of either a normal distribution (approximately) or the adequacy of the approximation of the normal distribution to another distribution. The consequences of such an assumption when the assumption is untenable will vary from chart to chart. These consequences are discussed when each chart is presented.

3.6.2 *t* Distribution

Although all of the control charts are based upon the assumption of a normal distribution or normal approximation, the statistical techniques presented in Part III utilize other distributions. One such distribution is the *t* distribution, which is often referred to as *Student's t distribution.* "Student" was the pseudonym used by W. S. Gosset (1876–1937) for the statistical papers that he wrote while employed as a brewer at St. James's Gate Brewery in Dublin, Ireland. The brewery had a rule that prohibited its employees from publishing papers under their own names, hence the need for a pseudonym.

Gossett worked with small samples, often in situations in which it was unreasonable to assume that σ was known. He was also concerned with probability statements on $\overline{X}$ instead of on X. Thus, he was more interested in, say, $P(\overline{X} > a)$ than $P(X > a)$. At the time of his work (circa 1900) it was well known that if X has a normal distribution with mean μ and variance σ^2 [frequently written as $X \sim N(\mu, \sigma^2)$ where $\sim$ is read "is distributed as"], then

$$Z = \frac{\overline{X} - \mu}{\sigma/\sqrt{n}} \tag{3.7}$$

has a normal distribution with $\mu = 0$ and $\sigma = 1$. This stems from the fact that $\overline{X} \sim N(\mu, \sigma^2/n)$ when $X \sim N(\mu, \sigma^2)$. Thus $\overline{X}$ is "standardized" in Eq. (3.7) by first subtracting its mean (which is the same as the mean of X),

Table 3.1 Sample Averages

Sample		$\bar{x}$
1	2	1.5
1	3	2.0
1	4	2.5
2	3	2.5
2	4	3.0
3	4	3.5

and then dividing by its standard deviation. This is the same type of standardization that was used for X in obtaining $Z = (X - \mu)/\sigma$. The fact that the mean of $\bar{X}$ is the same as the mean of X is a theoretical result which will not be proven here. It can be easily demonstrated, however, for a finite population using the following example. Assume that a (small) population consists of the numbers 1, 2, 3, and 4 and we want to find the average of the sample averages in which the averaging is performed over all possible samples of size two. We would then obtain the results given in Table 3.1.

There are six possible samples of size 2 and the average of the six values for $\bar{X}$ is 2.5. Notice that this is also the average of the numbers 1, 2, 3, and 4. This same result would be obtained for samples of any other size, as well as for populations of any other size.

It should also be observed that there is slightly less variability in the $\bar{X}$ values than in the X values. For infinite populations (or finite populations that are very large)

$$\sigma_{\bar{x}} = \frac{\sigma_x}{\sqrt{n}}$$

where n is the sample size.

When n is large (say, $n \geq 30$) the sample standard deviation, s, can be used as a substitute for σ in Eq. (3.7) so as to produce

$$Z = \frac{\bar{X} - \mu}{s/\sqrt{n}} \tag{3.8}$$

and Z will then be approximately normally distributed with $\mu = 0$ and $\sigma^2 \doteq 1$.

Gossett's 1908 paper, entitled "The Probable Error of a Mean," led to the t distribution in which

$$t = \frac{\bar{X} - \mu}{s/\sqrt{n}} \tag{3.9}$$

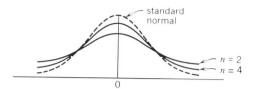

Figure 3.7 Student's t distribution for various n.

although his paper did not exactly give Eq. (3.9). The equation for the distribution is

$$f(t) = \frac{1}{\sqrt{(n-1)\pi}} \frac{\Gamma(n/2)}{\Gamma[(n-1)/2]} \left(1 + \frac{t^2}{n-1}\right)^{-n/2} \qquad -\infty < t < \infty$$

although the equation is not generally needed. (Γ refers to the gamma function.)

Unlike the standard normal distribution and other normal distributions, the shape of the t distribution depends upon the sample size. This is illustrated in Figure 3.7. It can be shown mathematically that the t distribution approaches the standard normal distribution as $n \to \infty$, as is illustrated graphically in Figure 3.7. There is very little difference in the two distributions when $n > 30$, so Eq. (3.8) might be used in place of Eq. (3.9).

Table C (at the end of the book) is used for the t distribution. Unlike the table for the standard normal distribution (Table B), Table C cannot be used to determine probabilities for any value of t.
illustrated in Part III.

It is worth noting that the t distribution arises not only when averages are used, but also for other statistics. In general

$$t = \frac{\hat{\theta} - \theta}{s_{\hat{\theta}}}$$

where θ is the parameter to be estimated, $\hat{\theta}$ is the estimator based upon a sample, and $s_{\hat{\theta}}$ is the sample estimator of $\sigma_{\hat{\theta}}$. The *degrees of freedom* for t are determined by the degrees of freedom for $s_{\hat{\theta}}$. Loosely speaking, a degree of freedom is used when a parameter is estimated. The t statistic in Eq. (3.9) has $n - 1$ degrees of freedom; other t statistics can have fewer degrees of freedom for fixed n.

3.6.3 Exponential Distribution

Another common distribution is the exponential distribution which is used extensively in the fields of life testing and reliability. It is not needed for any of the following chapters, but it is included here because the life of a manufactured product certainly depends upon its quality.

The equation for the distribution is

$$f(x) = \frac{1}{\theta} e^{-x/\theta} \qquad x > 0 \qquad (3.10)$$

where θ is the mean of the distribution. Readers interested in reliability and life testing are referred first to a survey paper by Lawless (1983), and then to books such as Lawless (1982), Nelson (1982), and Mann et al. (1974).

3.6.4 Lognormal Distribution

A distribution that is related to the normal distribution is the lognormal distribution. Specifically, if ln X (read "the natural logarithm of X") was normally distributed, then X would have a lognormal distribution where the equation for the latter is given by

$$f(x) = \frac{1}{\sqrt{2\pi}\,\sigma} \cdot \frac{1}{x} \exp\left[-\frac{1}{2\sigma^2} (\ln x - \mu)^2 \right] \qquad x > 0$$

where σ is the standard deviation of ln X, μ is the mean of ln X, and exp[ ] represents e raised to the bracketed power. (If we wished to transform the data and work with ln x, the distribution would then be normal rather than lognormal.) Like a normal distribution, the shape of a lognormal distribution depends upon σ. Unlike a normal, however, a lognormal is not symmetric, but a lognormal distribution will be close to a normal distribution when σ is small (say $\sigma \le 0.1$).

Ott (1975, p. 4) indicates that a lognormal distribution is oftentimes incorrectly assumed when data are unknowingly obtained from a mixture of two normal distributions with different means, with the proportion of data coming from each being considerably different. There is a very important message here. Assume that Figure 3.8 portrays part of a plant layout. There are thus two machines and two machine operators, but the data that are analyzed consist of mixed units from both machines. What if operator #1 is quite a bit faster than operator #2 so that most of the units come from machine #1? If the units produced with each machine have exactly the same distribution [say, normal ($\mu = 50$, $\sigma = 2$)] the fact that there are two different percentages of output coming from each machine will have no

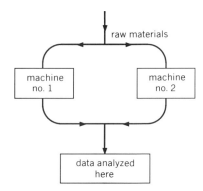

Figure 3.8 Product flow.

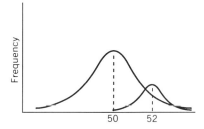

Figure 3.9 Distribution of units from machine #1 (μ_1 = 50) and machine #2 (μ_2 = 52).

effect on the distribution for the units from the two machines combined; it will still be normal (μ = 50, σ = 2). But what if machine #2 is out of adjustment so that μ_2 = 52 (Assume further that $\sigma_1 \doteq \sigma_2$.) The distribution for each machine might then be as in Figure 3.9.

When the units from the two machines are combined, the single distribution might appear as in Figure 3.10. If the data represented by the distribution in Figure 3.10 were standardized by subtracting the mean and dividing by the standard deviation, the resultant distribution would resemble a standardized lognormal distribution with σ = 0.5.

Thus, the data might appear to have come from a single lognormal distribution, whereas in actuality they came from two normal distributions.

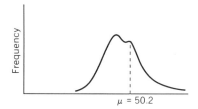

Figure 3.10 Distribution of units from the two machines combined.

For this example, the mixture of the two normal distributions will have a single "hump" (i.e., be unimodal) provided that $\sigma^2 > 32/27$, assuming that $\sigma_1^2 = \sigma_2^2$ and $\mu_1 = 50$ and $\mu_2 = 52$ [see Johnson and Kotz (1970, Vol. 2, p. 89)]. Since the lognormal distribution has only one hump, a mixture of two normals that produces two humps (i.e., in this case if $\sigma^2 \leq 32/27$) could not be mistaken for a lognormal.

This discussion of the lognormal distribution illustrates how easily erroneous conclusions can be drawn if data are not carefully analyzed. In general, data should be collected and analyzed in such a way that different causes of variation in the data (such as different machines) can be easily identified.

The lognormal distribution has found some application in quality improvement work, as is described, for example, in Morrison (1958).

3.6.5   Weibull Distribution

Like an exponential distribution, a Weibull distribution has been used extensively in life testing and reliability. The equation for the distribution is

$$f(x) = \alpha\beta(\alpha x)^{\beta-1}e^{-(\alpha x)^\beta} \qquad x > 0$$

where $\alpha > 0$ and $\beta > 0$ are parameters of the distribution. As with other distributions, the shape of a Weibull distribution depends upon the values of the parameters. When $\beta = 1$ a Weibull reduces to an exponential distribution. References on how a Weibull distribution can be used in quality improvement work include Berrettoni (1964).

3.6.6   Gamma Distribution

The gamma distribution is actually a family of distributions represented by the equation

$$f(x) = \frac{1}{\beta^\alpha \Gamma(\alpha)} x^{\alpha-1} e^{-x/\beta} \qquad x > 0 \qquad (3.11)$$

where $\alpha > 0$ and $\beta > 0$ are parameters of the distribution and Γ refers to the gamma function. In the special case in which $\alpha = 1$ we obtain the exponential distribution where β in Eq. (3.11) corresponds to θ in Eq. (3.10).

3.6.7 Chi-Square Distribution

This distribution is a special case of the gamma distribution. Specifically, the chi-square distribution is obtained by letting $\alpha = r/2$ and $\beta = 2$ in Eq. (3.11), where r is the degrees of freedom of the chi-square distribution.

3.6.8 Truncated Normal Distribution

This distribution has not been previously used to any extent in quality improvement work, but it is presented here because it is needed for the chapter on Taguchi methods (Chapter 14).

It results when a random variable has a normal distribution, but there is a lower bound and/or an upper bound for values of the random variable. When there is only a lower bound the distribution is said to be *left truncated*, and when there is only an upper bound the distribution is *right truncated*. When the truncation point is at the mean, this produces a half-normal distribution. When both bounds exist the distribution is said to be *doubly truncated*. The latter is discussed in detail by Johnson and Kotz (1970), whereas singly truncated normal distributions are discussed, at a more elementary level, by Meyer (1970), as well as in other statistical texts including Nelson (1982).

Only singly truncated normal distributions will be discussed here. A left-truncated normal distribution is represented by the equation

$$f(x) = \frac{k}{\sigma\sqrt{2\pi}} e^{-1/2[(x-\mu)/\sigma]^2} \qquad x \geq a$$

where

$$k = \left[1 - \Phi\left(\frac{a-\mu}{\sigma}\right)\right]^{-1}$$

a is the truncation point, and $\Phi[(a-u)/\sigma]$ is the cumulative area under the normal curve at the value of $(a-\mu)/\sigma$.

It can be shown that the mean of the distribution, $E(x)$, is given by

$$E(x) = \mu + k\sigma f[(a-\mu)/\sigma]$$

where k is as previously defined, and

$$f[(a-\mu)/\sigma] = \frac{1}{\sqrt{2\pi}} e^{-1/2[(a-\mu)/\sigma]^2}$$

The variance is given by the expression

$$\text{Var}(x) = \sigma^2\{1 + cf(c)[1 - \Phi(c)]^{-1} - [f(c)]^2[1 - \Phi(c)]^{-2}\} \quad (3.12)$$

where $c = (a - \mu)/\sigma$. [See Nelson (1982), p. 65.]

For a right-truncated normal distribution with truncation point a', the variance can be found by using Eq. (3.12), where the value of a would be chosen so that $a' - \mu = \mu - a$. The mean can be found from

$$E(x) = \mu - \sigma\left[\Phi\left(\frac{a' - \mu}{\sigma}\right)\right]^{-1} f\left(\frac{a' - \mu}{\sigma}\right)$$

where

$$f\left(\frac{a' - \mu}{\sigma}\right) = \frac{1}{\sqrt{2\pi}}e^{-1/2[(a'-\mu)/\sigma]^2}$$

The equation for the distribution is given by

$$f(x) = \frac{1}{(\sigma\sqrt{2\pi})\{\Phi[(a' - \mu)/\sigma]\}}e^{-1/2[(x-\mu)/\sigma]^2} \qquad x \leq a'$$

3.6.9 Bivariate and Multivariate Normal Distributions

These are other distributions that have not been used to any extent in quality improvement work. They are presented here because they are needed for the material on multivariate control charts in Chapter 9.

Recall that the equation for the normal distribution is

$$f(x) = \frac{1}{\sigma\sqrt{2\pi}}e^{-(x-\mu)^2/2\sigma^2} \qquad -\infty < x < \infty$$

If we have two *independent* process characteristics, x_1 and x_2, with means and standard deviations given by μ_1, μ_2 and σ_1, and σ_2, respectively, their joint distribution would be given by

$$f(x_1, x_2) = \frac{1}{2\pi\sigma_1\sigma_2}\exp\left[-(x_1 - \mu_1)^2/2\sigma_1^2 - (x_2 - \mu_2)^2/2\sigma_2^2\right] \quad (3.13)$$

where, as indicated previously, exp[ ] represents e raised to the bracketed power.

Using matrix notation, Eq. (3.13) becomes

$$f(\mathbf{x}) = \frac{1}{2\pi|\Sigma|^{1/2}} \exp\left[-\frac{1}{2}(\mathbf{x} - \mathbf{\mu})'\Sigma^{-1}(\mathbf{x} - \mathbf{\mu})\right]$$

where

$$\mathbf{x} = \begin{bmatrix} x_1 \\ x_2 \end{bmatrix} \qquad \mathbf{\mu} = \begin{bmatrix} \mu_1 \\ \mu_2 \end{bmatrix} \qquad \Sigma = \begin{bmatrix} \sigma_1^2 & 0 \\ 0 & \sigma_2^2 \end{bmatrix}$$

Σ^{-1} is the inverse of the matrix Σ and $|\Sigma|$ denotes the determinant of that matrix. For the general case of p variables the expression is

$$f(\mathbf{x}) = \frac{1}{(2\pi)^{p/2}|\Sigma|^{1/2}} \exp\left[-\frac{1}{2}(\mathbf{x} - \mathbf{\mu})'\Sigma^{-1}(\mathbf{x} - \mathbf{\mu})\right] \qquad (3.14)$$

where $\mathbf{x}$, $\mathbf{\mu}$, and Σ contain p, p, and p^2 elements, respectively.

The p variables $x_1, x_2, \ldots, x_p$ will generally not be independent, but Eq. (3.14) is the general expression for the *multivariate normal distribution*, regardless of whether the variables are independent.

When $p = 2$ and the variables are not independent, the *bivariate normal distribution* would be written as

$$f(x_1, x_2) = \frac{1}{2\pi\sigma_1\sigma_2\sqrt{1 - \rho^2}} \exp\left\{-\frac{1}{2(1 - \rho^2)}\left[\left(\frac{x_1 - \mu_1}{\sigma_1}\right)^2\right.\right.$$
$$\left.\left. -2\rho\frac{(x_1 - \mu_1)(x_2 - \mu_2)}{\sigma_1\sigma_2} + \left(\frac{x_2 - \mu_2}{\sigma_2}\right)^2\right]\right\}$$

which could also be written in the general matrix form given by Eq. (3.14). (Here ρ designates the correlation between x_1 and x_2.)

Readers requiring additional information on matrix algebra are referred to Searle (1982) and to a multivariate text such as Morrison (1976) for further reading on the multivariate normal distribution.

3.6.10 *F* Distribution

This is another distribution that is not generally used in control charting, but it is needed for a few of the statistical procedures covered in Part III, as well as in Chapter 9.

If two independent chi-square random variables are each divided by their respective degrees of freedom, and a fraction formed from these two fractions, the result is a random variable that has an F distribution. That is,

$$F_{v1,v2} = \frac{\chi^2_{v_1}/v_1}{\chi^2_{v_2}/v_2} \quad (0 < F < \infty)$$

where v_1 and v_2 are the degrees of freedom for each of the chi-square random variables, and are also the numerator and denominator degrees of freedom, respectively, for the random variable denoted here by F (which has an F distribution).

The shape of the distribution depends upon v_1 and v_2, so, as with the other distributions discussed in this chapter, there is not a single F distribution, but rather a family of such distributions.

Table D at the end of the book gives the values of F for different combinations of v_1 and v_2, as well as for $\alpha = 0.01, 0.05$, and 0.10, where α is the upper tail area (the upper tail is the only one that is used in most statistical procedures).

3.7 STATISTICAL INFERENCE

Various statistical distributions were presented in the preceding two sections. In this section we present methods of statistical inference that can be used for estimating the parameters of those distributions, and that are also needed to thoroughly understand control charts as well as the statistical methods that are presented in Part III.

3.7.1 Central Limit Theorem

It was stated in the section on the t distribution that $\overline{X} \sim N(\mu, \sigma^2/n)$ when $X \sim N(\mu, \sigma^2)$. When the distribution of X is unknown (the usual case), the distribution of $\overline{X}$ is, of course, also unknown. When the sample size is large, however, the distribution of $\overline{X}$ will be approximately normal. How large must the sample size be? That depends upon the shape of the distribution of X. If the distribution differs very little from a normal distribution (e.g., a chi-square distribution with a moderate number of degrees of freedom), a sample size of 15 or 20 may be sufficient. At the other extreme, for distributions that differ greatly from a normal distribution (e.g., an exponential distribution) sample sizes in excess of 100 will generally be required.

Stated formally, if $X_1, X_2, \ldots, X_n$ constitute a sequence of independent random variables (not necessarily identically distributed) with means $\mu_1, \mu_2, \ldots, \mu_n$ and variances $\sigma_1^2, \sigma_2^2, \ldots, \sigma_n^2$, then

$$Z = \frac{\sum_{i=1}^n X_i - \sum_{i=1}^n \mu_i}{\sqrt{\sum_{i=1}^n \sigma_i^2}}$$

will be approximately $N(0, 1)$ when n is sufficiently large and no single X_i has a dominant effect.

The central limit theorem forms the underlying foundation for many of the control charts that are presented in subsequent chapters.

3.7.2 Point Estimation

The distributions that were presented in Sections 3.5 and 3.6 all have one or more *parameters* that were, for the most part, represented by Greek letters. These (population) parameters are generally estimated by *sample statistics*. For example, μ is estimated by $\overline{X}$, σ^2 is estimated by S^2, and p is estimated by the sample proportion $\hat{p}$. In control chart methodology, however, the sample statistics are represented by slightly different symbols. This will be explained when the various control charts are presented in subsequent chapters. The important point is that the values of these parameters are generally unknown and must be estimated before control chart analyses and other types of statistical analyses can be performed. A *point estimate* is one type of estimate that can be obtained; in the next section another type of estimate is presented.

3.7.3 Confidence Intervals

A confidence interval is an *interval estimate* in which an experimenter knows that an interval that he is about to construct will contain the unknown value of a parameter with a specified probability. For example, a 95% confidence interval for μ is one in which an experimenter is 95% confident that the interval that he is about to construct will contain μ. The desired degree of confidence relates to the width of the interval—an increase in the width will increase the degree of confidence (for a fixed sample size).

Confidence intervals that utilize either t or z are always of the form

$$\hat{\theta} \pm t(\text{or } z) s_{\hat{\theta}}$$

where θ is the parameter to be estimated, $\hat{\theta}$ is the *point estimator* (the value of which is called the point estimate) of that parameter, and $s_{\hat{\theta}}$ is the estimated standard deviation of the point estimator.

For example, a large sample $100(1 - \alpha)\%$ confidence interval for μ would be of the form

$$\bar{x} \pm z_{\alpha/2} s_{\bar{x}}$$

so that a 95% confidence interval would be of the form

$$\bar{x} \pm 1.96 s_{\bar{x}}$$

Confidence intervals are not always symmetric about $\hat{\theta}$. One example is a confidence interval for σ^2 (using the chi-square distribution) where s^2 is not in the middle of the interval.

Confidence intervals can also be one sided. For example, a lower (large sample) 95% confidence bound for μ would be of the form

$$\bar{x} - 1.645 s_{\bar{x}}$$

where an experimenter would be 95% confident that μ is greater than or equal to the value that will be obtained for this lower bound.

In general, a 95% confidence interval means that if 100 samples were obtained and 100 intervals constructed, 95 of them should, theoretically, contain θ. If successive samples were taken, the results might appear as in Figure 3.11. A number of statistics texts contain a table that provides the general form of the confidence interval for a wide variety of different parameters [see, e.g., Hines and Montgomery (1980, p. 258)].

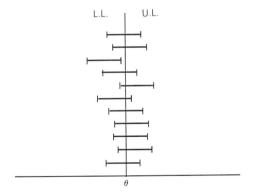

Figure 3.11 Confidence intervals. L.L., lower limit; U.L., upper limit.

3.7.4   Tolerance Intervals

Confidence intervals should not be confused with *statistical tolerance intervals*; the latter are statements on the *proportion* of the values in a population that will lie within an interval with a certain probability. For example, there is a probability of 0.90 that at least 95% of the population values for a normal distribution are contained in the interval $\bar{x} \pm 3.018s$, where $\bar{x}$ and s are computed from $n = 10$ observations. The reader is referred to Hahn (1970a, b) for a discussion of tolerance intervals and how they differ from confidence intervals and prediction intervals.

3.7.5   Hypothesis Tests

Hypothesis tests are covered in detail in introductory statistics texts, and will not be treated extensively here. The general idea is to formulate an hypothesis that is to be tested (e.g., hypothesizing that data have come from a normal distribution) and then use data to test the hypothesis and determine whether or not the hypothesis should be rejected. Hypothesis tests are used implicitly when control charts are employed.

Hypothesis tests using t or z are of the form

$$t(\text{or } z) = \frac{\hat{\theta} - \theta}{s_{\hat{\theta}}}$$

which is essentially a rearrangement of the components of the corresponding confidence interval.

3.7.6   Bonferroni Intervals

Bonferroni intervals are illustrated in Chapter 9 relative to multivariate control charts. They are based upon a common form of the Bonferroni inequality. When the latter is applied to confidence intervals the result is as follows: If k $100(1 - \alpha)\%$ confidence intervals are constructed for each of k parameters, the probability that every interval contains the unknown parameter value that it estimates is at least $1 - k\alpha$. Thus, if it is desired to have the probability of coverage for all k intervals equal to at least $1 - \alpha$, each interval should then be a $100(1 - \alpha/k)\%$ confidence interval. This has application in multivariate control charting in which there are p quality characteristics, and p intervals could be constructed to determine which characteristics are causing an apparent out-of-control condition.

See Alt (1982) for additional information on Bonferroni inequalities and intervals.

3.8 ENUMERATIVE STUDIES VERSUS ANALYTIC STUDIES

The basic concepts that have been presented in this chapter are primarily applicable to enumerative studies. An enumerative study is conducted for the purpose of determining the "current state of affairs" relative to a fixed frame (population). For example, if a large company wanted to estimate the number of clerical errors per hour made by clerical workers of a particular classification, a random sample from this class might be selected, and the average number of clerical errors made by *those* workers used as the estimate for all of the clerical workers of this type in the company.

By contrast, in an analytic study attention would be focused upon determining the *cause(s)* of the errors that were made with an eye toward reducing the number. Having an estimate of the number is obviously important, but trying to reduce the number is more important. Control charts could be used to monitor performance over time, and other graphical aids could also be employed. Special causes of variation in clerical errors might come to light, and some of the causes could be removable.

Statistical theory is not as easily applied to analytic studies as it is to enumerative studies. Even when an experiment is conducted to identify factors that may significantly affect process yield, so that process yield might be increased in the future, the results of the experiment can be applied, strictly speaking, only to future production in which the conditions are the same as those under which the experiment was conducted. (See Section 13.3 for additional discussion of this point.)

We may summarize by stating that the distinction between enumerative studies and analytic studies is essentially the difference between making inferential and descriptive statements regarding a fixed frame (a fixed list of population elements), versus determining how to improve future performance. Deming (1975) contains a detailed discussion of the difference between these two types of studies. See also Deming (1953), in which the author states that with an enumerative study one attempts to determine "how many," whereas with an analytic study one tries to determine "why."

REFERENCES

Alt, F. B. (1982). Bonferroni inequalities and intervals. In S. Kotz and N. Johnson, eds. *Encyclopedia of Statistical Sciences*, Vol. 1, pp. 294–300. New York: Wiley.

Army Materiel Command (1972). Tables of the cumulative binomial probabilities. AMC Pamphlet No. 706-109. Washington, D.C.: United States Army Materiel Command (Second printing: June, 1972).

Berrettoni, J. N. (1964). Practical applications of the Weibull distribution. *Industrial Quality Control 21*(1): 71–79 (August).

Deming, W. E. (1953). On the distinction between enumerative and analytic surveys. *Journal of the American Statistical Association 48*(262): 244–255 (June).

Deming, W. E. (1975). On probability as a basis for action. *American Statistician 29*(4): 146–152 (November).

Hahn, G. J. (1970a). Statistical intervals for a normal population. Part I. Tables, examples and applications. *Journal of Quality Technology 2*(3): 115–125 (July).

Hahn, G. J. (1970b). Statistical intervals for a normal population. Part II. Formulas, assumptions, some derivations. *Journal of Quality Technology 2*(4): 195–206 (October).

Harvard Computation Laboratory (1955). *Tables of the Cumulative Binomial Probability Distribution*. Cambridge, MA: Harvard University Press.

Hines, W. W., and D. C. Montgomery (1980). *Probability and Statistics in Engineering and Management Science*, 2nd ed. New York: Wiley.

Johnson, N. L., and S. Kotz (1970). *Distributions in Statistics: Continuous Univariate Distributions—1*. New York: Wiley.

Lawless, J. F. (1982). *Statistical Models and Methods for Lifetime Data*. New York: Wiley.

Lawless, J. F. (1983). Statistical methods in reliability. *Technometrics 25*(4): 305–316 (Discussion: pp. 316–335) (November).

Mann, N. R., R. E. Schafer, and N. D. Singpurwalla (1974). *Methods for Statistical Analysis of Reliability and Lifetime Data*. New York: Wiley.

Meyer, P. L. (1970). *Introductory Probability and Statistical Applications*, 2nd ed. Reading, MA: Addison-Wesley.

Morrison, D. F. (1976). *Multivariate Statistical Methods*, 2nd ed. New York: McGraw-Hill.

Morrison, J. (1958). The lognormal distribution in quality control. *Applied Statistics 7*(3): 160–172 (November).

Nelson, W. (1982). *Applied Life Data Analysis*. New York: Wiley.

Ott, E. R. (1975). *Process Quality Control*. New York: McGraw-Hill.

Rocke, D. M., G. W. Downs, and A. J. Rocke (1982). Are robust estimators really necessary? *Technometrics 24*(2): 95–101 (May).

Searle, S. R. (1982). *Matrix Algebra Useful for Statistics*. New York: Wiley.

"Student" (1908). On the probable error of the mean. *Biometrika 6*(1): 1–25 (March).

Weintraub, S. (1963). *Tables of Cumulative Binomial Probability Distribution for Small Values of p*. New York: Free Press of Glencoe (Macmillan Company).

EXERCISES

1. Compute S^2 for the sample $2, 6, 7, 8, 9$, and show that the same value of S^2 is obtained for the sample $72, 76, 77, 78, 79$. Comment.

2. Compute $\overline{X}$ for the numbers $23, 26, 27, 29, 30$.

3. Use Table A in the Appendix to produce a random sample of seven 2-digit numbers.

4. Use a hand calculator or computer software to determine the probability of observing at most one nonconforming unit in a sample of 100 if 1% nonconforming units are produced during that time period.

5. Determine the following probabilities for $X \sim N$ ($\mu = 40$, $\sigma = 5$) and $Z \sim N(0, 1)$.

   (a) $P(Z < 1.65)$ **(d)** $P(30 < X < 50)$
   (b) $P(Z > 1.30)$ **(e)** Find z_0 where $P(-z_0 < A < z_0) = 0.95$
   (c) $P(30 < X < 35)$ **(f)** $P(X = 43)$

6. Construct a 90% confidence interval for μ where $n = 100$, $s = 2$, and $\bar{x} = 20$. (Assume that X is approximately normally distributed.)

7. What is the probability of obtaining a head on a coin and a six on a die when a coin is tossed and a die is rolled?

8. Determine $P(t > 2.086$ or $t < -2.086)$ where a t statistic has 20 degrees of freedom.

9. Determine the approximate probability that a sample average ($\bar{x}$) taken from some population with $\mu = 50$ and $\sigma = 4$ exceeds 50.6, where the sample size is 100. Why is the probability approximate?

10. Explain the difference between a confidence interval and a tolerance interval.

11. Determine $\binom{8}{3}$ and explain what it means in words.

12. A sample is obtained from a normal population with $\bar{x} = 22.4$ and $s = 3.1$. We can say with probability 0.90 that at least 95% of the values in the population will be between what two numbers? (Assume $n = 10$.)

13. For a normal distribution, what percentage of values should be between $\mu - 2\sigma$ and $\mu + 2\sigma$?

14. What is the single parameter in the binomial distribution, and what sample statistic would be used to estimate it?

15. If we knew that a process was producing 0.5% nonconforming units, how many such units would we expect to observe if we inspected 400 units? What should we conclude about the process if we observed 12 nonconforming units?

16. Explain why we would generally not be able to compute σ^2?

17. Assume that the number of scratches per square yard of plate glass can be represented by the Poisson distribution. What is the probability of observing at most two scratches if it is known that the manufacturing process is producing a mean of 0.64 scratches per square yard?

PART II

Control Charts and Process Capability

CHAPTER 4

Introduction to Control Charts

In this chapter we discuss control charts in general; specific charts are covered in the succeeding chapters.

4.1 BASIC IDEA OF A CONTROL CHART

The construction of a control chart is based upon statistical principles. Specifically, the charts are based upon the statistical distributions that were presented in the preceding chapter, particularly the normal distribution. When used in conjunction with a manufacturing process, a control chart can indicate when a process is "out of control." Ideally, we would want to detect such a situation as soon as possible after its occurrence. Conversely, we would like to have as few "false alarms" as possible. The use of statistics allows us to strike a balance between the two. Basic control chart principles are illustrated in Figure 4.1. The center line of Figure 4.1 could represent an estimate of the process mean, or process standard deviation, or a number of other statistics to be illustrated in the following chapters. The curve to the left of the vertical axis should be viewed relative to the upper and lower control limits. The important detail to notice is that there is very little area under the curve below the lower control limit (LCL) and above the upper control limit (UCL). This is desirable since, as was mentioned in Chapter 3, areas under a curve for a continuous distribution represent probabilities. Since we look for a process that is out of statistical control when we obtain a value that is outside the control limits, we want the probability of conducting such a search to be quite small when the process is, in fact, in control.

A process that is not in a state of statistical control is one in which the variable being measured does not have a stable distribution. For example, a

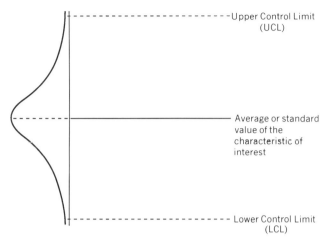

Figure 4.1 Basic form of a control chart.

plot of individual observations against time may indicate that the process mean may be fluctuating considerably over time.

If we are interested in controlling the process mean, μ, and the limits are given as $\mu \pm 3\sigma_{\bar{x}}$, the total probability outside the limits is .0027 (.00135 on each side) if X has a normal distribution. As explained in Chapter 3, $\bar{X}$ denotes a sample average and $\sigma_{\bar{x}}$ is its standard deviation. Thus, if we had exactly a normal distribution and if $\sigma_{\bar{x}}$ was known, the chances would be 27 in 10,000 of observing a plotted value of $\bar{X}$ outside the limits when the mean is at μ. We should not expect to have exactly a normal distribution, however, nor will we know the true process mean, μ, or $\sigma_{\bar{x}}$. Therefore, we should think of the limits as "3-sigma limits" (as they are usually called) rather than probability limits, since the exact probabilities are unknown. Some authors have provided probability limits for certain charts (as is discussed in Chapter 5), but the limits will not be true probability limits when the actual distribution is unknown (as is the usual case) and when parameters must be estimated. We can also argue that even if we knew μ (which will generally have to be estimated), we would not expect it to remain constant over a long period of time. Thus, when "probabilities" are applied to the future, they are only approximations—possibly poor approximations.

Nevertheless, if we take samples of at least size 4 or 5, the distribution of $\bar{X}$ will not differ greatly from a normal distribution as long as the distribution of X is reasonably symmetric and bell shaped. This results from the fact that the distribution of $\bar{X}$ will be more normal, in general, than the distribution of X. This is the result of the central limit theorem, mentioned in Chapter 3.

Even if the distribution is highly asymmetric so that the distribution of $\overline{X}$ will also be clearly asymmetric for small samples, data can usually be transformed (log, square root, reciprocal, etc.) so that the transformed data will be approximately normal.

4.2 PROCESS CONTROL VERSUS PROCESS CAPABILITY

Control charts can be used to determine if a process (e.g., a manufacturing process) has been in a state of statistical control by examining past data. More importantly, recent data can be used to determine control limits that would apply to future data obtained from a process, the objective being to determine if the process is being maintained in a state of statistical control. Control charts alone cannot produce statistical control; that is the job of the people who are responsible for the process. Control charts can indicate whether or not statistical control is being maintained and provide us with other signals from the data. They can also be used in studying process capability, as is illustrated in Chapter 7.

Control charts are essentially plots of data over time—a desirable way to plot any set of data. (See Section 11.6 for information on time sequence plots.) Figure 4.2 is an example of a control chart.

The asterisks in Figure 4.2 denote points that are outside the control limits. If control charts are being used for the first time, it will be necessary to determine *trial control limits*. To do so, the usual procedure is to obtain

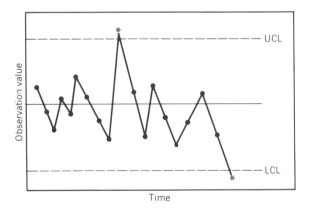

Figure 4.2 Typical control chart.

at least 20 subgroups or 20 individual observations (depending upon whether subgroups or individual observations are to be used) from either past data, if available, or from current data. If collected from past data, they should be relatively recent data so that they adequately represent the current process. The points in Figure 4.2 might represent such data. Because there are two points outside the control limits, these points should be investigated since they were included in the calculation of the trial control limits. Whether or not these trial limits should be revised depends upon the outcome of the investigation. If each of the points can be traced to a "special cause" (e.g., a machine out of adjustment), the limits should be recomputed *only* if the cause can be removed. If the cause cannot be removed it should be regarded (unfortunately) as a permanent part of the process, so the trial limits should not be recomputed. Thus, the trial limits should be recomputed only if the cause of points lying outside the limits can be both detected *and* removed. Occasionally, points will fall outside the limits because of the natural variation of the process. This is much more likely to happen when a *group* of points is plotted rather than the sequential plotting of individual points. This is discussed in detail in the next section.

The question arises as to what should be done when one or more points are outside the new limits that are obtained from deleting points that were outside the old limits. That could happen with the points in Figure 4.2, since deleting points outside the limits will cause the new limits to be closer together. Thus, the points that are just barely inside the old limits could be just barely outside the new limits. Technically, points that are outside the new limits should also be deleted and the limits recomputed if and only if an assignable cause can be both detected and removed, and this cycle should be continued until no further action can be taken.

After a process has been brought into a state of statistical control, a process capability study can be initiated to determine the capability of the process in regard to meeting the specifications. It would be illogical to undertake such a study if the process is not in control, since the objective should be to study the capability of the process after all problematic causes have been eliminated, if possible. Various methods can be employed for ascertaining process capability; these are discussed in Chapter 7.

4.3   REAL-TIME CONTROL CHARTING VERSUS ANALYSIS OF PAST DATA

Once the control limits are established, the charting should ideally be done in real time (i.e., plotting the data as it is collected), but this is not always possible. When a set of points is plotted all at once, the probability of

Table 4.1 Probabilities of Points Plotting Outside Control Limits

n	$.0027n$	Actual Probability (≥ 1 Point Outside Limits)
1	.0027	.0027
2	.0054	.0054
5	.0135	.0134
10	.0270	.0267
15	.0405	.0397
20	.0540	.0526
25	.0675	.0654
50	.1350	.1264
100	.2700	.2369
350	.9450	.6118

observing at least one point that is outside the control limits will obviously be much greater than 0.0027, which applies to points plotted individually. For n points, the probability of having at least one point outside the 3-sigma limits when the process is, in fact, in control is given in Table 4.1 for different values of n. The actual probability (assuming a normal distribution and independent points), can be approximated by $0.0027n$.

It can be observed from Table 4.1 that the approximation works quite well for moderate values of n. The reason for this is given in the Appendix to this chapter.

The important point is that there is a much higher probability of observing *at least* one point that is outside the limits when, say, 15 or 20 points are plotted together than when an individual point is plotted. When points are plotted individually in real time the .0027 probability applies to each point, so that there is indeed a very small probability of one particular point being outside the limits when the process is, in fact, in control. But when trial control limits are established, and periodically revised (using a set of observations each time), and when control charting is not performed in real time, the probability of observing one or more points outside the limits when the process is in control is clearly much greater.

This does not mean that we should ignore such points and not look for assignable causes; it simply means that we should not be too surprised if we cannot find them.

Although the use of 3-sigma limits has become quite customary, there is no reason they should always be used. If a particular work situation mandates that 20 points will always be plotted together on a chart whenever the charting is performed, the limits can be adjusted so that, if desired, the probability of observing at least one point out of 20 outside the limits when the process is in control is close to .0027.

Using the rule-of-thumb given in Table 4.1, we would use

$$np = .0027$$

so that with $n = 20$

$$20p = .0027$$

$$p = .000135$$

Thus, we would then look up $.50000 - .00007$ in Table B and observe that .49993 corresponds to approximately $z = 3.81$. We would then use 3.81-sigma limits. This is not to suggest that this should be done, but rather that it *could* be done.

4.4   CONTROL CHARTS: WHEN TO USE, WHERE TO USE, HOW MANY TO USE

General information has been given concerning how to use a control chart, and similar information is given in later chapters for each chart. When the decision is made to begin using control charts, various questions must be addressed, such as those indicated above.

It would be impractical to think of using a control chart at every work station in a plant. The nature of the product will often preclude measurements being made at various stages of production. There is also no need to use control charts at a point in a manufacturing process at which it is highly unlikely that the process could ever go out of control. Control charts should be used where trouble is likely to occur. When control charts are first implemented it is also important that they be used where the potential for cost reduction is substantial. This is desirable so that management can see the importance of the charts and support their continued use in a company.

The number of charts that can be handled in a plant may very well depend upon whether the control charting is to be performed manually or by computer. If it is done manually, more workers will have to understand the fundamentals of control charting than will be the case if the charting is to be handled by computer. Manual control charting could also be a problem if there is a need to use some of the mathematically sophisticated types of charts. There is also the problem of storing and displaying the charts when manual charting is used. The advantages of computerized control charting are discussed briefly in Chapter 10.

4.5   BENEFITS FROM THE USE OF CONTROL CHARTS

The benefits that result from the use of control charts are many and varied. One of the most important benefits is that they result in good record keeping. Whether charts are being used for administrative applications (as in Chapter 10) or for process control (or both), good records are essential if company-wide quality control is to become a reality. The mere maintenance of control charts often leads to a reduction in product variability simply because operators realize that management is placing considerable emphasis on product quality, and this causes them to exercise greater care. Control charts are invaluable as an aid in identifying special causes of variation, which often can be removed only through management action (e.g., replacing a faulty machine). Even if all special causes have been identified and removed, process improvement should still be sought. This is discussed further in Chapter 7.

4.6   LIST OF CONTROL CHARTS COVERED IN THIS BOOK

Many different types of control charts are covered in Chapters 5, 6, 8, and 9. They can be categorized as in Table 4.2.

Of these charts, which ones have been used the most often in the past? A partial answer to the question is contained in the results of a survey that was published in the May 1977 issue of *Quality Progress*. Part of the results are given in Table 4.3; the reader is referred to that source for additional results of the survey.

It can be seen that $\overline{X}$ and R charts have been used most often, and that multivariate charts and CUSUM charts are among the least-used charts. Chapter 9 of this book is devoted to multivariate charts and CUSUM charts are emphasized in Chapter 5. Why the emphasis on such little-used charts? Marquardt (1984, p. 12) states the following in discussing CUSUM procedures:

> But why, we may ask, are these more cost effective process control strategies so little used, so little researched, and so little understood? Some of the concerns that have been expressed are these strategies' complexity and their alleged difficulty to use on the factory floor and to teach to the production operators. Despite these expressed concerns, the tools for effective use are available. The tools are the current generation of computers and software knowhow.*

---

*Reprinted with permission of the American Statistical Association.

Table 4.2 Control Charts Covered in Subsequent Chapters

I. For Measurement Data with Subgrouping (One Variable)
    A. For Controlling Process Variability
        1. R Chart
            a. Without probability limits
            b. With probability limits
        2. s Chart
            a. Without probability limits
            b. With probability limits
        3. s^2 Chart
    B. For Controlling a Process Mean
        1. $\overline{X}$ chart
        2. CUSUM procedures
        3. Geometric moving average chart
        4. Acceptance chart
        5. Modified limits
        6. Difference charts
            a. For paired data
            b. For independent data

II. For Measurement Data without Subgrouping (One Variable)
    A. For Controlling Process Variability
        1. Moving range chart
        2. CUSUM for process variability
    B. For Controlling a Process Mean
        1. Individual observations chart (X chart)
        2. CUSUM for individual observations
        3. Moving average chart

III. For Attribute Data
    A. For Nonconforming Units
        1. NP Chart
        2. NP Chart with arcsin transformation
        3. P Chart
        4. Modified P and NP charts
        5. CUSUM procedures
    B. For Nonconformities
        1. c Chart
        2. c Chart with square root transformation
        3. u Chart
        4. ku Chart
        5. D Chart
        6. CUSUM procedures

IV. Multivariate Charts for Measurement Data
    A. With Subgrouping
    B. Without Subgrouping

Table 4.3 Percentage of Firms Using the Indicated Control Chart

	Firm size					
Technique	S_1	S_2	S_3	S_4	S_5	All
$\overline{X}$ chart (mean/average)	69	66	77	78	70	71
R chart (range)	56	61	67	71	67	64
s chart (standard deviation)	35	40	67	53	70	51
p chart (proportion)	13	47	43	61	67	48
c chart (number of defects)	35	53	39	43	59	45
u chart (defects per unit)	17	24	20	18	44	22
CUSUM chart (cumulative sum)	4	13	17	10	11	11
T^2 chart (multivariate average)	0	3	0	2	4	2
Moving average chart	13	31	27	35	44	32
Moving range chart	4	11	13	18	22	15
Test for runs	13	21	7	18	19	16
Median chart	9	13	10	6	26	12
Midrange chart	4	13	0	2	4	5
Geometric moving average	13	3	0	6	4	4
Lot plot method	0	16	2	12	11	9

*From E. M. Saniga and L. E. Shirland (1977). Quality control in practice...A survey. *Quality Progress 10*(5). © 1977 American Society for Quality Control. Reprinted by permission.

As was stated in the preface, this book was written under the assumption that a large percentage of its readers, if not a majority of readers, will be using a computer to implement the methods given in this book. Multivariate charts could not be easily handled without a computer and they are too complex to be taught to foremen and line operators, but CUSUM charts could conceivably be constructed manually. The latter are also not at all difficult to learn.

In summary, although $\overline{X}$ and R charts may still be the charts used most often in the immediate future, the availability of software for control charting will undoubtedly lead to increased usage of some of these superior and more sophisticated procedures.

APPENDIX TO CHAPTER 4:

Derivation of Entries in Table 4.1

The exact probability of observing one or more points outside the control limits when n points are plotted simultaneously is a binomial probability if the points are independent. The value of p in

$$P(x) = \binom{n}{x} p^x (1-p)^{n-x}$$

is taken to be .0027. Thus, since

$$P(x=0) + P(x \geq 1) = 1$$

we have the following when $n = 20$.

$$P(x \geq 1) = 1 - P(x=0)$$

$$= 1 - \binom{20}{0}(0.0027)^0(1-0.0027)^{20}$$

$$= 1 - (.9973)^{20}$$

$$= 1 - .9474$$

$$= .0526$$

The entries in Table 4.1 for other values of n were obtained in the same manner.

The reason that the approximation .0027n works so well for small to moderate values of n can be explained as follows: The actual probability can be written as

$$1 - (1-p)^n$$

which is equal to

$$1 - \left[1 - \binom{n}{1}p + \binom{n}{2}p^2 - \binom{n}{3}p^3 \cdots \binom{n}{n}p^n \right]$$

$$= \binom{n}{1}p - \binom{n}{2}p^2 + \binom{n}{3}p^3 - \binom{n}{4}p^4 \cdots \binom{n}{n}p^n$$

$$= np - \frac{n(n-1)}{2}p^2 + \frac{n(n-1)(n-2)}{6}p^3 \cdots$$

With $p = .0027$ and $n = 20$ this becomes

$$20(.0027) - \frac{(20)(19)}{2}(.0027)^2 + \cdots = .0540 - .001385 + .000224 \cdots$$

Thus, the first term is always np and the other terms will be comparatively small with alternating signs. When n is small the effect of ignoring these additional terms is almost negligible, but not so when n is large.

The approximation will thus be reasonably good when $n < 50$, and thus gives a quick estimate of the actual probability without having to compute $1 - (1 - p)^n$.

REFERENCE

Marquardt, D. W. (1984). New technical and educational directions for managing product quality. *The American Statistician 38*(1): 8–14 (February).

CHAPTER 5

Control Charts for Measurements with Subgrouping (for One Variable)

In this chapter we consider control charts that can be used when measurements are made and the values are obtained with sufficient speed to allow subgroups to be formed. Typical measurements are length, width, diameter, tensile strength, and Rockwell hardness.

As was indicated in Chapter 4, the $\overline{X}$ chart has been the most frequently used control chart. We shall first use a hypothetical data set to illustrate the construction and handling of an $\overline{X}$ chart and an R chart. An R (range) chart can be used for controlling the process variability and should generally indicate control before an $\overline{X}$ chart is constructed. The reason for this recommendation is that unless the variability of the process is in a state of statistical control we do not have a stable distribution of measurements with a single fixed mean.

5.1 ILLUSTRATIVE EXAMPLE

The data in Table 5.1 will be used to illustrate the construction of each chart.

If the data in Table 5.1 had been real data, they might have been obtained by measuring four consecutive units on an assembly line every 30 minutes until the 20 subgroups are obtained. (In general, 20 or more subgroups with at least four or five observations per subgroup should be obtained initially, so as to have enough observations to obtain a good estimate of the process mean and process variability.) The s is the sample

Table 5.1 Data in Subgroups Obtained at Regular Intervals

Subgroup	x_1	x_2	x_3	x_4	$\bar{x}$	R	s
1	72	84	79	49	71.00	35	15.47
2	56	87	33	42	54.50	54	23.64
3	55	73	22	60	52.50	51	21.70
4	44	80	54	74	63.00	36	16.85
5	97	26	48	58	57.25	71	29.68
6	83	89	91	62	81.25	29	13.28
7	47	66	53	58	56.00	19	8.04
8	88	50	84	69	72.75	38	17.23
9	57	47	41	46	47.75	16	6.70
10	13	10	30	32	21.25	22	11.35
11	26	39	52	48	41.25	26	11.53
12	46	27	63	34	42.50	36	15.76
13	49	62	78	87	69.00	38	16.87
14	71	63	82	55	67.75	27	11.53
15	71	58	69	70	67.00	13	6.06
16	67	69	70	94	75.00	27	12.73
17	55	63	72	49	59.75	23	9.98
18	49	51	55	76	57.75	27	12.42
19	72	80	61	59	68.00	21	9.83
20	61	74	62	57	63.50	17	7.33

standard deviation introduced in Chapter 3, namely,

$$s = \sqrt{\frac{\sum_{i=1}^{n}(x_i - \bar{x})^2}{n-1}}$$

We could use either R or s in controlling the process variability. The latter is preferable, particularly if a statistical quality control (SQC) operation is computerized, since it uses all the observations in each subgroup, whereas R is calculated from only two observations in each subgroup (the largest minus the smallest). Thus, although the range is much easier to calculate by hand than the standard deviation, it is wasteful of information. This loss of information is relatively inconsequential when the subgroup size is four (as in this example), but is much more serious when the subgroup size is somewhat larger. Therefore, when large subgroup sizes are used, the range should not be used to control the process variability. Instead, some statistic should be used that is calculated from all of the observations (such as s).

Another reason for preferring s over R is that other statistical methods that are useful in quality improvement work are generally based upon s (or s^2) rather than R.

A cursory glance at Table 5.1 reveals two comparatively small numbers in subgroup #10 (13 and 10), which cause the average for that subgroup to be much smaller than the other subgroup averages. At this point we might ask the following question: what is the probability of obtaining a subgroup average as small or smaller than 21.25 when, in fact, the process mean is in control at $\overline{\overline{x}}$, the average of the subgroup averages? Recall from Chapter 3 that we can "standardize" $\overline{X}$ as

$$Z = \frac{\overline{X} - \mu}{\sigma/\sqrt{n}}$$

so that $Z \sim N(0, 1)$ if $X \sim N(\mu, \sigma^2)$. The (usually) unknown process mean μ is estimated by $\overline{\overline{x}}$, where

$$\overline{\overline{x}} = \frac{\sum_{i=1}^{k} \overline{x}_i}{k}$$

for k subgroup averages. In this example $k = 20$ and the average of the 20 subgroup averages is 59.44, which is the same as the average of the 80 numbers. The process standard deviation σ could be estimated using either s or R. The latter will be illustrated first since that has been the conventional approach. How might we use the subgroup ranges to estimate σ? Could we use the average of the ranges to estimate σ, as we used the average of the subgroup averages to estimate μ? The answer to the latter question is "no." We would want our estimator of σ to be a statistic such that if we took a number k of samples from a large population of values whose standard deviation is σ, we would "expect" the average of the k values of the statistic to be equal to σ. That is, we would want the value of the statistic from a single sample to be an "unbiased" (in a statistical sense) estimate of the value of σ, such that the value of the statistic would be our best guess of the value of σ.

This will not happen if we use either the average of the subgroup ranges or the average of the subgroup standard deviations. Fortunately, however, tables have been constructed that allow the average of the ranges or the average of the standard deviations to be divided by a constant such that the resultant statistics are unbiased estimators of σ. Those constants, for different subgroup sizes, are given in Table E at the end of the book as d_2 and c_4. Thus, if we use ranges we would estimate σ by $\overline{R}/d_2$, where $\overline{R}$ is the average of the ranges. Similarly, if we use standard deviations we would estimate σ by $\bar{s}/c_4$, where $\bar{s}$ is the average of the standard deviations. (These and other constants are derived in the appendix to this chapter.) For the data in Table 5.1,

$$\hat{\sigma} = \overline{R}/d_2$$

$$= 31.30/2.059$$

$$= 15.20$$

where, as in Chapter 3, the "hat" ($\hat{}$) is used to indicate that σ is being estimated. If we were to use s our estimate would be

$$\hat{\sigma} = \bar{s}/c_4$$

$$= 13.90/.921$$

$$= 15.09$$

We can see that there is some difference in the two estimates, even though the subgroup size is quite small in this case. If we use the first estimator we would estimate $\sigma_{\bar{x}}$ as

$$\hat{\sigma}_{\bar{x}} = \frac{\overline{R}/d_2}{\sqrt{n}}$$

$$= \frac{15.20}{\sqrt{4}}$$

$$= 7.60$$

Then, $P(\overline{X} \leq 21.25)$ can be estimated using

$$z = \frac{\bar{x} - \hat{\mu}}{\hat{\sigma}_{\bar{x}}}$$

$$= \frac{21.25 - 59.44}{7.60}$$

$$= -5.02$$

where $\hat{\mu} = \bar{\bar{x}}$. We would estimate $P(Z < -5.02)$ as approximately zero since we cannot look up $z = 5.02$ in Table B. It clearly must be smaller than 0.00003 since that would be the probability for $z = -3.99$. In fact, the estimated probability can be shown to be 2.588×10^{-7}. (The word "estimated" is used since μ and σ are unknown, and the true distribution is almost certainly not exactly normal.)

Thus, before we even construct the $\overline{X}$ chart we have strong reason to suspect that the process was out of control (with respect to its mean) at the time the data in subgroup #10 were collected.

Are there other numbers that stand out? We observe that the range in subgroup #5 of Table 5.1 is considerably larger than any of the other ranges, and that this is due in large part to the existence of the number 97, which is the largest of the 80 numbers in Table 5.1. What is the probability of obtaining a value for the range that is at least as high as 71 (for this example) when the process variability is in a state of statistical control? This question cannot be answered as easily as the previous question.

5.1.1 R Chart

We can, however, construct an R chart for these data and see if 71 falls within the control limits. As with the other "standard" control charts that are given in this book, the control limits for an R chart are 3-sigma limits. Specifically, the control limits are obtained as

$$\overline{R} \pm 3\hat{\sigma}_R \tag{5.1}$$

The limits given by Eq. (5.1) can be shown to be equal to $D_3\overline{R}$ for the lower control limit (LCL) and $D_4\overline{R}$ for the upper control limit (UCL). (See the appendix to this chapter for the derivations.) Values of D_3 and D_4 for various sample sizes are contained in Table E.

Since we found that $\overline{R} = 31.30$ for the data in Table 5.1, the control limits are

$$\text{LCL} = D_3\overline{R}$$

$$= 0(31.3)$$

$$= 0$$

and

$$\text{UCL} = D_4\overline{R}$$

$$= 2.282(31.3)$$

$$= 71.43$$

It should be noted that the LCL for an R chart will always be 0 whenever the subgroup size is less than seven. The chart is given in Figure 5.1. We

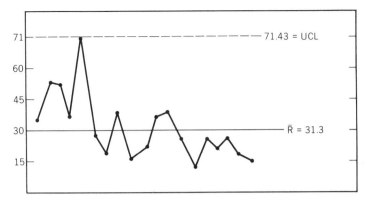

Figure 5.1 R chart obtained from the data in Table 5.1.

can see from Figure 5.1 that the range of 71 for subgroup #5 is (barely) inside the UCL. Nevertheless, we still might wish to investigate the values in subgroup #5 and try to determine why that range is considerably higher than the other ranges. There is also obvious evidence of a downward trend. Since this represents a reduction in variability (which is obviously desirable) we would certainly want to determine the cause (if possible), so that the cause could become a permanent part of the process.

The point to be made is that even though the chart indicates control, there is also evidence that some "detective work" might lead to further improvement. As Ott (1975) mentions in the preface: "Troubleshooting cannot be entirely formalized, and there is no substitute for being inquisitive and exercising ingenuity." Statements such as these apply to every type of control chart and every type of statistical procedure that we might use. No statistical quality control system should ever be so formalized that it does not leave room for the exercise of good judgment.

Implicit in the construction of an R chart is the assumption that the population of individual values from which the subgroups are obtained can be adequately represented by a normal distribution. Indeed, the D_3 and D_4 constants are tabulated under the assumption of a normal distribution. In practice, the "good judgment" referred to above should be used to see if the data are approximately normally distributed. Methods for doing so are discussed later in this chapter.

Even if the population was normally distributed, however, the distribution of the range is highly asymmetric and, thus, nowhere near a normal distribution. Nevertheless, whenever 3-sigma limits are used on any control chart there is the implicit assumption that whatever is being charted has a symmetric distribution, and that the "tail areas" are thus equal (and small).

The statistically proper approach would thus be to not use 3-sigma limits for an R chart if tables for "probability limits" are readily available. Grant and Leavenworth (1980, p. 292) do give an abbreviated table for this purpose; more extensive tables are given in Harter (1960). Table F at the end of the book contains some of the entries found in the latter.

5.1.2 R Chart with Probability Limits

One possibility in constructing an R chart would be to use $D_{.001}$ and $D_{.999}$ from Table F in place of D_3 and D_4. This would give equal tail areas (assuming normality) of .001. The probability limits would then be obtained as

$$\text{UCL} = D_{.999}\left(\overline{R}/d_2\right)$$

$$\text{LCL} = D_{.001}\left(\overline{R}/d_2\right)$$

If this approach had been used for the present example, the limits would have been

$$\text{UCL} = 5.31\left(\frac{31.3}{2.059}\right)$$

$$= 2.579(31.3)$$

$$= 80.72$$

$$\text{LCL} = 0.20\left(\frac{31.3}{2.059}\right)$$

$$= 0.097(31.30)$$

$$= 3.04$$

These limits obviously differ greatly from the 3-sigma limits. In particular, the (.001 and .999) probability limits will always be higher than the 3-sigma limits. Unlike the limits for the conventional R chart, the LCL using the probability limits will always be greater than zero since all of the values in the $D_{.001}$ column in Table F are greater than zero. This is a desirable feature since "significantly" small values of R can then show up as being below the LCL. Similarly, the UCL using $D_{.999}$ will always exceed the 3-sigma UCL. (This can be easily verified by calculating $D_{.999}/d_2$ for each value of n and observing that each of these values is greater than the corresponding value of D_4.)

Admittedly, $D_{.001}$ is used here rather than $D_{.00135}$ (there are no tables that give $D_{.00135}$), so the limits are not totally comparable. Nevertheless, the difference between the probability limits and the 3-sigma limits would not be this great if the distribution of the range was symmetric.

Which set of limits should be used in practice? Both sets are based upon the assumption of a normal distribution (of X), and the assumption that $\sigma = \overline{R}/d_2$. Neither assumption is likely to be met, and the statistical theory does not exist to allow the two approaches to be compared under other conditions. (In particular, the distribution of the range is not widely known for distributions other than the normal.) Nevertheless, the probability limits do have considerable appeal because the user of such limits is at least attempting to correct for the asymmetry in the distribution of the range.

5.1.3 s Chart

Although an s chart is generally preferable to an R chart when the computations are computerized, the former suffers from some of the same shortcomings as the latter. Specifically, the distribution of s is also asymmetric when the distribution of individual values is normal, although 3-sigma limits are typically used. Specifically, the control limits are

$$\bar{s} \pm 3\hat{\sigma}_s \qquad\qquad (5.2)$$

where $\bar{s}$ is the average of the subgroup standard deviations and $\hat{\sigma}_s$ is the estimate of the standard deviation of s. It can be shown that Eq. (5.2) leads to

$$\text{UCL} = B_4\bar{s}$$

$$\text{LCL} = B_3\bar{s}$$

where B_3 and B_4 are given in Table E. (See the appendix to this chapter for the derivation.) For the data in Table 5.1 we obtain

$$\text{UCL} = 2.266(13.899)$$

$$= 31.495$$

$$\text{LCL} = 0(13.899)$$

$$= 0$$

Like the two different types of limits for the R chart, these limits are also based upon the assumption of a normal distribution. We can also see from Table E that the LCL will always be zero when the subgroup size is less than six. (Recall that the LCL for the conventional R chart will always be zero when the subgroup size is less than seven.)

5.1.4 s Chart with Probability Limits

Can we improve upon these limits by using probability limits, as was done for the R chart? The answer is "yes"; the probability limits can be obtained by using the chi-square distribution discussed in Chapter 3, in conjunction with the following well-known theorem:

$$\text{If } X \sim N(\mu, \sigma^2), \quad \text{then } \frac{(n-1)S^2}{\sigma^2} \sim \chi^2_{n-1}$$

where $n - 1$ is the degrees of freedom. It follows from this result that

$$P\left(\chi^2_{.001} < \frac{(n-1)S^2}{\sigma^2} < \chi^2_{.999}\right) = .998$$

and so

$$P\left(\frac{\sigma^2}{n-1}\chi^2_{.001} < S^2 < \frac{\sigma^2}{n-1}\chi^2_{.999}\right) = 0.998$$

By taking square roots we obtain

$$P\left(\sigma\sqrt{\frac{\chi^2_{.001}}{n-1}} < S < \sigma\sqrt{\frac{\chi^2_{.999}}{n-1}}\right) = 0.998$$

Thus, if the process variability is in control at σ, 99.8% of the time the subgroup standard deviation, s, will fall between the endpoints of the interval. [The .998 is roughly equal to the (assumed) area between the 3-sigma limits on a standard chart, which is .9973.]

If an estimate, $\hat{\sigma}$, of σ is available from past experience or past (but relatively recent) data, that estimate could be used to obtain the control limits as

$$\text{LCL} = \hat{\sigma}\sqrt{\frac{\chi^2_{.001}}{n-1}}$$

$$\text{UCL} = \hat{\sigma}\sqrt{\frac{\chi^2_{.999}}{n-1}}$$

**Table 5.2 The .001 and .999 Percentage Points of
the χ^2 Distribution[a]**

n	$\chi^2_{.001,\, n-1}$	$\chi^2_{.999,\, n-1}$
2	1.570×10^{-6}	10.827
3	0.002	13.815
4	0.024	16.266
5	0.091	18.467
6	0.210	20.515
7	0.381	22.457
8	0.598	24.322
9	0.857	26.124
10	1.152	27.877
11	1.479	29.587
12	1.834	31.263

[a]The entries in this table (except for the first entry) were obtained using Minitab, a statistical software package. Minitab is a registered trademark of Minitab, Inc., 3081 Enterprise Drive, State College, PA 16801. Tel: (814) 238-3280, Telex 881612.

If σ is to be estimated from data collected in subgroups (as in the present example), an unbiased estimator of σ is $\bar{s}/c_4$ where c_4 is given in Table E. The control limits would then be

$$LCL = \bar{s}/c_4 \sqrt{\frac{\chi^2_{.001}}{n-1}}$$

$$UCL = \bar{s}/c_4 \sqrt{\frac{\chi^2_{.999}}{n-1}}$$

and the centerline would be $\bar{s}$. Table 5.2 gives the .001 and .999 percentage points of the χ^2 distribution for different values of n.

For the present example $n = 4$ so the limits would be

$$LCL = 13.899/0.921 \sqrt{\frac{.024}{3}}$$

$$= 1.350$$

$$UCL = 13.899/0.921 \sqrt{\frac{16.266}{3}}$$

$$= 35.140$$

Notice that these limits differ somewhat from the 3-sigma limits obtained previously (0 and 31.495).

Which set of limits should we use? The same kind of remarks that were made for the two types of R chart limits also apply to the two types of s chart limits. Specifically, both sets of limits are based upon the assumption of a normal distribution (of X), and the assumption that $\sigma = \bar{s}/c_4$. Neither assumption is likely to be met exactly, but the probability limits are more appealing than the 3-sigma limits since the area above the UCL for the latter will not be particularly close to the nominal value (0.00135).

This can be demonstrated as follows. The 3-sigma limits given by Eq. (5.2) can be converted from limits that give *nominal* tail areas of .00135 to limits that give nominal tail areas of .00100 by using 3.09 instead of 3.00. (The British actually use 3.09 instead of 3.00 for the various control charts.) The limits would then be obtained by using

$$\bar{s} \pm 3.09\hat{\sigma}_s$$

which is equivalent to

$$\bar{s} \pm 3.09\left(\frac{\bar{s}}{c_4}\right)\sqrt{1 - c_4^2}$$

For the present example the limits would be

$$\text{LCL} = \bar{s} - 3.09\left(\frac{\bar{s}}{c_4}\right)\sqrt{1 - c_4^2}$$

$$= 13.899 - 3.09\left(\frac{13.899}{.921}\right)\sqrt{1 - (.921)^2}$$

$$= -4.267$$

and

$$\text{UCL} = \bar{s} + 3.09\left(\frac{\bar{s}}{c_4}\right)\sqrt{1 - c_4^2}$$

$$= 13.899 + 3.09\left(\frac{13.899}{.921}\right)\sqrt{1 - (.921)^2}$$

$$= 32.065$$

Of course, the LCL would be set equal to zero, but notice that 32.065 differs considerably from the probability limit UCL of 35.140. Thus, *if* $\sigma = \bar{s}/c_4$

and we had exactly a normal distribution, attempting to obtain a nominal probability value of .001 by using $\bar{s} \pm 3.09\hat{\sigma}_s$ does not lead to a UCL that is particularly close to the .001 probability limit UCL.

Another way to view the difference would be to determine the χ^2 value that would cause the probability limit UCL to be equal to $\bar{s} \pm 3\hat{\sigma}_s$, and then compare the resultant upper tail area with .00135. Specifically,

$$\text{UCL} = \bar{s}/c_4 \sqrt{\frac{\chi_a^2}{n-1}} = 31.495$$

where χ_a^2 is the value that will result from solving the equation. Substituting in the values of $\bar{s}$, c_4, and n leads to

$$\chi_a^2 = 13.066$$

The value of a can be shown to be .0045. This is 3.33 times the nominal value of .00135.

What does all of this mean from a practical standpoint? It means that the number of "false alarms" will be much greater with 3-sigma limits than what the user would expect. Numerically, a false signal can be expected to occur once every 222 subgroups (1/.0045), whereas the user of the 3-sigma limits will naturally assume that a false signal will be received once every 741 subgroups (1/.00135). This is obviously a considerable difference, and could be a major consequence if the cost of looking for assignable causes is high. On the other hand, if the .001 probability limit is used a false signal will be received once every 1000 subgroups (1/.001).

Here again, this assumes that $\sigma = \bar{s}/c_4$ and that we have a normal distribution. Nevertheless, the type of data encountered in industry from which control charts are constructed is often reasonably close to a normal distribution, and we would certainly hope that the value of $\bar{s}/c_4$ is a good estimate of σ. Therefore, the probability limits for an s chart certainly have more appeal than the 3-sigma limits.

The reader should understand that a control chart or other statistical procedure is not invalidated just because the assumptions upon which it is based are not likely to be met. Rather, it is a matter of determining how "robust" the procedure is when the assumptions are not met (i.e., how insensitive is the procedure to a violation of the assumptions?). Some procedures will not be seriously affected by a slight-to-moderate departure from the assumptions, whereas other procedures will be seriously affected. These "robustness" considerations are discussed in each of the chapters on control charts.

The s chart will not be displayed here. Instead, the reader will be asked in Exercise 1 to construct the chart and to compare the configuration of points with the configuration of points on the R chart.

5.1.5 s^2 Chart

An s^2 chart is another chart that could be used for controlling the process variability. (With this chart the process variance would be controlled instead of the process standard deviation.) As would be expected, the control limits are similar to the control limits for the s chart. The limits are

$$\text{LCL} = \bar{s}^2 \left(\frac{\chi^2_{.001}}{n-1} \right)$$

$$\text{UCL} = \bar{s}^2 \left(\frac{\chi^2_{.999}}{n-1} \right)$$

The limits are not quite the same as the square of the limits for the s chart because $\bar{s}^2$ is an unbiased estimator of σ^2, not $(\bar{s}/c_4)^2$, where $\bar{s}^2$ is the average of the s^2 values.

5.1.6 $\bar{X}$ Chart

Regardless of which chart we select to control the process variability (R, s, or s^2), all of the points for the data in Table 5.1 lie within the control limits. Therefore, since the process variability is evidently in a state of statistical control, we can logically proceed to investigate whether or not the process mean is in control. An $\bar{X}$ chart will be used for that purpose.

The control limits for an $\bar{X}$ chart are obtained from

$$\bar{\bar{x}} \pm 3\hat{\sigma}_{\bar{x}}$$

where $\bar{\bar{x}}$ denotes the overall average of the subgroup averages, and $\hat{\sigma}_{\bar{x}}$ denotes an estimate of the standard deviation of the subgroup averages. It was established in Chapter 3 that $\sigma_{\bar{x}} = \sigma_x/\sqrt{n}$. Therefore,

$$\hat{\sigma}_{\bar{x}} = \frac{\hat{\sigma}_x}{\sqrt{n}}$$

The usual procedure for the $\bar{X}$ chart is to obtain $\hat{\sigma}_x$ from the subgroup ranges, namely,

$$\hat{\sigma}_x = \frac{\bar{R}}{d_2}$$

The control limits would then be written as

$$\bar{\bar{x}} \pm 3\hat{\sigma}_{\bar{x}}$$

$$= \bar{\bar{x}} \pm 3\frac{\hat{\sigma}_x}{\sqrt{n}}$$

$$= \bar{\bar{x}} \pm 3\frac{(\bar{R}/d_2)}{\sqrt{n}}$$

$$= \bar{\bar{x}} \pm A_2\bar{R}$$

where $A_2 = 3/(d_2\sqrt{n})$.

The control limits for the data in Table 5.1 are

$$\bar{\bar{x}} \pm A_2\bar{R}$$

$$= 59.4375 \pm 0.729(31.3)$$

$$= 59.4375 \pm 22.8177$$

so that

$$\text{LCL} = 36.6198$$

$$\text{UCL} = 82.2552$$

(The values of A_2 are given in Table E.)

There is no reason why the control limits must be obtained from $\bar{R}$, however. In particular, if the control chart user prefers an s chart over an R chart, it would make more sense to estimate σ from $\bar{s}$ instead of from $\bar{R}$. The control limits would then be obtained as

$$\bar{\bar{x}} \pm 3\frac{(\bar{s}/c_4)}{\sqrt{n}}$$

$$= \bar{\bar{x}} \pm A_3\bar{s}$$

where $A_3 = 3/(c_4\sqrt{n})$ and the values of A_3 are given in Table E.

The control limits for this example would then be

$$\bar{\bar{x}} \pm A_3\bar{s}$$

$$= 59.4375 \pm 1.628(13.899)$$

$$= 59.4375 \pm 22.6276 \tag{5.3}$$

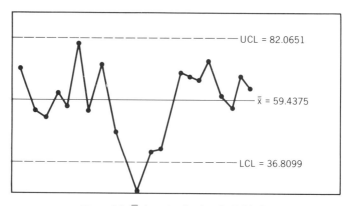

Figure 5.2 $\overline{X}$ chart for the data in Table 5.1.

so that

$$LCL = 36.8099$$

$$UCL = 82.0651$$

Thus, we see that there is some difference in the two sets of control limits, although the difference is fairly small.

The $\overline{X}$ chart with the limits obtained from using Eq. (5.3) is given in Figure 5.2. We observe that one of the 20 subgroup averages is below the LCL: the one corresponding to subgroup #10. Using the approximation given in Chapter 4, we would estimate the probability of observing at least one point outside the control limits when the process mean is in control as 20(.0027) = .0540. (The probability of observing exactly one point outside the limits when the process is in control is .0513, assuming normality.) Since this probability is not extremely small (say, less than .05), the process might have been in control at the time the data were collected, and the data may have been recorded correctly. Recall, however, that we previously estimated the probability of observing a subgroup average as small or smaller than 21.25 as being approximately zero. Therefore, by supplementing the control chart information with this extra detective work, we now have reason to believe that it is virtually impossible for the subgroup values to be valid numbers if the process was in control at that point. Perhaps the 13 and 10 should have been recorded as 43 and 40, respectively. If that were the case the limits could then be recomputed using the correct values.

5.1.7 Recomputing Control Limits

Assume, however, that the cause was detected as operator error, but there is no way to determine the correct value(s). The control limits should then be recomputed using the remaining 19 subgroups. Although this is the proper way to proceed (recall from Chapter 4 that a point should be removed from the control limit computations only if an assignable cause is both detected and removable), the question arises as to whether or not it will be worth the trouble. (The word "trouble" obviously has different meanings in this context depending upon whether or not the computations are computerized.)

Some generalizations can be made concerning the extent to which the recomputed limits will differ from the original limits. When the original data set contains n subgroups and one of the subgroup averages is below the LCL, it can be shown that the new UCL must exceed the old UCL by at least $(1/(n-1))A_3 \bar{s}_{(n)}$, provided that the value of s for the deleted subgroup is less than $\bar{s}_{(n)}$. (Here $\bar{s}_{(n)}$ denotes the average value of s for all n subgroups.) For this example, $s_{10} = 11.35 < \bar{s}_{(20)}$ so the difference must be at least $1/19(1.628)(13.899) = 1.191$.

Similar statements can be made when there is more than one point outside the control limits. In regard to the other control charts, if 30 samples of size four are used to compute the control limits for an R chart, and one of the ranges is above the UCL, the smallest possible difference between the original and recomputed UCL values is $.101\bar{R}$. Thus, if $\bar{R} = 50$ the difference would exceed 5. Again, that is not a small difference. (In Exercise 2 the reader will be asked to determine the difference for an s chart.)

The message is that not only is it proper to recompute the control limits when an assignable cause can be both detected and removed, it can also make a considerable difference in the limits.

When the $\bar{X}$ limits are recomputed we obtain

$$\bar{\bar{x}}_{19} \pm A_3 \bar{s}_{19}$$

$$= 61.447 \pm 1.628(14.033)$$

$$= 61.447 \pm 22.846$$

where $\bar{\bar{x}}_{19}$ and $\bar{s}_{19}$ indicate that the statistics are computed from the remaining 19 subgroups. The new limits are thus

$$\text{LCL} = 38.601$$

$$\text{UCL} = 84.293$$

We can see that the new limits are considerably different from the old ones. In particular, the new UCL exceeds the old UCL by 2.2279. This is considerably greater than the lower bound on the difference (1.191) since the average of the deleted subgroup was well below the old UCL, and, to a lesser extent, because $\bar{s}$ increased slightly.

5.1.8 Applying Control Limits to Future Production

We can tell by looking at the remaining 19 subgroup averages that all of them are contained by the new control limits. Thus, we could extend these limits and have them apply to future subgroups as they are plotted individually in real time, or to sets of future subgroups if for some reason real-time plotting is not feasible.

For how long should these limits be used? There is no simple answer to this question, but there are some guidelines that can be given. When control charts are implemented for the first time the process variability usually decreases. This is due not only to the removal of assignable causes, but also to the fact that workers become aware of the importance that management is attaching to quality improvement, and subsequently exercise greater care. Thus, variability that is due to workers will usually decrease even though it may have been "in control" initially.

Accordingly, the control limits should be revised from time to time by repeating the process of computing control limits from at least 20 subgroups. It is particularly important to revise the limits when there is evidence of a reduction in the process variability. The control limits for both $\bar{X}$ and s charts (and R charts) obviously depend greatly upon the process variability. If, for example, an s chart is being used and the limits are not revised (made tighter) when the variability decreases, a subsequent increase in variability (which would indicate that the process is probably out of control) might not be detected very quickly (if at all) if the points are within the (original) control limits. Similarly, a shift in the process mean might not be readily detected on an X chart if the limits on the chart are based upon a poor, outdated estimate of the current process variability.

5.1.9 Standards for Control Charts

Other writers have discussed the use of "standards" in conjunction with control charts. For example, if a machine can be adjusted so that the length of a bolt should be exactly 2 inches, the centerline of an $\bar{X}$ chart maintained for length should be set at 2 rather than some value of $\bar{\bar{x}}$. Similarly, if the variability has stabilized at σ', we could use that value in obtaining the control limits for an $\bar{X}$ and s (or R) chart rather than estimating σ by either $\bar{s}/c_4$ or $\bar{R}/d_2$.

The control limits for an $\bar{X}$ chart would then be set at $\mu' \pm A\sigma'$, where for the example just given $\mu' = 2$ and the values of A are given in Table E. For an s chart the centerline would be $c_4\sigma'$ and the control limits would be obtained from $B_5\sigma'$ and $B_6\sigma'$. For an R chart the centerline would be $d_2\sigma'$ and the control limits would be obtained from $D_1\sigma'$ and $D_2\sigma'$. The values for B_5, B_6, D_1, and D_2 are also given in Table E.

Some caution should be exercised when standards are used, however. For example, it might be desirable to control the process mean at a particular standard value but the current process may be incapable of meeting that standard. If the control limits are calculated from the standard, and, say, the current process mean exceeds the standard, subgroup averages could frequently exceed the UCL even when the process is in control. Another example would be where a company wanted to control the percentage of nonconforming items produced at a particular level (using one of the charts in Chapter 8). If the current percentage of nonconforming items exceeds this standard value by a sizable margin, many points will fall above the UCL and the "assignable cause" will be simply that there is a considerable difference between the current percentage of nonconforming items and the "hoped for" value.

Therefore, there can be serious consequences if standards are used unwisely. Even if the process mean and process variability do seem to have stabilized, the standard values do not have to be used. For a stabilized process we would expect $\bar{\bar{x}}$ and $\bar{s}/c_4$ to be very close to μ' and σ', respectively. Consequently, limits obtained using $\bar{\bar{x}}$ and $\bar{s}/c_4$ should differ very little from limits that would be obtained using μ' and σ'. Thus, nothing is lost by using the conventional approach. When in doubt as to whether or not to use standard values it is best not to use them since control chart limits should be based upon current conditions as reflected by recent data.

5.1.10 Deleting Points

A final word concerning the deletion of points and the recomputation of control limits. For the hypothetical example that was used, all of the points on the R and s charts fell within the limits, so it was not necessary to recompute the limits. What if a point had fallen outside the control limits on the s chart, with the point subsequently discarded and the limits recomputed; should that point also be excluded from the computations for the $\bar{X}$ control chart limits? Should it be included in computing $\bar{\bar{x}}$ but excluded in estimating σ? If a point is excluded on an s chart it should certainly not be used in estimating σ for the $\bar{X}$ chart, whether σ is estimated from $\overline{R}$ or $\bar{s}$. Technically, an assignable cause that affects σ need not have any effect on μ, and vice versa. (In particular, it is well known that $\bar{x}$ and s^2 are independent for a normal distribution.) Nevertheless, including a point for the estimation of $\mu(\sigma)$ and excluding it for the estimation of $\sigma(\mu)$ is apt to be more confusing than beneficial when charts are maintained by hand, and would make the programming somewhat tricky when a computerized system is used. The exclusion of such points will not make very much difference anyway unless the points are near one of the control limits.

5.1.11 Target Values

It is important to realize that a process can be in a state of statistical control and yet still be performing poorly if a target value is not met. For example, assume that a particular process characteristic should have a value of 12.0 for a product to function optimally, and the process appears to be in statistical control with $\bar{\bar{x}} = 13.3$. Having plotted points fall within 3-sigma limits is simply not good enough when $\bar{\bar{x}}$ is far removed from the target value. Target values are discussed in some detail in Chapter 14.

5.2 ILLUSTRATIVE EXAMPLE WITH REAL DATA

The hypothetical data set that was used to illustrate the $\overline{X}$, R, and s charts will be used later in this chapter to illustrate cumulative sum procedures. For the moment, however, we shall turn our attention to the real data set given in Table 5.3.

Table 5.3 Electrical Characteristics (in Decibels) of Final Assemblies from 11 Strips of Ceramic[a]

16.5	15.7	17.3	16.9	15.5	13.5	16.5	16.5	14.5	16.9	16.5
17.2	17.6	15.8	15.8	16.6	13.5	14.3	16.9	14.9	16.5	16.7
16.6	16.3	16.8	16.9	15.9	16.0	16.9	16.8	15.6	17.1	16.3
15.0	14.6	17.2	16.8	16.5	15.9	14.6	16.1	16.8	15.8	14.0
14.4	14.9	16.2	16.6	16.1	13.7	17.5	16.9	12.9	15.7	14.9
16.5	15.2	16.9	16.0	16.2	15.2	15.5	15.0	16.6	13.0	15.6
15.5	16.1	14.9	16.6	15.7	15.9	16.1	16.1	10.9	15.0	16.8
$\bar{x} =$ 16.0	15.8	16.4	16.5	16.1	14.8	15.9	16.3	14.6	15.7	15.8
$R =$ 2.8	3.0	2.4	1.1	1.1	2.5	3.2	1.9	5.9	4.1	2.8

[a] From Ellis R. Ott (1949). Variables and Control Charts in Production Research, *Industrial Quality Control* 6(3) 30. Reprinted with permission of the American Society for Quality Control.

The data were originally analyzed by Ott (1949), and can also be found on p. 32 of Ott (1975). The objective was to determine whether the variability (which was considered excessive) in a particular electrical characteristic that was involved in the assembly of electronic units was significant over the 11 ceramic sheets relative to the variability between the 7 strips within each sheet. If the variability between sheets turned out to be significant, inferior sheets could then be discarded.

Ellis R. Ott addressed this question by constructing an $\overline{X}$ and an R chart. The control limits for the R chart were

$$\text{LCL} = D_3\overline{R}$$
$$= 0.076(2.8)$$
$$= 0.2128$$

and

$$\text{UCL} = D_4\overline{R}$$
$$= 1.924(2.8)$$
$$= 5.3872$$

We observe that the range for subgroup #9 exceeds the UCL.

The limits for the $\overline{X}$ chart can be shown to be

$$\text{LCL} = \overline{\overline{x}} - A_2\overline{R}$$
$$= 15.81 - 0.419(2.8)$$
$$= 14.637$$
$$\text{UCL} = \overline{\overline{x}} + A_2\overline{R}$$
$$= 15.81 + 0.419(2.8)$$
$$= 16.983$$

It can be observed that the average for ceramic sheet #9 is just outside the LCL.

Thus, there is an apparent problem with subgroup #9 in regard to both average and variability. Closer examination of the data reveals that this is the result of the fact that there are two values for this ceramic sheet (10.9 and 12.9) that are smaller than any of the other values in the table.

In particular, the 10.9 is well below the average value for that sheet number. If that number was excluded, the average and range for that ceramic sheet would fall in line with the averages and ranges of the other ceramic sheets. Consequently, this value is perhaps one that was recorded incorrectly, rather than indicating that ceramic sheet #9 is inferior to the other sheets."

It is worth noting that if $\hat{\sigma}_{\bar{x}}$ had been obtained using s rather than R, $\bar{x}_9$ would have been slightly above the LCL, as the reader is asked to demonstrate in Exercise 3.

It should also be noted that this is an application to past data, as is also done when trial control limits are determined. The difference is that in this example there is no intent to apply the limits to future production.

5.3 CUSUM PROCEDURES FOR CONTROLLING A PROCESS MEAN

The amount of space devoted to $\bar{X}$, R, and s charts in this chapter is more in line with their popularity and frequency of usage than in accord with the author's view of their relative importance. Although Saniga and Shirland's (1977) survey indicated that these are the charts that were used most frequently, they can and should (in the opinion of the author and others) often be replaced by more efficient cumulative sum (CUSUM) procedures.

We would certainly want whatever procedure we use for controlling the process mean μ to enable us to detect a shift in the mean that is of any consequence as quickly as possible, but not give us a high rate of false signals. For example, we want to quickly detect a shift that would cause nonconforming units to be produced, but not to frequently receive signals indicating a shift when in fact there is no shift.

Assume for the moment that our only objective in process control is to prevent the production of nonconforming units, and that this objective will determine our control chart construction and usage.

We will assume that we have a process in which the process characteristic under scrutiny has parameter values of $\mu = 75$ and $\sigma = 5$ and the specifications are 55 and 95. The specifications cannot be altered and values outside these specs will result in the unit being nonconforming. If we assume that the process characteristic has virtually a normal distribution, the fact that the specs are four standard deviation units from the mean will result in about 6 of every 100,000 units produced being nonconforming. Idealistically, even that number is too high, as at most a small number of nonconforming parts per million is considered acceptable, but that might be the best performance that the current process can attain.

If an $\bar{X}$ chart is being used to control the process mean we will assume that the LCL = 67.5 and the UCL = 82.5. (This is what they would be if

$\bar{\bar{x}} = \mu$, $\hat{\sigma} = \sigma$, and $n = 4$.) If there is a $2\sigma_{\bar{x}}$ upward shift in the process mean (to 80), it would certainly be of interest to determine the effect that this will have on the number of nonconforming units that will be produced, and also how long it should take to detect this shift with an $\bar{X}$ chart.

The effect of the mean shift will result in a smaller percentage of units falling below the lower specification (3 out of 10 million instead of 3 out of 100,000), but a much higher percentage falling above the upper specification (1 out of 1,000 instead of 3 out of 100,000). The net effect is to increase the (expected) number of nonconforming units from 6 out of 100,000 to 135 out of 100,000. If the product is a high volume item such as a small steel ball, this shift would result in a considerable increase in the number of nonconforming units produced per day. Obviously it would be desirable to detect this shift as soon as possible. How long will it take to detect this shift with an $\bar{X}$ chart?

This question can be answered by determining $P(\bar{X} > 82.5)$ when $\mu = 80$. Thus,

$$z = \frac{82.5 - 80}{2.5}$$

$$= 1$$

and $P(Z > 1) = .1587$. [We can ignore $P(\bar{X} < 67.5)$ when $\mu = 80$ since that is virtually zero.] The concept of average run length (ARL) will be mentioned frequently in this section. This will refer to the expected number of subgroups that would be obtained before an out-of-control signal is received. For example, if with an $\bar{X}$ chart the process mean is in control at $\bar{\bar{x}}$, the probability that a subgroup average will fall outside the control limits is .0027 when the subgroup averages are plotted one at a time. The ARL is then $1/.0027 = 370.37$. Thus, we would "expect" to observe 371 subgroups before receiving an out-of-control signal. (Obviously we want this number to be high when the process is in control. The justification for this ARL calculation is given in the appendix to this chapter.)

Thus, for the mean shift to $\mu = 80$ the ARL $= 1/0.1587 = 6.30$. If samples (subgroups) are taken every 30 minutes, we would expect to detect the shift 3.5 hours after the shift had occurred. Accordingly, if 100,000 steel balls were produced per 8-hour day, we would expect about 60 nonconforming units to be produced before the shift is detected.

5.3.1 CUSUM Procedure versus $\bar{X}$ Chart

Could the shift be detected any faster by using a substitute for an $\bar{X}$ chart? The answer is "yes." With one of the CUSUM procedures to be presented

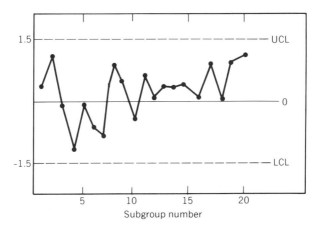

Figure 5.3 $\bar{X}$ chart for data generated from $N(0,1)$ and $N(0.5,1)$; $n = 4$.

in this section the ARL = 3.34 and with a slightly different CUSUM procedure the ARL = 3.226. With either procedure the shift would be detected within 2 hours as compared to 3.5 hours with the $\bar{X}$ chart. For this example about 26 fewer nonconforming units would be produced before the shift is detected.

Historically, the $\bar{X}$ chart has been considered effective in quickly detecting large mean shifts. For example, a 3-sigma mean shift (in this case to $\mu = 82.5$) would have an ARL = $1/.5 = 2$, and a 4-sigma shift would have an ARL = $1/.8413 = 1.19$. With the first CUSUM procedure alluded to the corresponding numbers are 2.19 and 1.71, and for the second CUSUM procedure the numbers are 1.922 and 1.322.

Thus, for detecting large mean shifts it is difficult to improve upon the performance of an $\bar{X}$ chart, but it is possible to design a CUSUM procedure that will be quite competitive (if not superior) to an $\bar{X}$ chart in detecting such shifts. For detecting small shifts (around one sigma), CUSUM procedures are far superior to an $\bar{X}$ chart.

The following example with simulated data should serve to illustrate how a small mean shift can be "camouflaged" by an $\bar{X}$ chart. Figure 5.3 is an $\bar{X}$ chart that consists of averages of four observations generated from a normal distribution. Initially, the distribution is $N(0,1)$ but beginning at some point the data are generated from a distribution that is $N(0.5,1)$. Can you determine visually the point at which the shift occurs?

Since $\sigma = 1$, $\sigma_{\bar{x}} = 1/\sqrt{4} = 0.5$ so that the shift is a 1-sigma shift. Yet all of the points are well within the control limits, and it may seem at first glance as though the chart contains a random configuration of points.

Closer examination, however, reveals that 10 consecutive averages are above the midline (11–20). The probability of that happening by chance if the mean is at $\mu = 0$ is (using the binomial distribution again) $(1/2)^{10} = .001$. Since this is a very small probability, we would certainly suspect that a shift had occurred by subgroup number 20. This is an application of what is referred to as *runs criteria* in conjunction with an $\overline{X}$ chart. This has been discussed by Duncan (1986, p. 434), Ott (1975, p. 49), and Grant and Leavenworth (1980, p. 91), among others. Criteria include seven consecutive points above or below the midline, and a number of consecutive points outside of 1-sigma limits or 2-sigma limits. Such criteria could easily be established so that the probability of meeting any of the criteria is quite small when the process is in control. Thus, if any of the criteria are met we would have reason to suspect that there has been a shift in the process mean.

If the control charts are being maintained by hand this would require that an operator look not only at the 3-sigma limits, but also at 1- and 2-sigma limits, and look for runs of points. Such an approach could, of course, be computerized, which would require that one set of criteria be selected from a number that have been proposed.

The choice of criteria would unquestionably be somewhat subjective, however, and it would be much easier to use some simple, straightforward procedure in place of runs criteria. Such a procedure will be given after discussing the development of CUSUM procedures.

But first, where did the shift occur? The random numbers from $N(0.5, 1)$ were generated starting with subgroup #13. We will see how quickly the shift would be detected with the suggested CUSUM procedures.

5.3.2 CUSUM Procedures: Principles and Historical Development

Cumulative sum charts were first proposed by Page (1954), and a number of modifications have resulted since then. As the name implies, sums are accumulated, but an observation (which may be a single reading or a statistic obtained from a sample) is "accumulated" only if it exceeds the goal value (e.g., the estimate of the process mean) by more than k units. Not all CUSUM procedures require the use of charts, but charts can nevertheless be used with any CUSUM procedure.

The survey article by Saniga and Shirland (1977) indicated that a relatively small percentage of firms in the United States used CUSUM procedures. A decade later, the author (of this book) finds that workers engaged in quality improvement are still primarily interested in learning about $\overline{X}$ and R charts.

Some CUSUM procedures are easy to learn (and to program) and are also quite intuitive, while others are somewhat more involved. The emphasis in this section will be on the former.

If quality control personnel are to make the transition from $\overline{X}$ charts to CUSUM procedures, it seems reasonable to assume that they will be drawn toward procedures that are easy to understand and that bear some relationship to an $\overline{X}$ chart. The methods proposed by Lucas (1982) and Lucas and Crosier (1982a) meet both requirements, and will now be examined extensively.

For an $\overline{X}$ chart a subgroup average will be outside the control limits if z is either greater than 3 or less than -3 where

$$z = \frac{\bar{x} - \bar{\bar{x}}}{\hat{\sigma}_{\bar{x}}} \tag{5.4}$$

This follows from the fact that if we solve Eq. (5.4) for $\bar{x}$ we obtain

$$\bar{x} = \bar{\bar{x}} + z\hat{\sigma}_{\bar{x}} \tag{5.5}$$

Notice that the right-hand side of Eq. (5.5) gives the UCL of an $\overline{X}$ chart if $z = 3$, and the LCL if $z = -3$. Thus, if the value of $\bar{x}$ in Eq. (5.4) produces $z = 2$, then $\bar{x} = \bar{\bar{x}} + 2\hat{\sigma}_{\bar{x}}$ is inside the UCL by the amount $\hat{\sigma}_{\bar{x}}$. If the value of $\bar{x}$ produces $z = 4$, then $\bar{x} = \bar{\bar{x}} + 4\hat{\sigma}_{\bar{x}}$ is outside the UCL by the amount $\hat{\sigma}_{\bar{x}}$.

Therefore, a worker who wanted to know whether or not a subgroup average would fall outside the control limits on an $\overline{X}$ chart could simply calculate the z-value and would not have to know the control limits. This might seem an awkward alternative to an $\overline{X}$ chart, but it is important to recognize that a list of z-values would indicate whether the corresponding subgroup averages are inside or outside the control limits. A list of such z-values is an integral part of the method proposed by Lucas (1982).

The pair of cumulative sums used is

$$S_{Hi} = \max\left[0, (z_i - k) + S_{Hi-1}\right]$$

and

$$S_{Li} = \max\left[0, (-z_i - k) + S_{Li-1}\right]$$

where the first is for detecting positive mean shifts and the second is for detecting negative mean shifts. The value of k is usually selected to be one-half of the mean shift (in z units) that one wishes to detect. We have seen that an $\overline{X}$ chart is effective in detecting a large mean shift such as a 3-sigma or 4-sigma shift. Therefore, there would be no point in setting $k = 1.5$ or $k = 2.0$. The usual choice is $k = 0.5$, which is the appropriate choice for detecting a 1-sigma shift. Two sums, S_{Hi} and S_{Li}, are computed for each z_i where z is as defined in Eq. (5.4), and i designates the ith subgroup. Notice that there is a minus sign in front of z_i in the formula for computing S_{Li}. This simply ensures that $-z_i$ will be positive whenever there is a negative mean shift. Notice also that neither S_{Hi} nor S_{Li} will ever be negative since they will always be the maximum ("max") of 0 and $(z_i - k) + S_{Hi-1}$ and $(-z_i - k) + S_{Li-1}$, respectively. The sums start with $S_{Ho} = 0$ and $S_{Lo} = 0$. The sums are generally reset after an out-of-control signal is received, but the sums do not have to be reset to zero. This will be explained later.

There obviously must be some "threshold" value such that when either sum exceeds that value an out-of-control signal will be given. This has been designated by h in the two papers that were previously cited. Typically, h is chosen to be either 4 or 5. The logic behind those choices will be discussed later.

Table 5.4 Simulated Data Charted in Figure 5.3

			From N(0, 1):				
1.54	0.86	−0.89	−1.88	−1.85	−2.53		
−0.09	0.57	0.21	−0.43	2.03	−0.59		
1.75	1.17	−1.23	−0.42	−0.64	0.60		
−1.58	1.82	1.77	−1.45	0.31	−0.22		
$\bar{x} = 0.41$	1.11	−0.04	−1.04	−0.04	−0.68		
−0.74	2.10	0.56	−1.53	0.53	−0.81		
−1.25	1.48	1.78	0.99	−0.52	0.67		
−0.40	0.86	−0.81	−2.38	1.71	0.42		
−1.01	−1.19	0.97	1.41	0.43	0.46		
$\bar{x} = -0.85$	0.81	0.62	−0.38	0.54	0.18		
			From N(0.5, 1):				
0.84	0.22	2.30	2.14	1.03	−0.90	1.56	1.28
−0.71	1.27	−0.33	0.51	0.30	1.71	−0.70	0.98
0.27	0.64	0.19	−1.65	0.55	−1.08	2.06	1.29
0.93	−0.83	−0.38	−0.14	1.65	0.93	0.88	0.81
$\bar{x} = 0.33$	0.32	0.44	0.22	0.88	0.16	0.95	1.09

Table 5.5 CUSUM Values

Subgroup Number	Subgroup Average	z	S_H	S_L
1	0.41	0.82	0.32	0
2	1.11	2.22	2.04	0
3	−0.04	−0.08	1.46	0
4	−1.04	−2.08	0	1.58
5	−0.04	−0.08	0	1.16
6	−0.68	−1.36	0	2.02
7	−0.85	−1.70	0	3.22
8	0.81	1.62	1.12	1.10
9	0.62	1.24	1.86	0
10	−0.38	−0.76	0.60	0.26
11	0.54	1.08	1.18	0
12	0.18	0.36	1.04	0
13	0.33	0.66	1.20	0
14	0.32	0.64	1.34	0
15	0.44	0.88	1.72	0
16	0.22	0.44	1.66	0
17	0.88	1.76	2.92	0
18	0.16	0.32	2.74	0
19	0.95	1.90	4.14^a	0
20	1.09	2.18	5.82	0

^{a}Exceeds $h = 4$.

We shall now illustrate this procedure with the simulated data that were graphed in Figure 5.3. The data are given in Table 5.4 and the cumulative sums are given in Table 5.5.

By studying Table 5.5 we can practically "see" how the $\overline{X}$ chart would look without having constructed it. For example, if we look at the first seven values for S_H and S_L, we see a string of nonzero numbers for S_H (and zeros for S_L), followed by a string of nonzero numbers for S_L (and zeros for S_H). This tells us that the first few subgroup averages are considerably above μ (or $\overline{\overline{x}}$, in general), and the next few averages are considerably below μ. The fact that the sums reach 2.04 for S_H and 3.22 for S_L indicates that at least one average had to be far above μ, and at least one average had to be far below μ. [If every average was within one-half sigma ($\sigma_{\overline{x}}$) of μ, all of the values for S_H and S_L would be zero.] Of course, we can see that much easier by looking at the averages in Table 5.5, but the important point is that whenever there is a trend it will be reflected by the values of S_H and/or S_L.

The trend begins to appear shortly after subgroup #7, and an out-of-control signal is received at subgroup #19, using $h = 4$. Recall that the

Table 5.6 Average Run Lengths for a CUSUM Procedure with $h = 4$ or $h = 5$ ($k = 0.5$)[a]

Mean Shift (in Standard Units)	$h = 4$	$h = 5$
0	168	465
0.25	74.2	139
0.50	26.6	38.0
0.75	13.3	17.0
1.00	8.38	10.4
1.50	4.75	5.75
2.00	3.34	4.01
2.50	2.62	3.11
3.00	2.19	2.57
4.00	1.71	2.01
5.00	1.31	1.69

[a] This table is adapted from Table 1 of James M. Lucas and Ronald B. Crosier, Fast Initial response for CUSUM quality control schemes: Give Your CUSUM a head start. *Technometrics* 24: 199–205, August, 1982. © 1982 American Statistical Association. Reprinted by permission.

shift actually began with subgroup 13 so the shift was detected after 7 subgroups.

How long would we expect the shift to go undetected using this approach? The answer is contained in Table 5.6, which gives the ARL values for various mean shifts with $h = 4$ and $h = 5$. We can see from Table 5.6 that we would expect the shift to be detected after the ninth subgroup (beyond 8 since the average is 8.38). These values are based upon the assumption that both S_H and S_L are zero at the time of the shift. In our example, however, $S_H = 1.04$ at the time of the shift. If S_H had been equal to zero at subgroup #12, then S_H would have been 4.78 at subgroup #20 and the shift would have been detected at that point. Thus, the shift would then be detected with the eighth subgroup.

How long would it have taken to detect this shift using an $\overline{X}$ chart without runs criteria? The answer is 43.96 subgroups. (It is 43.89 if the lower-tail area is ignored.) Thus, if subgroups were obtained every 15 minutes and a workday consists of 8 hours, it would take more than one full day longer when an $\overline{X}$ chart is used in this manner than with this particular CUSUM procedure.

This applies for *every* $\overline{X}$ chart—not just for this particular example. Granted, runs criteria could be constructed in such a way as to approximate the performance of this CUSUM procedure, but the latter would almost certainly be more straightforward and easier to apply.

For this example $h = 4$ was used, but this should not be taken to imply that $h = 4$ will always be the best choice. As Table 5.6 indicates, there is a considerable difference between the in-control ARL values for $h = 4$ and $h = 5$ (168 vs. 465). This is offset to some extent, however, by the fact that the ARL values are larger using $h = 5$ for every mean shift. For example, for a 1-sigma shift about two extra subgroups are required. Thus, if subgroups are obtained every 30 minutes it would require about 1 hour longer (with $h = 5$) to detect the shift. If the shift could cause a considerable increase in the number of nonconforming units (as was illustrated previously) that extra delay might be deemed critical. Conversely, if the cost of searching for assignable causes when none exists is substantial, the difference between the in-control ARL values might be of critical importance. Thus, the choice should be made after careful consideration of all the relevant factors—both statistical and nonstatistical. In practice, CUSUM schemes with $k = 0.5$ and $h = 5$ have been frequently used.

5.3.3 FIR CUSUM

The data in Table 5.5 illustrate how an out-of-control signal is obtained after a mean shift. When such a signal is received, the quality control person would search for an assignable cause just as he or she would when a subgroup average plots outside the limits on an $\overline{X}$ chart. After a search has been conducted, the sums could either be reset or left as is. If a cause was not found the sums might be left as is to see if the appropriate sum stays above the threshold value. If it does, that might mean that a cause does exist but it was simply not detected. Another search might then be initiated. The sums should definitely be reset, however, when an assignable cause is both detected and removed. The sums *could* be reset to zero. It could be, however, that the process was out of control because of multiple causes, and all of them might not have been removed. If the process is still out of control we would certainly want to detect that as soon as possible. The detection can be accomplished faster by using a "headstart" value as presented in Lucas and Crosier (1982a). They recommend a headstart value of $h/2$. Their method is generally referred to as FIR CUSUM, in which FIR stands for "fast initial response." As with any new CUSUM scheme, the objective should be to reduce the ARL for mean shifts, especially for the order of magnitude that one wishes to detect, without significantly reducing the in-control ARL. FIR CUSUM does have this property. For example, with $h = 5$ the ARL for a 1-sigma shift is reduced from 10.4 to

Table 5.7 Additional Data Generated from $N(0.5, 1)$ to Illustrate the Effect of FIR CUSUM vs. CUSUM without FIR ($k = 0.5$, $h = 5$)

Subgroup	$\bar{x}$	z	S_H (with FIR)	S_L (with FIR)	S_H (without FIR)	S_L (without FIR)
(RESET)	—	—	2.5	2.5	0	0
21	−0.08	−0.16	1.84	2.16	0	0
22	0.57	1.14	2.48	0.52	0.64	0
23	0.80	1.60	3.58	0	1.74	0
24	0.23	0.46	3.54	0	1.70	0
25	0.08	0.16	3.20	0	1.36	0
26	1.33	2.66	5.36[a]	0	3.52	0
27	1.23	2.46			5.48[a]	0

[a] Indicates out-of-control signal.

6.35, but the in-control ARL is reduced only from 465 to 430. In fact, this FIR CUSUM with $h = 5$ is far superior to the CUSUM with $h = 4$ without the headstart value since the in-control ARL is considerably longer and all but the one-fourth and one-half sigma shifts are shorter [See Lucas and Crosier (1982a) for the complete tables.]

The effect of the headstart value is illustrated in Table 5.7, which is produced from additional random numbers generated from $N(0.5, 1)$. We will now assume that $h = 5$ is being used and that Table 5.7 is a continuation of Table 5.5. If $h = 5$ had been used in Table 5.5 the out-of-control signal would have been received at subgroup #20, so we might assume that the cause was detected and removed at that point. Or, with $h = 4$, the source of the trouble might have remained undetected after subgroup 19, but was detected and removed after subgroup 20. In any event, the sums are reset before subgroup 21.

There are several important points to notice about Table 5.7. We see that with the FIR feature the fact that the process was still out of control was detected after six subgroups, whereas it took seven subgroups to detect this without the FIR feature. (The ARL values are 6.35 and 10.4, respectively, as can be seen from Table 5.9.) Notice also that the headstart value was used for both S_H and S_L even though we "knew" in this case that there was a positive shift and not a negative shift. In general, however, just because an assignable cause that resulted in a positive shift was removed does not preclude the possibility that the process might now be out of control in the other direction. For example, a machine could be overadjusted. If the shift is still positive the headstart value for S_L will not likely have any effect, as Table 5.7 illustrates.

The question arises as to the effect of the headstart value when the cause has been removed so that the process is subsequently in control. As

Table 5.8 Additional Data Generated from $N(0, 1)$ Illustrating Effect of FIR CUSUM When the Process Is in Control ($k = 0.5$, $h = 5$)

Subgroup	$\bar{x}$	z	With FIR		Without FIR	
			S_H	S_L	S_H	S_L
(RESET)	—	—	2.5	2.5	0	0
21	−0.28	−0.56	1.44	2.56	0	0.06
22	0.07	0.14	1.08	1.92	0	0
23	0.21	0.42	1.00	1.00	0	0
24	0.46	0.92	1.42	0	0.42	0
25	0.55	1.10	2.02	0	1.02	0
26	0.77	1.54	3.06	0	2.06	0
27	−0.30	−0.60	1.96	0.10	0.96	0.10
28	0.09	0.18	1.64	0	0.64	0
29	0.69	1.38	2.52	0	1.52	0
30	0.44	0.88	2.90	0	1.90	0
31	−0.26	−0.52	1.88	0.02	0.88	0.02
32	−0.34	−0.68	0.70	0.20	0	0.20
33	−0.28	−0.56	0	0.26	0	0.26

indicated previously, it causes only a slight decrease in the in-control ARL values; the decrease is from 465 to 430 for $h = 5$, and from 168 to 149 for $h = 4$ (see Table 5.9).

Additional data were generated from $N(0, 1)$ and we can see in Table 5.8 that for this particular set of data, the headstart values have no effect. The effect of the headstart values quickly dissipates to a difference of 1.00 by subgroup number 23, and it can be seen that there is a constant difference of 1.00 between S_H with FIR and S_H without FIR from that point until subgroup #32. The headstart for S_H then "zeros out" at the next subgroup.

By this time it should be apparent that the only way an $\bar{X}$ chart could ever be competitive with the CUSUM procedures described here (with and without FIR) for detecting small mean shifts would be for runs criteria to be designed in such a way as to approximate (or improve upon) the ARL values for a CUSUM scheme. This has not been done to date, and even if it could be done, a CUSUM procedure would still be the more structured and easily understood procedure.

5.3.4 Combined Shewhart–Cusum Scheme

Either of these two CUSUM procedures can be improved and made competitive with an $\bar{X}$ chart for detecting large mean shifts. This modifica-

Table 5.9 ARL Values for Various CUSUM Schemes Using $h = 5$ and $k = 0.5$[a]

Mean shift (in Standard Units)	1 Basic CUSUM	2 Shewhart– CUSUM ($z = 3.5$)	3 FIR CUSUM	4 Shewhart– FIR CUSUM ($z = 3.5$)
0	465	391	430	359.7
0.25	139	130.9	122	113.9
0.50	38.0	37.15	28.7	28.09
0.75	17.0	16.80	11.2	11.15
1.00	10.4	10.21	6.35	6.32
1.50	5.75	5.58	3.37	3.37
2.00	4.01	3.77	2.36	2.36
2.50	3.11	2.77	1.86	1.86
3.00	2.57	2.10	1.54	1.54
4.00	2.01	1.34	1.16	1.16
5.00	1.69	1.07	1.02	1.02

[a]Cols. 1 and 3 were adapted from James M. Lucas and Ronald B. Crosier (1982), Fast initial response for CUSUM quality control schemes: give your CUSUM a head start, *Technometrics* *24*, 199–205. © 1982 American Statistical Association. Reprinted by permission. Cols. 2 and 4 were adapted from James M. Lucas (1982), Combined Shewhart-CUSUM quality control schemes, *Journal of Quality Technology 14*(2) 51–59. © 1982 American Society for Quality Control. Reprinted by permission. The last five values in column 4 were obtained using the one-sided CUSUM scheme ARL values in Table 2 of Lucas (1982) as (more accurate) approximations to the two-sided values. All values in Table 5.9 are given to two decimal places, although the original sources often contained more decimals.)

tion entails using $\overline{X}$ chart limits in conjunction with a CUSUM scheme. The result is called a *combined Shewhart–CUSUM scheme* as introduced by Lucas (1982). The difference between this scheme and the other two CUSUM schemes is that an out-of-control signal can be received not just from S_H or S_L, but also from the z-value. We *could* select $z = 3$ as the threshold value so that an out-of-control signal would be received if either the absolute value of z exceeds 3 or either S_H or S_L exceeds h. This would then be, in essence, a modified $\overline{X}$ chart procedure since signals are also received from an $\overline{X}$ chart when z exceeds 3. Accordingly, the in-control ARL for the combined Shewhart–CUSUM scheme must be less than the in-control ARL for an $\overline{X}$ chart which, we recall, is approximately 370.

It can be seen [from Lucas (1982)] that the in-control ARL for a CUSUM scheme with $h = 5$, $k = 0.5$, $z = 3$, and without FIR is 223.4, whereas the in-control ARL for the same scheme *with* FIR is 206.5. Consequently, a z-value greater than 3 is preferable. Table 5.9 gives the ARL values for (1) a basic CUSUM scheme (the first type introduced), (2) a combined Shewhart–CUSUM scheme with $z = 3.5$, (3) an FIR CUSUM scheme, and (4) a combined Shewhart–FIR CUSUM scheme with $z = 3.5$. By comparing columns 1 and 2 we can see the effect of the Shewhart limits, especially in detecting shifts of at least 3-sigma. This improvement, however, is offset to some extent by a considerable reduction in the in-control ARL. By comparing columns 3 and 4, however, we can see that adding Shewhart limits to an FIR CUSUM has virtually no effect for mean shifts of any magnitude. Lucas (1982) shows the beneficial effects of adding Shewhart limits to a basic CUSUM, and of adding the FIR option to a combined Shewhart–CUSUM scheme. (Here this can be seen by comparing columns 2 and 4.) Thus, adding Shewhart limits can be beneficial if added to a basic CUSUM, but not if they are added to a FIR CUSUM. In particular, we can see that the addition of Shewhart limits to an FIR CUSUM has no effect on the ARL for shifts greater than 1-sigma, and decreases the in-control ARL considerably. Thus, the actual effect of the Shewhart limits is just the opposite of the intended effect.

To this point only integral values of h have been discussed. Lucas and Crosier (1982a) provide some insight into the effect that increasing h by 0.1 will have on the ARL values. For example, increasing h from 5.0 to 5.1 increases the in-control ARL for the FIR CUSUM from 430 to 478, but the ARL values for the various mean shifts increase very little, and they are virtually the same for shifts of at least 1-sigma.

One important point should be made in regard to ARL values for an FIR CUSUM scheme. These ARL values are valid only when one of the indicated shifts takes place at the time the sums are reset and the headstart value is applied. We saw in Table 5.8 that the effect of the headstart value can dissipate rather rapidly when the process is, in fact, in control. Thus, if a process is in control when the sums are reset but there is a mean shift quite some time later, these tabular ARL values do not apply. Instead, the appropriate ARL values are the ones that are given for the corresponding scheme without the FIR option. For example, if a combined Shewhart–FIR CUSUM is being used, the appropriate ARL values will then be the ones for the combined Shewhart–CUSUM scheme. Those values, however, are strictly applicable only when both S_H and S_L are zero at the time of the shift. That requirement will not always be met but the expected value of S_H and S_L is zero when the process is in control at the estimated value of μ.

In summary, if we knew that shifts occur only when the sums are reset, our best bet would be to use a FIR CUSUM without Shewhart limits. That would be very unrealistic, however, since it would mean that the process is constantly out of control. A better strategy would be to use a combined Shewhart–FIR CUSUM with either h slightly larger than 5 (e.g., 5.2) or z larger than 3.5 (e.g., 3.7), or both, the objective being to increase the in-control ARL somewhat without causing much of an increase in the ARL values for the various shifts. Again, such decisions must include considerations of nonstatistical factors such as the cost of searching for nonexistent assignable causes and the cost of not detecting shifts of various magnitudes. These factors should be considered in conjunction with the tables in Lucas (1982) and Lucas and Crosier (1982a).

The cumulative sums need not be displayed graphically, but they can be. A chart could be constructed that has a horizontal line at the value of h, and the values of S_H and S_L could be displayed on the same chart, or on separate charts. They are shown on the same chart in Dobben de Bruyn (1968). It would seem, however, that individual charts would be a better choice. The charts for the data in Table 5.5 are shown in Figure 5.4.

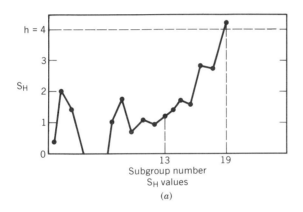

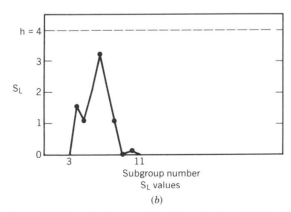

Figure 5.4 Charts for S_H (a) and S_L (b) for the data in Table 5.5.

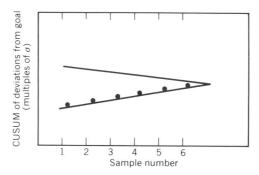

Figure 5.5 A V-mask for cumulative sums (indicating control).

We know that when either S_H or S_L increases the other will decrease or remain at zero, so that when the process is in control the lines (if the points are connected) will cross frequently, which could make the chart somewhat difficult to read. One way to circumvent this problem is to "invert" the chart for S_L by defining S_L in such a way that it will always be negative. This is done in Dobben de Bruyn (1968).

5.3.5   V-Mask CUSUM Scheme

Another graphical CUSUM procedure involves the use of a V-mask. Figure 5.5 illustrates such a mask. The general idea is to see if all of the points are within the arms of the mask after each sample point is plotted. The mask is moved backward after each point is plotted, with the slope of the arms of the mask remaining constant.

If a V-mask CUSUM scheme is to be used manually, a special transparency would have to be used so that the mask could be repositioned after each sample. Otherwise, the mask would have to be redrawn each time, which would be unduly laborious. The V-mask approach could also be computerized so that the mask would automatically appear in the proper position after each sample.

A modified V-mask can be used to increase the speed with which large shifts are detected. An example of such a mask is given in Figure 5.6. Other modified V-masks include a snub-nosed V-mask that is obtained by superimposing two straight V-masks, and a polygonal mask that is obtained by superimposing more than two straight V-masks. (It should be noted that what is typically plotted with these V-masks is the cumulative sum of the deviations from the target value.)

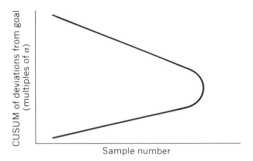

Figure 5.6 A parabolic V-mask.

Are any of these various types of V-masks superior to the other CUSUM procedures discussed previously? In some cases they are equivalent. The straight V-mask procedure described in Lucas (1976) has the same ARL values as the basic CUSUM procedure presented in this section. Parabolic, snub-nosed, and polygonal V-masks are competitive with $\overline{X}$ charts for detecting large mean shifts, but so is a combined Shewhart–CUSUM scheme. Lucas (1982) showed that the combined Shewhart–CUSUM scheme is quite competitive with the "semiparabolic" scheme given by Bissell (1979). The latter is essentially a Shewhart–CUSUM scheme with extra decision rules. Specifically, the Shewhart–CUSUM values are $z = 3.1$ and $h = 5$. The additional rules are (1) two consecutive z-values whose average exceeds 2.3, (2) three whose average exceeds 1.9, and (3) four whose average exceeds 1.7.

One would expect such a scheme to be slightly superior to a combined Shewhart–CUSUM scheme simply because of the extra criteria (provided that these extra criteria are chosen intelligently). Nevertheless, the advantage is probably not great enough to warrant using the more involved procedure. Also, as Lucas (1982) points out, parabolic CUSUM schemes require more computer storage than Shewhart–CUSUM schemes. All things considered, a Shewhart–CUSUM scheme may be the better choice, particularly if CUSUM schemes are computerized. More numerical work is needed, however, to compare Shewhart–CUSUM schemes with various types of V-masks for speed in detecting mean shifts of various magnitudes.

Readers interested in the construction and use of V-masks are referred, in particular, to Lucas (1973, 1976), Wadsworth, Stephens, and Godfrey (1986), Johnson and Leone (1977), Bissell (1979, 1981), Rowlands, Nix, Abdollahian, and Kemp (1982), and Dobben de Bruyn (1968).

The use of a combined Shewhart–CUSUM scheme in clinical chemistry is described by Westgard, Groth, Aronsson, and de Verdier (1977). Another reference not previously mentioned is Lucas and Crosier (1982b).

It should be noted that the superiority of the CUSUM procedures discussed in this section is for sudden jumps in the process mean. The advantage of these procedures over an $\overline{X}$ chart is somewhat less, but still significant, when the change is a slow drift (see Bissell 1984, 1986).

5.4   CUSUM PROCEDURES FOR CONTROLLING PROCESS VARIABILITY

Although much attention has been given to CUSUM procedures for controlling a process mean, CUSUM procedures for controlling process variability have received relatively little attention. Johnson and Leone (1977) illustrate a CUSUM procedure for the sample range (R), and one for the sample variance (s^2). These methods are based upon the theory developed in the three-part series of Johnson and Leone (1962a–c).

More recently, Hawkins (1981) proposed a CUSUM procedure for detecting changes in the process variability. That procedure utilizes individual observations rather than subgroups, however, so discussion of the procedure will be deferred to Chapter 6.

In addition to the Johnson and Leone (1977) methodology, CUSUM procedures for controlling process variability are contained in the British Standards as published by the British Standards Institution.* These procedures are illustrated in Wadsworth, Stephens, and Godfrey (1986).

The approach is to compute cumulative sums using essentially the same general form as was presented earlier in this chapter for controlling the process mean. Specifically,

$$S_i = \max\left(0,\ SD_i - k\,\overline{SD} + S_{i-1}\right)$$

where SD_i denotes the ith standard deviation, and $\overline{SD}$ denotes the value at which the standard deviation is to be controlled. (As with the other control procedures, this might be the average of a reasonable number of previous standard deviations.) The out-of-control signal is received when the sum exceeds h, as with the other CUSUM procedures.

---

*British Standards 5703 covers CUSUM procedures and consists of four parts: Part 1—Introduction to CUSUM Charting (1980, amended August 1982, 32 pages); Part 2—Decision Rules and Statistical Tests for CUSUM Charts and Tabulations (1980, 40 pages); Part 3—CUSUM Methods for Process/Quality Control by Measurement (1981, 44 pages); and Part 4—CUSUMS for Counted Attribute Data (1982, 36 pages). These can be purchased from the American National Standards Institute, 1430 Broadway, New York, NY 10018. (As of 1988, the cost of each part exceeds $50.)

Table 5.10 Simulated Data

		From N(0, 1):			
1.54	0.86	−0.89	−1.88	−1.85	−2.53
−0.09	0.57	0.21	−0.43	2.03	−0.59
1.75	1.17	−1.23	−0.42	−0.64	0.60
−1.58	1.82	1.77	−1.45	0.31	−0.22
s = 1.56	0.54	1.35	0.74	1.64	1.33
−0.74	2.10	0.56	−1.53	0.53	−0.81
−1.25	1.48	1.78	0.99	−0.52	0.67
−0.40	0.86	−0.81	−2.38	1.71	0.42
−1.01	−1.19	0.97	1.41	0.43	0.46
s = 0.37	1.43	1.08	1.86	0.91	0.67
		From N(0, 4):			
3.42	7.01	2.09	−1.13	−2.16	−3.58
2.55	−2.97	−1.69	0.27	−3.29	−1.53
−2.22	−0.34	3.78	1.05	−0.22	−1.12
0.55	−3.04	−1.42	−1.60	1.42	−2.40
s = 2.50	4.73	2.68	1.51	2.08	1.09

It should be noted that this h and k are quite different from those used in the CUSUM schemes discussed previously. In particular, here the standard deviation is not standardized in that the standard deviation of SD is not used. Choices for h and k are discussed in the British Standards.

This approach will be illustrated using the data in Table 5.10. The first 12 subgroups are the same as in Table 5.4. The next 6 subgroups are generated from $N(0, 4)$. Table 5.11 contains the CUSUM calculations that enable us to see how quickly the change from $\sigma = 1$ to $\sigma = 2$ is detected. We can see that the shift is detected immediately using scheme C2, whereas the shift is detected on the second subgroup using C1. Scheme C2 will lead to quicker detection of an increase in σ than scheme C1, but will also give more false signals. (The ARL values for each scheme are given in BS 5703, Part 3.)

It is of interest at this point to determine how long we would expect to have to wait before the shift is detected on an s chart with .001 probability limits. Recall from an earlier section of this chapter that

$$\frac{(n-1)S^2}{\sigma^2} \sim \chi^2_{n-1}$$

Table 5.11 CUSUM Values[a]

Subgroup Number	S_i for Scheme C1[a]	S_i for Scheme C2:[b]
1	0.04	0.22
2	0	0
3	0	0.01
4	0	0
5	0.12	0.30
6	0	0.29
7	0	0
8	0	0.09
9	0	0
10	0.34	0.52
11	0	0.09
12	0	0
—	—	—
13	0.98	1.16[c]
14	4.19[c]	4.55[c]
15	5.35[c]	5.89[c]
16	5.34[c]	6.06[c]
17	5.90[c]	6.80[c]
18	5.47[c]	6.55[c]

[a] For Scheme C1 $k = 1 + f = 1.35$, $\overline{SD} = 1.12$, $k\overline{SD} = 1.52$, $h = 1.15$.
[b] For Scheme C2 $k = 1 + f = 1.20$, $\overline{SD} = 1.12$, $k\overline{SD} = 1.344$, $h = 1.15$. h = threshold value, f = slope of the mask, and $\overline{SD}$ = target value for the standard deviation.
[c] —Exceeds threshold value.

so that

$$P\left[\frac{(n-1)S^2}{\sigma^2} > \chi^2_{.999}\right] = .001$$

It then follows

$$P\left(S^2 > \frac{\sigma^2}{n-1}\chi^2_{.999}\right) = .001$$

and

$$P\left(S > \frac{\sigma}{\sqrt{n-1}}\chi_{.999}\right) = .001$$

In this instance $\sigma = 2$ and $n = 4$, so

$$P\left(S > \frac{2}{\sqrt{3}}\chi_{.999}\right) = .001$$

We need to determine $P[S > (1/\sqrt{3})\chi_{.999}]$. This can be done by using the more familiar chi-square distribution. We know from Table 5.2 that $\chi^2_{.999}$ for $n = 4$ is 16.2660. Thus,

$$P\left[S^2 > \left(\frac{2}{\sqrt{3}}\right)^2 \chi^2_{.999}\right] = .001$$

so that

$$P\left[S^2 > \frac{4}{3}(16.2660)\right] = .001$$

where $S^2 \sim \frac{4}{3}\chi^2_3$. What we need is $P[S^2 > 1/3(16.2660)]$ since σ is assumed to equal one. It can be determined that

$$P\left[S^2 > \frac{1}{3}(16.2660)\right] = P\left[S^2 > (4)\left(\frac{1}{3}\right)\left(\frac{16.2660}{4}\right)\right]$$

$$= P\left[S^2 > \frac{4}{3}(4.0665)\right]$$

$$= .25437$$

Accordingly, the ARL for the UCL is $(1/.25437) = 3.93$. Therefore, using an s chart (or an s^2 chart) with .001 probability limits, we would expect the shift from $\sigma = 1$ to $\sigma = 2$ to be detected with the fourth subgroup, as compared with detection on the first subgroup using scheme C2, and the second subgroup using scheme C1.

It should be noted that both of these schemes are for detecting an *increase* in σ, and cannot be used for detecting a decrease. Johnson and Leone (1977) give both a one-sided chart for detecting an increase in σ^2 and a two-sided chart for detecting either an increase or a decrease in σ^2. The details of the construction of these charts are beyond the intended mathematical level of this book, however, so they will not be given here. The interested reader is referred to pp. 374–377 of Johnson and Leone.

5.5   GEOMETRIC MOVING AVERAGE CHART

This type of control chart is similar to a CUSUM procedure in that it has utility in detecting small shifts in the process mean. It is due to Roberts (1959), and has also been referred to as an *exponentially weighted moving average chart* (EWMA).

The general idea is to plot the value of a statistic that we will designate as w_t where

$$w_t = r\bar{x}_t + (1 - r)w_{t-1} \qquad (5.6)$$

The expression given by Eq. (5.6) is essentially a weighted average in which the subgroup average at time t, $\bar{x}_t$, is given a weight $r(0 < r \le 1)$ and the value of the expression at time $t - 1$ is given a weight $1 - r$.

The iterative calculations begin with $w_0 = \bar{\bar{x}}$. The control limits could be obtained from

$$\bar{\bar{x}} \pm 3\frac{\hat{\sigma}}{\sqrt{n}} \sqrt{\left(\frac{r}{2-r}\right)\left[1 - (1-r)^{2t}\right]} \qquad (5.7)$$

which follows from the fact that

$$\sigma_{w_t}^2 = \frac{\sigma^2}{n}\left(\frac{r}{2-r}\right)\left[1 - (1-r)^{2t}\right]$$

The use of the exact expression for σ_{w_t} in Eq. (5.7) will thus produce variable control limits, which will become wider over time. If $r \ge 0.2$, however, $(1 - r)^{2t}$ will be close to zero if $t \ge 5$, so $\sigma_{w_t}^2$ could then be approximated by $\sigma^2/n[r/(2 - r)]$. Constant control limits could then be obtained using

$$\bar{\bar{x}} \pm 3\frac{\hat{\sigma}}{\sqrt{n}} \sqrt{\frac{r}{2-r}} \qquad (5.8)$$

Accordingly, the exact variance could be used in producing the control limits for the first four or five time periods [i.e., using Eq. (5.7)] and then Eq. (5.8) used thereafter to produce constant limits.

The value of r would have to be determined. As with any control chart or CUSUM procedure, the general idea is to detect a shift that is of any consequence as quickly as possible without having an unacceptably high probability of receiving false alarms.

We consider the general case of L-sigma limits, where $L = 3$ in Eqs. (5.7) and (5.8). Similar in spirit to the tables that are available for designing

Table 5.12 Geometric Moving Average Calculations with $r = 0.25$

Subgroup Number	Subgroup Average	w_t	Exact Control Limits	Approximate Control Limits
1	0.41	0.1025	±0.3750	
2	1.11	0.3544	±0.4688	
3	−0.04	0.2558	±0.5140	
4	−1.04	−0.0682	±0.5378	
5	−0.04	−0.0612	±0.5508	
6	−0.68	−0.2159	±0.5579	
7	−0.85	−0.3744	±0.5619	
8	0.81	−0.0783		±0.5669
9	0.62	0.0963		
10	−0.38	−0.0228		
11	0.54	0.1179		
12	0.18	0.1134		
13	0.33	0.1826		
14	0.32	0.2170		
15	0.44	0.2728		
16	0.22	0.2596		
17	0.88	0.4147		
18	0.16	0.3510		
19	0.95	0.5008		
20	1.09	0.6481		

a CUSUM procedure, Robinson and Ho (1978) gives tables of ARL values that provide some guidance in the selection of L, r, and n, and also discuss the selection from an economic standpoint.

We will assume that n has been determined and use the data in Table 5.4 to illustrate this technique. For detecting a 1-sigma shift, the tables in Robinson and Ho (1978) suggest that one reasonable combination of L and r would be $L = 3.00$ and $r = 0.25$. This combination would provide an in-control ARL of 492.95 and an ARL of 10.95 for detecting the 1-sigma shift. (Note that these are very close to the corresponding values for a CUSUM procedure with $h = 5$ and $k = 0.5$ that are 465 and 10.4, respectively.)

We can see from Table 5.12 that the shift would be detected with subgroup #20, which is also when the shift would be detected using a CUSUM procedure with $k = 0.5$ and $h = 5$ (as can be seen from Table 5.5). This should come as no surprise in light of the ARL values for the two procedures. [The calculations were started using $w_0 = 0$ since the data were initially generated from an $N(0,1)$ distribution, and recall that the shift occurred with subgroup #13.]

Thus, a geometric moving average procedure with good choices for L and r should provide results that closely parallel the results obtained using a CUSUM procedure with good choices for h and k. So which one should be used? The amount of required computation is about the same for each, but the CUSUM procedure has a few advantages. First, the S_H and S_L values are not scale dependent, so the values can be compared for different products and for different processes. The geometric moving averages are, of course, scale dependent, although that problem could be easily remedied by standardizing the averages, which would then require changing the general form of the control limits. The CUSUM procedure also incorporates z-values that indicate how many standard deviations a subgroup average is from the midline, whereas z-values are not an inherent part of the geometric moving average calculations (but could be easily added).

One advantage of the EWMA (geometric moving average) procedure is that it provides a forecast of where the process mean will be at the next time period, as illustrated in Hunter (1986). Lorenzen and Vance (1986) indicate, however, that the CUSUM approach of Lucas is superior to a geometric moving average chart with $r = 0.25$ when economic considerations are employed.

5.6 ACCEPTANCE CONTROL CHART

Control chart users have employed modified forms of an $\overline{X}$ chart when the specification limits are well beyond the endpoints of the interval $\mu \pm 3\sigma$. The rationale for doing so can be explained as follows. Assume that the specification limits are at $\mu \pm 6\sigma$, and that a value outside this interval will result in a nonconforming unit of production. What will be the effect of a shift in the process mean from μ to $\mu + 2\sigma_{\overline{x}}$ for $n = 4$? Before the shift occurs, only about one of every one billion units will be judged nonconforming ($z = 6$) by having exceeded the upper specification limit (assuming approximate normality). Since $\sigma_{\overline{x}} = \sigma/2$ when $n = 4$, it follows that $2\sigma_{\overline{x}} = \sigma$ so that the new mean is at $\mu' = \mu + \sigma$. It then follows that the proportion of nonconforming units will be given by $P(Z > 5)$ where $Z \sim N(0,1)$. The answer is that slightly less than 3 of every 10 million units will be nonconforming because of having exceeded the upper specification limit. Such a small increase is not likely to cause any real concern.

With an $\overline{X}$ chart the 2-sigma shift would produce an ARL of approximately 3 for the UCL. Nevertheless, in this instance the shift would be relatively inconsequential in terms of the increase in the percentage of nonconforming units.

Accordingly, when the specifications are well outside $\mu \pm 3\sigma$, which is the natural variability of the process, an argument could be made for not using the conventional $\overline{X}$ chart. A similar argument could be made regarding a CUSUM procedure for averages, since there would apparently not be a need to detect a small mean shift (but read Section 5.6.2). The control limits on an $\overline{X}$ chart could, of course, be increased from 3-sigma to, say, 5-sigma, but it would be far more logical to design a chart for plotting subgroup averages in which the control limits are determined from the specification limits. An *acceptance control chart* is such a chart. Recall, however, that the specification limits should not be displayed on an $\overline{X}$ chart, or, in general, on any control chart on which averages are plotted. Thus, they should not be displayed on an acceptance chart either; they should be used only in obtaining the control limits.

The acceptance control chart was developed by Freund (1957), and reviewed later by Woods (1976). The limits are obtained from the same components that are used in acceptance sampling procedures. They are:

APL (Acceptable Process Level). This is the process level farthest from standard that yields product quality that is to be accepted $(1 - \alpha)\%$ of the time that the level is attained. There will be two APL values when there is both an upper and lower specification limit.

α (Alpha). This is the probability of rejecting an APL.

RPL (Rejectable Process Level). This is the process level closest to the standard that yields product quality that is to be rejected $(1 - \beta)\%$ of the time it occurs. There will be two RPL values when there is both an upper and lower specification limit.

β (Beta). This is the probability of accepting an RPL.

p_1. The acceptable percentage of units falling outside of the specifications.

p_2. The rejectable percentage of units falling outside of the specifications.

In general, all six must not be specified. Doing so would most likely result in inconsistent solutions for the acceptance control limits because of the way in which the limits are computed. Specifically, the upper acceptance control limit (UACL) could be computed as

$$\text{UACL} = \text{USL} - z_{p_1}\sigma + z_\alpha\sigma / \sqrt{n} \qquad (5.9)$$

where USL is the upper specification limit, and z_{p_1} and z_α denote the z-values (for the standard normal distribution) corresponding to tail areas of p_1 and α, respectively. The UACL could also be computed as

$$\text{UACL} = \text{USL} - z_{p_2}\sigma - z_\beta\sigma\big/\sqrt{n} \qquad (5.10)$$

Equality between Eqs. (5.9) and (5.10) would require that $z_{p_2}\sigma + z_\beta\sigma/\sqrt{n} = z_{p_1}\sigma - z_\alpha\sigma/\sqrt{n}$, which will not hold for most choices of p_1, p_2, α, and β.

Similarly, the lower acceptance control limit (LACL) could be computed as

$$\text{LACL} = \text{LSL} + z_{p_1}\sigma - z_\alpha\sigma\big/\sqrt{n} \qquad (5.11)$$

or as

$$\text{LACL} = \text{LSL} + z_{p_2}\sigma + z_\beta\sigma\big/\sqrt{n} \qquad (5.12)$$

In essence, an acceptance control chart is a modified $\overline{X}$ chart, but is not necessarily the same as charts obtained from "modified control limits" as discussed in Hill (1956). Those modified charts do not allow for the specification of β and p_2. They are discussed later in the chapter.

5.6.1 Acceptance Chart with $\overline{X}$ Control Limits

The acceptance chart can be constructed with the $\overline{X}$ (chart) control limits either shown or not shown on the chart. It would be advantageous to have them displayed on the chart. The reason for this is that the $\overline{X}$ control limits would enable the user to determine whether or not the process is in control at the assumed mean. Evidence of a mean shift would not necessarily cause any action to be taken, however. This use of $\overline{X}$ limits would be for detecting a "tolerable shift" before the shift becomes larger and causes major consequences.

An example will be given to illustrate the determination of the acceptance control limits. In Table 5.1 the smallest value was 10 and the largest was 97. Let us assume that the specification limits are 4 and 108, and that we will specify p_1 and α. Readers familiar with acceptance sampling will recognize that p_1 is the same as the acceptable quality level (AQL). Since arguments against use of the latter were given in Chapter 1, this begs the question of whether the same arguments apply to the use of p_1. They do, but not to the same extent. We can make p_1 as small as we want, but we do not have that luxury with AQL. The smallest possible AQL value that can be used in the various sampling plans is .001. Stating a value for p_1 implies that we are willing to tolerate some nonconforming units, so we would probably want to counteract that by making p_1 very small. If we make it too small, however, the acceptance control limits will be *inside* the $\overline{X}$ limits, which is not in accordance with the way that the chart is designed to function. To illustrate this we will use $p_1 = .00001$, which means that 1 nonconforming unit of every 100,000 units will be considered an acceptable rate. We will also use $\alpha = .05$, which means that we will run the risk of rejecting a process that has this value of p_1 5% of the time. A value of $p_1 = .00001$ corresponds to $z = 4.265$ and $\alpha = .05$ corresponds to $z = 1.645$. The limits are

$$\text{LACL} = \text{LSL} + z_{p_1}\hat{\sigma} - z_{\alpha}\hat{\sigma}/\sqrt{n}$$

$$= 4 + 4.265(15.202) - 1.645\left(15.202/\sqrt{4}\,\right)$$

$$= 56.333$$

and

$$\text{UACL} = \text{USL} - z_{p_1}\hat{\sigma} + z_{\alpha}\hat{\sigma}/\sqrt{n}$$

$$= 108 - 4.265(15.202) + 1.645\left(15.202/\sqrt{4}\,\right)$$

$$= 55.667$$

Thus, not only are both limits well *inside* the $\overline{X}$ limits, but the LACL is actually larger than the UACL! This occurs, in part, because a small value of p_1 was chosen, but primarily because the specification limits were not very far outside the natural variability of the process. The USL was at $\hat{\mu} + 3.19\hat{\sigma}$ and the LSL was at $\hat{\mu} - 3.65\hat{\sigma}$, where $\hat{\sigma} = \overline{R}/d_2$.

We will now assume that the data in Table 5.1 are "coded" (e.g., by subtracting 1000 from the original observations) so that a negative value for LSL is possible for the coded data. Can we use a very small value for p_1 when the specification limits are at, say, $\hat{\mu} \pm 6\hat{\sigma}$? The answer is "yes" and can be demonstrated as follows. The specification limits would be

$$\hat{\mu} \pm 6\hat{\sigma}$$

$$= 59.4375 \pm 6(15.202)$$

$$= 59.4375 \pm 91.2120$$

so that USL = 150.6495 and LSL = -31.7745. The acceptance control

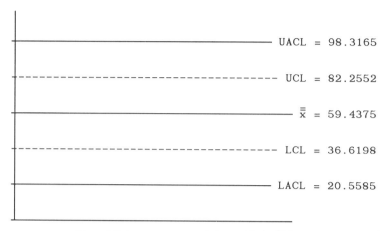

UACL = 98.3165

UCL = 82.2552

$\bar{\bar{x}}$ = 59.4375

LCL = 36.6198

LACL = 20.5585

Figure 5.7 Acceptance control chart with the $\bar{X}$ limits.

limits for these specification limits can be shown to be

$$LACL = 20.5585$$

$$UACL = 98.3165$$

Notice that these values are well outside the $\bar{X}$-chart limits of 36.6198 and 82.2552 that were given much earlier in the chapter. Recall that the average for subgroup #10 in Table 5.1 is 21.25, which is well below the LCL of 36.6198. It is not, however, below the LACL, so a search for an assignable cause would not necessarily be initiated. The acceptance chart with the $\bar{X}$ limits would appear as in Figure 5.7. Notice in this case that the acceptance control limits are equidistant from the estimated process mean. This is the result of the fact that the specification limits were assumed to be at $\hat{\mu} \pm 6\hat{\sigma}$. Obviously, the specification limits will not always be equidistant from the estimated process mean, and when they are not the acceptance control limits will not be equidistant, nor will they be equidistant from their respective $\bar{X}$ limits.

These $\bar{X}$ limits essentially serve as "warning limits" on the acceptance chart. A CUSUM procedure could be used as a substitute for an acceptance control chart. It would require, though, a value of k somewhat larger than 0.5 since the latter is used when the objective is to detect a 1-sigma shift. In Figure 5.7 the acceptance control limits are at $\bar{\bar{x}} \pm 5.115\hat{\sigma}_{\bar{x}}$ so $k = 1.0$ might be suitable. Tables that contain ARL values for CUSUM schemes with k greater than 0.5 can be found in Lucas and Crosier (1982a). Readers interested in acceptance control charts are referred to Woods (1976) for further reading.

5.6.2 Acceptance Charts versus Target Values

The focus for acceptance charts has been on the location of the specification limits relative to the variability of the variable being measured. There has been no mention of a "target value" for the mean of that variable. If, on the other hand, a target value does exist and a "loss" of some sort will be incurred if there is even a slight deviation from that target value, then an acceptance chart should not be used. (The reader is referred to Chapter 14 for additional information concerning target values and loss functions.)

5.7 MODIFIED LIMITS

These comments also apply if modified limits are used. As stated previously, these do not allow for the use of β and p_2. Accordingly, the control limits would be obtained using Eqs. (5.9) and (5.11). Figure 5.8 illustrates a possible configuration. Here the USL $= \mu + 8\sigma$ and LSL $= \mu - 8\sigma$ (assuming for simplicity that μ and σ are known). Since the USL and LSL are well beyond $\mu \pm 3\sigma$, there is considerable room for the distribution of $\overline{X}$ to shift without causing an appreciable increase in the percentage of nonconforming units. If it is desired to use 3-sigma limits relative to the midlines for the two distributions of $\overline{X}$ shown in Figure 5.8 (as is the usual case), the effect is to widen the usual $\overline{X}$ control limits by, in this case, 5σ since

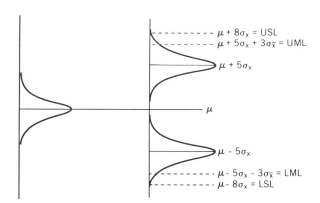

$8 - 3 = 5$. In general, if the specification limits were at $\mu \pm k\sigma$, the limits would be widened by $(k - 3)\sigma$. Thus, we would not want to use modified limits unless $k > 3$. (Of course, the specification limits will not necessarily be equidistant from μ or $\overline{\overline{x}}$.)

Modified limits, acceptance control charts, and a modified version of acceptance control charts are discussed in detail by Wadsworth, Stephens, and Godfrey (1986).

5.8   DIFFERENCE CONTROL CHARTS

Two types of difference charts have been proposed. Grubbs (1946) proposed a difference chart for ballistics testing during World War II. The general idea is to separate process instability caused by uncontrollable factors (e.g., humidity) from process instability due to assignable causes. This is accomplished by taking samples (subgroups) from the current production and also samples from what is referred to as a reference lot. The reference lot consists of units that are produced under controlled process conditions except for possibly being influenced by uncontrollable factors. Since samples from the current production and the reference lot are equally susceptible to influence by uncontrollable factors, any sizable differences between subgroup averages should reflect process instability in the current production due to controllable factors. The 3-sigma control limits are obtained from

$$0 \pm A_2\sqrt{\overline{R}_r^2 + \overline{R}_c^2}$$

where A_2 is the same constant that is used for $\overline{X}$ charts; $\overline{R}_r$ and $\overline{R}_c$ designate the average range for the reference lot and the current lot, respectively, for the (20 or more) subgroups that are used in determining the control limits.

Each point that is plotted on the chart represents $\overline{x}_r - \overline{x}_c$ for each subgroup, where $\overline{x}_r$ and $\overline{x}_c$ denote a subgroup average for the reference and current lot, respectively.

This chart would be used in place of an $\overline{X}$ chart. An R chart could be kept on the current production or an R chart of differences could be maintained if it is believed that the uncontrollable factors affect the within-sample variability for the current production. The limits on such a chart would be obtained from

$$0 \pm 3\sqrt{\mathrm{Var}(R_r - R_c)}$$

$$= 0 \pm 3\sqrt{\mathrm{Var}(R_r) + \mathrm{Var}(R_c)}$$

$$= 0 \pm \frac{3d_3}{d_2}\sqrt{\overline{R}_r^2 + \overline{R}_c^2}$$

and each point plotted on the chart would represent $R_r - R_c$ for each subgroup (d_3 is explained in the Appendix to this chapter).

Readers familiar with statistics will recognize that this difference chart for averages is analogous to a pooled-t test. In fact, when each point is plotted separately and compared with the limits, it is comparable to a pooled-t test for testing the equality of population means with a significance level of 0.0027 provided that $\bar{x}_r - \bar{x}_c$ is approximately normally distributed. (A pooled-t test does not utilize ranges, however.)

Another type of difference chart was proposed by Ott (1947). With this chart differences are obtained between paired observations within each subgroup, and what is plotted on the chart is the average difference for each subgroup. The control limits are obtained from

$$0 \pm A_2\overline{R}$$

where $\overline{R}$ is the average of the ranges of the differences. (That is, there is one range per subgroup, and that range is the difference between the largest difference between the pairs in a subgroup and the smallest difference.) Notice that the limits are obtained in essentially the same way as they are obtained for an $\overline{X}$ chart, except that the centerline is 0 instead of $\bar{\bar{x}}$.

This type of difference chart is of particular value in calibration work in which test equipment is to be kept in good working order. See Ott (1975, pp. 64–68) for further reading.

5.9 OTHER CHARTS

As was indicated in Table 4.3 in Chapter 4, median charts have been used by a modest percentage of the companies that were included in the survey of Saniga and Shirland (1977), particularly large companies. A median chart is a substitute for an $\overline{X}$ chart, and could be used, in particular, when the subgroup size is an odd number (e.g., $n = 5$). The median was defined in Chapter 3 as the middle value in a set of ordered observations (from smallest to largest), or the average of the two middle values when there is an even number of observations.

The median is easy to determine and easily understood, but it is not as efficient as the average since not all of the observations are being used. References on the median chart include Nelson (1982), which gives the factors for calculating the 3-sigma limits and also gives efficiency figures for the median relative to the average. With a computerized SQC system a chart that uses averages is to be preferred over a median chart, but the latter will probably continue to be used by a number of companies that use manual charting.

Ferrell (1953) proposed a midrange chart for controlling the process mean and provided tables to be used in constructing such charts. (The midrange is defined as the average of the largest and smallest observations in a subgroup.) Midrange charts have been used very little as indicated by the Saniga and Shirland survey results.

5.10   UNEQUAL SAMPLE SIZES

Although unequal sample sizes frequently occur with charts for nonconformities and nonconforming units (discussed in Chapter 8), they should occur less frequently for the procedures presented in this chapter since the subgroup sizes are typically small and the sampling is usually performed in real time. Nevertheless, missing data can occur. The presence of unequal subgroup sizes can be handled for an $\bar{X}$, R, or s chart by using the approach given in Burr (1969).

5.11   ASSUMPTIONS FOR THE CHARTS IN THIS CHAPTER

This section should be studied by those readers who are interested in the statistical foundation of the control charts presented in this chapter, and who are interested in control chart modifications that should be used under certain conditions.

There are various assumptions that must be (at least) approximately satisfied before the control chart methodologies given in this chapter can be considered valid. These are not often stated, and are checked even less frequently, but they are very important.

We shall now consider the assumptions for each of the procedures in the order in which the procedures appeared in the chapter.

For the R, s, and s^2 charts the basic assumptions are that the individual observations are independent and are (approximately) normally distributed. We have seen that the usual 3-sigma limits can be off considerably from the actual probability limits due to the fact that the distributions of R, s, and s^2 differ considerably from a normal distribution. The charts for R and s that were illustrated with probability limits will also have incorrect probability limits, however, when the individual observations are not normally distributed.

Burr (1967) investigated the effect of nonnormality on the control limits of an R chart (and an $\overline{X}$ chart) and concluded that nonnormality is not a serious problem unless there is a considerable deviation from normality. He provides constants that should be used (instead of D_3 and D_4) for 28 (nonnormal) distributions in the family of Burr distributions. These constants, however, simply facilitate the construction of 3-sigma limits in the presence of nonnormality. The resultant limits are not probability limits and the probability of a point falling outside the limits will, in general, be unknown. This is due to the fact that the distribution of the range is known only for a few nonnormal distributions. Consequently, since the distribution of the range is generally unknown for nonnormal distributions, probability limits cannot be determined analytically.

The same general problem exists with s and s^2 charts since the distributions of s and s^2 are not generally known for nonnormal distributions. As Hahn (1970) points out, confidence intervals and hypothesis tests on σ or σ^2 are highly sensitive to slight-to-moderate departures from normality, and an s chart and an s^2 chart correspond to hypothesis tests on σ and σ^2, respectively. [See also Box (1953) for a discussion of the sensitivity of tests on σ and σ^2 to the normality assumption.]

Since there is no general way to obtain probability limits for an R, s, or s^2 chart for every type of nonnormal data, what can a user do who would like to have control limits such that the probability of a point falling outside one of the control limits when the process is in control is approximately the same for each limit, and a good estimate can be obtained of each of the two probabilities? A logical approach would be to transform the data such that the transformed data are approximately normally distributed, and then use the probability-limit approach to obtain the limits on the desired chart. Such limits would then be approximate probability limits. The variability of the transformed variable would then be controlled—not the variability of the original variable. Transformed variables will often have physical meaning when simple transformations are used (e.g., log, reciprocal, square root). Simple transformations will not necessarily lead to normality, whereas more sophisticated transformations that produce approximate normality will often produce new variables that do not have any physical meaning. For example, what is the physical interpretation of $X^{2.6}$ when X is measured in feet? The user might thus be faced with the choice between approximate probability limits for a less-than-desirable trans- formed variable and false probability limits for the original variable where the limits may result in highly different tail probabilities.

This choice need be made, however, only if there is evidence that the distribution may be more than slightly nonnormal. This can be checked in various ways, as was discussed briefly in Chapter 2. These methods are described in detail in Shapiro (1980). Suggested methods include plotting all of the observations on normal probability paper and observing if the points form approximately a straight line. (Alternatively, a systematic sample of every ith observation might be plotted if the data set is large.) Another commonly used test is the Shapiro–Wilk W test. (A normal probability plot is illustrated in Chapter 11.)

The assumption of independent observations can be checked by calculat- ing autocorrelation coefficients of various lags [see, for example, Box and Jenkins (1976)]. The control limits should be adjusted when there is strong evidence of correlated observations. This is discussed later in the chapter.

For an $\overline{X}$ chart it is assumed that the observations are independent, and the *averages* are approximately normally distributed. Thus, the individual observations need not be approximately normally distributed as is the case for an R, s, or s^2 chart. It is often assumed, however, that the subgroup averages are approximately normally distributed for subgroup sizes of 4 or 5, regardless of the way the individual observations are distributed. This implicit assumption can be traced to the work of Dr. Walter A. Shewhart, who took samples of size four from various nonnormal distributions and constructed empirical distributions of the sample averages. The results were reported in Shewhart (1931). They indicate that the distribution of the sample averages does not differ greatly from a normal distribution, even when the observations come from a highly nonnormal distribution such as a right triangular distribution. The right triangular distribution used by Shewhart was obtained from a population that consisted of 820 chips, with 40 chips marked -1.3, 39 chips marked -1.2, 38 chips marked -1.1, etc., with the pattern continued so that one chip is marked 2.6. The mean of this distribution can be shown to be zero, the coefficient of skewness, α_3, is 0.5661, and the coefficient of kurtosis, α_4, is 2.3978. These are measures of the asymmetry and "peakedness" of a distribution. For a normal distribu- tion $\alpha_3 = 0$ (since the distribution is symmetric) and $\alpha_4 = 3.0$.

Our interest, however, should be in α_3 and α_4 for $\overline{X}$ not X, and to see the extent to which these differ from 0 and 3.0, respectively. Measures of skewness and kurtosis are perhaps more frequently given as β_1 and β_2, respectively, where $\beta_1 = \alpha_3^2$ and $\beta_2 = \alpha_4$. For the distribution of $\overline{X}$ we have

$$\beta_{1:\bar{x}} = \frac{\beta_{1:x}}{n}$$

and

$$\beta_{2:\bar{x}} = \frac{\beta_{2:x} - 3}{n} + 3$$

For the right triangular distribution, $\beta_{1:\bar{x}} = 0.0801$ and $\beta_{2:\bar{x}} = 2.84945$ when $n = 4$. Since these are very close to 0 and 3, respectively, Shewhart's sampling distribution of $\overline{X}$ obtained from 1000 samples of size 4 from the population of 820 chips was expectedly very close to a normal distribution in shape.

Samples drawn from a less asymmetric, "mound-shaped" distribution could be expected to have values of $\beta_{1:\bar{x}}$ and $\beta_{2:\bar{x}}$ that are closer to 0 and 3, respectively, than the values for the right triangular distribution.

Our attention, however, should be focused on the effect that the nonnormal distributions have on the probabilities outside the 3σ limits on an $\overline{X}$ chart. These "tail probabilities" have been examined by Schilling and Nelson (1976) who showed that the sum of the two tail probabilities differs very little from the nominal value (.0027) even when the distribution of X differs considerably from a normal distribution.

The individual tail probabilities have been examined by Moore (1957) in addition to Schilling and Nelson (1976). A much different picture emerges when the tail probabilities are examined separately rather than combined. Examination of the individual tail areas can reveal how unequal the tail probabilities are.

Moore examined, in particular, what happens to the tail probabilities when the data are drawn from either a chi-square distribution with 4 degrees of freedom, or a chi-square distribution with 8 degrees of freedom (the former is more asymmetric that the latter). Such an analysis, however, begs the question, "Are these distributions likely to arise in practice when control charts are constructed?" As Moore (1957, p. 171) points out, data received from W. A. Shewhart resulting from work at Bell Labs had considerable skewness and kurtosis, roughly equal to that of a chi-square distribution with 8 degrees of freedom.

Although Moore examined the true tail probabilities for samples of size 5 from the latter distribution when normality is assumed, the smallest nominal tail probability given in his appropriate table is .005, which corresponds to 2.575 σ limits. Therefore, it is necessary to derive the results for 3σ limits.

The derivation will now be given. It can be easily shown that if

$$X \sim \chi_r^2$$

then $\overline{X}_n \sim (1/n)\chi_{nr}^2$. Thus, for samples of size 5 drawn from a chi-square distribution with r degrees of freedom, the distribution of the sample average will be $1/5$ times a chi-square variable with $5r$ degrees of freedom. In this case $r = 8$ so $\overline{X}_5 \sim (1/5)\chi_{40}^2$. It follows that $E(\overline{X}_5) = 8$ and $\mathrm{Var}(\overline{X}_5) = 3.2$ since the mean and the variance of a chi-square random variable are the degrees of freedom and twice the degrees of freedom, respectively. Also, the variance of a constant times a random variable is equal to the constant squared times the variance of the random variable. The 3σ control limits would then be obtained from $8 \pm 3\sqrt{3.2}$ so that the UCL = 13.3666 and LCL = 2.6334. It is then a matter of determining $P(\overline{X}_5 > 13.3666)$ and $P(\overline{X}_5 < 2.6334)$. Since $5\overline{X}_5 \sim \chi_{40}^2$, this is equivalent to determining the tail area of χ_{40}^2 above 66.8328 and below 13.1672. These probabilities can be shown to be .0049 and .000019, respectively. These probabilities follow the general pattern of probabilities reported in Moore (1957). Specifically, for small nominal tail probabilities the actual tail probabilities differ greatly, with the lower tail probability being virtually zero. Furthermore, the actual upper tail probability in this case is almost four times the nominal upper tail probability (.00135), and is thus almost double the nominal probability for both tails. [This differs somewhat from the results reported by Schilling and Nelson (1976) for the distributions they considered.]

The practical significance of these results is that if $X \sim \chi_8^2$, the expected frequency of "false alarms" above the UCL is actually 1 per 204 subgroups instead of the assumed expected frequency of 1 per 741 subgroups. Thus, if samples of size 5 are selected every 30 minutes, a false signal will be received about once every 13 work days (assuming an 8-hour day), instead of the assumed rate of once every 46 work days. If it is costly to search for assignable causes, this would obviously increase those costs considerably.

How can this problem be avoided? *If* we knew the actual distribution from which we are sampling, we could obtain the actual limits from that distribution such that the tail areas are 0.00135. For the present example the actual limits would be (approximately)

$$\mathrm{UCL} = \tfrac{1}{5}(72.20) = 14.44$$

$$\mathrm{LCL} = \tfrac{1}{5}(18.38) = 3.676$$

Notice that these differ considerably from the 3σ limits.

We will not generally know the type of distribution from which we are sampling, however. One possible solution would be to fit a distribution to the data (such as a member of the Pearson family of distributions), and then use the percentage points of that distribution to obtain control limits for equal tail probabilities (.00135 or some other value). Another possible solution, as mentioned earlier, would be to transform the data so that the transformed data seem to be approximately normally distributed, and then follow the basic procedure for controlling the transformed variable. For a detailed discussion of these two suggested approaches the reader is referred to Chapter 21 of Cowden (1957). Burrows (1962) also believes that nonnormality is a problem and suggests that data be simulated from the parent distribution for determining the control limits for an $\overline{X}$ chart.

Another possible problem is lack of independence of observations made in sequential order. Is the weight of a ball bearing coming off an assembly line correlated with the weight of the preceding ball bearing, for example? In particular, is that ball bearing likely to be nonconforming because the preceding one was nonconforming? The distorting effect that correlated data can have on the control limits of $\overline{X}$, R, and other control charts has received very little attention.

The problem has been considered by Vasilopoulos and Stamboulis (1978), who showed that the limits for an $\overline{X}$ chart, in particular, can be off by a wide margin when the correlation structure of the data is ignored. To remedy this problem, they provide factors that should be used with an s chart or an $\overline{X}$ chart when the data can be fit with either a first- or second-order autoregressive model [AR(1) or AR(2)]. Figure 5.9 illustrates what can happen when an obvious trend in the data is ignored when determining control limits for an $\overline{X}$ chart. If subgroups are obtained in such a way that the n observations in each subgroup all happen to be at either

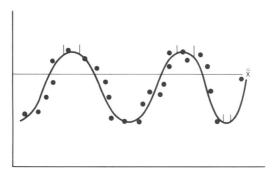

Figure 5.9 Nonrandom data.

Table 5.13 100 Consecutive Values from AR(1)
$[\phi_1 = 0.5, \varepsilon \sim NID(0, 1)]$

1.30	0.06	−1.63	1.28	0.52
1.59	−1.46	0.03	0.48	−0.29
0.17	−1.75	0.52	−0.50	2.22
0.01	−1.46	1.21	0.99	1.21
0.07	0.19	0.87	1.00	−0.20
−1.18	−0.60	1.23	−0.05	0.59
−3.36	−0.67	0.78	−1.55	0.42
−3.35	1.10	0.86	−0.88	0.63
0.50	1.15	2.71	0.79	0.52
−0.26	1.30	1.68	1.04	−0.89
−2.07	1.61	−0.52	2.52	−0.50
−2.02	0.12	−1.40	1.79	−0.99
−1.77	1.11	−0.59	3.72	−2.02
−0.12	0.76	−1.15	2.65	−1.40
0.32	−0.21	−0.48	1.92	0.39
−1.16	−0.73	0.13	0.90	1.36
−0.89	0.17	0.33	−0.60	1.24
−0.80	0.45	0.07	−1.70	−1.10
0.08	0.27	0.34	−0.75	−1.98
1.74	−0.78	0.78	0.76	−0.41

the top or the bottom of the curve (as indicated by the vertical lines), σ^2 would be poorly estimated since there would be hardly any variability within each subgroup. Although we would usually not expect any trend in the data to be quite as obvious as in Figure 5.9, the intent here is to show that ignoring trended data can cause serious problems.

A simple example will now be given to illustrate this point. Assume that data obtained for some quality characteristic can be represented by a *first-order autoregressive process* of the form

$$X_t = \phi_1 X_{t-1} + \varepsilon_t$$

where $-1 < \phi_1 < 1$ and $\varepsilon_t \sim NID(0, \sigma_\varepsilon^2)$. (The requirement on ϕ_1 is necessary for the process to be stationary, and NID indicates that the errors are normally and independently distributed.) Successive observations will obviously be uncorrelated if $\phi_1 = 0$ but will be highly correlated if $|\phi_1|$ is close to 1.

One hundred consecutive values generated from a first-order autoregressive [AR(1)] process are displayed in Table 5.13, and a time-sequence plot of that data is given in Figure 5.10. If subgroups of size four or five are

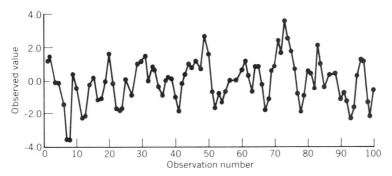

Figure 5.10 Time-sequence plot of the data in Table 5.13.

formed from these data (preserving the time order of the data), σ will be underestimated if subgroup ranges are used. For example, if subgroups of size five are formed and σ is estimated by $\overline{R}/d_2$, the estimate is 0.9190 compared to the known value of 1.1547. (See Chapter 6 for explanation of the latter.) A better estimate would be obtained if the data were not put into subgroups, and this applies, in general, to trended data. This is discussed at greater length in Chapter 6.

Although the data in Figure 5.10 exhibit a very obvious trend, even stronger trends have been encountered in practice. A somewhat classic article on this subject is McCoun (1949), which was reprinted in the October 1974 issue of *Quality Progress*. The article describes an actual study of a tooling problem in which the individual values graphed similar to Figure 5.9. Subgroups were unknowingly taken at the bottom of each cycle and σ was badly underestimated because $\overline{R}$ was close to zero. Nevertheless, in spite of the fact that the resultant control limits were very narrow, the subgroup averages when plotted provided evidence that the process was in control. This was because the averages also differed very little because of the way that the data were obtained. In spite of this control-chart message, many of the individual values did not even meet engineering specifications. The fact that the trend was fouling up the $\overline{X}$ chart limits was not detected until the individual values were plotted and the trend became apparent.

It should be pointed out that Vasilopoulos and Stamboulis did not consider the possibility that σ could be poorly estimated as a result of the correlated observations. Instead, they just considered the appropriate expression for $\sigma_{\overline{x}}$ for an AR(2) process and contrasted what the control limits would be for that expression with the usual $\overline{X}$ chart limits obtained from using $3(\sigma/\sqrt{n})$.

Berthouex, Hunter, and Pallesen (1978) found that the use of a standard Shewhart or CUSUM chart for certain environmental data was unsatisfactory in that the charts gave too many false alarms. This was due to the fact that the data were correlated. The problem was remedied by fitting a time-series model to the data, and using the *residuals* from the model in monitoring the process. (A residual is the difference between an observed value and the corresponding predicted value. Residuals are discussed and illustrated in Chapters 12 and 13.) Using residuals to monitor a process is thus an alternative to the use of adjustment factors such as those given by Vasilopoulos and Stamboulis (1978), and is a more general approach. Its value results from the fact that it is much easier to fit an adequate model to a set of data than to construct tables of adjustment factors for every type of model that might be fit to data from some process. There is one drawback, however, in that it is harder to relate to a residual than to an $\overline{X}$ value. Consequently, if residuals are used, the $\overline{X}$ values should probably also be plotted (without control limits).

If an $\overline{X}$ chart of residuals begins to exhibit a lack of control, this would be evidence that the fitted model is no longer appropriate, and, in particular, the mean of the measured variable is no longer at the assumed value.

Readers interested in fitting time series models to data should consult Box and Jenkins (1976).

The different types of CUSUM procedures presented in this chapter are also adversely affected by nonnormality and serial correlation. The methods that employ the two cumulative sums (S_H and S_L) are based upon the assumption that the z-values that are computed have an $N(0, 1)$ distribution. This assumption will not be strictly valid if $\overline{X}$ is not normally distributed.

In particular, the discussion concerning the problems created by assuming that $\overline{X} \sim$ Normal when $X \sim \chi_8^2$ also applies here. Specifically, $P(Z > 3) = .0049$ instead of $.00135$, $P(Z > 1.96) = .0362$ instead of $.025$, etc. This means that, in this case, the ARL tabulated values are not exact, and the actual (unknown) ARL values may be considerably different, particularly the ARL values for detecting large shifts. The value of h could be adjusted to compensate for this if there were guidelines for adjusting h for various nonnormal situations. Alternatively, the data could be transformed so that at least $\overline{X}$ would be approximately normally distributed.

If the data appear to be approximately normally distributed but are obviously correlated, this presents a different type of problem. The estimation of $\sigma_{\overline{x}}$ by $\hat{\sigma}_x / \sqrt{n}$ is appropriate only when the data are independent. Assume that the available data can be fit by an AR(1) model. As implied previously, $\sigma_{\overline{x}}$ will expectedly be underestimated, perhaps by a considerable amount, if ϕ_1 is positive (and overestimated if ϕ_1 is negative) when $\hat{\sigma}_x / \sqrt{n}$ is used. The process standard deviation, σ_x, might also be poorly estimated by $\overline{R}/d_2$ in the presence of autocorrelation. When there is strong evidence of autocorrelation it is preferable to estimate σ_x by s_x, the sample standard deviation, calculated from at least 50 consecutive observations. The appropriate expression for $\sigma_{\overline{x}}$ will be determined by the time series model that is fit to the data, and $\hat{\sigma}_{\overline{x}}$ would then be obtained by substituting sample estimates for the parameters in the expression for $\sigma_{\overline{x}}$.

The consequence of not doing this is that the z-values in the CUSUM procedure could be seriously inflated or deflated, thus necessitating a different value for h so as to keep the ARL values within reason for various mean shifts.

As far as the other charts are concerned, the assumptions of normality and independence are also important for the acceptance chart, the two types of difference charts that were presented, as well as the median and midrange charts that were mentioned.

SUMMARY

The control chart user has many different types of control charts to select from when subgroups can be formed. Although $\overline{X}$ and R charts are the types that have been most frequently used, they are inferior to other procedures even if the assumptions of normality and independence are satisfied. CUSUM procedures are far superior to an $\overline{X}$ chart for detecting small mean shifts (unless the shift results from a slow drift), and a combined Shewhart–CUSUM scheme is competitive with an $\overline{X}$ chart in detecting large mean shifts. The main problem with the conventional R chart is that the 3σ limits will result in highly unequal tail probabilities since the distribution of the sample range is highly asymmetric even when the individual observations are normally distributed This problem can be overcome by using an R chart with probability limits, provided that the original or transformed observations are approximately normally distributed. An s chart with probability limits would be a better choice under such conditions, however, since an s chart is superior to an R chart even for small sample sizes. An acceptance chart can be used in place of an $\overline{X}$ chart when the specification limits are much wider than the inherent process variability, and a target value is not being specified. A difference chart for paired data can be used in calibration work, and the "grouped" difference chart can be used to adjust for the influence of extraneous factors.

Data that exhibit a discernible trend should be treated differently from data that appear to be reasonably random.

APPENDIX TO CHAPTER 5

A. Derivation of Control Chart Constants

(1) d_2:

Assuming $Y \sim N(\mu, \sigma^2)$, it is well known that

$$E(R) = \int_{-\infty}^{\infty} (y_{(n)} - y_{(1)}) f(R) \, dR = d_2 \sigma_y$$

where $y_{(n)}$ is the largest value in a sample of size n, $y_{(1)}$ is the smallest value, $f(R)$ represents the probability function for the range, and d_2 depends upon n. Thus, since

$$\mu_R = d_2 \sigma_y$$

it follows that we would estimate σ_y as

$$\hat{\sigma}_y = \hat{\mu}_R / d_2 = \overline{R} / d_2$$

where $\overline{R}$ is the average of the ranges for a set of subgroups.

(2) c_4:

Again, assuming $Y \sim N(\mu, \sigma^2)$, we can utilize the result given in this chapter; that is,

$$\frac{(n-1)s_y^2}{\sigma_y^2} \sim \chi_{n-1}^2$$

It then follows that

$$\frac{s\sqrt{n-1}}{\sigma}$$

has a chi distribution with $(n-1)$ degrees of freedom, so that

$$E(s) = \frac{\sigma}{\sqrt{n-1}} E(\chi_{n-1})$$

Since the expected value of a chi random variable with $(n - 1)$ degrees of freedom can be shown to be equal to

$$\sqrt{2} \; \frac{\Gamma(n/2)}{\Gamma[(n-1)/2]}$$

where $\Gamma(n) = \int_0^\infty y^{n-1} e^{-y} \, dy$, it follows that

$$E(s) = \sqrt{\frac{2}{n-1}} \; \frac{\Gamma(n/2)}{\Gamma[(n-1)/2]} \sigma$$

$$= c_4 \sigma$$

where c_4 is given in Table E for different values of n. Thus, $\hat{\sigma} = \bar{s}/c_4$.

(3) D_3 and D_4:
Assuming a normal distribution, it can be shown that the control limits for the R chart are $D_3 \overline{R}$ and $D_4 \overline{R}$, by starting with the expression

$$\overline{R} \pm 3 \hat{\sigma}_R$$

that produces the control limits. As with $E(R)$, it is also well known that the standard deviation of R can be written as $\sigma_R = d_3 \sigma_y$ where d_3 depends on n. It then follows that

$$\hat{\sigma}_R = d_3 \hat{\sigma}_y$$

$$= d_3 (\overline{R}/d_2)$$

so that the 3-sigma limits could be written as

$$\overline{R} \pm 3(d_3/d_2)\overline{R}$$

but are generally written as $D_3 \overline{R}$ and $D_4 \overline{R}$, where $D_3 = 1 - 3(d_3/d_2)$ and $D_4 = 1 + 3(d_3/d_2)$.

Values of D_3, D_4, and d_3 are given in Table E for different values of n.

(4) B_3 and B_4:
It was shown in **(2)** of this Appendix that $E(s) = c_4 \sigma$. Since the variance of s equals $E(s^2) - [E(s)]^2$, it follows that

$$\text{Var}(s) = E(s^2) - [E(s)]^2$$

$$= \sigma^2 - (c_4 \sigma)^2$$

$$= \sigma^2 (1 - c_4^2)$$

With σ^2 estimated as $(\bar{s}/c_4)^2$, it follows that an estimate of the standard deviation of s is given by

$$\hat{\sigma}_s = \frac{\bar{s}}{c_4}\sqrt{1 - c_4^2}$$

so that the 3-sigma limits for the s chart could be written as

$$\bar{s} \pm 3\frac{\bar{s}}{c_4}\sqrt{1 - c_4^2}$$

but could be more conveniently written as $B_3\bar{s}$ and $B_4\bar{s}$ where $B_3 = 1 - (3/c_4)\sqrt{1 - c_4^2}$ and $B_4 = 1 + (3/c_4)\sqrt{1 - c_4^2}$.

B. ARL Calculations

The probability of obtaining the first out-of-control message on the nth subgroup is $p(1 - p)^{n-1}$ $n = 1, 2, \ldots$, which is the general form for the geometric distribution. Thus, with $f(n) = p(1 - p)^{n-1}$ $n = 1, 2, \ldots$, we need the expected value of n. Specifically, $E(n) = \sum_{n=1}^{\infty}np(1 - p)^{n-1} = p\sum_{n=1}^{\infty}n(1 - p)^{n-1}$. Using the fact that $\sum_{n=1}^{\infty}(1 - p)^{n-1}$ is an infinite geometric series so that

$$\sum_{n=1}^{\infty}(1 - p)^{n-1} = \frac{1}{p}$$

we can take the derivative of each side of this last equation and then multiply by p to obtain

$$p\sum_{n=1}^{\infty}(n - 1)(1 - p)^{n-2} = \frac{1}{p} = p\sum_{n=1}^{\infty}n(1 - p)^{n-1}$$

so that the expected subgroup number is $1/p$, where p is the probability associated with a single subgroup.

REFERENCES

Berthouex, P. M., W. G. Hunter, and L. Pallesen (1978). Monitoring sewage treatment plants: Some quality control aspects. *Journal of Quality Technology* 10(4): 139–149 (October).

Bissell, A. F. (1979). A semi-parabolic mask for CUSUM charts. *The Statistician* *28*(1): 1–7.

Bissell, A. F. (1981). Correction to a semi-parabolic mask for CUSUM charts. *The Statistician*, *30*: 77.

Bissell, A. F. (1984). The performance of control charts and cusums under linear trend. *Applied Statistics 33*(2): 145–151.

Bissell, A. F. (1986). "Corrigendum" (to Bissell, 1984). *Applied Statistics 35*(2): 214.

Box, G. E. P. (1953). Non-normality and tests on variances. *Biometrika 40*: 318–335 (June).

Box, G. E. P., and G. M. Jenkins (1976). *Time Series Analysis: Forecasting and Control*, Revised Edition. San Francisco: Holden-Day.

Burr, I. W. (1967). The effect of non-normality on constants for $\overline{X}$ and R charts, *Industrial Quality Control 23*(11): 563–569 (May).

Burr, I. W. (1969). Control charts for measurements with varying sample sizes. *Journal of Quality Technology 1*(3): 163–167 (July).

Burrows, P. M. (1962). $\overline{X}$ control schemes for a production variable with skewed distribution. *The Statistician 12*(4): 296–312.

Cowden, D. J. (1957). *Statistical Methods in Quality Control*. Englewood Cliffs, NJ: Prentice-Hall.

Dobben de Bruyn, C. S. (1968). *Cumulative Sum Tests: Theory and Practice*. Griffin's Statistical Monographs and Courses No. 24. New York: Hafner.

Duncan, A. J. (1986). *Quality Control and Industrial Statistics*, 5th ed. Homewood, IL: Irwin.

Ferrell, E. B. (1953). Control charts using midranges and medians. *Industrial Quality Control 9*(5): 30–34.

Freund, R. A. (1957). Acceptance control charts. *Industrial Quality Control 14*(4): 13–23 (October).

Grant, E. L., and R. S. Leavenworth (1980). *Statistical Quality Control*, 5th ed. New York: McGraw-Hill.

Grubbs, F. E. (1946). The difference chart with an example of its use. *Industrial Quality Control 3*(1): 22–25 (July).

Hahn, G. J. (1970). How abnormal is normality. *Journal of Quality Technology 3*(1): 18–22 (January).

Harter, H. L. (1960). Tables of range and studentized range. *The Annals of Mathematical Statistics 31*(4): 1122–1147 (December).

Hawkins, D. M. (1981). A CUSUM for a scale parameter. *Journal of Quality Technology 13*(4): 228–231 (October).

Hill, D. (1956). Modified control limits. *Applied Statistics 5*(1): 12–19 (March).

Hunter, J. S. (1986). The exponentially weighted moving average. *Journal of Quality Technology*, *18*(4): 203–210 (October).

Johnson, N. L., and F. C. Leone (1962a). Cumulative sum control charts. *Industrial Quality Control 18*(12): 15–21 (June).

Johnson, N. L., and F. C. Leone (1962b). Cumulative sum control charts. *Industrial Quality Control 19*(1): 29–36 (July).

Johnson, N. L., and F. C. Leone (1962c). Cumulative sum control charts. *Industrial Quality Control 19*(2): 22–28 (August).

Johnson, N. L., and F. C. Leone (1977). *Statistics and Experimental Design in Engineering and the Physical Sciences*, Volume I, 2nd ed. New York: Wiley.

Lorenzen, T. J., and L. C. Vance (1986). Economic comparisons of control charts. *ASQC Annual Quality Congress Transactions*: 255–263.

Lucas, J. M. (1973). A modified V-mask control scheme. *Technometrics 15*(4): 833–847 (November).

Lucas, J. M. (1976). The design and use of V-mask control schemes. *Journal of Quality Technology 8*(1): 1–12 (January).

Lucas, J. M. (1982). Combined Shewhart-CUSUM quality control schemes. *Journal of Quality Technology 14*(2): 51–59 (April).

Lucas, J. M., and R. B. Crosier (1982a). Fast initial response for CUSUM quality control schemes: Give your CUSUM a head start. *Technometrics 24*(3): 199–205 (August).

Lucas, J. M., and R. B. Crosier (1982b). Robust CUSUM. *Communications in Statistics, Part A—Theory and Methods 11*(23): 2669–2687.

McCoun, V. E. (1974). The case of the perjured control chart. *Quality Progress 7*(10): 17–19. (Originally published in *Industrial Quality Control*, May 1949.)

Moore, P. G. (1957). Normality in quality control charts. *Applied Statistics 6*(3): 171–179 (November).

Nelson, L. S. (1982). Control chart for medians. *Journal of Quality Technology 14*(4): 226–227 (October).

Ott, E. R. (1947). An indirect calibration of an electronic test set. *Industrial Quality Control 3*(4): 11–14 (January).

Ott, E. R. (1949). Variables control charts in production research. *Industrial Quality Control 6*(3): 30–31 (November).

Ott, E. R. (1975). *Process Quality Control*. New York: McGraw-Hill.

Page, E. S. (1954). Continuous inspection schemes. *Biometrika 41*: 100–115.

Roberts, S. W. (1959). Control chart tests based on geometric moving averages. *Technometrics 1*(3): 239–250 (August).

Robinson, P. B., and T. Y. Ho (1978). Average run lengths of geometric moving average charts by numerical methods. *Technometrics 20*(1): 85–93 (February).

Rowlands, R. J., A. B. J. Nix, M. A. Abdollahian, and K. W. Kemp (1982). Snub-nosed V-mask control schemes. *The Statistician 31*(2): 133–142.

Saniga, E. M., and L. E. Shirland (1977). Quality control in practice...A survey. *Quality Progress 10*(5): 30–33 (May).

Schilling, E. G., and P. R. Nelson (1976). The effect of non-normality on the control limits of $\overline{X}$ charts. *Journal of Quality Technology 8*(4): 183–188 (October).

Shapiro, S. S. (1980). How to test normality and other distributional assumptions, Volume 3, *Basic References in Quality Control: Statistical Techniques.* Milwaukee: American Society for Quality Control.

Shewhart, W. A. (1931). *Economic Control of Quality of Manufactured Product.* New York: Van Nostrand.

Vasilopoulos, A. V., and A. P. Stamboulis (1978). Modification of control chart limits in the presence of data correlation. *Journal of Quality Technology 10*(1): 20–30 (January).

Wadsworth, H. M., K. S. Stephens, and A. B. Godfrey (1986). *Modern Methods for Quality Control and Improvement.* New York: Wiley.

Westgard, J. O., T. Groth, T. Aronsson, and C. de Verdier (1977). Combined Shewhart–CUSUM control chart for improved quality control in clinical chemistry. *Clinical Chemistry 23*(10): 1881–1887.

Woods, R. F. (1976). Effective, economic quality through the use of acceptance control charts. *Journal of Quality Technology 8*(2): 81–85 (April).

EXERCISES

1. Construct the s chart for the data in Table 5.1. Compare the configuration of points with the R chart given in Figure 5.1.

2. Deleting points and recomputing the control limits can cause the limits to change considerably. Show this for the s chart with 3-sigma limits by determining the smallest possible difference between the original and recomputed UCL values for $n = 4$ when one point out of 30 plots above the UCL and is subsequently discarded.

3. For the data in Table 5.3 show that $\bar{x}_9$ would have been inside the control limits if σ had been estimated using subgroup standard deviations rather than subgroup ranges. Comment.

4. Explain the purpose of an acceptance control chart, and indicate one or more conditions under which it should not be used.

5. What are the guiding factors for determining the values of h and k that are to be used in a CUSUM scheme?

6. Assume that a CUSUM scheme is being used to monitor the process mean, and a $1.5\sigma_{\bar{x}}$ increase in the process mean suddenly occurs.

   a. If $h = 5$ and $k = 0.5$ are being used, how many subgroups would we expect to observe before a signal is received?

   b. How many subgroup averages would we expect to have to plot with an $\bar{X}$ chart before observing an average above the UCL?

   c. Explain why your answers to (a) and (b) do not depend upon the subgroup size.

7. Indicate when it might be inadvisable to reset S_H and S_L to zero after an out-of-control signal has been received.

8. Discuss the alternatives that an experimenter has when constructing an $\overline{X}$ chart for correlated data.

9. Twenty subgroups of size five are obtained for the purpose of determining trial control limits for an $\overline{X}$ and an R chart. The data are given below.

Subgroup number	$\overline{X}$	R	Subgroup Number	$\overline{X}$	R
1	23	5	11	26	5
2	22	3	12	21	4
3	24	2	13	22	4
4	20	4	14	20	4
5	18	3	15	23	3
6	17	4	16	21	6
7	24	4	17	20	5
8	10	3	18	18	4
9	16	5	19	15	3
10	20	4	20	17	2

   a. Determine the (3-sigma) trial control limits for each chart.

   b. Explain why there are so many subgroup averages outside the control limits for the $\overline{X}$ chart in spite of the fact that the averages do not vary greatly.

   c. What should be done with those subgroups whose average is beyond the limits?

   d. Since the number of points outside the control limits on the $\overline{X}$ chart is quite high relative to the number of points that are plotted, what might this suggest about the type of distribution from which the data could have come?

10. Fill in the blanks below where a CUSUM procedure is being used to control the process mean, with $k = 0.5$.

z	S_H	S_L
0.48	0	0
—	3.0	—
—	—	1.3
2.13	—	—

11. Construct an R chart with probability limits for the data in Problem #9, and compare with the conventional R chart.

12. Construct an $\overline{X}$ chart for the following data:

Subgroup Number	Observations	Subgroup Number	Observations
1	3.1 3.2 3.6 3.8	11	3.2 3.6 2.9 3.4
2	3.3 3.4 3.1 3.7	12	3.0 3.5 3.1 3.3
3	3.0 2.9 3.6 3.5	13	3.2 3.7 3.4 3.1
4	3.2 3.2 3.1 3.5	14	3.4 3.1 2.8 3.5
5	3.7 3.8 3.4 4.0	15	3.6 3.3 3.4 3.9
6	3.3 3.5 3.2 3.0	16	3.8 3.2 3.4 3.5
7	3.4 3.1 3.6 3.0	17	3.7 3.5 3.2 3.3
8	3.3 3.9 3.7 3.6	18	3.5 3.4 3.1 3.0
9	3.5 3.8 3.1 3.3	19	3.6 3.7 3.9 3.2
10	4.1 3.7 3.5 3.2	20	3.4 3.8 3.5 3.1

Control Charts for Measurements *without* Subgrouping (for One Variable)

The control charts given in the preceding chapter can be used when subgroups can be formed. This is not always possible or practical, however. Items coming off an assembly line may be produced at such a slow rate so as to preclude the forming of subgroups. If items are produced every 30 minutes it would take 2.5 hours to form a subgroup of size 5; by then the process might already have gone out of control. Variables such as temperature and pressure could also not be charted with subgrouping since, for example, a "subgroup" of five temperature readings made in quick order would likely be virtually the same. Thus, nothing would be gained. Clerical and accounting data would also have to be charted using individual numbers rather than subgroups. (This will be discussed further in Chapter 10.)

6.1 INDIVIDUAL OBSERVATIONS CHART

Charts based upon individual observations are not as sensitive as an $\overline{X}$ chart or CUSUM procedure in detecting a mean shift, however. This can be demonstrated as follows. Assume that there is a shift in the process mean of $a\sigma$ where $a > 0$. The control limits on an individual observations chart are at (estimates of) $\mu \pm 3\sigma$. The probability of an individual observation plotting above the upper control limit (UCL) is equal to $P(X > \mu + 3\sigma)$ given that the actual mean is equal to $\mu + a\sigma$. For the $\overline{X}$ chart we need to

150

determine $P(\overline{X} > \mu + 3\sigma_{\overline{x}})$ when the mean is $\mu + a\sigma$. The two z-values are

$$z = \frac{\mu + 3\sigma - (\mu + a\sigma)}{\sigma} = 3 - a$$

and

$$z = \frac{\mu + 3\sigma_{\overline{x}} - (\mu + a\sigma)}{\sigma_{\overline{x}}} = 3 - a\sqrt{n}$$

(The latter results from the fact that $\sigma_{\overline{x}} = \sigma/\sqrt{n}$.) $P(Z > 3 - a\sqrt{n})$ is clearly greater than $P(Z > 3 - a)$, so for an $a\sigma$ increase in μ, we would expect to observe a subgroup average above its UCL before we would observe an individual observation above its UCL. (The same type of result would hold when $a < 0$.)

This is not only intuitive, it is also in line with general statistical theory, which holds that the "power" of a hypothesis test increases as the sample size increases. (Here we are comparing a sample size of 1 with a sample size of $n > 1$.)

The important point is that when conditions are such that either an X (individual observations) chart or an $\overline{X}$ chart (or a CUSUM procedure) *could* be used, it would be unwise to use an X chart.

This does not mean, however, that the two charts could not be used together. A subgroup average could be above the UCL on an $\overline{X}$ chart because of the presence of one exceedingly large observation. The individual observations which comprise that subgroup could be plotted on an X chart, and the magnitude of that one large observation could be assessed relative to the control limits for the individual observations. A subsequent investigation might reveal that the value was recorded in error. An X chart could be used in conjunction with a CUSUM procedure for the same purpose, as well as with an R, s, or s^2 chart.

6.1.1 Control Limits for the X Chart

The control limits for an X chart are obtained from

$$\hat{\mu} \pm 3\hat{\sigma}$$

The estimate of the mean should be obtained from a sample of at least 50 observations. The estimation of σ is another matter. Obviously subgroup ranges cannot be used since we have no subgroups. The commonly accepted procedure is to "create" ranges by taking differences of successive observations (second minus first, third minus second, etc.) and dropping the sign of the difference when it is negative. The average of these "moving ranges" of size 2 is then used in the same manner that $\overline{R}$ is used in estimating σ for an $\overline{X}$ chart. Specifically,

$$\hat{\sigma} = \overline{MR}/d_2$$

where $\overline{MR}$ denotes the average of the moving ranges.

6.1.2 Trended Data

This approach is objectionable because a moving range of size 2 will smooth out whatever trend may be present in the data. This is desirable if the trend is only temporary, but undesirable if the trend is a relatively permanent part of the data.

A disciple of Shewhart might argue, however, that a process is out of control if there is *any* trend in the data. Nevertheless, it is unreasonable to assume that every out-of-control condition is immediately correctable, or that data will always be uncorrelated over time when a process is in control. For the McCoun (1974) data, a cam mechanism had to be reworked twice before the trend was removed. If an X chart had been constructed with sigma estimated from the moving ranges, the chart after the first rework would have likely indicated that the process was out of control, whereas the graph of the data was similar to that shown in Figure 5.9, so that the process was very much in control, relative to the trend.

The use of an X chart in this manner would simply identify the existence of a trend, but that could be seen just by plotting the data. It seems preferable to separate the detection of the trend from the detection of any points that might represent an out-of-control condition in addition to the trend.

A better approach would be to take a sample of at least 50 consecutive observations, calculate s and $\bar{x}$, and then obtain the limits as

$$\bar{x} \pm 3\frac{s}{c_4}$$

where s/c_4 is an unbiased estimator of σ when the observations are independent, and will likely provide a better estimate of σ than $\overline{MR}/d_2$ when the observations are not independent. This would be a reasonable approach as long as the 50 observations typify the data generated by the process.

Regardless of the way in which σ is estimated, it is very important that the data be almost normally distributed. If not, the tail probabilities outside the limits could differ greatly and render the chart virtually useless. Consequently, it is imperative that approximate normality be checked before an X chart is used. As indicated previously, this can be accomplished by using a normal probability plot, or by one of several other tests. (The problem of nonnormality when an $\overline{X}$ chart is used was discussed in Section 5.11. Nonnormality is a more serious problem when only individual observations are plotted.)

6.1.3 Illustrative Example: Random Data

Two sets of simulated data and one set of real data will be used to illustrate an X chart and the other charts presented in this chapter. Table 6.1 contains 50 random numbers generated from a normal distribution with $\mu = 25$ and $\sigma = 3$.

Assume that the random numbers in Table 6.1 constitute 50 consecutive observations from a manufacturing process. (The consecutive observations are obtained by reading down each column.) In this instance we know that the data are normally distributed. Nevertheless, the normal probability plot is given in Figure 6.1 since a test for normality should be the first step in a typical application. It should be observed that the points do not form exactly a straight line even though the data came from a normal distribution, but neither does it depart greatly from a straight line. (We should not expect exactly a straight line, however. See the discussion in Section 13.8.)

For the sake of illustration, σ (which we know is 3) will be estimated using both s and $\overline{MR}/d_2$ for a moving range of size 2. It can be shown that $s/c_4 = 2.9872/0.9949 = 3.0025$ and $\overline{MR}/d_2 = 3.1484/1.128 = 2.7911$.

Table 6.1 Random Numbers from $N(\mu = 25, \sigma^2 = 9)$

28.30	17.89	26.45	24.69	24.18
23.64	28.38	26.83	24.35	24.54
26.92	22.71	23.75	16.79	21.35
30.53	24.35	24.26	24.00	27.09
26.68	23.80	27.60	25.66	24.30
25.87	30.80	25.74	30.70	29.54
24.26	25.54	29.16	21.27	27.11
20.03	24.85	25.86	21.27	21.50
21.58	23.58	27.03	26.43	23.89
22.24	24.14	24.28	28.01	24.33

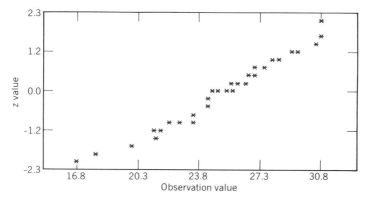

Figure 6.1 Normal probability plot of Table 6.1 data.

Thus, the two estimates differ noticeably, even though the observations are normally distributed random numbers.

The control limits using s would be

$$\bar{x} \pm 3\frac{s}{c_4} = 24.96 \pm 3(3.0025)$$

so that UCL = 33.9675 and LCL = 15.9525. The control limits using the moving range would be

$$\bar{x} \pm 3\left(\overline{MR}/d_2\right) = 24.96 \pm 3(2.7911)$$

so that UCL = 33.3333 and LCL = 16.5867. Thus, the two sets of limits

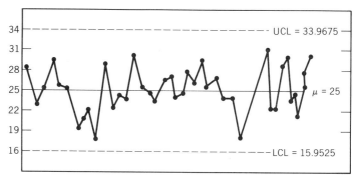

Figure 6.2 X chart for Table 6.1 data.

differ somewhat, and this is due to the comparatively poor estimate of σ obtained by using the moving range. The X control chart is displayed in Figure 6.2, and it can be observed that all of the points lie within the limits (which are the limits using s).

6.1.4   Illustrative Example: Trended Data

Limits obtained from the two approaches can be expected to differ greatly when the data contain a nonremovable trend. This will be illustrated by using part of the data for the AR(1) process used in Chapter 5.

Recall that the data (in Table 5.13) were generated using

$$x_t = \phi_1 x_{t-1} + \varepsilon_t$$

where ϕ_1 was set equal to 0.5 and we assumed $\varepsilon \sim \text{NID}(0, 1)$. The first 50 of those 100 values are listed in Table 6.2 with the corresponding moving ranges.

Although data from an AR(1) with $\phi_1 = 0.5$ should not show as strong a trend as would be the case if $0.5 < \phi_1 < 1.0$, there is nevertheless some evidence of a trend when the data in Table 6.2 are graphed in Figure 6.3.

Table 6.2   Fifty Consecutive Values from AR(1) [$\phi_1 = 0.5$, $\varepsilon \sim \text{NID}(0, 1)$]

Value	Moving Range ($n = 2$)	Value	Moving Range ($n = 2$)	Value	Moving Range ($n = 2$)
1.30		-0.80		-0.21	
	0.29		0.88		0.52
1.59		0.08		-0.73	
	1.42		1.66		0.90
0.17		1.74		0.17	
	0.16		1.68		0.28
0.01		0.06		0.45	
	0.06		1.52		0.18
0.07		-1.46		0.27	
	1.25		0.29		1.05
-1.18		-1.75		-0.78	
	2.18		0.29		0.85
-3.36		-1.46		-1.63	
	0.01		1.65		1.66
-3.35		0.19		0.03	
	3.85		0.79		0.49
0.50		-0.60		0.52	
	0.76		0.07		0.69
-0.26		-0.67		1.21	
	1.81		1.77		0.34
-2.07		1.10		0.87	
	0.05		0.05		0.36
-2.02		1.15		1.23	
	0.25		0.15		0.45
-1.77		1.30		0.78	
	1.65		0.31		0.08
-0.12		1.61		0.86	
	0.44		1.49		1.85
0.32		0.12		2.71	
	1.48		0.99		1.03
-1.16		1.11		1.68	
	0.27		0.35		
-0.89		0.76			
	0.09		0.97		

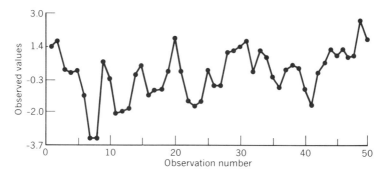

Figure 6.3 Time-sequence plot of Table 6.2 data.

It is well known (see, e.g., p. 58 of Box and Jenkins, 1976) that the variance of an AR(1) process is

$$\sigma_x^2 = \frac{\sigma_\varepsilon^2}{1 - \phi_1^2}$$

Thus, with $\sigma_\varepsilon^2 = 1$ and $\phi_1 = 0.5$, $\sigma_x^2 = 1.33$. Therefore, we *know* the actual process variance, and with a sample consisting of a large number of consecutive values we would expect the sample variance, s_x^2, to be reasonably close to 1.33. For the 50 observations in Table 6.2 it can be determined that $s_x^2 = 1.679$.

We would expect the estimator of σ_x that is based upon moving ranges of size 2 would underestimate σ_x, however. In particular, successive values will not differ greatly, in general, when ϕ_1 is close to one, which will cause the moving ranges to be close to zero. Consequently, the average moving range will also be close to zero, and since $d_2 = 1.128$ for $n = 2$, the estimate of σ_x will differ only slightly from the average moving range.

For fixed σ_ε, $\sigma_x = \sigma_\varepsilon/\sqrt{1 - \phi_1^2}$ will increase rapidly as ϕ_1 approaches one, but the estimate of σ_x obtained using moving ranges will not track σ_x. For example, if $\sigma_\varepsilon = 1$ and $\phi_1 = 0.99$ then $\sigma_x = 7.09$, but the estimate obtained using the moving range approach should be close to 0.71. (See the Appendix to this chapter for details.)

In this example $\phi_1 = 0.5$ and the average moving range is 0.85, so the estimate of σ_x is thus

$$\hat{\sigma}_x = \overline{MR}/d_2$$
$$= 0.85/1.128$$
$$= 0.754$$

Thus, $\sigma_x = \sqrt{1.33} = 1.155$ is estimated by 0.754 using the moving range, and by $s_x = \sqrt{1.679}/0.9949 = 1.296/0.9949 = 1.302$. Since the control

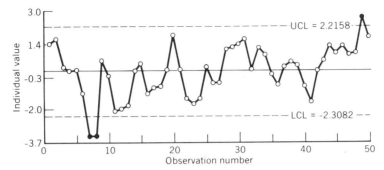

Figure 6.4 X chart of Table 6.2 data; limits obtained using moving ranges.

limits for the X chart are generally obtained using the moving range, the limits in this instance will be much too narrow. In general, limits that are too narrow can give a false signal that a process is out of control when, in fact, the process is actually in control.

This is exactly what happens in this case as can be seen from Figure 6.4.

Three of the fifty values are outside the control limits even though the process that generated the values is a stationary (i.e., in control) process. With the nominal tail areas of .00135 we would expect 50(0.0027) = .135 values to be outside the control limits. (In other words, we would expect all of the values to be within the control limits.)

If the limits had been obtained from $\bar{x} \pm 3s/c_4$, however, they would have been

$$\text{UCL} = \bar{x} + 3\frac{s}{c_4} = -0.0462 + 3\left(\frac{1.296}{0.9949}\right) = 3.8617$$

and

$$\text{LCL} = \bar{x} - 3\frac{s}{c_4} = -0.0462 - 3\left(\frac{1.296}{0.9949}\right) = -3.9541$$

Inspection of Table 6.2 reveals that all of the values lie between these limits. This can be seen more easily by viewing the X chart with the new limits as shown in Figure 6.5.

The important point is that the use of the moving range to estimate σ for an X chart is inadvisable when data contain a nonremovable trend. On the other hand, the use of s to estimate σ is also inadvisable if s is calculated from data that contain a trend that is due to an assignable cause that is (immediately) removable. Thus, considerable caution should be exercised in determining the limits for an X chart. The problem in determining trial

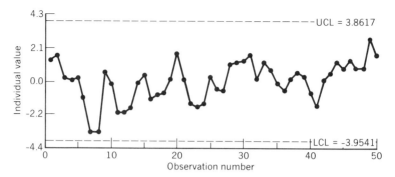

Figure 6.5 X chart with limits obtained from $\bar{x} \pm 3s/c_4$.

limits when an X chart is first used is that it may be difficult to determine whether or not a trend is removable. Nevertheless, if a trend exists at the time the data are collected, it is appropriate to use s in analyzing *that* set of data. If the trend is subsequently removed the limits should then be recomputed, and it should not make much difference whether σ is estimated from s or from the moving range. (Recall that there was some difference for the data in Table 6.1, however.)

An alternative approach which could be used when data display a trend would be to fit an appropriate time series model, and then use the residuals (the difference between the observed and predicted values) in monitoring the process. That is, the residuals would be used in constructing the control charts rather than the observed values. If lack of control was indicated for the residuals, or if a nonrandom pattern existed, this would indicate that the assumed model was no longer an appropriate model. As was indicated in Section 5.11, the residuals do not have engineering significance, however, so it would be desirable to also plot the individual values. Control charts for residuals are discussed in Alwan and Roberts (1988).

Time series models are not treated in detail in this text; the reader interested in such models is referred to Box and Jenkins (1976). The explicit use of such models is not mandatory for control charting, however. Rather, one can use adjustment factors such as those given by Vasilopoulos and Stamboulis (1978), which were discussed in Chapter 5. To use any adjustment factors, the control chart user must know what general model(s) would be appropriate for the data.

6.1.5 Trended Real Data

The fact that what was discussed in the preceding section can happen with real data can be illustrated by analyzing the data in Table 6.3. The data are measurements of color for some actual chemical data. The control chart

Table 6.3 Trended Real Data

Observation Number	Value	Observation Number	Value	Observation Number	Value
1	0.67	35	0.67	69	0.77
2	0.63	36	0.73	70	0.76
3	0.76	37	0.69	71	0.77
4	0.66	38	0.73	72	0.71
5	0.69	39	0.73	73	0.74
6	0.71	40	0.74	74	0.66
7	0.72	41	0.71	75	0.65
8	0.71	42	0.65	76	0.68
9	0.72	43	0.67	77	0.69
10	0.72	44	0.68	78	0.66
11	0.83	45	0.71	79	0.71
12	0.87	46	0.64	80	0.74
13	0.76	47	0.66	81	0.74
14	0.79	48	0.71	82	0.72
15	0.74	49	0.69	83	0.76
16	0.81	50	0.73	84	0.73
17	0.76	51	0.77	85	0.73
18	0.77	52	0.78	86	0.78
19	0.68	53	0.70	87	0.76
20	0.68	54	0.67	88	0.77
21	0.74	55	0.77	89	0.66
22	0.68	56	0.77	90	0.70
23	0.69	57	0.78	91	0.66
24	0.75	58	0.77	92	0.73
25	0.80	59	0.80	93	0.74
26	0.81	60	0.79	94	0.85
27	0.86	61	0.80	95	0.66
28	0.86	62	0.75	96	0.70
29	0.79	63	0.85	97	0.66
30	0.78	64	0.74	98	0.73
31	0.77	65	0.74	99	0.74
32	0.77	66	0.71	100	0.85
33	0.80	67	0.74	101	0.57
34	0.76	68	0.76	102	0.62

with σ estimated using moving ranges is shown in Figure 6.6. We can observe that 7 of the 102 points are outside the control limits. In particular, 6 of those points are above the upper control limit. We would not expect this from a process that is in control.

A histogram of the data (not shown) reveals that the data are slightly skewed—there are more large values than small values. This coupled with

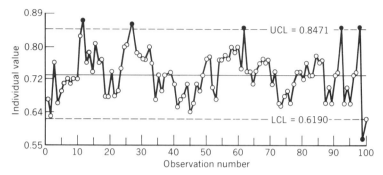

Figure 6.6 X chart for Table 6.3 data; limits obtained using moving ranges.

the fact that the data are obviously correlated (and hence σ is underestimated) causes so many points to be above the upper control limit. (The fact that the data are correlated can be seen from the runs of points above and below the midline.) The company's process engineers believed that the process was not operating properly, but it was also known that the company's chemical data were naturally correlated because of the nature of the chemical process. Thus, there may be some question as to whether or not the process was really out of control.

In any event, since $s = 0.0574$ the control limits obtained using s would be 0.9052 and 0.5608, and none of the points is outside these limits. Thus, whether or not the process is out of control for these 102 values depends on whether or not successive values should be correlated.

6.2   MOVING RANGE CHART

A moving range chart has been used in conjunction with an X chart for controlling the process variability. This chart thus complements an X chart similar to the way that an R chart complements an $\overline{X}$ chart. A moving range chart has considerable shortcomings, however. The control limits obtained from $D_3\overline{MR}$ and $D_4\overline{MR}$ are, strictly speaking, invalid since the values for D_3 and D_4 are tabulated under the assumption that the ranges are independent. (The two constants are obtained from Table E using $n = 2$.) A related problem is interpreting points on a moving range chart which are correlated. It is for the latter reason that Nelson (1982) recommends that the moving ranges not be plotted. The moving ranges might still be compared against the control limits, however. A CUSUM alternative will be discussed later in the chapter.

6.3 MOVING AVERAGE CHART

A moving average chart suffers from essentially the same deficiencies as a moving range chart; namely, σ is estimated from moving ranges, and the points on the moving average chart are correlated. The control limits are obtained from

$$\bar{x} \pm \frac{3}{\sqrt{n}} \frac{\overline{MR}}{d_2}$$

where $\bar{x}$ represents the average of the individual observations, n is the number of observations from which each moving average is computed, and $\overline{MR}/d_2$ is the estimate of σ (with d_2 obtained using $n = 2$).

The moving averages that are plotted on the chart are obtained as follows. If averages of size 5 are to be used, the first average would be the average of the first five observations, the second average would be the average of observations 2–6, the third would be the average of observations 3–7, and so on.

For the data in Table 6.1 the moving average chart is given in Figure 6.7. (Recall that the data are ordered sequentially by columns.) Notice that the graph indicates somewhat of a trend despite the fact that the data were generated from a stable process. Nelson (1983) illustrates how moving averages can be quite deceiving; Figure 6.7 is a perfect example of that.

For the three basic types of control charts considered so far in this chapter, an X chart with the control limits obtained from s would be easier to justify than a moving average chart, and a moving range chart for controlling the process variability must be used with caution, if at all.

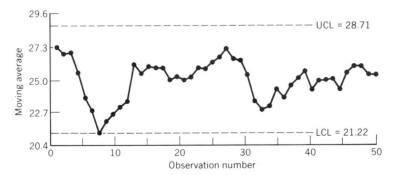

Figure 6.7 Moving average chart for the data in Table 6.1.

As mentioned previously, there is a CUSUM alternative to a moving range chart, and also a CUSUM alternative to an X chart. The latter will be considered first.

6.4   CUSUM FOR INDIVIDUAL OBSERVATIONS

The CUSUM methods of Lucas (1982) and Lucas and Crosier (1982), which were illustrated in Chapter 5, are also applicable to individual observations. Specifically, one would compute

$$Z = \frac{X - \overline{X}}{\hat{\sigma}_x}$$

and then proceed as in Chapter 5 once the z-values are obtained. As with the X chart, the standard deviation of an individual observation, σ_x, could be estimated using either $\overline{MR}/d_2$ or s/c_4.

The data in Table 6.1 will be used first to illustrate the approach. The calculations are shown in Table 6.4 (s/c_4 is used for $\hat{\sigma}_x$, with c_4 obtained for $n = 50$). Notice that none of the S_H or S_L values exceeds 5, or even comes close to 5. This should be expected since the data are from a stable process, and do not exhibit a trend.

The corresponding calculations obtained from using $\hat{\sigma} = \overline{MR}/d_2 = 2.7911$ are given in Table 6.5. Notice that some of the values for S_H and S_L differ considerably from those in Table 6.4. In particular, $S_{L(11)}$ is 4.49 in Table 6.5 compared with 4.03 in Table 6.4. Thus, when there is a string of z-values all of which either exceed 0.5 or are less than -0.5, the difference in two different estimates of σ will be essentially compounded at each sum (except when the sums zero out). Consequently, it is important that a good estimate of σ be obtained, whether it be from s/c_4, $\overline{MR}/d_2$, from prior experience, or in some other manner.

We have seen the deleterious effect that the use of $\hat{\sigma} = \overline{MR}/d_2$ can have on the control limits of an X chart when the data are trended. As stated in Chapter 5, it is inadvisable to strictly apply a CUSUM procedure for controlling the process mean in the presence of trended data. This also applies when individual observations are being used. The use of a CUSUM procedure for trended data could simply lead to detection of the trend that is known to exist in the first place. This is illustrated in Table 6.6 using the data in Table 6.2 with $\hat{\sigma} = s/c_4 = 1.303$. The threshold value of h is

Table 6.4 CUSUM Calculations Using the Data in Table 6.1
($k = 0.5$, $h = 5$, $\hat{\sigma} = s/c_4$)

Number	Observation	z	S_H	S_L
1	28.30	1.11	0.61	0
2	23.64	−0.44	0	0
3	26.92	0.65	0.15	0
4	30.53	1.86	1.51	0
5	26.68	0.57	1.58	0
6	25.87	0.30	1.38	0
7	24.26	−0.23	0.65	0
8	20.03	−1.64	0	1.14
9	21.58	−1.13	0	1.77
10	22.24	−0.91	0	2.18
11	17.89	−2.35	0	4.03
12	28.38	1.14	0.64	2.39
13	22.71	−0.75	0	2.64
14	24.35	−0.20	0	2.34
15	23.80	−0.39	0	2.23
16	30.80	1.95	1.45	0
17	25.54	0.19	1.14	0
18	24.85	−0.04	0.60	0
19	23.58	−0.46	0	0
20	24.14	−0.27	0	0
21	26.45	0.50	0	0
22	26.83	0.62	0.12	0
23	23.75	−0.40	0	0
24	24.26	−0.23	0	0
25	27.60	0.88	0.38	0
26	25.74	0.26	0.14	0
27	29.16	1.40	1.04	0
28	25.86	0.30	0.84	0
29	27.03	0.69	1.03	0
30	24.28	−0.23	0.30	0
31	24.69	−0.09	0	0
32	24.35	−0.20	0	0
33	16.79	−2.72	0	2.22
34	24.00	−0.32	0	2.04
35	25.66	0.23	0	1.31
36	30.70	1.91	1.41	0
37	21.27	−1.23	0	0.73
38	21.27	−1.23	0	1.46
39	26.43	0.49	0	0.47
40	28.01	1.02	0.52	0
41	24.18	−0.26	0	0
42	24.54	−0.14	0	0
43	21.35	−1.20	0	0.70
44	27.09	0.71	0.21	0
45	24.30	−0.22	0	0
46	29.54	1.53	1.03	0
47	27.11	0.72	1.25	0
48	21.50	−1.15	0	0.65
49	23.89	−0.36	0	0.51
50	24.33	−0.21	0	0.22

Table 6.5 CUSUM Calculations Using the Data in Table 6.1
$(k = 0.5, h = 5, \hat{\sigma} = \overline{MR}/d_2)$

Number	Observation	z	S_H	S_L
1	28.3	1.196	0.70	0.00
2	23.64	−0.473	0.00	0.00
3	26.92	0.702	0.20	0.00
4	30.53	1.995	1.70	0.00
5	26.68	0.616	1.81	0.00
6	25.87	0.326	1.64	0.00
7	24.26	−0.251	0.89	0.00
8	20.03	−1.767	0.00	1.27
9	21.58	−1.211	0.00	1.98
10	22.24	−0.975	0.00	2.45
11	17.89	−2.533	0.00	4.49
12	28.38	1.225	0.72	2.76
13	22.71	−0.806	0.00	3.07
14	24.35	−0.219	0.00	2.79
15	23.8	−0.416	0.00	2.70
16	30.8	2.092	1.59	0.11
17	25.54	0.207	1.30	0.00
18	24.85	−0.040	0.76	0.00
19	23.58	−0.495	0.00	0.00
20	24.14	−0.294	0.00	0.00
21	26.45	0.533	0.03	0.00
22	26.83	0.670	0.20	0.00
23	23.75	−0.434	0.00	0.00
24	24.26	−0.251	0.00	0.00
25	27.6	0.946	0.45	0.00
26	25.74	0.279	0.22	0.00
27	29.16	1.504	1.23	0.00
28	25.86	0.322	1.05	0.00
29	27.03	0.741	1.29	0.00
30	24.28	−0.244	0.55	0.00
31	24.69	−0.097	0.00	0.00
32	24.35	−0.219	0.00	0.00
33	16.79	−2.928	0.00	2.43
34	24.0	−0.344	0.00	2.27
35	25.66	0.250	0.00	1.52
36	30.7	2.056	1.56	0.00
37	21.27	−1.322	0.00	0.82
38	21.27	−1.322	0.00	1.64
39	26.43	0.526	0.03	0.62
40	28.01	1.092	0.62	0.00
41	24.18	−0.280	0.00	0.00
42	24.54	−0.151	0.00	0.00
43	21.35	−1.294	0.00	0.79
44	27.09	0.763	0.26	0.00
45	24.3	−0.237	0.00	0.00
46	29.54	1.641	1.14	0.00
47	27.11	0.770	1.41	0.00
48	21.5	−1.240	0.00	0.74
49	23.89	−0.384	0.00	0.62
50	24.33	−0.226	0.00	0.35

Table 6.6 CUSUM Calculations Using the Data in Table 6.2 ($k = 0.5$, $h = 5$, $\hat{\sigma} = s/c_4$)

Number	Observation	z	S_H	S_L
1	1.30	1.03	0.53	0
2	1.59	1.26	1.29	0
3	0.17	0.17	0.96	0
4	0.01	0.04	0.50	0
5	0.07	0.09	0.09	0
6	−1.18	−0.87	0	0.37
7	−3.36	−2.54	0	2.41
8	−3.35	−2.54	0	4.45
9	0.50	0.42	0	3.53
10	−0.26	−0.16	0	3.19
11	−2.07	−1.55	0	4.24
12	−2.02	−1.51	0	5.25[a]
13	−1.77	−1.32	0	6.07[a]
14	−0.12	−0.06	0	5.63[a]
15	0.32	0.28	0	4.85
16	−1.16	−0.85	0	5.20[a]
17	−0.89	−0.65	0	5.35[a]
18	−0.80	−0.58	0	5.43[a]
19	0.08	0.10	0	4.83
20	1.74	1.37	0.87	2.96
21	0.06	0.08	0.45	2.38
22	−1.46	−1.09	0	2.97
23	−1.75	−1.31	0	3.78
24	−1.46	−1.09	0	4.37
25	0.19	0.18	0	3.69
26	−0.60	−0.43	0	3.62
27	−0.67	−0.48	0	3.60
28	1.10	0.88	0.38	2.22
29	1.15	0.92	0.80	0.80
30	1.30	1.03	1.33	0
31	1.61	1.27	2.10	0
32	0.12	0.13	1.73	0
33	1.11	0.89	2.12	0
34	0.76	0.62	2.24	0
35	−0.21	−0.13	1.61	0
36	−0.73	−0.52	0.59	0.02
37	0.17	0.17	0.26	0
38	0.45	0.38	0.14	0
39	0.27	0.24	0	0
40	−0.78	−0.56	0	0.06
41	−1.63	−1.22	0	0.78
42	0.03	0.06	0	0.22
43	0.52	0.43	0	0
44	1.21	0.96	0.46	0
45	0.87	0.70	0.66	0
46	1.23	0.98	1.14	0
47	0.78	0.63	1.27	0
48	0.86	0.70	1.47	0
49	2.71	2.12	3.09	0
50	1.68	1.32	3.91	0

[a] Exceeds $h = 5$.

Table 6.7 CUSUM Calculations Using the Data in Table 6.2
$(k = 0.5, h = 5, \hat{\sigma} = \overline{MR}/d_2)$

Number	Observation	z	S_H	S_L
1	1.3	1.786	1.29	0.00
2	1.59	2.171	2.96	0.00
3	0.17	0.287	2.74	0.00
4	0.01	0.075	2.32	0.00
5	0.07	0.154	1.97	0.00
6	− 1.18	− 1.504	0.00	1.00
7	− 3.36	− 4.397	0.00	4.90
8	− 3.35	− 4.383	0.00	8.78
9	0.5	0.725	0.22	7.56
10	− 0.26	− 0.284	0.00	7.34
11	− 2.07	− 2.685	0.00	9.53
12	− 2.02	− 2.619	0.00	11.65
13	− 1.77	− 2.287	0.00	13.43
14	− 0.12	− 0.098	0.00	13.03
15	0.32	0.486	0.00	12.05
16	− 1.16	− 1.478	0.00	13.02
17	− 0.89	− 1.120	0.00	13.64
18	− 0.8	− 1.000	0.00	14.14
19	0.08	0.167	0.00	13.48
20	1.74	2.370	1.87	10.61
21	0.06	0.141	1.51	9.97
22	− 1.46	− 1.876	0.00	11.34
23	− 1.75	− 2.261	0.00	13.10
24	− 1.46	− 1.876	0.00	14.48
25	0.19	0.313	0.00	13.66
26	− 0.6	− 0.735	0.00	13.90
27	− 0.67	− 0.828	0.00	14.23
28	1.1	1.521	1.02	12.21
29	1.15	1.587	2.11	10.12
30	1.3	1.786	3.39	7.83
31	1.61	2.197	5.09	5.13
32	0.12	0.221	4.81	4.41
33	1.11	1.534	5.85	2.38
34	0.76	1.070	6.42	0.81
35	− 0.21	− 0.217	5.70	0.53
36	− 0.73	− 0.907	4.29	0.94
37	0.17	0.287	4.08	0.15
38	0.45	0.658	4.24	0.00
39	0.27	0.420	4.16	0.00
40	− 0.78	− 0.974	2.68	0.47
41	− 1.63	− 2.101	0.08	2.07
42	0.03	0.101	0.00	1.47
43	0.52	0.751	0.25	0.22
44	1.21	1.667	1.42	0.00
45	0.87	1.216	2.13	0.00
46	1.23	1.693	3.33	0.00
47	0.78	1.096	3.92	0.00
48	0.86	1.202	4.63	0.00
49	2.71	3.657	7.78	0.00
50	1.68	2.290	9.57	0.00

initially exceeded at observation 12, and the value of S_L remains above $h = 5$ for 5 of the next 6 values. Thus, a false signal is received because of the trend. The problem is compounded in this instance when σ is estimated by $\overline{MR}/d_2$. The results are shown in Table 6.7.

Obviously there is an enormous difference between the S_L values in Table 6.7 and the S_L values in Table 6.6. The effect of the two different estimates of σ is perhaps best seen by the fact that $S_{L(27)} = 3.60$ in Table 6.6. and 14.23 in Table 6.7.

The reader is referred to Johnson and Bagshaw (1974), Bagshaw and Johnson (1975), and Kartha and Abraham (1978) for additional reading on the effects of correlated data and poor estimates of sigma on the performance of CUSUM procedures.

6.5 CUSUM FOR PROCESS VARIABILITY

A CUSUM procedure for controlling σ using individual observations has been proposed by Hawkins (1981). The approach is as follows. Let

$$Z_i = \frac{|X_i/\sigma|^{1/2} - 0.82218}{0.34914}$$

where $E(|X_i/\sigma|^{1/2}) = 0.82218$ and $\text{Var}(|X_i/\sigma|^{1/2}) = (0.34914)^2$ when $X \sim N(0, \sigma^2)$. If X has a nonzero mean, successive differences between the X values (i.e., $X_i - X_{i-1}$) would be used in place of X_i.

The reason for using $|X/\sigma|^{1/2}$ is that this will have approximately a normal distribution when $X \sim N(0, \sigma^2)$. Therefore, Z will be approximately $N(0, 1)$. Consequently, the general CUSUM procedure that has been used in the previous section and elsewhere could also be used here, but Hawkins (1981) presented the procedure in which the cumulative sum of deviations from the mean (0.82218) was used.

APPENDIX TO CHAPTER 6

For a first-order autoregressive [AR(1)] process, the constraint on ϕ_1 is $-1 < \phi_1 < 1$. If, however, we let $\phi_1 = 1$ for the sake of illustration, then successive observations can be expressed very simply. If x_t and x_{t-1} denote deviations from μ at times t and $t - 1$, respectively, then $x_2 = x_1 + \varepsilon_2$,

$x_3 = x_1 + \varepsilon_2 + \varepsilon_3$, $x_4 = x_1 + \varepsilon_2 + \varepsilon_3 + \varepsilon_4$, etc. Thus,

$$|x_t - x_{t-1}| = |\varepsilon_t|$$

generates the moving ranges for successive values of t. By assumption, $\varepsilon_t \sim NID(0, \sigma_\varepsilon^2)$ so it is a matter of evaluating $E|\varepsilon_t|$, which, using direct integration of the normal distribution function, can be shown to equal $\sigma_\varepsilon\sqrt{2/\pi}$.

Since each moving range has the same expected value, it follows that

$$E\left(\overline{MR}/d_2\right) = \sigma_\varepsilon/\sqrt{2}$$

since $d_2 = 2/\sqrt{\pi}$ for $n = 2$. In particular, if $\sigma_\varepsilon = 1$ the $E(\overline{MR}/d_2) = 0.71$. When ϕ_1 is close to 1, $(1 - \phi_1^2)^{-1}$ will be much larger than 0.71, so the moving range approach will badly underestimate σ_x.

REFERENCES

Alwan, L. C., and H. V. Roberts (1988). Time series modeling for statistical process control. *Journal of Business and Economic Statistics* 6(1): 87–95 (January).

Bagshaw, M., and R. A. Johnson (1975). The effect of serial correlation on the performance of CUSUM tests II. *Technometrics* 17(1): 73–80 (February).

Box, G. E. P., and G. M. Jenkins (1976). *Time Series Analysis: Forecasting and Control*, Revised Edition. San Francisco: Holden-Day.

Hawkins, D. M. (1981). A CUSUM for a scale parameter. *Journal of Quality Technology* 13(4): 228–231 (October).

Johnson, R. A., and M. Bagshaw (1974). The effect of serial correlation on the performance of CUSUM tests. *Technometrics* 16(1): 103–112 (February).

Kartha, C. P., and B. Abraham (1978). Effect of bias in estimating process variability on ARL for CUSUM charts. *ASQC Technical Conference Transactions*, pp. 669–672.

Lucas, J. M. (1982). Combined Shewhart-CUSUM quality control schemes. *Journal of Quality Technology* 14(2): 51–59 (April).

Lucas, J. M., and R. B. Crosier (1982). Fast initial response for CUSUM quality control schemes: Give your CUSUM a head start. *Technometrics* 24(3): 199–205 (August).

McCoun, V. E. (1974). The case of the perjured control chart. *Quality Progress* 7(10): 17–19 (October). (Originally published in *Industrial Quality Control*, May 1949.)

Nelson, L. S. (1982). Control charts for individual measurements. *Journal of Quality Technology 14*(3): 172–173 (July).

Nelson, L. S. (1983). The deceptiveness of moving averages. *Journal of Quality Technology 15*(2): 99–100 (April).

Vasilopoulos, A. V., and A. P. Stamboulis (1978). Modification of control chart limits in the presence of data correlation. *Journal of Quality Technology 10*(1): 20–30 (January).

EXERCISES

1. Reorder the data in Table 6.2 in the following manner: Put the data in ascending order grouped by the last digit, ignoring the sign of the number. (Thus, the first 12 numbers are 0.50, -0.60, -0.80, 1.10, 1.30, 1.30, 0.01, -0.21, 1.11, 1.21, 1.61, 2.71. Put 0.12 before -0.12.)

   a. Would you expect the estimate of σ obtained from $\overline{MR}/d_2$ to be satisfactory, or should σ be estimated using s/c_4?

   b. Construct the X chart and display the 3-sigma limits obtained using both $\overline{MR}/d_2$ and s/c_4 as estimates of σ.

   c. Comment on the difference in the two sets of control limits.

2. Obtain the first 10 S_H and S_L values for the data in Problem #1. (Use the s for all 50 values, however.)

3. Assume that there has been a 1.6σ upward shift in the process mean. How many individual observations would we expect to obtain before finding one that is above the UCL. Compare this with the number of subgroups of $n = 4$ that we would expect to observe before a subgroup average plots above its UCL.

4. List the objections to the use of moving range and moving average charts.

5. The model that is implied by the use of a conventional X chart is $y_i = \mu + \varepsilon_i$ where $\varepsilon \sim \text{NID}(0, \sigma^2)$ and the y_i are the values that are charted. If, however, the data actually come from an AR(1) process with $\phi_1 = 0.6$, by what amount would we expect σ_y^2 to be underestimated when $\overline{MR}/d_2$ is used to obtain the estimate?

6. Explain why a control chart user should select an $\overline{X}$ chart over an X chart if a process is such that either could be used.

7. Construct an X chart for the following data set, using s/c_4 as the estimate of σ. (The data are ordered in columns.)

14.2	14.1	14.5	14.1	15.7
15.3	13.9	14.8	14.7	15.1
14.4	13.7	14.0	13.5	13.9
13.6	14.4	13.9	13.8	14.2
13.2	15.1	13.5	14.2	14.3
15.0	14.8	15.3	14.4	14.5

8. The following 50 observations have been generated from a normal distribution with $\mu = 75$ and $\sigma = 10$.

78.2	92.6	74.7	83.9	54.3
67.6	75.2	67.4	71.7	77.3
54.8	79.2	75.1	88.1	83.8
67.2	87.0	56.8	83.6	78.5
85.4	65.4	91.8	74.1	66.8
64.4	75.5	84.8	72.0	86.4
69.2	69.1	71.0	87.2	90.5
79.7	59.2	96.8	86.3	85.5
80.7	58.4	75.7	80.0	75.8
64.3	100.1	75.0	77.5	79.2

Construct the set of 46 moving averages of size 5. Note the trend in the moving averages, even though the individual observations are randomly generated. (The data are ordered in columns.)

9. The following 50 observations have been generated from an AR(1) process with $\phi_1 = 0.4$.

13.0	10.2	10.4	10.2	11.2
8.9	9.9	9.6	10.9	8.8
7.6	11.1	9.2	10.0	9.0
8.0	10.2	9.2	9.6	9.3
10.9	11.5	11.9	10.3	10.3
10.2	11.9	11.4	11.1	9.9
10.2	10.9	10.0	10.2	9.1
10.5	12.3	11.3	10.3	9.6
9.4	10.9	9.7	11.6	8.7
8.8	9.5	8.1	10.6	9.3

Construct the set of 46 moving averages of size 5, after first plotting the individual observations. Compare the trend in the moving averages with the trend in the individual observations. Merging this result with the outcome from the preceding problem, what does this suggest about the effect created by moving averages, whether the individual observations are independent or not? (The data are ordered in columns.)

CHAPTER 7

Process Capability

The concept of process capability was mentioned briefly in Chapter 4. What is process capability and how is it measured? *Process capability* generally refers to whether or not a process is operated in a manner such that one or more of the variables being measured have distributions that lie almost completely within the specification limits, where the latter determine whether the unit of production is conforming or nonconforming. (These limits are generally determined from engineering specifications, whereas control limits are determined using data obtained from a process.)

A capable process has often been thought of as one whose lower specification limit (LSL) is at or below $\hat{\mu} - 3\hat{\sigma}$, and whose upper specification limit (USL) is at or above $\hat{\mu} + 3\hat{\sigma}$. If the limits were exactly at these two points, this would mean that for an approximately normal distribution, roughly 27 of every 10,000 units would be classified as nonconforming.

Heretofore, such process capability has been considered acceptable in the Western world. As Sullivan (1984) emphasizes, however, the goal should be a continual effort to improve process capability for all processes.

7.1 PROCESS CAPABILITY INDICES

To facilitate such improvement, it is helpful to define one or more process capability indices. The Japanese use several such indices, as Sullivan (1985) points out, but the two indices which probably have been used most frequently in the Western world are those designated by C_{pk} and C_p.

The former is defined as

$$C_{pk} = \frac{Z_{min}}{3}$$

where Z_{min} is defined as the minimum of $(USL - \hat{\mu})/\hat{\sigma}$ and $(\hat{\mu} - LSL)/\hat{\sigma}$. (It is assumed that both quantities are positive.) In words, if the USL and LSL are equidistant from $\hat{\mu}$, Z_{min} can be thought of as the number of standard deviations that the specification limits are from $\hat{\mu}$. If the distances are not the same, Z_{min} will then equal the number of standard deviations that the closest specification limit is to $\hat{\mu}$.

In particular, if the limits are at $\hat{\mu} \pm 3\hat{\sigma}$, then $Z_{min} = 3$ and $C_{pk} = 1.0$ which can be seen from simple substitution. In general, if the limits are at $\hat{\mu} \pm j\hat{\sigma}$, then $Z_{min} = j$ and $C_{pk} = j/3$. Thus, process capability for equidistant limits could be expressed in terms of either $\hat{\mu} \pm j\hat{\sigma}$ or $C_{pk} = j/3$. The use of C_{pk} is clearly preferable when the limits are not equidistant, however, and in general, has obvious intuitive appeal.

In Japan, the minimum acceptable C_{pk} value is 1.33 (Sullivan, 1984), with many processes having a higher minimum. (This assumes that the distribution for the variable being measured is at the target value.) A process with a C_{pk} value of 1.33 would, assuming approximately a normal distribution, produce at most 6 of every 100,000 units that would be classified as nonconforming. Thus, if 10,000 units were produced each day, we would expect to encounter about 3 nonconforming units each week. On the other hand, if $C_{pk} = 2.67$ we would expect to have to wait about 306 million years between the occurrence of nonconforming units. Hence, we should strive to continually increase the C_{pk} value.

The other index, C_p, is defined as

$$C_p = \frac{USL - LSL}{6\hat{\sigma}}$$

If the process mean is centered at $(USL + LSL)/2$, then $C_p = C_{pk}$. This can be seen as follows. The two z-values will be the same, therefore C_{pk} can be written as

$$C_{pk} = \frac{(USL - \hat{\mu})/\hat{\sigma}}{3}$$

$$= \frac{USL - \hat{\mu}}{3\hat{\sigma}}$$

Then, $USL - \hat{\mu} = 1/2(USL - LSL)$ since the process is centered. It then follows that

$$C_{pk} = \frac{1/2(USL - LSL)}{3\hat{\sigma}}$$

$$= \frac{USL - LSL}{6\hat{\sigma}}$$

Thus, for a centered process the two indices are equivalent. When a process is not centered, the use of C_p could be quite misleading, however, as is illustrated in Sullivan (1985). The problem results from the fact that C_p is not a function of the process mean. Specifically, a process that is badly off target would have the same C_p value as it would if it were on target if $\hat{\sigma}$ was the same in each case.

Assume, for example, that a process should have $\hat{\mu} = 50$ with LSL = 40 and USL = 60 so that the distribution is centered relative to the specification limits. If $\hat{\sigma} = 1.0$, $C_{pk} = C_p = 3.33$ and the process capability is excellent. Now if $\hat{\mu}$ shifts to 60, about 50% of the product will be nonconforming, but we still have $C_p = 3.33$ if we assume that $\hat{\sigma}$ remains unchanged. We would have $C_{pk} = 0$, however, which will happen whenever the distribution is centered at one of the specification limits. Accordingly, C_{pk} is a superior measure of process capability.

In addition to the references previously cited, readers are referred to Kane (1986) for additional information on process capability indices.

7.2   DETERMINING PROCESS CAPABILITY WITH CONTROL CHARTS

7.2.1   Using an $\overline{X}$ Chart

It was stated in Chapter 4 that process capability can be logically determined only after a process has been brought into a state of statistical control. Once control has been established, capability can be assessed in a variety of ways.

It is essentially a matter of estimating μ and σ. This could be handled by using data that had previously been used in producing an $\overline{X}$ chart or an X chart. Most SPC (statistical process control) software packages provide the values of various capability indices, but they can also be easily calculated.

With an $\overline{X}$ chart, μ would be estimated from $\overline{\overline{x}}$ and σ estimated from $\bar{s}/c_4$ or $\overline{R}/d_2$. If a user is viewing a control chart, μ would be estimated by the midline, and σ would be estimated by $(\sqrt{n}/6)(UCL - LCL)$.

For an X chart, μ would be estimated by $\bar{x}$ and σ estimated from s/c_4 or $\overline{MR}/d_2$. From a control chart, μ would be estimated by the midline, and σ would be estimated by (UCL − LCL)/6.

To illustrate the computation of C_{pk} from an $\bar{X}$ chart, we shall use the data of Table 5.1, but shall exclude the tenth subgroup since its average plotted below the LCL. The control limits using s in estimating σ were found to be

$$\bar{\bar{x}}_{19} \pm A_3 \bar{s}_{19}$$

$$= 61.447 \pm 1.628(14.033)$$

$$= 61.447 \pm 22.846$$

so that the UCL = 84.293 and the LCL = 38.601. Thus, σ would be estimated by $(\sqrt{n}/6)(\text{UCL} - \text{LCL})$, i.e.,

$$\hat{\sigma} = (\sqrt{4}/6)(84.293 - 38.601)$$

$$= 15.231$$

If we assume that the specification limits are USL = 106 and LSL = 8, we then have

$$Z_{\text{USL}} = \frac{\text{USL} - \bar{\bar{x}}}{\hat{\sigma}}$$

and

$$Z_{\text{LSL}} = \frac{\bar{\bar{x}} - \text{LSL}}{\hat{\sigma}}$$

Thus,

$$Z_{\text{USL}} = \frac{106 - 61.447}{15.231}$$

$$= 2.93$$

and

$$Z_{\text{LSL}} = \frac{61.447 - 8}{15.231}$$

$$= 3.51$$

so that $Z_{\text{min}} = 2.93$ and $C_{pk} = 2.93/3 = 0.98$.

Notice that $Z_{\text{USL}} \neq Z_{\text{LSL}}$. It would be only by sheer coincidence that they would be the same, as we would not expect $\bar{\bar{x}}$ to fall exactly halfway between the USL and the LSL.

More importantly, we observe that the C_{pk} value is somewhat low, in spite of the fact that all of the values in Table 5.1 are well below the USL, and, after excluding the tenth subgroup, all of the values are also well above the LSL. Yet the process capability is relatively poor. If we were to assume (approximately) a normal distribution, we would expect roughly 0.17% of the values to exceed the USL, and about 0.02% to be below the LSL. Thus, about 2 of every 1000 units would be labeled as nonconforming.

We thus have a process that the control charts indicate is in control, but the process is not capable. How could the process capability be improved? Some improvement would be afforded by causing the distribution of the output to shift to the left so that $\bar{\bar{x}}$ would be closer to the halfway point between the USL and LSL. For example, if $\bar{\bar{x}} = 57$ (the halfway point), we would then have $Z_{USL} = Z_{LSL} = 3.22$ so that $C_{pk} = 1.07$ and, again assuming approximately a normal distribution, about 1.3 of every 1000 units would be nonconforming. (Note that such a shift could conceivably make matters worse if the distribution of the output was asymmetric.)

It is easy to show the benefit of a shift in the distribution under certain situations, but it seems logical to ask how a shift could be effected in an actual physical setting. This could be accomplished by changing the settings of the design parameters. This would usually be undertaken after attempting to reduce the process variability, however. This is discussed in some detail in Chapter 14.

The initial effort should thus be directed at reducing the process variability, which requires the identification of those factors that contribute to process variability. Thus, process improvement will generally require the use of experimental designs, which are discussed in detail in Part III.

For the present example, by how much should $\hat{\sigma}$ be reduced to have excellent process capability? If $\hat{\sigma} = 7.4255$ (roughly one-half of its present value), we would then have $C_{pk} = 2.00$ and the proportion of nonconforming units would then be extremely small (about 10^{-9}).

For high-volume products (e.g., steel balls) such a C_{pk} value might still result in a few nonconforming units being produced over the course of a year, however, and if the product is a critical part even one nonconforming unit is excessive. Consequently, the objective should be to try to continually increase the C_{pk} value, rather than striving to attain a particular goal value.

7.2.2 Using an X Chart

C_{pk} can also be computed from an individual observations chart. It was shown in Chapter 6 that an X chart produced from the data in Table 6.1 would have control limits of UCL = 33.3333 and LCL = 16.5867, where σ was estimated using moving ranges of size 2. We would estimate σ from

(UCL − LCL)/6, so that

$$\hat{\sigma} = \frac{33.3333 - 16.5867}{6}$$

$$= 2.7911$$

which is the value that was given for $\overline{MR}/d_2$ in Chapter 6. (Of course, it was known that $\sigma = 3$ in generating the data for Table 6.1, but the usual estimator of σ obtained from an X chart will be employed here.)

If we assume that the LSL = 12 and the USL = 36, the z-values would then be calculated from

$$z_{\text{USL}} = \frac{\text{USL} - \bar{x}}{\hat{\sigma}}$$

and

$$z_{\text{LSL}} = \frac{\bar{x} - \text{LSL}}{\hat{\sigma}}$$

Thus,

$$z_{\text{USL}} = \frac{36 - 24.9}{2.7911}$$

$$= 3.98$$

and

$$z_{\text{LSL}} = \frac{24.9 - 12}{2.7911}$$

$$= 4.62$$

Therefore, $C_{\text{pk}} = 3.98/3 = 1.33$ so the process would have moderately good capability.

In summary, there is more to process improvement than just running the various processes in a state of statistical control. Improvement also entails reducing process variability and the C_{pk} statistic can be used to measure the extent to which this is being accomplished. The objective should be to try to achieve continual increases in the C_{pk} value.

REFERENCES

Kane, V. E. (1986). Process capability indices. *Journal of Quality Technology 18*(1): 41–52 (January).

Sullivan, L. P. (1984). Reducing variability: A new approach to quality. *Quality Progress 17*(7): 15–21 (July).

Sullivan, L. P. (1985). Reply to a letter to the Editor. *Quality Progress 18*(4): 7–8 (April).

EXERCISES

1. A manufacturing process has specification limits of 0.99 and 1.02 and a standard deviation of 0.005.

   a. What is the value of C_{pk} if the distribution of measurements is centered at the target value of 1.00?

   b. Will C_{pk} increase or decrease if the mean shifts to 1.005 (i.e., halfway between the specification limits)?

   c. Assuming a normal distribution, will the proportion of nonconforming units increase or decrease with a mean shift to 1.005? What is the expected proportion before and after the shift?

   d. If, rather than being normal, the distribution is actually highly asymmetric with most of the area under the curve lying to the right of the mean, will the answer to Part (c) still hold? What does this imply about the steps that should be followed when trying to improve process capability?

2. An $\overline{X}$ chart exhibits control for the control limits of UCL = 30.26 and LCL = 26.34. If subgroup sizes of $n = 4$ were used and the specification limits are 20 and 36, what is the value of C_{pk}? What would you recommend to this company?

3. An X chart exhibits control for 50 observations with UCL = 75.8 and LCL = 64.4. To what value will $\hat{\sigma}$ have to be reduced to produce a C_{pk} of 1.33 if the specification limits are 76 and 62, and $\hat{\mu}$ remains unchanged? Could a C_{pk} value of at least 1.33 be obtained by centering the distribution so that $\hat{\mu} = 69$? Comment.

CHAPTER 8

Control Charts for Attributes

It is not always possible or practical to use measurement data in quality improvement work. Instead, *count data* (often referred to as *attribute data*) are used where, for example, the number of nonconforming parts for a given time period may be charted instead of measurements charted for one or more quality characteristics. Although automatic measuring devices have greatly simplified the measurement process, it is still often easier to classify a unit of production as conforming or nonconforming than to obtain the measurement for each of many quality characteristics.

Before studying and implementing charts for the number of nonconforming units, it is important to remember the quotes given near the end of Chapter 1. Ideally, nonconforming units should not be produced. Consequently, attempting to control the number of nonconforming units at a particular level would generally be counterproductive. The objective should be, of course, to continually reduce the number of such units. When used for that purpose, such charts can be of value in indicating the extent to which the objective is being achieved over time. Thus, such charts might be used in *conjunction* with measurement charts, rather than simply in place of them. If either type of chart could be used in a particular situation, it would be wasteful of information to use an attribute chart by itself. Accordingly, such charts should be used alone only when there is no other choice.

Several different types of attribute charts are presented in this chapter. Before examining these charts in detail, there is the question of which terminology to adopt. For example, should a chart that displays the fraction or percentage of defective units be called a chart for fraction rejected, fraction defective, or fraction of nonconforming units? The latter will be adopted in accordance with the national and international standards (see, e.g., ANSI/ASQC A1–1987). In particular, *nonconforming unit* will be used in place of *defective*. A unit could also have a number of defects (e.g.,

179

scratches) that might not be severe enough to cause it to be classified as a nonconforming unit, but a chart of each type of defect might be maintained. *Defect* will not be used; it will be replaced by *nonconformity*.

8.1 CHARTS FOR NONCONFORMING UNITS

When interest centers on nonconforming units, the user can employ a chart for either the fraction or number of such units. These are labeled the *p* chart and *np* chart, respectively. Each of these is based upon the assumed adequacy of the normal approximation to the binomial distribution that was alluded to in Chapter 3. Specifically, if X represents the number of nonconforming units in a sample of size n, and $\hat{P} = X/n$ is the proportion of such units

$$\frac{X - np}{\sqrt{np(1-p)}} \tag{8.1}$$

and

$$\frac{\hat{P} - p}{\sqrt{\dfrac{p(1-p)}{n}}} \tag{8.2}$$

will be approximately distributed as $N(\mu = 0,\ \sigma = 1)$ when n is at least moderately large and p does not differ greatly from 0.5. In practice, the first requirement is generally met; in fact, n has often been equal to an entire day's production. We would certainly hope that the second requirement is never met, however, since anything close to 50% nonconforming units would be disastrous.

8.1.1 *np* Chart

As mentioned in Chapter 3, the rule of thumb generally advanced is that for Eqs. (8.1) and (8.2) to be approximately $N(0,1)$, both np and $n(1-p)$ should exceed 5. We would certainly expect p to be quite small, so it is the first requirement that is of interest. A company embarking upon a statistical quality control program might well have p approximately equal to .10 for some products. The rule of thumb would then require n greater than 50. Assume that $n = 400$ and $p = .10$ so that the requirement is easily satisfied. In general, the control limits for an *np* chart would be obtained (if p

was known) from

$$np \pm 3\sqrt{np(1-p)} \tag{8.3}$$

where p will usually have to be estimated. For this example we assume p to be known so the limits would be

$$400(.10) \pm 3\sqrt{400(.1)(.9)} = 40 \pm 18$$

Thus, the UCL = 58 and the LCL = 22. If the normal approximation was quite good, we would expect $P(X > 58)$ and $P(X < 22)$ to be close to .00135 (recall that this is the area in each tail for an $\overline{X}$ chart when normality is assumed). Unfortunately, the probabilities differ greatly even though $np = 40$. Specifically, $P(X > 58) = .0017146$ and $P(X < 22) = .0004383$, using the binomial distribution. Thus, although the first probability is fairly close to the nominal value, the second one is not.

The practical implication of this is that when the actual lower tail area is very close to zero, sizable reductions in p will not be immediately reflected by points falling below the LCL. For example, $P(X < 22) = .02166$ when $p = .08$ and $P(X < 22) = .00352$ when $p = .09$. Thus, for a 10% reduction in the percentage of nonconforming units we expect to have to obtain $1/.00352 = 284$ samples of size 400 before observing a value of X that is below the LCL of 22. Similarly, for a 20% reduction to $p = .08$ we would expect to observe $1/.02166 = 46$ samples before observing a value of X less than 22. This means that the LCL will have very little value in many practical situations as a benchmark for indicating quality improvement. The problem can even be more acute when p is smaller than in the preceding example.

The fact that the actual upper tail area is close to the nominal value is virtually irrelevant because that would have meaning only if an np chart was being used for *defensive* purposes, i.e., to keep the quality from deteriorating any further. (Recall that this is essentially the objective of acceptance sampling.) Thus, if an np chart is to be used in a quality *improvement* program, it is certainly desirable to have an LCL value such that points which begin appearing below that value will reflect a significant reduction in p; conversely, a significant reduction in p will cause points to begin immediately appearing below that value.

A related problem is the fact that the LCL will often be set at 0 since $np - 3\sqrt{np(1-p)}$ can easily be negative. For example, with $n = 400$, $np - 3\sqrt{np(1-p)}$ will be negative if $p < .022$. In general, it can be stated that $np - 3\sqrt{np(1-p)}$ will be negative if $p < 9/(9+n)$, which is equivalent to $n < 9(1 - p)/p$. Since it will typically be easier to change n than to change p, it would be wise to select n so that the LCL > 0.

8.1.2 Arcsin Transformation for Proportions Data

These two types of problems with the LCL can also be avoided by simply using a better method for obtaining the LCL for an np (or p) chart. One such method would be to transform the binomial data so that the transformed data are approximately normally distributed, and then use 3-sigma limits for the transformed variable. Some of these suggested transformations will now be briefly discussed.

Some (almost identical) arcsin transformations have been proposed. Johnson and Kotz (1969) state that

$$y = \sin^{-1}\sqrt{\left(x + \frac{3}{8}\right)\Big/\left(n + \frac{3}{4}\right)} \tag{8.4}$$

will be approximately normally distributed with mean $\sin^{-1}\sqrt{p}$ and variance $1/4n$, where $\sin^{-1}$ denotes the inverse of the sine function in trigonometry (generally referred to as the arcsin). Thus, for each sample of size n, one would plot the value of y on a control chart with the midline at $\sin^{-1}\sqrt{p}$ (if p is known) and the control limits given by

$$\sin^{-1}\sqrt{p} \pm 3\sqrt{\frac{1}{4n}}$$

$$= \sin^{-1}\sqrt{p} \pm \frac{3}{2\sqrt{n}} \tag{8.5}$$

For the example with $n = 400$ and $p = .10$, the control limits would be

$$\sin^{-1}\sqrt{0.10} \pm \frac{3}{2\sqrt{400}}$$

$$= 0.32175 \pm 0.075$$

so that the LCL = 0.24675 and the UCL = 0.39675.

A simple way to compare the worth of this approach for this particular example would be to determine the value of x such that $P(X \leq x) \doteq .00135$ (from the binomial distribution), and then see if that value of x produces a value of y that is quite close to the LCL of 0.24675. $P(X \leq 23) = .00168$ and for $x = 23$, $y = 0.2439$. Thus, since y is indeed almost equal to the

LCL, we can see the value of obtaining the control limits by using the arcsin transformation—at least for this example.

Comparing this arcsin result with the result obtained using the conventional approach, the LCL using the arcsin transformation would correspond to $x = 23$ (to the nearest integer), whereas the conventional approach yielded $x = 22$ for the LCL.

These values will differ by a somewhat larger amount, however, when p is much smaller than .10, as is shown later in Table 8.2. Notice in Table 8.1 that the actual tail areas, for the 3-sigma limits are off considerably from .00135, although we should not expect that value to be met exactly since the binomial random variable is discrete instead of continuous. Of particular concern, however, is the fact that the lower tail areas are quite close to zero when p is around .02 for $n \leq 1000$. In particular, when $n = 600$ and $p = .02$ the lower tail area is .00007. As indicated earlier, the problem this creates is that a considerable reduction in p could go undetected for quite some time when an np chart (or p chart) is used in the conventional manner. For example, if there is a subsequent reduction in p from .02 to .015 (a 25% improvement), the probability of a point falling below the LCL obtained using $p = .02$ is only .0012, so it would require, on the average, 856 samples before a point would fall below the LCL. (Notice that this is even a higher ARL value than would exist with a nominal tail area of .00135 and no change in p.) Similarly, a drop to $p = .01$ would produce a tail area of .01698 and an ARL value of approximately 59.

In general, by comparing Table 8.1 with Table 8.2 we can see that the LCL values for the 3-sigma limits differ from the probability limit LCL values by either 1 or 2 units in all cases, but for the UCL values the two differ by only 1 unit in almost all cases. Specifically, the 3-sigma limit LCL is too low by 2 units roughly half the time (and by 1 unit the rest of the time), and the UCL is generally 1 unit too low.

The limits obtained from use of the arcsin transformation fare somewhat better. The UCL values on the original scale agree exactly (in terms of the possible integer values of X) for 21 of the 35 combinations, and differ by 1 unit for the other 14. For the LCL values there is exact agreement for 19 of the combinations, and a difference of 1 unit for the other 16. We should not always expect exact agreement, however, since the use of 3-sigma limits with the arcsin transformation is designed to hit the .00135 probability limits almost exactly, *if* they existed. We should not expect them to exist for a discrete random variable, however. For these combinations of n and p some of the tail probabilities are not particularly close to .00135 (see, e.g., the LCL for $n = 600$ and $p = .02$), even though they are the *closest* to .00135 for each combination. Notice, however, that when the tail probability is very close to .00135, the arcsin-based limit for the LCL is almost

Table 8.1 np **Chart Control Limits**

		3-Sigma Limits		Actual Tail Areas	
n	p	LCL	UCL	LCL	UCL
100	.12	2.250	21.750	.00030	.00341
	.10	1.000	19.000	.00003	.00198
	.09	0.415	17.586	.00008	.00342
200	.10	7.272	32.728	.00048	.00292
	.08	4.490	27.510	.00027	.00276
	.06	1.924	22.076	.00006	.00221
	.05	0.753	19.247	.00004	.00266
300	.10	14.412	45.588	.00057	.00242
	.08	9.903	38.097	.00028	.00196
	.06	5.660	30.340	.00024	.00246
	.05	3.675	26.325	.00016	.00257
	.04	1.818	22.182	.00006	.00247
	.03	0.136	17.864	.00011	.00464
400	.10	22.000	58.000	.00044	.00171
	.05	6.923	33.077	.00020	.00207
	.03	1.765	22.235	.00007	.00261
600	.10	37.955	82.045	.00058	.00169
	.05	13.984	46.016	.00031	.00189
	.03	5.464	30.536	.00028	.00288
	.02	1.712	22.288	.00007	.00275
800	.10	54.544	105.456	.00081	.00190
	.05	21.507	58.493	.00057	.00226
	.03	9.525	38.475	.00037	.00257
	.02	4.121	27.879	.00036	.00374
1000	.10	71.540	128.460	.00086	.00184
	.05	29.324	70.676	.00072	.00233
	.03	13.817	46.183	.00035	.00210
	.02	6.718	33.282	.00023	.00243
	.01	0.561	19.439	.00004	.00329
2000	.10	159.751	240.249	.00094	.00162
	.05	70.760	129.240	.00076	.00178
	.03	37.113	82.887	.00084	.00245
	.02	21.217	58.783	.00067	.00263
	.01	6.650	33.349	.00024	.00256
	.007	2.814	25.186	.00009	.00252

Table 8.2 np Chart Probability Limits and Arcsin Transformation (Values of x that give Areas Closest to .00135)

n	p	LCL	Tail Area[a]	UCL	Tail Area[a]	LCL[b]	UCL[b]
100	.12	4	.00145	22	.00151	3.750	23.100
	.10	3	.00194	20	.00081	2.568	20.432
	.09	2	.00087	18	.00140	2.017	19.058
200	.10	9	.00139	33	.00154	8.820	34.180
	.08	6	.00099	28	.00137	6.108	29.042
	.06	4	.00184	23	.00101	3.612	23.688
	.05	2	.00040	20	.00116	2.476	20.899
300	.10	16	.00127	46	.00141	15.951	47.049
	.08	12	.00184	39	.00108	11.513	39.636
	.06	7	.00080	31	.00128	7.341	31.959
	.05	5	.00069	27	.00127	5.391	27.984
	.04	4	.00199	23	.00115	3.568	23.882
	.03	2	.00111	19	.00086	1.921	19.604
400	.10	24	.00168	59	.00105	23.534	59.466
	.05	9	.00172	34	.00110	8.635	34.740
	.03	4	.00206	23	.00123	3.546	23.979
600	.10	40	.00166	83	.00112	39.482	83.518
	.05	16	.00158	47	.00111	15.692	47.683
	.03	7	.00092	31	.00153	7.243	32.282
	.02	4	.00214	23	.00131	3.525	24.075
800	.10	56	.00125	106	.00134	56.068	106.930
	.05	23	.00112	59	.00143	23.212	60.163
	.03	11	.00095	39	.00147	11.301	40.223
	.02	6	.00128	29	.00100	5.932	29.668
1000	.10	73	.00127	129	.00134	73.061	129.939
	.05	31	.00128	71	.00154	31.027	72.348
	.03	16	.00172	47	.00125	15.591	47.934
	.02	9	.00193	34	.00133	8.528	35.072
	.01	2	.00048	20	.00150	2.405	21.270
2000	.10	161	.00123	241	.00128	161.266	241.734
	.05	72	.00111	130	.00131	72.458	130.917
	.03	39	.00139	84	.00115	38.884	84.641
	.02	23	.00128	60	.00107	23.024	60.576
	.01	8	.00075	34	.00141	8.493	35.182
	.007	5	.00176	26	.00125	4.667	27.030

[a] These values for tail areas are binomial probabilities such that $P(X < \text{LCL})$ = tail area and $P(X > \text{UCL})$ = tail area.

[b] Values of X in the arcsin transformation $y = \sin^{-1}\sqrt{(x + 3/8)/(n + 3/4)}$ that cause y to equal the upper and the lower limits obtained from $\sin^{-1}\sqrt{p} \pm 3\sqrt{1/4n}$.

identical to the probability limit, even when the decimal places are considered. For example, for the LCL with $n = 1000$ and $p = .05$ there is hardly any difference between 31 and 31.027.

All factors considered, the superiority of the suggested approach over the traditional approach should be apparent.

Other forms of the arcsin transformation have also been used. One is

$$y_1 = \sin^{-1} \sqrt{\frac{x}{n}}$$

[see, e.g., Ehrenfeld and Littauer (1964, p. 310), Brownlee (1960, p. 115), or Hald (1952, p. 685)]. Another variation is

$$y_2 = \frac{1}{2} \left(\sin^{-1} \sqrt{\frac{x}{n+1}} + \sin^{-1} \sqrt{\frac{x+1}{n+1}} \right)$$

The latter is generally referred to as the average angular transformation, and is discussed, for example, in Nelson (1983). (But note misprint-omission of the $1/2$.) It was originally suggested by Freeman and Tukey (1950), where $1/2$ was also omitted.

If either of these two transformations were to be used instead of Eq. (8.4), the control limits would still be obtained from Eq. (8.5).

Since the three transformations differ only slightly, the results obtained from using any of the transformations should be virtually the same.

It is also possible that the LCL could be 0 when using the arcsin transformation, but this will happen for a smaller range of values for p and n than with the traditional approach. This is illustrated in Table 8.3.

The minimum sample size needed using the arcsin approach is thus roughly one-fourth the size needed for the traditional approach. Although an entire day's production has often constituted the sample size, it would generally be impractical to inspect 22,499 items for each sample. Therefore, regardless of the approach that is used, a very small percentage of nonconforming units will cause the LCL to be 0 for reasonable values of n.

8.1.3 *np* Chart with Runs Criteria

Suggested approaches to this problem include using runs criteria in lieu of the conventional 3-sigma LCL. Burr (1979, p. 96) and Duncan (1986, p. 444) discuss the use of runs criteria above and below the midline (on a *p* chart). (Recall that the use of runs criteria for an $\overline{X}$ chart was discussed in

Table 8.3 Comparison of Minimum Sample Size Necessary to Make LCL > 0 for Traditional Approach and Arcsin-Transformation Approach

p	Arcsin Method: n Must Exceed:	Traditional Method: n Must Exceed:
.10	21	81
.08	27	103
.06	36	141
.05	44	171
.04	55	216
.03	74	291
.02	111	441
.01	224	891
.005	449	1,791
.002	1,124	4,491
.001	2,249	8,991
.0001	22,499	89,991
.00001	224,999	899,991

Chapter 5 as an alternative to a CUSUM procedure.) This can be helpful, although it should be borne in mind that the probability of a point falling above the midline is not generally the same as the probability of a point falling below the midline. For example, if $n = 100$ and $p = .10$ we would use 10 as the midline, but $P(X \leq 9) = .45129$ and $P(X \geq 11) = .41684$. We would thus be more likely to have points falling below the midline when the process is in control at $p = .10$. Unfortunately, this is also a problem when n is much larger than 100 since the distribution of X will still be skewed when p is small. For example, with $n = 1000$ and $p = .01$, $P(X \leq 9) = .45730$ and $P(X \geq 11) = .41696$ with the midline at $x = 10$. The probability of five consecutive points falling above the midline is thus $(.41696)^5 = .0126$, and $(.4573)^5 = .0200$ for the five points falling below the midline.

Similar problems exist when runs criteria are used relative to 1-sigma and 2-sigma limits; the tail probabilities can differ considerably, and also differ greatly from the assumed probabilities from the normal distribution. For example, with $n = 1000$ and $p = .01$, the probability that X will fall below a 1-sigma LCL is .1289 compared with the nominal area of .1587, and .01007 and .0228, respectively for a 2-sigma LCL.

This is not to suggest that runs criteria should never be used with a traditional np chart, but rather the actual tail probabilities for individual points should be carefully considered when using such criteria.

The binomial tail probabilities that have been given to this point in the chapter can be obtained in several ways: (1) by computer, (2) by a hand calculator that contains a binomial subroutine, and (3) some of the probabilities could have been obtained from extensive tables that have been prepared. [A listing of some of these tables can be found in Hahn (1981, p. 107).] Most tables, however, do not contain large values of n (> 100) nor small values of p ($< .01$) and there are no widely available tables that contain both.

8.1.4 p Chart

In the preceding section attention was focused upon the number of nonconforming units in each sample. Alternatively, a chart could be used that shows the percentage of nonconforming units in each sample. Such a chart is called a *p chart*. Neither type of chart is superior to the other from a statistical standpoint. Some users may wish to plot the number of nonconforming units per sample (which would be reasonable if the sample size is constant), whereas others may prefer to see the percentage of such units.

The control limits for a p chart would be obtained (with p known) from

$$p \pm 3 \sqrt{\frac{p(1-p)}{n}}$$

Notice that if these limits are multiplied by n the result will be equal to the limits given by Eq. (8.3), and if the points that are plotted on a p chart are also multiplied by n, the numerical values would be equal to the values of the points plotted on an np chart. Thus, a p chart is simply a scaled version of an np chart, with the same configuration of points on each chart. Thus, there is no need to use both charts.

Since a p chart is simply a scaled version of an np chart, it is subject to the same general weakness as an np chart. Namely, the tail probabilities will be the same as for the np chart, so the arcsin approach (using the same transformation) would also be preferable to a p chart.

It should be borne in mind, however, that numbers on a transformed scale will, in general, not be as easy to relate to as numbers on the original scale. In particular, the arcsin transformation will not produce numbers that have a direct physical interpretation. If this is of concern to the user, it would be preferable to use a regular p or np chart with the actual tail probabilities used as a guide in determining the control limits, rather than automatically using the 3-sigma limits.

For example, Table 8.2 indicates that the approximate 3-sigma limits for an np chart with $n = 400$ and $p = 0.10$ are 24 and 59 rather than 22 and 58. The corresponding limits for the p chart would then be $24/400 = .06$ and $59/400 = .1475$, instead of $22/400 = .055$ and $58/400 = .1450$.

8.1.5 Modified p and np Chart Limits

If a p chart or np chart is to be used continuously, it would be desirable to determine the proper limits exactly using an appropriate calculating device. As a rough rule of thumb, the results of Table 8.2 indicate that the following should be sufficient. The limits for an np chart would be determined as

$$\text{LCL} = np - 3\sqrt{np(1-p)} + 1.25$$

$$\text{UCL} = np + 3\sqrt{np(1-p)} + 1.15$$

for the range of values of n and p covered in Table 8.2. This leads to general agreement with virtually all of the appropriate UCL and LCL values.

The corresponding p chart limits would then be modified as

$$\text{LCL} = p - 3\sqrt{\frac{p(1-p)}{n}} + \frac{1.25}{n}$$

$$\text{UCL} = p + 3\sqrt{\frac{p(1-p)}{n}} + \frac{1.15}{n}$$

8.1.6 p Unknown

To this point it has been implicitly assumed that p is known. If p is unknown it must be estimated, and it would be reasonable to estimate it by obtaining a number of samples of a given size, analogous to the way that μ and σ are estimated for an $\overline{X}$ chart.

To obtain a good estimate of p we initially need a rough estimate of p, or at least a lower bound on p, so that we can select a sample size large enough to ensure that each sample will contain at least a few nonconforming units. If, for example, we believed that p was approximately .005, it would be unwise to use samples of size $n = 100$ since we would expect most of the samples to have zero nonconforming units. Instead, we could use Table 8.3 as a guide. Thus, if p was approximately .005, we might wish to use samples of size 500 or larger so as to have some assurance that the LCL will be positive (if an arcsin transformation is used). This should also provide at least one or two nonconforming units in each sample since the expected number is 2.5.

The construction of a p chart and an np chart can be illustrated using the fictitious data in Table 8.4. An estimate of p would be obtained as

$$\bar{p} = \frac{\text{total number of nonconforming units}}{\text{total number inspected}}$$

where $\bar{p}$ will be used instead of $\hat{p}$ to designate the estimate of p, in accordance with standard notation. The data in Table 8.4 produce

$$\bar{p} = \frac{318}{30,000} = .0106$$

so that 1.06% of the units examined were nonconforming. The standard 3-sigma limits for the np chart are

$$np \pm 3\sqrt{n\bar{p}(1 - \bar{p})}$$

$$= 1000(.0106) \pm 3\sqrt{1000(.0106)(1 - .0106)}$$

$$= 10.6 \pm 9.715$$

so that the UCL = 20.315 and the LCL = 0.885.

The corresponding limits obtained from use of the adjustment factors mentioned previously would be 21.465 and 2.135, whereas Table 8.2 would suggest the use of limits that are slightly above 20 and 2. Since, with $p = .0106$, $P(X < 3) = .00163$, and $P(X > 21) = .00135$, the appropriate (integer-valued) probability limits would be 21 and 3. These are operationally equivalent to the limits obtained from the adjustment factors since $X < 2.135$ is equivalent to $X < 3$, and $X > 21.465$ is equivalent to $X > 21$.

For whichever set of limits is to be used, the next step is to plot the points on the p chart or np chart. The former is given in Figure 8.1 and the latter in Figure 8.2, with the limits being the modified limits given in the preceding section. We can see that the configuration of points is the same for the two charts, as will always be the case. All of the points are within the control limits on each chart, although the last five points being above the midline could indicate (with real data) that the number (percentage) of nonconforming units has increased.

The point that was made in Chapter 4 should be borne in mind, however, when a set of samples is used to determine trial control limits.

Table 8.4 Number of Nonconforming Transistors of 1000 Inspected Each Day During the Month of April

Day	No. of Nonconforming Units
1	7
2	5
3	11
4	13
5	9
6	12
7	10
8	10
9	6
10	14
11	9
12	13
13	8
14	11
15	12
16	10
17	9
18	12
19	14
20	12
21	13
22	7
23	9
24	12
25	8
26	14
27	12
28	12
29	11
30	13

Namely, the probability of observing at least one of k points outside the control limits is aproximately kp, where p is the sum of the two tail probabilities. Thus, using a nominal value of $p = .0027$, $kp = .081$ so that at least one point would easily fall outside the limits due strictly to chance.

Since all of the points are within the limits for the current example, the limits would be extended and applied to future samples provided that $n = 1000$.

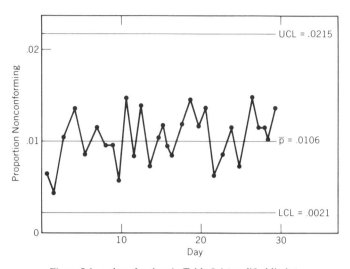

Figure 8.1 p chart for data in Table 8.4 (modified limits).

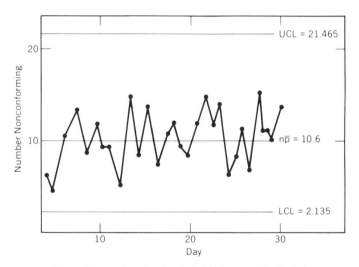

Figure 8.2 np chart for data in Table 8.4 (modified limits).

8.1.7   Unequal Sample Sizes

What if it is likely that n will vary instead of being fixed? If each sample is comprised of a full-day's production, we would certainly not expect production to be constant from day to day. (Of course, this would be 100% inspection, which would be impractical for very long.) On the other hand, management might later decide that it is too expensive to inspect 1000 units in each sample. Or perhaps there is a decision to inspect more than 1000 units.

Whatever the reason, it would be inadvisable to use an np chart when n varies, but a p chart could be used. The reason for this is as follows. With an np chart both the limits and the centerline will vary with n, whereas with a p chart only the limits will vary. Thus, with a "jagged centerline" on an np chart it would be difficult to compare adjacent points to see, for example, if there is evidence of a downward trend.

The (variable) limits for the p chart would be obtained from

$$\bar{p} \pm 3 \sqrt{\frac{\bar{p}(1 - \bar{p})}{n_i}} \qquad (8.6)$$

where n_i is the size of the ith sample. Thus, the limits will vary as the n_i vary. This means that the limits would have to be computed for each different sample size. To circumvent this problem some authors have suggested using the average sample size ($\bar{n}$) in place of n_i in Eq. (8.6) so as to produce constant limits, provided that the n_i vary only slightly. Such "approximate" limits can be a time saver if the charting is performed by hand, but would be unnecessary if a computer is used. If such limits are used, it would be highly desirable to compute the exact (variable) limits and compare a point with those limits whenever the point plots close to one of the approximate limits. (It should be noted that $\bar{p}$ would be obtained by adding the number of nonconforming units for the different samples, and dividing by the sum of the sample sizes.)

8.1.8   CUSUM For Binomial Data

It is also possible to use a CUSUM procedure as an alternative to a p chart or an np chart. To use the same general procedure that was illustrated in Chapter 5 for measurement data, it would be necessary to use a transformed variable that is approximately normally distributed. Thus, one possibility would be to define

$$z_i = \frac{\sin^{-1} \sqrt{(x_i + 3/8)/(n + 3/4)} - \sin^{-1} \sqrt{\bar{p}}}{\sqrt{\frac{1}{4n}}} \qquad (8.7)$$

and then use the z_i values the same way they were used in Chapter 5.

Table 8.5 Illustration of the Proposed CUSUM Procedure ($n = 400$, $k = 0.5$, $h = 5$)

Sample Number	p	x^a	LCL^b	UCL^b	$z_A{}^c$	$z_{NA}{}^c$	Arcsin transformation S_H	Arcsin transformation S_L	Normal approximation S_H	Normal approximation S_L
1	.10	47	22	58	1.17	1.17	0.67	0	0.67	0
2		38			−0.29	−0.33	0	0	0	0
3		39			−0.12	−0.17	0	0	0	0
4		46			1.01	1.00	0.51	0	0.50	0
5		42			0.38	0.33	0.39	0	0.33	0
6		36			−0.63	−0.67	0	0.13	0	0.17
7		46			1.01	1.00	0.51	0	0.50	0
8		37			−0.46	−0.50	0	0	0	0
9		40			0.05	0	0	0	0	0
10		35			−0.80	−0.83	0	0.30	0	0.33
11	.08	34	22	58	−0.98	−1.00	0	0.78	0	0.83
12		31			−1.53	−1.50	0	1.81	0	1.83
13		33			−1.16	−1.17	0	2.47	0	2.50
14		29			−1.90	−1.83	0	3.87	0	3.83
15		33			−1.16	−1.17	0	4.53	0	4.50
16		39			−0.12	−0.17	0	4.15	0	4.17
17		29			−1.90	−1.83	0	5.55[d]	0	5.50[d]
18		39			−0.12	−0.17				
19		34			−0.98	−1.00				

[a] Simulated values.
[b] 3-Sigma np chart limits.
[c] z_A represents the z-value using the arcsin transformation; z_{NA} designates the z-value from the normal approximation.
[d] Value exceeds h.

Namely, one would compute

$$S_{Hi} = \max\left[0, (z_i - k) + S_{Hi-1}\right]$$

and

$$S_{Li} = \max\left[0, (-z_i - k) + S_{Li-1}\right]$$

and then search for an assignable cause of the apparent increase or decrease in p whenever S_H or S_L exceeds the selected value of h.

The value of such a CUSUM procedure can be illustrated as follows. It was stated earlier in the chapter that for $n = 400$ a reduction in p from 0.10 to 0.08 would not be detected, on the average, until after 46 samples, when a p chart or np chart is used. In Table 8.5 values for X are randomly generated for two binomial distributions with $n = 400$: first for $p = 0.10$

and then for $p = 0.08$. The two sets of values for z, S_H, and S_L are for the arcsin method given in Eq. (8.7) and for the normal approximation given by

$$z_i = \frac{x_i - np}{\sqrt{np(1 - p)}} \tag{8.8}$$

Notice that the two sets of z values differ somewhat, and the S_H and S_L values differ by a similar amount. (We should expect the differences to be much greater, however, when p is considerably less than .10.) Thus, although the arcsin method will be generally preferable, the use of the normal approximation z in Eq. (8.8) gives the same result in this instance. The specific result is that sample #17 provides evidence that there has been a decrease in p, as indicated by the fact that $S_L > h$. Since the change actually occurred with the eleventh sample, six additional samples were required to detect the change. Since

$$\sigma_{\bar{p}} = \sqrt{\frac{p(1 - p)}{n}}$$

which equals .015 when $n = 400$ and $p = .10$, the decrease in p from .10 to .08 is equal to $1.33\sigma_{\bar{p}}$. Interpolating in Table 5.6 produces 7.331 as the expected number of samples needed to detect a mean shift equal to 1.33σ. Thus, the result for this illustrative example is in general agreement with the theory. Notice that the z_{NA} values for samples 11–17 are all within $(-3, 3)$, so a signal would not be received from a p chart or np chart.

As indicated earlier in this chapter, runs criteria could also be used to detect such a shift, but it should be remembered that the probability of a point lying outside of 1-, 2-, or 3-sigma limits can differ considerably from the assumed normal distribution probabilities. Consequently, this should be kept in mind if runs criteria are to be used with the x values.

In spite of the fact that the runs-criteria probabilities can be off considerably, we would certainly suspect that a decrease in p had occurred by sample #17 since there are 8 consecutive points below the midline (10–17). The "assumed" probability of this occurring due to chance is $(0.5)^8 = .0039$, whereas the actual probability is .0026.

Other CUSUM procedures have been proposed for detecting a change in the number or percentage of nonconforming units. Johnson and Leone (1977, pp. 375–379) present a mask-type graphical procedure for detecting a change in p of a specified amount. Wadsworth, Stephens, and Godfrey (1986, p. 253) discuss a CUSUM alternative to an np chart that is found in the British Standards.

8.2   CHARTS FOR NONCONFORMITIES

8.2.1 c Chart

This chart can be used to control the number of nonconformities per inspection unit, where the latter may be comprised of one or more than one physical unit. For example, the inspection unit may consist of a single bolt, or a container of bolts. The chart can be used for controlling a single type of nonconformity, or for controlling all types of nonconformities without distinguishing between types. (Another chart that can be used for controlling multiple types of nonconformities is the demerit chart, D chart, which is discussed at the end of this chapter.)

As mentioned earlier in the chapter, a physical unit could have one or more (generally minor) nonconformities without being labeled (and discarded) as a nonconforming unit. Examples would include a minor blemish on a tire and wrapping on a food item that is not fastened properly. Ideally, such nonconformities should not occur, but elimination of all types of imperfections might be too expensive to be practical. (This relates to Deming's contention that product quality should be just good enough to meet the demands of the market place.)

The 3-sigma limits for a c chart, where c represents the number of nonconformities, are obtained from

$$\bar{c} \pm 3\sqrt{\bar{c}} \qquad (8.9)$$

where the adequacy of the normal approximation to the Poisson distribution is assumed, in addition to the appropriateness of the Poisson distribution itself. (C is assumed to have a Poisson distribution.) Specifically, the probability of observing a nonconformity in the inspection unit should be small, but a large number of nonconformities should be theoretically possible. The size of the inspection unit should also be constant over time.

The mean and variance of the Poisson distribution are the same, and $\bar{c}$ is the estimate of each. The "± 3" implies the use of a normal approximation, as was the case with the p and np charts. With those two charts, the normal approximation to the binomial distribution was assumed to be adequate, although it was shown that this will often not be true. The normal approximation to the Poisson distribution has been assumed to be adequate when the mean of the Poisson distribution is at least five, but that really applies to estimating Poisson probabilities rather than to the related problem of determining control limits.

When applied to the c chart, this requires that $\bar{c}$ should be at least 5. Although this requirement will often be met in practice, control limits obtained from Eq. (8.9) should not automatically be used when it is met. In particular, when $5 \leq \bar{c} < 9$, zero would be used for the lower limit since $\bar{c} - 3\sqrt{\bar{c}}$ would be negative. Thus, the lower limit could not be used as a possible indicator of a reduction in the number of nonconformities since the plotted values of c, the number of nonconformities, could not fall below the lower limit. (Recall that this is the same type of problem that can exist with a p chart and np chart.) The tail areas beyond the control limits can also be off considerably from the assumed (nominal) areas of .00135. For example, when $\bar{c} = 10$ the lower limit is approximately 0.5, but $P(X = 0)$ = .000045 when the Poisson mean is 10, which is one-thirtieth of the assumed area. If the objective was to come as close as possible to .00135, the lower limit would be set at 2, and the tail area would be .00050. This type of problem can be avoided by using probability limits obtained from tables such as those given in Kitagawa (1952) and Molina (1973).

8.2.2 Transforming Poisson Data

Alternatively, a transformation could be used analogous to the transformations discussed for the p chart. One such transformation is to let $Y = 2\sqrt{c}$, which will be, for a large sample, approximately normally distributed with mean $2\sqrt{\lambda}$ and variance 1, where λ is the mean of the Poisson distribution. Y would be plotted on the chart and the control limits would be obtained as $\bar{y} \pm 3$. Similar transformations have been proposed by Anscombe (1948) and Freeman and Tukey (1950). When applied to a c chart, the transformations would be $y_1 = 2\sqrt{c + 3/8}$ and $y_2 = \sqrt{c} + \sqrt{c + 1}$, respectively, and the control limits would be obtained as $\bar{y}_1 \pm 3$ and $\bar{y}_2 \pm 3$, respectively.

There is obviously very little difference between these three transformations. The following considerations should be made in choosing between the use of probability limits or some type of transformation. Probability limits allow the user to work with the data on the original scale, but they do require special tables. Limits obtained with transformed variables are easier to construct, but they are for data on a different scale. Another important factor is whether or not a CUSUM procedure is to be used to supplement (or replace) the c chart. Since CUSUM procedures are generally quite sensitive to departures from normality, a normalizing transformation would be highly desirable.

8.2.3 Illustrative Example

The regular (untransformed) c chart, one of the three transformations, and two CUSUM procedures will be illustrated using the data in Table 8.6. It can be determined that $\bar{c} = 189/25 = 7.56$, so the control limits for the

Table 8.6 Nonconformity Data[a]

Number of nonconformities (c)	Bolt Number	Date
9	1	November 9
15	2	
11	3	
8	4	
17	5	
11	1	November 10
5	2	
11	3	
13	1	November 16
7	2	
10	3	
12	4	
4	5	
3	1	November 17
7	2	
2	3	
3	4	
3	1	November 18
6	2	
2	3	
7	4	
9	5	
1	1	November 19
5	2	
8	3	

[a] From Ford Motor Co., (1985), *Continuing Process Control and Process Capability Improvement*, p. 46a. Ford Motor Co., Statistical Methods Publications, Plymouth, MI. Copyright 1985. Reprinted with permission.

regular c chart are obtained from

$$7.56 \pm 3\sqrt{7.56}$$
$$= 7.56 \pm 8.25$$

The control limits are thus 0 and 15.81. The chart is shown in Figure 8.3. It can be observed that one point is above the UCL, and there is evidence of a downward trend. Notice, however, that there is no LCL (since $\bar{c} < 9$), so other methods would have to be used to determine if there has indeed been a true downward shift in the number of nonconformities.

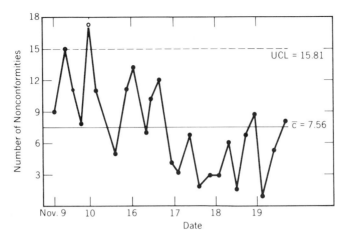

Figure 8.3 c chart with data from Table 8.6.

It is interesting to note that if any of the three transformations had been used, the fifth point would have been inside the UCL, but the twenty-third point (bolt no. 1 on November 19) would have been below the LCL. The results for each of the transformations are given in Table 8.7. In particular, there is very little difference between the values for the last two transformations.

Can the use of one of these transformations instead of the regular c chart be justified in this instance? The answer is yes. If interest had centered upon determining the control limits in such a way that they are as close as possible to being .00135 probability limits, the limits would have been set in such a way that $c \geq 18$ would fall above the UCL, and $c < 1$ (i.e., $c = 0$) would be below the LCL. It can be determined using the results in Table 8.7 that the UCL will be exceeded for each of the transformations when $c \geq 18$, although $c \leq 1$ will be below the LCL. It can be shown that $P(C \geq 16) \doteq .005$ when the mean of the Poisson distribution is 7.56. Therefore, the actual probability is roughly four times the nominal prob-

Table 8.7 Nonconformity Data (Table 8.6) Using Transformations

Transformation	Value of 5th Point	Value of 23rd Point	LCL	UCL
$y = 2\sqrt{c}$	8.246	2.0	2.257	8.257
$y = 2\sqrt{c + 3/8}$	8.337	2.345	2.415	8.415
$y = \sqrt{c} + \sqrt{c + 1}$	8.366	2.414	2.459	8.459

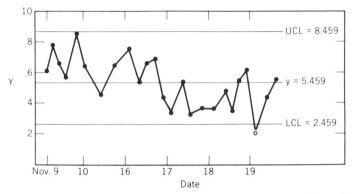

Figure 8.4 c chart with data from Table 8.6 using transformation: $y = \sqrt{c} + \sqrt{c+1}$.

ability. Thus, although the requirement of $\bar{c} \geq 5$ is met for this example, the UCL is nevertheless off by about two units relative to the probability limit. (Recall that this is the same type of problem that occurred with the p chart.) In general, any of the transformations can be expected to produce control limits that are closer to the desired probability limits than those obtained from use of the regular c chart. The c chart obtained from using the transformation $y = \sqrt{c} + \sqrt{c+1}$ is shown in Figure 8.4. The configuration of points is essentially the same as for the regular c chart in Figure 8.3, as should be expected.

Kittlitz (1979) has proposed modified c chart limits that could be used rather than employing one of these transformations. Specifically, the author suggests using

$$\text{LCL} = \bar{c} - 3\sqrt{\bar{c}} + 2$$

and

$$\text{UCL} = \bar{c} + 3\sqrt{\bar{c}} + 5$$

We might ask how a control chart with limits of this form would compare with a chart obtained using the transformation $y = \sqrt{c} + \sqrt{c+1}$. For the present example with $\bar{c} = 7.56$, it could be shown that the control limits on the original scale that would be equivalent to the limits on the transformed scale are

$$\text{LCL} = \bar{c} - 3\sqrt{\bar{c}} + 1.74$$

and

$$\text{UCL} = \bar{c} + 3\sqrt{\bar{c}} + 1.59$$

Thus, the two UCL values differ considerably. The latter would seem to be preferable for $\bar{c} = 7.56$, however, since $P(C \geq 18 | \mu = 7.56)$ is about .00085, whereas $P(C \geq 21)$ is less than .0001. (The vertical line before $\mu = 7.56$ is read "given.")

Therefore, for moderate values of $\bar{c}$ it would appear that the adjustment factor for the UCL should be smaller than what has been proposed.

One way to avoid the need for transformations or adjustment factors would be to define the sample size so that it would consist of more than one inspection unit. This will naturally cause $\bar{c}$ to be larger than it would be if the sample size equaled one inspection unit. The chart user would then have to be satisfied with charting the number of nonconformities per sample, however, and $\bar{c}$ would have to be quite large before the tail areas would be close to .00135. Consequently, the use of a transformation or adjustment factor seems preferable.

Some authors [see, e.g., Grant and Leavenworth (1980, p. 256)] have pointed out that there are many instances in which the requirements for using the Poisson distribution will not be strictly met. For example, the area of opportunity for the occurrence of nonconformities may not be constant over time, or a distribution similar to the Poisson might be more appropriate. When the first requirement is violated, a u chart can be used (to be discussed later). When a c chart is being maintained where c is the count of different types of nonconformities, c will not necessarily have a Poisson distribution. [See Grant and Leavenworth (1980, p. 259) for an extended discussion.] In particular, if different types of nonconformities with different opportunities for occurrence comprise the value of c, it can be shown that c will not have a Poisson distribution, even if each type of nonconformity has a Poisson distribution.

8.2.4 CUSUM Procedures for Nonconformity Data

CUSUM procedures can also be used with nonconformity data. Several such procedures are discussed in this section. *If* the normal approximation to the Poisson distribution could be assumed to be adequate, a CUSUM procedure could be used with

$$z_{\text{NA}} = \frac{c - \bar{c}}{\sqrt{\bar{c}}}$$

where "NA" designates normal approximation. The superiority of the transformation approach was demonstrated in the preceding section, however, so it would be logical to use one of those transformations in a CUSUM procedure. For example, if the transformation $y = \sqrt{c} + \sqrt{c + 1}$

is used, this would lead to

$$z_T = \frac{(\sqrt{c} + \sqrt{c+1}) - \sqrt{4\bar{c}+1}}{1}$$

$$= \sqrt{c} + \sqrt{c+1} - \sqrt{4\bar{c}+1}$$

since the mean of $(\sqrt{c} + \sqrt{c+1})$ is estimated by $\sqrt{4\bar{c}+1}$.

The results for the standard approach and the transformation approach are given in Table 8.8. Recall that this same type of comparison was made for a p chart example, and the results did not differ greatly since p was not extremely small. There is obviously a big difference with this nonconformity data, however. In particular, the z values differ considerably at the two extremes; namely, $c \geq 15$ and $c \leq 2$. This causes the cumulative sums to differ greatly, and results in the two out-of-control messages being received

Table 8.8 CUSUM Calculations ($k = 0.5$, $h = 5$)

c	$z_{NA} - (c - \bar{c})/\sqrt{\bar{c}}$	$z_T = \sqrt{c} + \sqrt{c+1}$ $-\sqrt{4\bar{c}+1}$	$S_H(z_{NA})$	$S_H(z_T)$	$S_L(z_{NA})$	$S_L(z_T)$
9	0.52	0.57	0.02	0.07	0	0
15	2.71	2.28	2.23	1.85	0	0
11	1.25	1.19	2.98	2.54	0	0
8	0.16	0.24	2.64	2.28	0	0
17	3.43	2.78	5.57[a]	4.56	0	0
11	1.25	1.19	6.32	5.25[a]	0	0
5	−0.93	−0.90	4.89	3.85	0.43	0.40
11	1.25	1.19	5.64	4.54	0	0
13	1.98	1.76	7.12	5.80	0	0
7	−0.20	−0.12	6.42	5.18	0	0
10	0.89	0.89	6.81	5.57	0	0
12	1.61	1.48	7.92	6.55	0	0
4	−1.29	−1.35	6.13	4.70	0.79	0.85
3	−1.66	−1.86	3.97	2.34	1.95	2.21
7	−0.20	−0.12	3.27	1.72	1.65	1.83
2	−2.02	−2.44	0.75	0	3.17	3.77
3	−1.66	−1.86	0	0	4.33	5.13[a]
3	−1.66	−1.86	0	0	5.49[a]	6.49
6	−0.57	−0.49	0	0	5.56	6.48
2	−2.02	−2.44	0	0	7.08	8.42
7	−0.20	−0.12	0	0	6.78	8.04
9	0.52	0.57	0.02	0.07	5.76	6.97
1	−2.39	−3.18	0	0	7.65	9.65
5	−0.93	−0.90	0	0	8.08	10.05
8	0.16	0.24	0	0	7.42	9.31

[a] Value exceeds $h = 5$.

at different points. (Note: $\sqrt{4\bar{c} + 1}$ was used in computing z_T because $\mu_y = \sqrt{4\lambda + 1}$ where $y = \sqrt{c} + \sqrt{c + 1}$ and $\bar{c}$ is the estimator of the Poisson mean, λ. Alternatively, $\bar{y}$ could have been used. The two values will not differ much, particularly when the c values do not differ greatly.)

Lucas (1985) presents a CUSUM procedure for Poisson data that does not utilize a normal approximation and differs somewhat from the procedure given in Lucas and Crosier (1982) for variables data. Specifically, the cumulative sums are obtained from the formulas

$$S_{Hi} = \max\left[0, (c_i - k_H) + S_{Hi-1}\right]$$

and

$$S_{Li} = \max\left[0, -(c_i - k_L) + S_{Li-1}\right]$$

where the first formula is for detecting an increase in the number of nonconformities, and the second is for detecting a decrease. It is stated that the value of k_H should be chosen to be close to

$$(\mu_d - \mu_a)/\left[\ln(\mu_d) - \ln(\mu_a)\right]$$

where μ_a is the acceptable level (number of nonconformities), and μ_d is the level such that a shift to this level is to be detected quickly. This is actually for a one-sided CUSUM in which an upward shift is to be detected. For a two-sided CUSUM, which is generally recommended, a second value of k, k_L, would be calculated using the level that corresponds to a shift in the opposite direction.

Applying this method to the nonconformity data in Table 8.6, we might set μ_d at 10.31 and compare the results with the results for the other CUSUM procedures. This would provide a fair comparison with the other CUSUM procedures, as $\mu_d = 10.31$ is one standard deviation above $\mu_a = 7.56$, and the use of $k = 0.5$ with the other (normal approximation) procedures is appropriate when a one standard deviation shift is to be detected quickly. For a downward shift, $\mu_d = 4.81$ is one standard deviation below the mean. These two values of μ_d will produce different k values, however. Using $\mu_d = 10.31$,

$$k_H = \frac{10.31 - 7.56}{\ln(10.31) - \ln(7.56)}$$

$$= 8.86$$

whereas $\mu_d = 4.81$ produces

$$k_L = \frac{4.81 - 7.56}{\ln(4.81) - \ln(7.56)}$$

$$= 6.08$$

Thus, different k values will be used in the two cumulative sums. Following Lucas' recommendation, we round these to the nearest integer, so that the two sets of cumulative sums will be obtained using

$$S_{Hi} = \max[0, (c_i - 9) + S_{Hi-1}]$$

and

$$S_{Li} = \max[0, -(c_i - 6) + S_{Li-1}]$$

This will also require the use of two different h values, denoted by Lucas as h_H and h_L. As with measurement data, h is determined from a table of average run length (ARL) values. Using the tables in Lucas (1985), $h_H = 8$ and $h_L = 7$ could be used, although there appears not to be an obvious choice for h_H such that the in-control ARL at $\mu_a = 7.56$ will be large, and the out-of-control ARL at $\mu_d = 10.31$ will be small. The CUSUM calculations for the Lucas approach are given in Table 8.9. Notice that the upward-shift signal from S_H is received sooner than with either of the transformations used in Table 8.8, and the downward-shift signal from S_L is also received sooner.

Alternative CUSUM procedures for handling Poisson data include the V-mask approach illustrated in Johnson and Leone (1977) and the method illustrated in the British Standard on CUSUMS for Counted Data: BS 5703, Part 4. The latter are also described in Wadsworth, Stephens, and Godfrey (1986, p. 251).

8.2.5 *u* Chart

When the area of opportunity for the occurrence of nonconformities does not remain constant, a u chart should be used rather than a c chart, where $u = c/n$ and n is the number of inspection units from which c is obtained. When n is constant, either a u chart or a c chart can be used, but when n varies a u chart must be used. (It can be noted that U does not have a Poisson distribution, however, so it does differ from C in that respect.)

The control limits for a u chart are obtained from the limits for a c chart. Specifically, $\mathrm{Var}(c/n) = (1/n^2)\mathrm{Var}(c)$ which is estimated by $(1/n^2)\bar{c}$.

Table 8.9 CUSUM Calculations for Lucas Approach
$(k_H = 9, k_L = 6, h_H = 8, h_L = 7)$

c	S_H	S_L
9	0	0
15	6	0
11	8^a	0
8	7	0
17	15	0
11	17	0
5	13	1
11	15	0
13	19	0
7	17	0
10	18	0
12	21	0
4	16	2
3	10	5
7	8	4
2	1	8^a
3	0	11
3	0	14
6	0	14
2	0	18
7	0	17
9	0	14
1	0	19
5	0	18
8	0	16

^{a}Threshold value is reached or exceeded.

The latter is obviously equal to $(\bar{c}/n)/n$, which equals $\bar{u}/n$. Thus, the control limits are obtained from

$$\bar{u} \pm 3\sqrt{\frac{\bar{u}}{n}} \qquad (8.10)$$

where $\bar{u} = \bar{c}/n$ and n is assumed to be constant. When the sample size varies, n_i would replace n in Eq. (8.10). The control limits will thus vary as n_i varies, but the center line will still be constant. When the n_i do not vary greatly, the average sample size, $\bar{n}$, can be used in place of n. One suggested rule of thumb is that this approach can be used as long as no individual sample size differs from the average by more than 25% [Ford Motor Company (1985)]. As was discussed for a p chart, when a point falls near a control limit based upon $\bar{n}$, the exact limit using n_i should be calculated to see if the point falls inside or outside the exact limit.

A u chart can thus be used under each of the following conditions:

1. As a substitute for a c chart when the (constant) sample size contains more than one inspection unit, and there is a desire to chart the average number of nonconformities per inspection unit.
2. When the sample size varies so that a c chart could not be used. The control limits would then be
   a. Variable limits using individual sample sizes, or
   b. Constant limits using the average sample size when the sample sizes do not differ greatly.

It should be noted that a u chart could be produced when a transformation is used for c. For example, if $y = \sqrt{c} + \sqrt{c + 1}$ and n is constant, the control limits would then be obtained from

$$\frac{\bar{y}}{n} \pm \frac{3}{n}$$

where $\bar{u} = \bar{y}/n$ is the average number of "transformed nonconformities" per inspection unit. Similarly, when the sample size varies, the exact variable limits would be obtained from

$$\frac{\sum y}{\sum n_i} \pm \frac{3}{n_i}$$

The motivation for using transformations in conjunction with a u chart is the same as the motivation for using them with a c chart. Specifically, if the normal approximation is not adequate for nonconformity data, it is not going to be adequate for nonconformities per unit.

8.2.6 CUSUM Alternative to a u Chart

A CUSUM alternative to a u chart could be easily developed. When n is constant, one simple approach would be to use

$$z = \frac{u - \bar{u}}{\sqrt{\bar{u}/n}}$$

It can easily be seen, however, that this is equivalent to the first suggested CUSUM alternative to a c chart. Specifically,

$$z = \frac{(c/n) - (\bar{c}/n)}{\sqrt{(\bar{c}/n)/n}}$$

$$= \frac{(c/n) - (\bar{c}/n)}{\sqrt{\bar{c}}/n}$$

$$= \frac{c - \bar{c}}{\sqrt{\bar{c}}}$$

Similarly, if a transformation such as $y = \sqrt{c} + \sqrt{c + 1}$ were used, the z statistic would reduce to the same z statistic as was given for the second suggested CUSUM alternative to a c chart.

Therefore, a CUSUM alternative to a u chart would actually be the same as the alternative to a c chart.

8.2.7 *ku* Chart

If the occurrence of nonconformities per sample is quite small, it might be desirable to scale the data so that the center line and control limits will not be very close to zero. For example, if the inspection unit is a typewritten page, and the sample size consists of 20 pages, the number of typing errors per sample, c, could be small so that $u = c/20$ could be close to zero. Therefore, instead of using

$$\frac{\bar{c}}{20} \pm 3\frac{\sqrt{\bar{c}}}{20}$$

as the regular u chart limits, a scaling factor such as $k = 10$ could be used so that the limits would be

$$10\left(\frac{\bar{c}}{20}\right) \pm 3(10)\frac{\sqrt{\bar{c}}}{20}$$

In general, the control limits will be obtained from

$$k\bar{u} \pm 3k\sqrt{\frac{\bar{u}}{n}}$$

(The use of c and u charts in administrative applications is mentioned in Chapter 10.)

8.2.8 D Chart

It was previously stated that a c chart can be used to chart a single type of nonconformity, or to chart the sum of different types of nonconformities. If the latter is being used, each type of nonconformity is implicitly assigned the same weight. This will be unsuitable in some applications because some nonconformities could be very minor. Consequently, many companies have used demerit charts (D charts) in which different weights (demerits) can be assigned to nonconformities of differing severity.

For example, assume that there are three different types of nonconformities, expressed as 1, 2, and 3, with the number of nonconformities of each type expressed as c_1, c_2, and c_3. If the corresponding weights are expressed as w_1, w_2, and w_3, and D represents the number of demerits per inspection unit, we then have

$$D = w_1 c_1 + w_2 c_2 + w_3 c_3$$

Assuming that $w_i \geq 1$, $i = 1, 2, 3$, D will not have a Poisson distribution unless all $w_i = 1$, which would be rather meaningless. Nevertheless, control chart limits can be easily constructed (recall that u does not have a Poisson distribution either).

In general, if we assume that there are k different types of nonconformities, and the nonconformities are independent, we then have

$$\text{Var}(D) = \sum_{i=1}^{k} w_i^2 \lambda_i$$

where λ_i is the mean of c_i. This variance would be estimated by $\sum_{i=1}^{k} w_i^2 \bar{c}_i$, where $\bar{c}_i$ is obtained by averaging over the n inspection units (which may or may not equal the number of samples). Specifically, if we let c_{ij} represent the number of nonconformities of type i in inspection unit j, then

$$\bar{c}_i = \frac{\sum_{j=1}^{n} c_{ij}}{n}$$

The control limits are obtained from

$$\bar{D} \pm 3 \sqrt{\sum_{i=1}^{k} w_i^2 \bar{c}_i}$$

where

$$\overline{D} = \frac{\sum_{j=1}^{n}\sum_{i=1}^{k} w_i c_{ij}}{n} = \frac{\sum_{j=1}^{n} D_j}{n}$$

and $D_j = \sum_{i=1}^{k} w_i c_{ij}$ is the number of demerits for the jth inspection unit.

This would be the counterpart to a c chart. If each sample contains more than one inspection unit and it is desired to chart the number of demerits per inspection unit, then the counterpart to the u chart would be produced. Specifically,

$$D_u = \sum_{i=1}^{k} w_i u_i$$

where $u_i = c_i/n_\ell$ is the number of nonconformities of type i per inspection unit in a sample that contains n_ℓ such units.

If m samples are available for computing the control limits, it follows that we would compute

$$\overline{D}_u = \sum_{i=1}^{k} w_i \overline{u}_i$$

where

$$\overline{u}_i = \frac{\sum_{\ell=1}^{m} c_{i\ell}}{\sum_{\ell=1}^{m} n_\ell}$$

Here $c_{i\ell}$ denotes the number of nonconformities of type i in sample ℓ, which contains n_ℓ inspection units.

Assuming again that the k nonconformities are independent, we have

$$\text{Var}(D_u) = \frac{1}{n_\ell^2} \sum_{i=1}^{k} w_i^2 \lambda_i$$

Since c_i is assumed to have a Poisson distribution with mean (and variance) of λ_i, a weighted average of the c_i (assuming that the n_ℓ differ) would be used in estimating λ_i.

Thus,

$$\bar{c}_i = \frac{\sum_{\ell=1}^{m} n_\ell c_{i\ell}}{\sum_{\ell=1}^{m} n_\ell}$$

where the average would be an unweighted average if the n_ℓ are equal.
The control limits are obtained from

$$\bar{D}_u \pm \frac{3}{n_\ell} \sqrt{\sum_{i=1}^{k} w_i^2 \bar{c}_i}$$

SUMMARY

Several different types of control charts for attribute data were presented in this chapter. It was observed that the usual Shewhart charts will often have lower control limits that are zero, as well as tail areas that differ greatly.

Some new charts were proposed to remedy these problems. It was observed that transformations can be used to equalize (approximately) the tail areas of the standard charts, and adjustment factors can be employed if the user prefers not to transform the data.

We also saw that CUSUM procedures can be applied just as easily to attribute data as they can to measurement data.

We need to keep in mind, however, that the use of these charts will not help improve the quality of products and processes. They will merely show the extent to which progress is being achieved.

REFERENCES

Anscombe, F. J. (1948). The transformation of Poisson, binomial, and negative binomial data. *Biometrika 35*: 246–254 (December).

Brownlee, K. A. (1960). *Statistical Theory and Methodology in Science and Engineering*. New York: Wiley.

Burr, I. W. (1979). *Elementary Statistical Quality Control*. New York: Marcel Dekker.

Duncan, A. J. (1986). *Quality Control and Industrial Statistics*, 5th ed. Homewood, IL: Irwin.

Ehrenfeld, S., and S. B. Littauer (1964). *Introduction to Statistical Method*. New York: McGraw-Hill.

Ford Motor Company (1985). *Continuing Process Control and Process Capability Improvement*. (Available from Ford Motor Company, Statistical Methods Publications, P.O. Box 1000, Plymouth, MI 48170.)

Freeman, M. F., and J. W. Tukey (1950). Transformations related to the angular and the square root. *Annals of Mathematical Statistics 21*: 607–611.

Grant, E. L., and R. S. Leavenworth (1980). *Statistical Quality Control*, 5th ed. New York: McGraw-Hill.

Hahn, G. J. (1981). Tolerance intervals for Poisson and binomial variables. *Journal of Quality Technology 13*(2): 100–110 (April).

Hald, A. (1952). *Statistical Theory with Engineering Applications*. New York: Wiley.

Johnson, N. L., and S. Kotz (1969). *Discrete Distributions* (Vol. 1 of the 4-volume set: *Distributions in Statistics*). New York: Wiley.

Johnson, N. L., and F. C. Leone (1977). *Statistics and Experimental Design in Engineering and the Physical Sciences*, Vol. I, 2nd ed. New York: Wiley.

Kitagawa, T. (1952). *Tables of Poisson Distribution*. Tokyo, Japan: Baifukan Pub. Co.

Kittlitz, R. G. (1979). Poisson distribution and textile mill problems. *ASQC Technical Conference Transactions*, pp. 126–133.

Lucas, J. M. (1985). Counted data CUSUM's. *Technometrics 27*(2): 129–144 (May).

Lucas, J. M., and R. B. Crosier (1982). Fast initial response for CUSUM quality control schemes: Give your CUSUM a head start. *Technometrics 24*(5): 199–205 (August).

Molina, E. C. (1973). *Poisson's Exponential Binomial Limit*. Huntington, NY: R. E. Krieger.

Nelson, L. S. (1983). Transformations for attribute data. *Journal of Quality Technology 15*(1): 55–56 (January).

Wadsworth, H. M., K. S. Stephens, and A. B. Godfrey (1986). *Modern Methods for Quality Control and Improvement*. New York: Wiley.

EXERCISES

1. An experimenter has collected 20 samples of size 200 for the purpose of constructing trial control limits for a p chart, and finds that $\bar{p} = .023$. Determine the control limits using the transformation

$$y = \sin^{-1}\sqrt{(x + 3/8)/(n + 3/4)}\,.$$

2. Consider the data in Table 8.4. For each of the last 5 days the number of nonconforming units plot above the midline on the np chart in Figure 8.2. Does this provide evidence that p has increased? What would runs

criteria suggest? A logical approach to answering the question would be to compute S_H for the last 5 days after first using the transformation given in Problem #1. (Assume that $S_H = 0$ at the beginning of day #26, which is approximately what it will be anyway.)

3. Explain why an experimenter should not attempt to construct an "untransformed" p chart for $n = 100$ and $p = .001$.

4. A soft drink company wishes to control the number of nonconformities per bottle of its product. The data on nonconformities for 30 days are as follows, where 100 inspection units (bottles) constitute the sample size.

6	7	3	5	2	2
3	8	4	6	4	9
4	5	5	8	4	2
3	3	8	3	10	5
8	4	7	2	6	6

  a. Could either a c chart or u chart be used here? Explain.
  b. If a c chart is used, will the LCL be zero?
  c. Consider the transformation $y = \sqrt{c} + \sqrt{c + 1}$ and determine the control limits using that transformation.
  d. What would be reasonable adjustment factors to use for these data if the chart user preferred to adjust the conventional c chart limits rather than using a transformation?
  e. Plot the points on a chart using your results from Part (c).

5. Could we determine the largest value of $\bar{c}$ that would make the LCL zero using the transformation $y = \sqrt{c} + \sqrt{c + 1}$? Why or why not?

6. Construct a u chart for the following data. (Use the conventional approach.)

c	n	c	n	c	n
12	125	15	145	14	135
13	140	12	130	19	195
15	150	14	150	16	180
10	115	18	175	15	160
11	135	17	180	13	155
14	145	15	155	12	115

7. The following 50 numbers are random values generated from a binomial distribution with $n = 500$ and $p = 0.008$

1	4	5	3	3	3	3	5	8	4
4	3	5	5	2	3	3	4	7	8
3	1	1	3	6	2	4	1	3	4
5	5	6	2	2	3	2	5	6	5
7	8	6	3	2	3	3	5	8	2

Construct the p chart using the standard approach and the p chart using modified limits and compare the results. (Successive values are in columns.)

8. The following 40 numbers have been produced as follows. The first 30 numbers were generated from a Poisson distribution with $\lambda = 9$ and the next 10 were generated from a Poisson distribution with $\lambda = 12$.

$\lambda = 9$						$\lambda = 12$	
7	9	10	12	9	9	11	8
8	7	11	8	12	13	14	11
9	5	8	14	6	9	11	13
11	9	12	9	7	11	18	14
7	11	8	9	9	9	12	13

Use the first 30 values (successive values are in columns) to determine the control limits using the following:

a. The standard c chart approach

b. The transformation $y = \sqrt{c} + \sqrt{c + 1}$

and apply these to the next 10 values.

c. Then apply a CUSUM approach to the last 10 observations using $z = \sqrt{c} + \sqrt{c + 1} - \sqrt{4\bar{c} + 1}$ with $\bar{c}$ obtained from the first 30 observations, and use $S_{H30} = S_{L30} = 0$.

Compare the results.

9. Assume that a demerit chart is to be produced, and the numbers of demerits assigned to each of three types of nonconformities are 5, 4, and 8, respectively. The data for 20 inspection units are as follows, where c_1,

c_2, and c_3 denote the number of nonconformities of each of the three types.

Unit number	c_1	c_2	c_3	Unit number	c_1	c_2	c_3
1	3	5	2	11	2	3	1
2	2	4	5	12	4	4	2
3	1	2	3	13	3	1	0
4	2	4	1	14	2	0	1
5	3	2	3	15	3	2	3
6	4	3	2	16	4	1	2
7	2	1	2	17	5	3	4
8	2	0	3	18	2	3	6
9	3	2	2	19	1	2	4
10	0	3	1	20	3	1	1

a. Construct the D chart (that corresponds to a c chart) and test for control.

b. Would three separate c charts have indicated statistical control? [Note that this can be easily determined since the three $\bar{c}$ values were computed in Part (a).]

CHAPTER 9

Multivariate Control Charts for Measurement Data

When there are a number of quality characteristics that are to be controlled simultaneously, the usual practice has been to maintain a separate (univariate) chart for each characteristic. Unfortunately, this can give misleading results when the characteristics are highly correlated.

It should be noted that the control charts presented in this chapter are quite different from the Multi-Vari Chart proposed by Seder (1950). The latter is actually not a type of control chart. It is primarily a graphical tool for displaying variability due to different factors, and is covered in Chapter 11.

The mathematics in this chapter is (unavoidably) at a higher level than in the preceding chapters. Nevertheless, every effort has been made to minimize the amount of advanced mathematics and statistical theory. The reader with a good knowledge of statistical theory is referred, in particular, to Alt (1973) for details that are not given in this chapter.

As with the univariate charts, multivariate charts can be used when there is subgrouping, or when individual (multivariate) observations are to be used. For both cases, what is calculated and plotted on a chart when monitoring the process mean is the value of a *quadratic form*. In general, a quadratic form can be written as

$$\mathbf{x}'A\mathbf{x}$$

where A is a matrix (a rectangular array of numbers arranged in rows and columns), $\mathbf{x}'$ is a row vector, and $\mathbf{x}$ is a column vector which contains the elements of $\mathbf{x}'$ written in a column. Numerically, if we let

$$A = \begin{bmatrix} 6 & 4 \\ 4 & 3 \end{bmatrix}$$

and

$$\mathbf{x} = \begin{bmatrix} 2 \\ 5 \end{bmatrix}$$

it can be shown that

$\mathbf{x}'A\mathbf{x}$

$$= \begin{bmatrix} 2 & 5 \end{bmatrix} \begin{bmatrix} 6 & 4 \\ 4 & 3 \end{bmatrix} \begin{bmatrix} 2 \\ 5 \end{bmatrix}$$

$$= \left[(2 \times 6) + (5 \times 4) \right] \times 2 + \left[(2 \times 4) + (5 \times 3) \right] \times 5$$

$$= 179$$

Readers unfamiliar with matrix algebra are referred to books such as Searle (1982).

9.1 CHARTS FOR THE PROCESS MEAN USING SUBGROUPS

Multivariate procedures for control charts are based heavily upon Hotelling's T^2 distribution, which was introduced in Hotelling (1947). This is the multivariate analogue of the univariate t distribution that was covered in Chapter 3. Recall that

$$t = \frac{\bar{x} - \mu}{s/\sqrt{n}}$$

has a t distribution. If we wanted to test the hypothesis that $\mu = \mu_0$, we would then have

$$t = \frac{\bar{x} - \mu_0}{s/\sqrt{n}}$$

so that

$$t^2 = \frac{(\bar{x} - \mu_0)^2}{s^2/n}$$

$$= n(\bar{x} - \mu_0)(s^2)^{-1}(\bar{x} - \mu_0) \qquad (9.1)$$

When Eq. (9.1) is generalized to p variables it becomes

$$T^2 = n(\bar{\mathbf{x}} - \mu_0)'S^{-1}(\bar{\mathbf{x}} - \mu_0)$$

where

$$\bar{\mathbf{x}} = \begin{bmatrix} \bar{x}_1 \\ \bar{x}_2 \\ \vdots \\ \bar{x}_p \end{bmatrix} \qquad \mu_0 = \begin{bmatrix} \mu_1^0 \\ \mu_2^0 \\ \vdots \\ \mu_p^0 \end{bmatrix}$$

S^{-1} is the inverse of the sample variance–covariance matrix, S, and n is the sample size upon which each $\bar{x}_i$, $i = 1, 2, \ldots, p$, is based. (The diagonal elements of S are the variances and the off-diagonal elements are the covariances for the p variables.)

It is well known that when $\mu = \mu_0$

$$T^2 \sim \frac{p(n-1)}{n-p} F_{(p, n-p)}$$

where $F_{(p, n-p)}$ refers to the F distribution (covered in Chapter 3) with p degrees of freedom for the numerator and $n - p$ for the denominator.

Thus, if μ was specified to be μ_0, this could be tested by taking a single p-variate sample of size n, then computing T^2 and comparing it with

$$\frac{p(n-1)}{n-p} F_{\alpha(p, n-p)}$$

for a suitably chosen value of α. (Here α denotes the upper tail area for the F distribution.) A suggested approach for determining α is to select α so that $\alpha/2p = .00135$—the 3-sigma value for a univariate chart. Accordingly, this approach would lead to $\alpha = .0054$ when $p = 2$. If $T^2 > F_{\alpha(p, n-p)}$, we would then conclude that the multivariate mean is no longer at μ_0.

9.2 VARIATIONS OF HOTELLING'S T^2

In practice, μ is generally unknown, so it is necessary to estimate μ analogous to the way that μ is estimated when an $\bar{X}$ chart is used. Specifically, when there are rational subgroups μ is estimated by $\bar{\bar{x}}$ where

$$\bar{\mathbf{x}} = \begin{bmatrix} \bar{\bar{x}}_1 \\ \bar{\bar{x}}_2 \\ \vdots \\ \bar{\bar{x}}_p \end{bmatrix}$$

Each $\bar{\bar{x}}_i$, $i = 1, 2, \ldots, p$, is obtained the same way as with an $\bar{X}$ chart, namely, by taking k subgroups of size n and computing $\bar{\bar{x}}_i = (1/k)\sum_{j=1}^{k}\bar{x}_{ij}$. (Here $\bar{x}_{ij}$ is used to denote the average for the jth subgroup of the ith variable.) As with an $\bar{X}$ chart (or any other chart) the k subgroups would be tested for control by computing k values of T^2 [Eq. (9.2)] and comparing each against the upper control limit. If any T^2 value falls above the UCL (there is no LCL), the corresponding subgroup would be investigated.

Thus, one would plot

$$T_j^2 = n(\bar{\mathbf{x}}^{(j)} - \bar{\bar{\mathbf{x}}})' S_p^{-1} (\bar{\mathbf{x}}^{(j)} - \bar{\bar{\mathbf{x}}}) \tag{9.2}$$

for the jth subgroup ($j = 1, 2, \ldots, k$), where $\bar{\mathbf{x}}^{(j)}$ denotes a vector with p elements that contains the subgroup averages for each of the p characteristics for the jth subgroup. (S_p^{-1} is the inverse of the "pooled" variance–covariance matrix, S_p, which is obtained by averaging the subgroup variance–covariance matrices over the k subgroups.)

Each of the k values of Eq. (9.2) would be compared with

$$\text{UCL} = \left(\frac{knp - kp - np + p}{kn - k - p + 1} \right) F_{\alpha(p, kn - k - p + 1)} \tag{9.3}$$

[See Alt (1973, p. 173) or Alt (1982a, p. 890).] If any of the T_j^2 values exceed the UCL from Eq. (9.3), the corresponding subgroup(s) would be investigated. The investigation would proceed somewhat differently, however, than it would for, say, an $\bar{X}$ chart in which only one quality characteristic is involved. Specifically, it is necessary to determine which quality characteristic(s) is causing the out-of-control signal to be received. There are a number of possibilities, even when $p = 2$. Assume for the moment that we have two quality characteristics that have a very high positive correlation (i.e., ρ close to 1.0). We would then expect their average in each subgroup to almost always have the same relationship in regard to their respective averages in $\bar{\bar{\mathbf{x}}}$. For example, if $\bar{x}_1^{(j)}$ exceeds $\bar{\bar{x}}_1$ then $\bar{x}_2^{(j)}$ will probably exceed $\bar{\bar{x}}_2$. Similarly, if $\bar{x}_1^{(j)} < \bar{\bar{x}}_1$, we could expect to observe $\bar{x}_2^{(j)} < \bar{\bar{x}}_2$, i.e., we would not expect them to move in opposite directions relative to their respective averages since the two characteristics have a very high *positive* correlation (assuming that ρ has not changed). If they do start moving in opposite directions this would indicate that the "bivariate" process is probably out of control. This out-of-control state could result in a value of Eq. (9.2) that far exceeds the value of Eq. (9.3). Unless one of the two deviations, $\bar{x}_1^{(j)} - \bar{\bar{x}}_1$ or $\bar{x}_2^{(j)} - \bar{\bar{x}}_2$ in absolute value exceeds $\bar{\bar{x}}_1 + 3(\bar{R}_1/d_2\sqrt{n})$ or $\bar{\bar{x}}_2 + 3(\bar{R}_2/d_2\sqrt{n})$, respectively, the individual $\bar{X}$ charts will not give an out-of-control message, however. This will be illustrated later with a numerical example.

There are a variety of other out-of-control conditions that *could* be quickly detected using an $\bar{X}$ chart or CUSUM procedure, however. For example, if the two deviations are in the same direction and one of the deviations is more than three standard deviations from the average ($\bar{\bar{x}}$) for that characteristic, the deviation will show up on the corresponding $\bar{X}$ chart. It is *not* true, however, that a deviation that causes an out-of-control signal to be received on at least one of the $\bar{X}$ charts will also cause a signal to be received on the multivariate chart. (This will also be illustrated, later.) Thus, it is advisable to use a univariate procedure (such as an $\bar{X}$ chart or Bonferroni intervals) in conjunction with the multivariate procedure.

The latter are described in various sources including Alt (1973, p. 95) as well as an encyclopedia article on Bonferroni inequalities (Alt, 1982b). They essentially serve as a substitute for individual $\bar{X}$ charts, and will usually be as effective as $\bar{X}$ charts in identifying the quality characteristic(s) that causes the out-of-control message to be emitted by the multivariate chart.

The general idea is to construct p intervals (one for each quality characteristic) for each subgroup that produces an out-of-control message on the multivariate chart. Thus, for the jth subgroup the interval for the ith characteristic would be

$$\bar{\bar{x}}_i - t_{\alpha/2p,\,k(n-1)}s_{p_i}\sqrt{\frac{k-1}{kn}}$$

$$\leq \bar{x}_i^{(j)} \leq \bar{\bar{x}}_i + t_{\alpha/2p,\,k(n-1)}s_{p_i}\sqrt{\frac{k-1}{kn}} \tag{9.4}$$

where s_{p_i} designates the square root of the pooled sample variance for the ith characteristic, and the other components of Eq. (9.4) are as previously defined. If Eq. (9.4) is not satisfied for the ith characteristic, the values of that characteristic would then be investigated for the jth subgroup. If an assignable cause is detected and removed, the entire subgroup would be deleted (for all p characteristics) and the UCL recomputed.

Recomputing the UCL that is to be subsequently applied to *future* subgroups entails recomputing S_p and $\bar{\bar{x}}$, *and* using a constant and an F-value that are different from the form given in Eq. (9.3). The latter results from the fact that a different distribution theory is involved since future subgroups are assumed to be independent of the "current" set of subgroups that is used in calculating S_p and $\bar{\bar{x}}$. (The same thing happens with $\bar{X}$ charts; the problem is simply ignored through the use of 3-sigma limits.)

For example, assume that a subgroups had been discarded so that $k - a$ subgroups are used in obtaining S_p and $\bar{\bar{x}}$. We shall let these two values be represented by S_p^* and $\bar{\bar{x}}^*$ to distinguish them from the original values, S_p and $\bar{\bar{x}}$, before any subgroups are deleted. Future values to be plotted on the multivariate chart would then be obtained from

$$n\left(\bar{x}^{(\text{future})} - \bar{\bar{x}}^*\right)'\left(S_p^*\right)^{-1}\left(\bar{x}^{(\text{future})} - \bar{\bar{x}}^*\right) \tag{9.5}$$

where $\bar{x}^{(\text{future})}$ denotes an arbitrary vector containing the averages for the p characteristics for a single subgroup obtained in the future. Each of these future values would be plotted on the multivariate chart and compared with

$$\text{UCL} = \left(\frac{p(k - a + 1)(n - 1)}{(k - a)n - k + a - p + 1} \right) F_{\alpha[p,(k-a)n-k+a-p+1]} \quad (9.6)$$

where a is the number of the original subgroups that is deleted before computing S_p^* and $\bar{\bar{x}}^*$. Notice that Eq. (9.6) does *not* reduce to Eq. (9.3) when $a = 0$, nor should we expect it to since Eq. (9.3) is used when testing for control of the entire *set* of subgroups that is used in computing S_p and $\bar{\bar{x}}$. [Note: Eqs. (9.5) and (9.6) are variations of a result given in Alt (1973, p. 112), which can also be found on pp. 891–892 of Alt (1982a)]

9.2.1 Illustrative Example

An example will now be given for $p = 2$ which illustrates how an out-of-control condition can be detected with the multivariate chart, but would not be detected with the two $\bar{X}$ charts. The data set to be used is contained in Table 9.1. Assume that each pair of values represents an observation on

Table 9.1 Data for Multivariate Example[a] ($p = 2$, $k = 20$, $n = 4$)

Subgroup Number	First Variable				Second Variable			
1	72	84	79	49	23	30	28	10
2	56	87	33	42	14	31	8	9
3	55	73	22	60	13	22	6	16
4	44	80	54	74	9	28	15	25
5	97	26	48	58	36	10	14	15
6	83	89	91	62	30	35	36	18
7	47	66	53	58	12	18	14	16
8	88	50	84	69	31	11	30	19
9	57	47	41	46	14	10	8	10
10	26	39	52	48	7	11	35	30
11	46	27	63	34	10	8	19	9
12	49	62	78	87	11	20	27	31
13	71	63	82	55	22	16	31	15
14	71	58	69	70	21	19	17	20
15	67	69	70	94	18	19	18	35
16	55	63	72	49	15	16	20	12
17	49	51	55	76	13	14	16	26
18	72	80	61	59	22	28	18	17
19	61	74	62	57	19	20	16	14
20	35	38	41	46	10	11	13	16

[a] The multivariate observations are $(72, 23), (84, 30), \ldots, (46, 16)$.

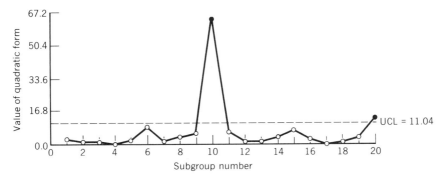

Figure 9.1 Multivariate chart for Table 9.1 data.

Table 9.2 T^2 **Values in Figure 9.1**

Subgroup Number	Subgroup Averages		T^2
	First Variable	Second Variable	
1	71.00	22.75	2.24
2	54.50	15.50	0.65
3	52.50	14.25	1.27
4	63.00	19.25	0.22
5	57.25	18.75	1.53
6	81.25	29.75	8.98
7	56.00	15.00	1.32
8	72.75	22.75	3.77
9	47.75	10.50	4.95
10	41.25	20.75	63.76
11	42.50	11.50	6.55
12	69.00	22.25	1.37
13	67.75	21.00	1.36
14	67.00	19.25	3.26
15	75.00	22.50	7.41
16	59.75	15.75	2.76
17	57.75	17.25	0.12
18	68.00	21.25	1.33
19	63.50	17.25	3.50
20	40.00	12.50	13.04
$\bar{\bar{x}}$	60.38	18.49	

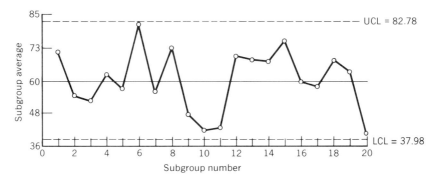

Figure 9.2a $\overline{X}$ chart for Table 9.1 data (first variable).

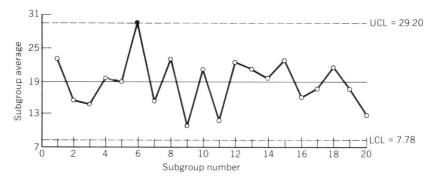

Figure 9.2b $\overline{X}$ chart for Table 9.1 data (second variable).

each of the two variables. Thus, there are 20 subgroups (represented by the 20 rows of the table), with four observations in each subgroup for each variable.

When, for this data set, the values obtained using Eq. (9.2) are plotted against the UCL given by Eq. (9.3), with $\alpha = 0.0054$, the result is the chart given in Figure 9.1. There are two points that exceed the UCL; in particular, the value for subgroup #10 far exceeds the UCL. (The T^2 values are given in Table 9.2.) Before explaining why the value for subgroup #10 is so much larger than the other values, it is of interest to view the individual $\overline{X}$ charts. These are given in Figure 9.2a and Figure 9.2b.

It should be observed that at subgroup #10 the average that is plotted on each chart is inside the control limits. Thus, the use of two separate $\overline{X}$ charts would not have detected the out-of-control condition at that point. But how can the process be out of control at that point when the $\overline{X}$ charts indicate control? The answer is that the *bivariate* process is out of control.

At subgroup #10 the positions of the two averages relative to their respective midlines differ greatly; one is well below its midline whereas the other is somewhat above its midline. If two variables have a high positive correlation (as they do in this case) we would expect their relative positions to be roughly the same over time. That is, they should either be both above their respective midlines or below their midlines, and the distances to the midline should be about the same on each chart. Notice that this holds true for virtually every other subgroup except #10.

Thus, if these were real data and the points were being plotted in real time, there would be reason to suspect that something is wrong with the process when the data in subgroup #10 were obtained.

Conversely, no out-of-control message is received at subgroup #6 on the multivariate chart, but Figure 9.2b shows that the subgroup average for the second variable is above the UCL.

9.3 MULTIVARIATE CHART VERSUS INDIVIDUAL $\overline{X}$ CHARTS

This illustrates one of the primary advantages of a single multivariate chart over p separate (univariate) $\overline{X}$ charts, which relates to an important general advantage that can be explained as follows. For a multivariate chart with p characteristics, the probability that the chart indicates control when the process is actually in control at the multivariate average $\overline{\overline{x}}$ is $1 - \alpha$, which equals $1 - .0027p$ when α is chosen in accordance with the suggested procedure of selecting α so that $\alpha/2p = .00135$. As Alt (1982a) demonstrates, the use of Bonferroni's inequality leads to the result that with p separate $\overline{X}$ charts the probability that each of the p averages (in a given subgroup) will fall within the control limits is at least $1 - .0027p$ when the multivariate process is in control. Thus, the p separate charts could conceivably indicate that the process is in control more often than it actually is in control. The difference between the two probabilities is virtually zero when the p variables are independent. Specifically, for the p separate charts the probability is $(1 - .0027)^p$ compared to $1 - .0027p$ for the multivariate chart. Recall that in Chapter 4 it was demonstrated that $.0027n$ gives a reasonably good approximation of $1 - (1 - .0027)^n$ when $n \leq 50$. That result applies directly here since if $.0027n$ is used to estimate $1 - (1 - .0027)^n$, then $1 - .0027n$ would be used to estimate $(1 - .0027)^n$, and the estimate would be with the same accuracy.

What this implies is that when the p quality characteristics are virtually unrelated (uncorrelated), it will not make much difference whether a single multivariate chart is used or p separate $\overline{X}$ charts. However, when the characteristics are highly correlated it can make a considerable difference; the illustrative example showed how the difference can occur.

When $p = 2$, as in the preceding example, a *bivariate control ellipse* could be constructed, with the bivariate averages plotted in a two-dimensional graphical display. The area that represents an in-control bivariate process would be that enclosed by an ellipse. A point that falls outside of the ellipse would indicate that the bivariate process may be out of control. This approach has one serious shortcoming, however, in that the time order of the subgroups is not preserved. Readers interested in the use of control ellipses are referred to Jackson (1959). (But note that control ellipses are illustrated there for individual observations, not for subgroup averages.)

9.4 CHARTS FOR PROCESS VARIABILITY

Multivariate charts for controlling the process variability have been developed by Alt (1973, Chapter 7), and are also described in Alt (1986). These are based upon $|S|$, the determinant of S. These charts can be useful in detecting an increase in one or more of the individual variances, but should always be supplemented by the corresponding Bonferroni intervals. This is due to the fact that one or more of the individual variances could be out of control (on, say, an s^2 chart) but $|S|$ could remain virtually the same. Assume that the variability of two quality characteristics is being controlled by the use of a multivariate chart. If an assignable cause results in an increase in both variances, but the cause affects both characteristics in essentially the same way so that the correlation coefficient for the two characteristics remains unchanged, $|S|$ will also remain unchanged.

For example, if the values of one of the characteristics change from $1, 2, 3, 4$ to $2, 4, 6, 8$ and the values of the other characteristic change from $1, 3, 5, 7$ to $2, 6, 10, 14$ in going from subgroup j to subgroup $j + 1$, $|S|$ will remain unchanged. Such a shift might also be due to a change in the process mean, which might show up on the multivariate chart for averages. The variances are being quadrupled, however, whereas the means are doubled, so this could be indicative more of an increase in variability than an increase in μ. How likely this is to occur in practice is conjectural since such charts have not been used to any extent in practice.

In addition to the multivariate charts for controlling the process variability developed by Alt (1973), a multivariate range procedure has been given by Siotani (1959a, b).

9.5 CHARTS CONSTRUCTED USING
INDIVIDUAL OBSERVATIONS

The multivariate charts presented to this point in the chapter are applicable when subgrouping is used. A multivariate analogue of the X chart was presented by Jackson (1956, 1957, 1959). The UCL is an approximation, however, that should be used only for a large number of observations. The exact UCL is given by Alt (1973, p. 114; 1982a, p. 892). Using Alt's notation, if m individual multivariate observations are to be used for estimating the mean vector and variance–covariance matrix (the estimates denoted by $\bar{\mathbf{x}}_m$ and S_m, respectively), each future observation vector, $\mathbf{x}$, would, in turn, be used in computing

$$(\mathbf{x} - \bar{\mathbf{x}}_m)'S_m^{-1}(\mathbf{x} - \bar{\mathbf{x}}_m) \tag{9.7}$$

and comparing it against the UCL. The latter is

$$\frac{p(m+1)(m-1)}{m^2 - mp} F_{\alpha(p, m-p)} \tag{9.8}$$

where, as before, p denotes the number of characteristics. It is important to note that this can be used only for controlling future multivariate observations; it cannot be used in testing each $\mathbf{x}$ that is used in calculating $\bar{\mathbf{x}}_m$. There is presently no exact method for doing the latter.

It would be reasonable to use one of two approximate methods, however, when m is large. For example, if $m = 75$, $\bar{\mathbf{x}}_{75}$ should give a reasonable estimate of μ. Jackson's suggested method of plotting

$$(\mathbf{x}^j - \bar{\mathbf{x}}_{75})'S_{75}^{-1}(\mathbf{x}^j - \bar{\mathbf{x}}_{75}) \tag{9.9}$$

for $j = 1, 2, \ldots, 75$ against the UCL of

$$\frac{p(m-1)}{m-p} F_{\alpha(p, m-p)} \tag{9.10}$$

would be a fair approximate procedure, although it was not originally proposed as such. Also, the value of Eq. (9.7) can be thought of as an approximation for

$$(\mathbf{x}^j - \mu)'\Sigma^{-1}(\mathbf{x}^j - \mu)$$

where the latter is distributed as χ_p^2. The value of Eq. (9.7) would then be compared with the UCL of $\chi_{\alpha, p}^2$.

Which approximate procedure should be used? When m is large (say, $m > 100$) the results will be virtually the same. This is due to the well-known result [see, e.g., Johnson and Kotz (1970, Vol. 3, p. 78)] that $F_{\nu_1, \nu_2} \to \chi_{\nu_1}^2/\nu_1$ as $\nu_2 \to \infty$. Applied in the present context it means that

$$\frac{p(m-1)}{m-p} F_{\alpha(p, m-p)} \to \chi_{\alpha, p}^2$$

as $m \to \infty$. Thus, when m is large the UCL values from each of the two approximate procedures will be approximately equal, and either procedure could justifiably be used only when m is large.

Unfortunately, there is no multivariate analogue to a moving range chart or the CUSUM procedure for controlling variability that was mentioned in Chapter 6. Thus, to control the multivariate process variability the user would need to maintain p separate univariate charts using whichever procedure is desired.

Additional information on multivariate control chart procedures can be found in Alt (1985).

9.6   WHEN TO USE EACH CHART

In summary, multivariate charts were presented for controlling the multivariate process mean using either subgroups or individual observations. Multivariate dispersion charts were mentioned only briefly; the details are given in Alt (1973, 1986). When subgroups are being used, the value of Eq. (9.2) is plotted against the UCL of Eq. (9.3) when testing for control of the "current" set of subgroups. For control using future subgroups obtained individually, Eq. (9.5) is computed for each future subgroup and compared with the UCL given by Eq. (9.6). When individual observations are used rather than subgroups, control using future observations is checked by comparing the value of Eq. (9.7) with Eq. (9.8). When a current set of individual observations is being tested for control, the value of Eq. (9.9) would be compared with either Eq. (9.10) or $\chi^2_{\alpha,\, p}$. Analogous to the case with subgrouping, vectors would be discarded if removable assignable causes are detected so that, in general, one would actually compute

$$\left(\mathbf{x} - \bar{\mathbf{x}}_{m-a}\right)' S_{m-a}^{-1} \left(\mathbf{x} - \bar{\mathbf{x}}_{m-a}\right) \tag{9.11}$$

where $m - a$ denotes the number from the original m observations that are retained. [Equation (9.7) assumes that they are all retained.] If a vectors are discarded, the value of Eq. (9.11) would then be compared with

$$\frac{p(m - a + 1)(m - a - 1)}{(m - a)^2 - (m - a)p} F_{\alpha(p,\, m-a-p)}$$

for testing future multivariate observations.

As indicated previously in the material on multivariate procedures for subgroups, a bivariate control ellipse could be used when $p = 2$. Such an ellipse can also be constructed when individual observations are plotted, as is illustrated in Jackson (1959). But it has the same shortcoming as the ellipse for subgroups; that is, the time order of the individual observations is lost when they are plotted.

9.7 ACTUAL ALPHA LEVELS FOR MULTIPLE POINTS

The remarks made concerning the α value for an $\overline{X}$ chart when one point is plotted versus the plotting of multiple points also applies here. Specifically, the α given in this chapter as a subscript for F and χ^2 applies, strictly speaking, when one (individual) observation or one subgroup is being used. When current control is being tested for a set of individual observations or a set of subgroups and the process is in control, the probability that at least one point exceeds the UCL far exceeds α. For example, if $\alpha = .0054$ for $p = 2$ (in accordance with the suggested approach of having $\alpha/2p = .00135$), the probability that at least one value of Eq. (9.9) exceeds Eq. (9.10), assuming $\overline{x}_{75} \doteq \mu$, is approximately .334 when the process is in control. (The probability cannot be determined exactly since the procedure is only approximate.) To make $\alpha = .0054$ for the entire set of 75 observations would require using $\alpha = .000072$ in Eq. (9.10).

9.8 REQUISITE ASSUMPTIONS

The multivariate procedures presented in this chapter are also based upon the assumptions of normality and independence of observations. Everitt (1979) examined the robustness of Hotelling's T^2 to multivariate nonnormality, and concluded that the (one-sample) T^2 statistic is quite sensitive to skewness (but not kurtosis) and the problem becomes worse as p increases. Consequently, it is reasonable to conclude that multivariate control chart procedures that are similar to Hotelling's T^2 (such as those given by Alt) will also be sensitive to multivariate nonnormality).

A number of methods have been proposed for assessing multivariate nonnormality, including those given by Royston (1983) and Koziol (1982).

REFERENCES

Alt, F. B. (1973). *Aspects of Multivariate Control Charts*. M.S. Thesis, Georgia Institute of Technology, Atlanta, Georgia.

Alt, F. B. (1982a). Multivariate quality control: State of the art. *ASQC Annual Quality Congress Transactions*, pp. 886–893.

Alt, F. B. (1982b). Bonferroni inequalities and intervals. In S. Kotz and N. Johnson, eds. *Encyclopedia of Statistical Sciences*, Vol. 1, pp. 294–300. New York: Wiley.

Alt, F. B. (1985). Multivariate quality control. In S. Kotz and N. Johnson, eds. *Encyclopedia of Statistical Sciences*, Vol. 6, pp. 110–122. New York: Wiley.

Alt, F. B. (1986). SPC of dispersion for multivariate data. *ASQC Annual Quality Congress Transactions*, pp. 248–254.

Everitt, B. S. (1979). A Monte Carlo investigation of the robustness of Hotelling's one and two-sample T^2 tests. *Journal of the American Statistical Association* *74*(365): 48–51 (March).

Hotelling, H. (1947). Multivariate quality control. In C. Eisenhart, M. W. Hastay, and W. A. Wallis, eds. *Techniques of Statistical Analysis*. New York: McGraw-Hill.

Jackson, J. E. (1956). Quality control methods for two related variables. *Industrial Quality Control 12*(7): 4–8 (January).

Jackson, J. E., and R. H. Morris (1957). An application of multivariate quality control to photographic processing. *Journal of the American Statistical Association 52*(278): 186–189 (June).

Jackson, J. E. (1959). Quality control methods for several related variables. *Technometrics 1*(4): 359–377 (November).

Johnson, N. L., and S. Kotz (1970). *Continuous Univariate Distributions* (Vol. 3 in the 4-volume set: *Distributions in Statistics*). New York: Wiley.

Koziol, J. A. (1982). A class of invariant procedures for assessing multivariate normality. *Biometrika 69*: 423–427.

Royston, J. P. (1983). Some techniques for assessing multivariate normality based on the Shapiro-Wilk W. *Applied Statistics 32*(2): 121–133.

Searle, S. R. (1982). *Matrix Algebra Useful for Statistics*. New York: Wiley.

Seder, L. A. (1950). Diagnosis with diagrams—Part I. *Industrial Quality Control 6*(4): 11–19 (January).

Siotani, M. (1959a). On the range in the multivariate case. *Proceedings of the Institute of Statistical Mathematics 6*: 155–165 (in Japanese).

Siotani, M. (1959b). The extreme value of the generalized distances of the individual points in the multivariate normal sample. *Annals of the Institute of Statistical Mathematics 10*: 183–203.

EXERCISES

1. Assume that there are two correlated process characteristics, and the following values have been computed; $\bar{\bar{x}}_1 = 47$, $\bar{\bar{x}}_2 = 53$, and $S_p^{-1} = \begin{bmatrix} 1.5 & -1 \\ -1 & 1 \end{bmatrix}$.

   a. What would the UCL for *future* control of the bivariate process be if $k = 25$, $n = 5$, $\alpha = 0.0054$, and no subgroups were deleted from the original set (i.e., $a = 0$). (Use $F_{.0054(2, 99)} = 5.51$ in calculating the UCL.)

b. Which of the following (future) subgroup averages would cause an out-of-control signal: (1) $\bar{x}_1 = 48$, $\bar{x}_2 = 54$; (2) $\bar{x}_1 = 46$, $\bar{x}_2 = 54$; (3) $\bar{x}_1 = 47$, $\bar{x}_2 = 54$; and (4) $\bar{x}_1 = 50$, $\bar{x}_2 = 56$.

c. It can be shown (using S_p) that the sample correlation coefficient is 0.816 (i.e., the two characteristics have a high positive correlation). Use this fact to explain why one of the subgroups in Part (b) caused an out-of-control signal even though $\bar{x}_1 - \bar{\bar{x}}_1$ and $\bar{x}_2 - \bar{\bar{x}}_2$ were both comparatively small.

2. What assumptions must be made (and should be verified) before a multivariate chart can be used for controlling the multivariate process mean (using either individual observations or subgroups)?

3. An experimenter wishes to test a *set* of (past) individual observations for control. What approach would you recommend?

4. It was stated that the use of Bonferroni intervals in conjunction with a multivariate chart for subgroups is essentially a substitute for individual $\bar{X}$ charts. The two approaches will not necessarily produce equivalent results, however, due in part to the fact that standard deviations are used in computing Bonferroni intervals, whereas ranges are used (typically) with $\bar{X}$ charts. For the data given in Table 9.1, construct the two intervals for subgroup #6 and subgroup #10. Notice that there is agreement for the latter, but that the results differ slightly for the former. (Use $s_{p_1} = 14.90$, $s_{p_2} = 7.52$, and $t_{.00135, 60} = 3.13$ in constructing the Bonferroni intervals.)

5. The "standards given" approach for an $\bar{X}$ chart was discussed in Chapter 5. Could a T^2 value be compared against a UCL in the form of $p(n - 1)/(n - p)F_{p, n-p}$ when a target value of μ is to be used? Explain.

6. An experimenter wishes to construct a multivariate chart for individual observations with three process characteristics.

a. What value of α should be used?

b. What is the numerical value of the constant that would be multiplied times $F_{\alpha(p, m-p)}$ in determining the UCL when m = 20?

c. To which observations should this UCL be applied, past or future?

7. A bivariate control ellipse could be used with either subgroups or individual observations, but what is one major shortcoming of that approach?

CHAPTER 10

Miscellaneous Control
Chart Topics

In this chapter we discuss several topics that, although important, would generally not be presented in individual chapters. These include (1) the economic design of control charts, (2) administrative applications of control charts, (3) software for control charting, and (4) applications of control charts in specific industries and for specific company functions.

10.1 ECONOMIC DESIGN OF CONTROL CHARTS

The control charts that have been presented in the preceding chapters were not based upon economic considerations. Specifically, the sample size and 3-sigma control limits were presented without being determined from cost criteria. These factors, in addition to the sampling interval, could just as well be determined from cost considerations.

The design of control charts using cost criteria has received very little attention in industry, although it has received some attention in the literature. Concerning the latter, a review is given by Montgomery (1980). One reason given for not using economically designed control charts is that actual costs are difficult to obtain. This is not really a valid reason, however, as the economic models that have been proposed will work fairly well when only estimates of the actual costs are available.

The costs that need to be determined or estimated include the cost of sampling, the cost of searching for an assignable cause when none exists (i.e., a false signal), the cost of detecting and removing an assignable cause, and the cost of producing nonconforming units.

230

Admittedly, many of the economic models that have been proposed are somewhat complicated (as compared to, say, an $\overline{X}$ chart), but computer programs can prevent this from being an impediment to their use. An example of such a program for an $\overline{X}$ chart can be found in Montgomery (1982).

Most of the models that have been proposed have been for an $\overline{X}$ chart, and the work dates from Duncan (1956), which is also described in Montgomery (1980). Chiu and Wetherill (1974) presented a simple model as an alternative to the model proposed by Duncan (1956). The latter assumed a model in which the process is presumed to start in control, with a subsequent mean shift due to a single assignable cause. The time until the assignable cause occurs is assumed to have an exponential distribution with parameter λ, so the process is assumed to operate in control for λ^{-1} hours. Samples of size n are drawn h hours apart, and the control limits are "k-sigma" limits. As usual, a search for the assignable cause is initiated when a point falls outside the control limits, and the process continues in operation until the cause is detected. The repair cost is not charged against the income from the process. Duncan (1956) has shown that the expected loss (cost) per hour of operation is

$$L = \left[(\lambda BM + \alpha T/h + \lambda w)/(1 + \lambda B)\right] + (b + cn)/h$$

where

$$B = (1/p - 1/2 + \lambda h/12)h + en + D$$

and the other symbols are defined as follows:

α is the probability of a point falling outside the control limits when the process is in control

M is the increased net loss per hour attributable to a greater percentage of unacceptable items when the assignable cause occurs

$b + cn$ is the cost of taking a sample of size n and maintaining the control chart

T is the average cost of looking for an assignable cause when none exists

w is the average cost of looking for an assignable cause when one exists

en is the time required to take a sample and compute the results

D is the average time required to discover the assignable cause after a signal has been received.

The general idea is to determine the values of h, k, and n that will minimize the expected loss. The minimization procedure proposed by Duncan is somewhat involved, but Chiu and Wetherill (1974) gave a simple procedure for approximating the minimum of Duncan's loss function.

More recently, Lorenzen and Vance (1986) have presented a general approach for the economic design of any control chart.

10.2 ADMINISTRATIVE APPLICATIONS OF CONTROL CHARTS

If a business is to run efficiently, more than just the manufactured products need to be "in control." Other factors such as clerical errors, accounts receivable, salesmen's expenses, and a host of other factors can be charted with the purpose of keeping them in a state of statistical control.

Although the use of control charts for administrative applications has not received very much attention, some actual applications are discussed in this section with the intention of providing the reader with some insight as to their (relatively untapped) potential value.

It is important to remember, however, that statistical quality control consists of more than just control charts, so general SQC principles can still be applied in situations in which control charts cannot be used without modification. For example, if clerical errors are being charted with the objective of keeping them "in control," would a c chart with 3-sigma limits be suitable, or would management prefer to establish an upper limit based upon what it considers to be an excessive number of errors, or perhaps not even use an upper limit? Whichever the case may be, the mere maintenance of some type of control chart will certainly indicate the variability of clerical errors over time, and should lead to the detection of assignable causes when the variability is judged to be excessive.

One such assignable cause could be inadequate training. Lobsinger (1954) describes the use of np-type charts in the airline industry that uncovered the need for additional training for certain individuals. The end result was that basic training time was cut in half, and this was accomplished by using the feedback from the control charts.

Another interesting account of the use of an np chart for clerical errors (using 2σ limits) in a mail order plant can be found in Ballowe (1950), where the application is described in considerable detail.

The use of an $\overline{X}$ chart for cost control, by controlling the number of work hours per thousand units produced, is described in Schiesel (1956).

Pringle (1962) gives a detailed account of the successful application of $\overline{X}$ and R charts for controlling the volume of speech transmitted on a switched telephone call.

Bicking (1955) describes the application of X and R charts to (1) inventory control, (2) rating of technical personnel, and (3) analysis of indirect expense. Enrick (1973) also discusses the use of statistical control limits for inventory control.

Latzko (1977) discusses the use of control charts for controlling the encoding of bank checks. See also Latzko (1986).

There have been many applications of SQC principles to accounting data, although the method used has often been some acceptance sampling procedure. See, e.g., Buhl (1955) and Dalleck (1954).

10.3 SOFTWARE FOR CONTROL CHARTING

Many of the control charts that were presented in the previous chapters could be easily maintained by hand and/or hand calculator. For example, the points to be plotted on an $\overline{X}$, R, or c chart can be easily determined. At the other extreme, determining the points to be plotted on a multivariate chart for averages could not easily be performed without a computer, and determining the trial control limit for the chart would be extremely laborious without a computer.

In general, the more sophisticated (and superior) control chart procedures could not be used very efficiently without a computer. Even when the simpler control charts are used, it is easier to view and analyze historical data with a computer than when the charts are maintained by hand.

SPC software developers have concentrated on the microcomputer, and the IBM-PC in particular. In the early 1980s there were very few such packages on the market, but by the middle of the decade the number had increased to several dozen. On the whole, they were generally easy to use, and could thus be easily used by plant personnel. The developers generally concentrated on the standard control charts for measurement and attribute data. Although user friendly, many packages were somewhat limited in terms of data input flexibility, as well as the way in which the data could be handled.

One software package which does not have these limitations, and which could be used to produce almost all of the control charts presented in previous chapters is SQCS[a] (Statistical Quality Control System).

Several software directories have been published to aid people who are searching for SPC software. One such directory is published in the March issue of *Quality Progress* each year, starting in 1984. Other directories have appeared in *Quality* and *Industrial Engineering*.

[a]SQCS is the trademark of SQC Systems, Inc. 2351 College Station Rd., Suite 475, Athens, Georgia 30605

These packages are generally in the price range of $500–$1000, with a few packages above $1000, and software for computers larger than micros is also above $1000.

SPC software reviews of any length (e.g., at least one page) have been virtually nonexistent, and short reviews have also been rather scarce.

10.4 APPLICATIONS OF CONTROL CHARTS IN SPECIFIC INDUSTRIES

Although extensive control chart usage in the Western world is of relatively recent origin, there are many published examples of control chart applications in various fields. Listed in the references are papers that describe such applications. This is by no means intended to be a complete listing; the intent is simply to provide readers with references to specific applications that they may be able to relate to in their own environment. (Included in the listing are those papers mentioned in the preceding sections of this chapter.)

The vast majority of the papers were gleaned from the *Quality Control and Applied Statistics Abstracts* published by Executive Sciences Institute, Inc. There are similar bibliographies that can be found in the literature. Vardeman and Cornell (1987) provide a list of applications articles, in addition to a list of SQC books, booklets, and other materials. Vance (1983) gives a bibliography of control chart papers categorized by charts.

REFERENCES

Armour, N., R. Morey, R. Kleppinger, and K. Pitts (1985). Statistical process control for LSI manufacturing: What the handbooks don't tell you. *RCA Engineer*, *30*(3): 44–53 (May/June).

Ballowe, J. M. (1950). Results obtained during five years of operation in a mail order plant. *ASQC Annual Quality Control Conference Papers*, Paper #10.

Beall, G. (1956). Control of basis weight in the machine direction. *Tappi 39*:26–29 (January).

Beaudry, J. P. (1956). Statistical quality control methods in the chemical industry. *ASQC National Convention Transactions*, pp. 626–627.

Bicking, C. A. (1955). Quality control as an administrative aid. *ASQC National Convention Transactions*, pp. 347–357.

Bingham, R. S. (1957). Control charts in multi-stage batch processes. *Industrial Quality Control 13*(12): 21–26 (June).

Breunig, H. L. (1964). Statistical control charts in pharmaceutical industry. *Industrial Quality Control 21*(2): 79–86 (August).

Buhl, W. F. (1955). Statistical controls applied to clerical and accounting procedures. *ASQC National Convention Transactions*, pp. 9–25.

Chiu, W. K., and G. B. Wetherill (1974). A simplified scheme for the economic design of $\bar{X}$-charts. *Journal of Quality Technology* 6(2): 63–69 (April).

Cyffers, B. (1957). Setting snuff packing machines under control. *Revue de Statistique Appliquee* 5(1): 67–76.

Dalleck, W. C. (1954). Quality control at work in airline accounting. *ASQC Quality Control Convention Papers*, pp. 489–498.

Deile, A. J. (1956). How General Foods prevents accidents—by predicting them. *Management Methods* 10(4): 45–48 (July).

Desmond, D. J. (1961). The testing of ceiling fans. *Quality Engineering* 25(3): 77–80 (May-June).

Doornbos, R. (1959). Efficient weight control of margarine packets. *Statistica Neerlandica* 13(3): 323–328.

Duffy, D. J. (1960). A control chart approach to manufacturing expense. *Journal of Industrial Engineering* 11(6): 451–458 (Nov.-Dec.).

Duncan, A. J. (1956). The economic design of $\bar{X}$-charts used to maintain current control of a process. *Journal of the American Statistical Association* 51(274): 228–242 (June).

Duncan, J. M. (1957). Statistical quality control in a petroleum control laboratory. *ASTM Bulletin No. 219*, pp. 40–43 (January).

Enrick, N. L. (1956). Survey of control chart applications in textile processing. *Textile Research Journal* 26: 313–316 (April).

Enrick, N. L. (1973). Control charts in operations research. *ASQC Annual Quality Conference Transactions*, pp. 17–26.

Erdman, E. J., and L. E. Bailey (1969). The production line SQC helped. *Quality Progress* 2(8): 20–22 (August).

Field, E. G. (1957). How to determine yarn strength control limits. *Textile Industry* 121: 109–112 (January).

Gadzinski, C., and R. W. Hooley (1957). The control of magnesium alloy castings. *Industrial Quality Control* 14(5): 14–19 (November).

Hance, L. H. (1956). Statistical quality control, a modern management tool. *Modern Textiles* 37: 61–64 (December).

Harrison, H. B. (1956). Statistical quality control will work on short-run jobs. *Industrial Quality Control* 13(3): 8–11 (September).

Harrison, P. J. (1964). The use of cumulative sum (Cusum) techniques for the control of routine forecasts of product demand. *Operations Research* 12(2): 325–333 (March-April).

Hart, R. F. (1984). Steel by Shewhart. *Quality* 23(6): 66–69 (June).

Hoogendijk, J. (1962). Quality care of a graphic product. *Sigma* 8(1): 10–12.

Hull, A. M. (1956). Optimizing maintenance costs through quality control. *Industrial Quality Control* 12(2): 4–8 (June).

Kornetsky, A., and A. Kramer (1957). Quality control program for the processing of sweet corn. *Food Technology* 11: 188–192 (March).

Kreft, I. J. (1980). Control charts help set firm's energy management goals. *Industrial Engineering 12*(12): 56–58 (December).

Kroll, F. W. (1957). Effective quality control program for the industrial control laboratory. *Statistical Methods in the Chemical Industry, ASQC*, pp. 1–14 (January 12).

Latzko, W. J. (1977). Statistical quality control of MICR documents. *ASQC Annual Quality Conference Transactions*, pp. 117–123.

Latzko, W. J. (1986). Quality and productivity for bankers and financial managers. New York: Marcel Dekker.

Lee, E. P. (1956). A statistical quality control approach to weights and measures. *ASQC National Convention Transactions*, pp. 543–551.

Littauer, S. B. (1956). The application of statistical control techniques to the study of industrial and military accidents. *Transactions of the New York Academy of Sciences, Series II 18*(3): 272–277 (January).

Llewellyn, R. W. (1960). Control charts for queueing applications. *Journal of Industrial Engineering 11*(4): 332–335 (July-August).

Lobsinger, D. L. (1954). Some administrative attributes of SQC. *Industrial Quality Control 10*(6): 20–24 (May).

Lobsinger, D. L. (1957). Application of statistical quality control in administrative areas of a company. *TAPPI 40*: 209A–211A (November).

Lorenzen, T. J., and L. C. Vance (1986). The economic design of control charts: A unified approach. *Technometrics 28*(1): 3–10 (February).

Mandel, B. J. (1975). C-chart sets mail fines. *Quality Progress 8*(10): 12–13 (October).

Mansfield, E., and H. H. Wein (1958). A regression control chart for costs. *Applied Statistics 7*(2): 48–57 (March).

Meddaugh, E. J. (1975). The bias of cost control charts toward type II errors. *Decision Sciences 6*(2): 367–382 (April).

Meyer, J. J. (1963). Statistical sampling and control and safety. *Industrial Quality Control 19*(12): 14–17 (June).

Meyer, T. R., J. H. Zambone, and F. L. Curcio (1957). Application of statistical quality control in glass fabrication. *Industrial Quality Control 14*(2): 21–24 (August).

Montgomery, D. C. (1980). The economic design of control charts: A review and literature survey. *Journal of Quality Technology 12*(2): 75–87 (April).

Montgomery, D. C. (1982). Economic design of an $\overline{X}$ control chart. *Journal of Quality Technology 14*(1): 40–43 (January).

Newchurch, E. J., J. S. Anderson, and E. H. Spencer (1956). Quality control in petroleum research laboratory. *Analytical Chemistry 28*: 154–157 (February).

Osinski, R. V. (1962). Use of median control charts in the rubber industry. *Industrial Quality Control 19*(2): 5–8 (August).

Oxenham, J. P. (1957). An application of statistical control techniques to a post office. *Industrial Quality Control 14*(3): 5–10 (September).

Patte, W. E. (1956). General techniques in pulp and paper mills, *ASQC National Convention Transactions*, pp. 185–193.

Preston, F. W. (1956). A quality control chart for the weather. *Industrial Quality Control 12*(10): 4–6 (April).

Pringle, J. B. (1962). SQC methods in telephone transmission maintenance. *Industrial Quality Control 13*(2): 6–11 (July).

Rhodes, W. L., and J. F. Petrycki (1960). Experience with control charts on ink-film thickness and sharpness. *TAPPI 43*: 429–433 (May).

Sandon, F. (1956). A regression control chart for use in personnel selection. *Applied Statistics 5*(1): 20–31 (March).

Schiesel, E. E. (1956). Statistical cost control and analysis. *ASQC National Convention Transactions*, pp. 553–558.

Schreiber, R. J. (1956). The development of engineering techniques for the evaluation of safety programs. *Transactions of the New York Academy of Sciences, Series II 18*(3): 266–271 (January).

Schumacher, R. B. F. (1976). Quality control in a calibration laboratory, Part II. *Quality Progress 9*(2): 16–20 (February).

Vance, L. C. (1983). A bibliography of statistical quality control chart techniques, 1970–1980. *Journal of Quality Technology 15*(2): 59–62 (April).

Vardeman, S., and J. A. Cornell (1987). A partial inventory of statistical literature on quality and productivity through 1985. *Journal of Quality Technology 19*(2): 90–97 (April).

Walter, J. T. (1956). How reliable are lab analyses? *Petroleum Refiner 35*: 106–108 (February).

Way, C. B. (1961). Statistical quality control applications in the food industry. *Industrial Quality Control 17*(11): 30–34 (May).

Yegulalp, T. M. (1975). Control charts for exponentially distributed product life. *Naval Research Logistics Quarterly 22*(4): 697–712 (December).

PART III

Beyond Control Charts: Graphical and Statistical Methods

CHAPTER 11

Graphical Methods

The cliché "a picture is worth a thousand words" could perhaps be modified to "a picture is often better than several numerical analyses" when adapted to the field of statistics. In this chapter we present some standard graphical tools for displaying data, which have been used for decades, in addition to some newer and in many instances, more powerful methods, which have been introduced and have gained acceptance within the past 10 years.

The book *How to Lie with Statistics* by Huff (1954) is replete with examples of misleading graphical displays which can serve to remind us of the much-quoted statement of Disraeli concerning different types of lies and statistics. The problem, of course, is not with statistics but rather in the way in which they are used. Football experts have been prone to say that statistics are for losers, but *all* of the game statistics generally indicate why a team was the loser. One issue that must be faced when using graphical displays is that there is generally not going to be one right way to proceed in terms of choosing appropriate graphical methods or in terms of how a particular method is used.

The graphical tools discussed in this chapter all have value as stand-alone procedures, but can and should be used in conjunction with the statistical techniques discussed in the succeeding chapters, as well as with control charts.

The numerous control charts illustrated in Part II are graphical displays of a two-dimensional type, in which whatever is being charted is generally graphed against the sample number (i.e., against time).

If, however, we have a set of, say, 100 numerical values that were all obtained at the same time, we should address the question of determining a meaningful way to portray the data graphically so as to provide some insight into the process that generated the numbers. Assume that the 100

Table 11.1 100 Data Values

24	45	36	59	48
31	70	85	62	87
81	57	68	60	78
27	25	37	56	65
42	50	53	39	57
51	51	40	34	63
58	66	54	46	43
82	55	55	75	66
21	32	49	69	79
54	23	50	68	64
53	64	74	30	65
60	58	52	61	44
32	52	40	59	49
83	84	35	76	67
55	56	41	59	47
64	52	28	76	71
33	33	56	51	69
51	43	72	73	45
41	45	61	42	46
58	58	63	52	62

numbers are those given in Table 11.1. Such a table, by itself, tells us very little. By looking at Table 11.1, we can determine the largest value and the smallest value, and that is about all.

One or more good graphical displays of the data will tell us much more, however. In particular, we would want a graphical display to provide us with answers to questions such as the following: What is the general shape of the distribution of the data? Is it close to the shape of a normal distribution, or is it markedly nonnormal? Are there any numbers that are noticeably larger or smaller than the rest of the numbers?

11.1 HISTOGRAM

A commonly used starting point in summarizing data is to put the data into classes and then to construct a *histogram* from the data that have been thus grouped. This is what is generally covered in the first week or two in an introductory statistics course; it was discussed briefly in Chapter 2. We will construct a histogram for the data in Table 11.1, but our choice of a histogram as the first graphical tool to illustrate should not be interpreted

Table 11.2 **Frequency Distribution for the Data in Table 11.1**

Class	Frequency
20–29	6
30–39	11
40–49	18
50–59	29
60–69	20
70–79	10
80–89	6

as an indication that a histogram is superior to other graphical tools. It isn't. There are alternative displays that have clear advantages over the histogram, particularly for small data sets. It is illustrated first simply because it is an often-used display that is well understood by both statisticians and nonstatisticians.

As indicated, a histogram is produced from grouped data. Before data can be grouped, however, there is an obvious need to determine the number of classes that is to be used. From Table 11.1 we can see that the smallest number is 21 and the largest number is 87, so it might seem reasonable to use the following set of classes: 20–29, 30–39, 40–49, . . . , 80–89. This selection of classes produces the following *frequency distribution* given in Table 11.2, from which a histogram is then constructed and displayed in Figure 11.1.

It can be observed that the histogram is simply a bar chart in which the height of each of the seven rectangles corresponds to the frequency of the class that the rectangle represents. Notice that the values along the horizontal axis of the histogram do not correspond to the values of the class intervals in Table 11.2. That is because these are *class boundaries*, which are defined as the average of adjacent class limits (e.g., 29.5 is the average of 29 and 30). To illustrate their use, we might think of the data in Table 11.1 as being rounded to the nearest integer so that values between 29.0 and 29.5 would be rounded down to 29 and thus appear in the first class, whereas values above 29.5 and less than 39.5 would be put in the second class. Also, if the class limits had been used to construct the histogram there would have been gaps between the rectangles because there is a one-unit gap between 29 and 30, 39 and 40, etc. If the classes are of equal width, which is generally desirable, the rectangles will then be of equal width.

In this example the number of classes was implicitly determined from the selection of what seemed to be logical class intervals. The use of the latter is desirable whenever possible, but it is not always possible. What if there had

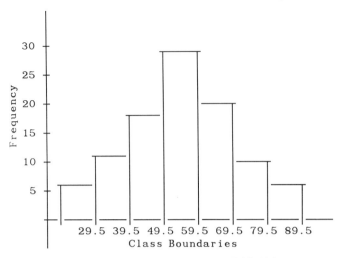

Figure 11.1 Histogram of the data in Table 11.2.

been only 30 values rather than 100, but the largest and smallest values were still 21 and 87, respectively. If we tried to spread 30 values over 7 classes, we might have some empty classes, and/or the shape of the histogram could be rather flat. We should keep in mind that one of the main reasons for constructing a histogram is to provide some insight into the shape of the distribution of population values from which the sample values were obtained. We will have a distorted view of that shape if we use either too many or not enough classes.

Therefore, we need a rule for determining the number of classes that is based upon the number of observations. One rule that works well is called the "power of 2 rule": for n observations we would use a classes where $2^{a-1} < n \le 2^a$. Thus, for $n = 100$ we have $2^6 < 100 < 2^7$ so that seven classes would be used, which is the number that was actually used in Figure 11.1. Another rule of thumb that has been advanced is to let the number of classes equal $\sqrt{n}$, but this will produce quite a few classes when n is well in excess of 100. The first rule seems to be better suited for giving us a good view of the distribution of values.

Histograms can also be constructed using frequencies of individual values. Velleman and Hoaglin (1981) provide a histogram of the chest measurements of 5738 Scottish militiamen; the measurements were recorded to the nearest inch and ranged from 33 inches to 48 inches. With only 16 different values (33–48) there is certainly no need to group them into classes, and, in fact, the "power of 2" rule would specify 13 classes anyway. We would expect such anthropometric measurements to be roughly normally distributed, and the histogram did have that general shape.

When used in process capability studies, specification limits can be displayed on a histogram to show what portion of the data exceeds the specifications. Ishikawa (1976) displays these as dotted vertical lines.

11.2 STEM-AND-LEAF DISPLAY

A stem-and-leaf display is one of the newer graphical techniques alluded to in the first paragraph of this chapter. It is one of many techniques that are generally referred to as exploratory data analysis (EDA) methods, as popularized in the book on EDA by Tukey (1977).

We want our graphical displays to be reasonably compact, but not to sacrifice important details about the data while providing a summarization of the data. With a histogram we lose information about the individual values after we put them into classes and display the histogram. A stem-and-leaf display, however, provides us with essentially the same information as a histogram, *without* losing the individual values.

There are many different ways to create a stem-and-leaf display, depending upon the type of data that are to be displayed and what the user wishes to show. We shall illustrate a basic display using the data in Table 11.1 and compare the result with the histogram in Figure 11.1. The basic idea is to display "leaves" that correspond to a common "stem," and to do this in such a way that the display does not require much space. With a two-digit number the choice for the "stem" is the first digit, and the second digit for the leaf. This leads to the stem-and-leaf display in Figure 11.2.

In Figure 11.2 the numerals to the left of the vertical line represent tens. The numerals to the right of the vertical line represent, when combined with

```
2 | 1 3 4 5 7 8
3 | 0 1 2 2 3 3 4 5 6 7 9
4 | 0 0 1 1 2 2 3 3 4 5 5 5 6 6 7 8 9 9
5 | 0 0 1 1 1 1 2 2 2 2 3 3 4 4 5 5 5 6 6 6 7 7 8 8 8 8 9 9 9
6 | 0 0 1 1 2 2 3 3 4 4 4 5 5 6 6 7 8 8 9 9
7 | 0 1 2 3 4 5 6 6 8 9
8 | 1 2 3 4 5 7
```

Figure 11.2 Stem-and-leaf display of the data in Table 11.1.

the tens digit, the actual numbers that are distributed within that range (e.g., from 20–29). Thus if we look at the "2" line we see 1 (representing 21), 3 (representing 23), 4 (representing 24), etc. These are taken from the actual data values in Table 11.1. If a data value occurred more than once, the numeral is repeated the number of times that it occurred in the sample. For example, in Table 11.1 there are two data values of 32; thus on the "3" line of the stem-and-leaf chart there are two numeral "2's" to the right of the vertical line—each representing 32.

We can observe that this particular stem-and-leaf display requires roughly the same amount of space as the corresponding histogram, and when turned on its side has exactly the same shape as the histogram. Thus, it provides the same information as a histogram, but with the advantage that it also allows us to see the individual values. Obviously this provides us with better insight into the data and the data collection procedures. For example, if we look at the stem "6" and the corresponding leaves, we can see that all of the digits are listed twice except for the four and the seven. If this had been actual data we would certainly want to question those numbers, as we would expect to see more variation in the digit counts.

Velleman and Hoaglin (1981, p. 14) discuss an example in which the pulse rates of 39 Peruvian Indians were displayed in a histogram and in a stem-and-leaf display. The latter revealed that all of the values except one were divisible by four, thus leading to the conjecture that 38 of the values were obtained by taking 15-second readings and multiplying the results by 4, with the other value obtained by doubling a 30-second reading resulting (perhaps) from missing the 15-second mark. Thus, the stem-and-leaf display provided some insight into how the data were obtained, whereas this information was not provided by the histogram.

An interesting industrial use of stem-and-leaf displays is described by Godfrey (1985) who relates that the Japanese train schedules are actually stem-and-leaf displays in which the hours are the stems and the leaves are the minutes, and the display runs in two directions—one for arrivals and the other for departures.

Another example is the Atlanta phone directory, which took the general form of a stem-and-leaf display starting with the December 1985 issue. Instead of each last name being listed as many times as there are phone numbers of people with that last name, the last name was listed only once. Thus, the last name was the stem, and the leaves were the various combinations of the first two names and initials.

Readers interested in further reading on stem-and-leaf displays are referred to Velleman and Hoaglin (1981) and to Emerson and Hoaglin (1983).

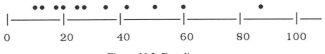

Figure 11.3 Dot diagram.

11.3 DOT DIAGRAMS

Another way to display one-dimensional data is through the use of dot diagrams, which have also been termed one-dimensional scatter plots [Chambers, Cleveland, Kleiner, and Tukey (1983)]. The first label seems slightly better; it will be used later in Chapter 13, and is also used in Box, Hunter, and Hunter (1978).

A dot diagram is simply a one-dimensional display in which a dot is used to represent each point. For example, Figure 11.3 is a dot diagram of the numbers 60, 20, 24, 10, 12, 17, 26, 35, 42, 50, and 87. The dot diagram portrays the relationship between the numbers and, in this instance, allows us to see the separation between the number 87 and the rest of the numbers. This might cause us to question whether or not that number was recorded correctly. If so, the number might be classified as an *outlier*: an observation that is far removed from the main body of the data. (The classification of outliers is somewhat subjective. If the distribution of 100 or so numbers is reasonably symmetric, we might classify a number as an outlier if it differs from $\bar{x}$ by more than $3s$, where $\bar{x}$ and s are the average and standard deviation, respectively, of the numbers.)

A dot diagram does have some limitations, however. In particular, we would not want to use it if we have a large number of observations [Box, Hunter, and Hunter (1978, p. 25) suggest at most 20 observations], as the dots would tend to run together and give rather poor resolution. We also cannot accurately determine the individual values from the diagram. It simply shows us the relationship between the numbers for a small set of numbers.

11.4 BOXPLOT

We should perhaps start by pointing out that this type of display was not named for G. E. P. Box. Rather, it is another EDA tool that was introduced and popularized by Tukey (1977). It derives its name from the fact that the middle half of a set of data is depicted by the area between the top and bottom of a box (rectangle). It is an easily constructed display which may be as routinely used in the years to come as a histogram is today. Quoting from Heyes (1985): "An increasing number of workshops and statistics courses are including boxplots (and other EDA tools) in their agendas." The fact that Heyes' article appeared in a "nonstatistical" publication (*Quality Progress*) is indicative of the widespread exposure that the technique is receiving. Heyes' article serves as a good introduction to boxplots and contains an industrial application (although the reader should note that the illustration of quartiles is apparently motivated more by convenience than by statistical rigor).

There are several ways to construct a boxplot; we shall begin with what has been termed a *skeletal boxplot* by Velleman and Hoaglin (1981, p. 66). Assume that we have a sample of 16 numbers as follows: 18, 19, 23, 24, 26, 29, 31, 33, 35, 37, 39, 40, 42, 45, 47, and 49. Notice that these numbers have been placed in ascending order and that there are no large gaps between any of the numbers.

The first step in constructing the box is to calculate the median, which was defined in Chapter 3 as the middle value when there is an odd number of observations and the average of the two middle values when there is an even number of observations. Here we have an even number so the median is 34 (the average of 33 and 35). The next step is to compute the two *hinges* which are equivalent to the two medians for each half of the data when there is an even number of observations, but cannot be explained quite so simply when there is an odd number of observations. This is illustrated later.

We can observe that the median of the first eight numbers is 25 $[(24 + 26)/2]$, and the median for the second eight numbers is 41 $[(40 + 42)/2]$. These two "hinges" determine the top and bottom of the box, and the overall median is indicated by a horizontal line running across the box. A vertical line is then drawn from the top of the box to a point representing the largest value, and a line is similarly drawn down from the bottom of the box to reach the smallest value. The skeletal boxplot for these 16 values is shown in Figure 11.4.

The fact that the two vertical lines are short relative to the length of the box indicates that there are no values that are either much larger or much smaller than the other values. Also, the midline being slightly closer to the top than to the bottom of the box indicates that the numbers above the median are, as a group, closer to the median than the group of numbers below the median. The box will generally contain roughly half of the observations, so the display also indicates how the middle half of the data are dispersed. We can see from Table B that for a normal distribution roughly 50% of the data are contained within $\mu \pm 0.67\sigma$. Thus, for a normal distribution the length of the box will be close to 1.34σ. Therefore, the

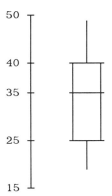

Figure 11.4 Skeletal boxplot for 16 numbers.

display could also provide us with a rough estimate of σ for data that are approximately normally distributed.

The formal name for the plot in Figure 11.4 is a "box-and-whiskers plot," with the vertical lines being thought of as representing whiskers. The shortened name is what is generally used, however.

When there is an odd number of observations, the two hinges cannot be explained quite as simply and intuitively as when there is an even number. If we think about assigning the median to both halves of the data (only for the purpose of explanation), we would then have an even number of observations in each half. The hinges would then be the averages of the two middle values in each half. To illustrate, if we were to modify the previous example by deleting the 49 so as to produce 15 observations, the hinges would then be 25 and 39.5. Notice that only the upper hinge changes since the largest value is the one that is being deleted.

Some authors have presented a boxplot in which the bottom and the top of the box are the first and third quartiles, respectively (i.e., the 25th and 75th percentiles). [See, for example, Chambers et al. (1983, p. 21).] The endpoints of the box should be about the same when they are obtained from the quartiles (for the 15 observations the quartiles are 24.5 and 39.75), but the quartiles require more work to obtain. Thus, if the necessary calculations are being performed with pencil and paper (which is what EDA tools were originally intended for), the use of hinges is preferable, whereas with a computer it really doesn't make much difference. (Of course, if there are more than 20 or so numbers, the use of a computer becomes essential since the data have to be sorted into ascending order before the plot can be constructed.)

There are other variations of boxplots that are more sophisticated and thus provide more information than skeletal boxplots. Two uses of these other types of boxplots deserve special mention: (1) the determination of outliers, and (2) the comparison of groups. The latter will be illustrated in the chapter on design of experiments (Chapter 13); the former can be illustrated as follows.

Following Velleman and Hoaglin (1981, p. 68), we will call the difference between the two hinges the *H-spread*. An observation is then considered to be an outlier if it either exceeds the upper hinge plus (1.5 × H-spread) or is less than the lower hinge minus (1.5 × H-spread). Remembering that for a normal distribution (1) mean = median, (2) H-spread $\doteq$ 1.34σ, and (3) the distance from each hinge to the mean is approximately equal to 0.67σ, it then follows that this rule for classifying outliers is roughly equivalent to classifying a value as an outlier if it is outside the interval $\mu \pm 2.68\sigma$. (Notice that this is in general agreement with the statement made earlier in the chapter.)

To illustrate, we shall modify the original example with 16 observations by adding one very small number (2) and one very large number (75). The 18 numbers are thus 2, 18, 19, 23, 24, 26, 29, 31, 33, 35, 37, 39, 40, 42, 45, 47, 49, and 75. The question to be addressed at this point is whether or not these two additional values would be classified as outliers. If we let UH = upper hinge, LH = lower hinge, and H-S = H-spread, we thus have

$$UH + (1.5 \times \text{H-S})$$
$$= 42 + (1.5 \times 18)$$
$$= 69$$

and

$$LH - (1.5 \times \text{H-S})$$
$$= 24 - (1.5 \times 18)$$
$$= -3$$

Since 75 exceeds 69 we would thus classify the former as an outlier, and try to determine whether or not it is a valid data point. These two boundary values, −3 and 69, are termed *inner fences* by Velleman and Hoaglin (1981, p. 68). Their *outer fences* are obtained by using 3.0 rather than 1.5 as the multiplier of H-S, which is equivalent to using boundaries of approximately $\mu \pm 4.69\sigma$ for data that are roughly normally distributed.

The boxplot for the 18 observations is shown in Figure 11.5. The dashed horizontal lines represent the two values 18 and 49, which are the most extreme values of those that lie within the inner fences. (The latter are not shown on the plot.) The value 75 that is outside the inner fences is designated by a circle or some other symbol, and identifying information provided so that the validity of the value can be investigated.

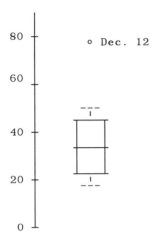

Figure 11.5 Boxplot for 18 numbers.

11.5 NORMAL PROBABILITY PLOT

Most of the statistical procedures used in quality improvement work are based upon the assumption that the population of data values from which a sample is obtained is approximately normally distributed. There are various ways to check this assumption; one such method is to construct a *normal probability plot*, which was discussed briefly in Chapter 2. This is easy to do with appropriate computer software, but a bit laborious to do by hand. Nevertheless, we shall discuss and illustrate hand-generated normal plots so that readers who will be using software will have some understanding of how the plots are generated.

Normal probability paper is generally used for hand-constructed normal plots, although such paper is by no means essential. We shall not illustrate the construction of normal paper since such paper is readily available. The best source for obtaining normal probability paper and other types of probability paper is probably TEAM (Technical Engineering Aids for Management).[†] Readers interested in the construction of normal probability paper are referred to Nelson (1976).

We shall concentrate on explaining the meaning of the points that are plotted, and shall then plot a set of such points without using normal paper. We would generally want to have at least 20 observations before constructing a normal probability plot, but, for the sake of simplicity, we will use a sample consisting of the following 10 observations: 8, 10, 12, 14, 15, 15, 16, 18, 19, 20. Could these data have come from a normal distribution with

---

*Catalogue and price list available from TEAM, Box 25, Tamworth, New Hampshire 03886.

some (unknown) values of μ and σ? This is the question that we wish to address. We are not interested in estimating μ and σ from a normal plot, although that can be done. Remembering from Chapter 3 that we can always transform a random variable X where $X \sim N(\mu, \sigma^2)$ into a random variable Z where $Z \sim N(0, 1)$, we wish to determine what the z-values would be if the sample data were *exactly* normally distributed. We should not expect the sample data to be exactly normally distributed, however, as there will be sampling variability even if the population was normally distributed. Thus, even when the latter is true, there will generally not be an exact linear relationship between the sample values and the theoretical z-values, but when they are plotted against each other the result should be something close to a straight line.

We will define a plotting position p_i for the ith ordered observation as $p_i = (i - 0.5)/n$ where n is the number of observations. (It might seem more logical to use i/n, which would then give the exact fraction of the sample values that are less than or equal to the ith ordered value, but when $i = n$ the fraction would be 1.0, and the z-value that corresponds to an area of 1.0 under the standard normal curve is plus infinity, i.e., not a real number.) We then compute the z-value that would correspond to a cumulative area of p_i under the standard normal curve. These z-values are sometimes called "inverse (standard) normal values," and could be obtained (approximately) by interpolating in Table B. For example, $p_1 = (1 - 0.5)/10 = 0.05$ corresponds to $z = -1.645$. The other values are given in Table 11.3. (It should be noted that other expressions for p_i are also used, but they differ very little from what is given here.)

We can observe that the differences between the z-values are not always equal for constant differences between the sample values (e.g., the difference

Table 11.3 Values for a Normal Probability Plot

Sample Value	p	z
8	.05	−1.645
10	.15	−1.036
12	.25	−0.674
14	.35	−0.385
15	.45	−0.126
15	.55	0.126
16	.65	0.385
18	.75	0.674
19	.85	1.036
20	.95	1.645

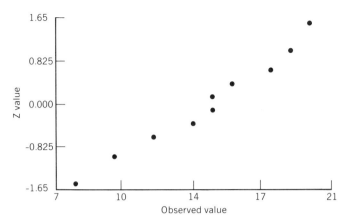

Figure 11.6 Normal probability plot of the data in Table 11.3.

between 8 and 10 is the same as the difference between 10 and 12, but the differences in the corresponding z-values are unequal.) Thus, we will not obtain a straight line when we plot the sample values against the z-values, but closer observation of the differences between adjacent pairs for all 10 numbers reveals that it should be fairly close to a straight line. The actual plot is shown in Figure 11.6. A variation of the normal plot is the half-normal plot (Daniel, 1959), which utilizes the half-normal (also called *folded normal*) distribution, with only positive z-values being used. See also Zahn (1975a, b).

11.6 SCATTER PLOT

The graphical methods discussed to this point in the chapter are applicable to one-dimensional data (i.e., one variable). When bivariate data are to be graphed, the most commonly used display is a *scatter plot*. (A basic scatter plot was discussed in Chapter 2; variations of the basic plot are also discussed in this section.) Consider the hypothetical data in Table 11.4, which are assumed to be for a large company that has recently initiated a quality improvement program. A scatter plot of "cost of training" vs. "number of employees trained" might be expected to show points that virtually form a straight line, so that points that deviate from that pattern might require further investigation. The scatter plot is shown in Figure 11.7. (Note that the horizontal axis has a wider scale than the vertical axis. This is done to produce horizontal separation of the points. A wider vertical scale would have produced more vertical separation.) From the plot we can

Table 11.4 Data for Quality Improvement Program

Month	Number of Employees Trained (000)	Cost of Training (000)
January	12	23
February	10	19
March	10	27
April	11	20
May	9	15
June	6	10
July	8	14
August	5	8
September	6	9
October	3	5
November	2	3
December	2	4

see rather clearly that there is one point that does not fit in with the others, namely, the point that corresponds to March. (One way to illustrate that it represents the figures for March will be explained shortly.) Perhaps during that month there was a deviation from the usual training program in that outside consultants were used. In any event, the point is highlighted by the scatter plot.

The label for each axis is oftentimes determined by whether or not one of the variables could be logically classified as the "dependent" variable. For example, in Figure 11.7 "cost of training" is dependent upon the

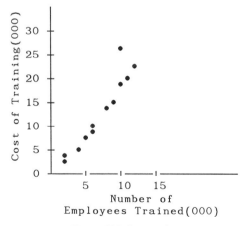

Figure 11.7 Scatter plot.

number of employees trained. Traditionally the dependent variable is placed on the vertical axis.

The scaling of the two axes is somewhat arbitrary, although we should use the same scaling for each axis when the data for each variable are of the same order of magnitude. When this is not the case, we should keep in mind that two variables that are not strongly related can often be depicted as having a linear relationship just by increasing the scale of the axes, which will tend to squeeze the data together. [See Cleveland, Diaconis, and McGill (1982).] Therefore, some thought needs to be given to the choice of scaling.

A *time sequence plot* is a type of scatter plot in that data on one variable are plotted against a second variable, time, where time could be in hours, days, months, etc. Thus, if either of the two variables used in Figure 11.7 was to be graphed against "month" (which would be on the horizontal axis), the result would be a time sequence plot. A control chart can also be thought of as a time sequence plot since sample number or time is generally used for the horizontal axis label. The use of time sequence plots with data from designed experiments is illustrated in Chapter 13.

A time sequence plot will often reveal peculiarities in a data set. It is an important graphical tool that should be routinely used whenever data have been collected over time, and the time order has been preserved. A convincing argument of the importance of this type of plot can be found in Ott (1975, pp. 34–36).

11.6.1 Variations of Scatter Plots

Although it was not a problem in Figure 11.7, when a sizable number of points are plotted in a scatter plot, some of the points will likely have the same value for the two variables. There are several ways to handle this situation. One approach is to use a number instead of the dot, where the number indicates how many values are at that point. When multiple values occur at different points in the same area, however, there will generally be a need to show multiple values using other symbolism. One such approach is to use lines through the dot to designate additional values at that point. For example, ⦙ might represent two values at one point, and ∗ might represent five values at one point. Such symbols are referred to as "sunflowers" in Chambers et al. (1983, p. 107), and the reader is referred to that text for more details.

Although a scatter plot is generally in the form of either a "half box" (two sides) as in Figure 11.7, or a full box where the points are enclosed in a box, Tufte (1983) claims that a range-frame is more informative. The latter is similar to a half box, but differs in that the two lines cover only the range

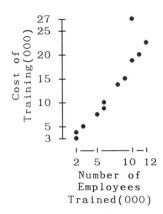

Figure 11.8 Range frame.

of the data, and thus do not meet. A range-frame for the data in Table 11.4 is given in Figure 11.8. Such a display is obviously more informative than the regular scatter plot in that the reader can easily observe that the cost of training ranged from 3,000 to 27,000, and the number of employees trained ranged from 2,000 to 12,000. Such information is not available from the conventional scatter plot in Figure 11.7. Additional information can be provided by using staggered line segments for the axes so as to show the quartiles and the median for each variable (Tufte, 1983).

11.7   PLOTTING THREE VARIABLES

Table 11.4 contains data on three variables, and the third variable, month, can be displayed using a slight alteration of Figure 11.7 or Figure 11.8. Specifically, the months could be numbered 1 through 12, and the numbers could be used in place of the dots. Another obvious possibility would be to use letters instead of numbers (e.g., ja could represent January).

Another technique for displaying three-dimensional data is a *casement display*, introduced by Tukey and Tukey (1983) and discussed by Chambers et al. (1983). A casement display is a set of two-variable scatter plots. If the third variable is discrete (and possibly categorical), a scatter plot is produced for each value of that variable, and the plots assembled in logical order. If the third variable is continuous, intervals for that variable would be constructed and the scatter plots then produced.

A similar technique introduced by Tukey and Tukey (1981) is a *draftsman's display*, which is the set of the three two-variable scatter plots arranged in a particular manner.

A multi-vari chart is a graphical device that is helpful in assessing variability due to three or more factors. This should not be confused with the multivariate control charts that were discussed in Chapter 9. Seder (1950) presented the multi-vari chart and gave several examples. The chart is essentially a way of presenting analysis of variance data in graphical form, thus making it more easily understood by a quality control engineer. (Analysis of variance is covered in Chapter 13, and another alternative to analysis of variance is presented in Chapter 16.)

11.8 DISPLAYING MORE THAN THREE VARIABLES

Much of the work that has been done on the display of four or more variables has been motivated by Chernoff (1973) who introduced the concept of faces for displaying multivariate data. For example, the following two faces

would represent multivariate data that differ only on the variable represented by the mouth.

Other methods for displaying many variables include a *star plot* in which the length of each ray of a star would represent the value of each of the variables. This is essentially the same idea as a *glyph* (Anderson, 1960), which has also been called a metroglyph. There are various other techniques for displaying multivariate data, including the use of *weathervanes* and *trees*. These various methods are discussed in some detail in Chambers et al. (1983) and in Chapter 9 of Wadsworth, Stephens, and Godfrey (1986). Boardman (1985) discusses variations of some of these methods that can be used in plotting hourly data.

11.9 PLOTS TO AID IN TRANSFORMING DATA

One important function of graphical methods is to provide the user of statistical methods with some insight into how data might be transformed so as to simplify the analysis. Assume that we are provided with data as in Table 11.5. If we graph these data in a scatter plot, we obtain the plot shown in Figure 11.9. Notice that only a small fraction of the horizontal axis is used with this scaling convention. Assume that our objective is to

Table 11.5 Sample Data

Y	X
9	3
15	4
24	5
3	2
36	6
65	8

transform Y and/or X so that we have approximately a linear relationship between the new variables that is of the form $Y^* = mX^* + b$.

We can see from Figure 11.9 that Y increases sharply as X approaches 10. How do you think the plot would have looked if the 10 on the horizontal axis had been placed at the end of the line that represents that axis? The result would be that the curve would not only be bent down considerably, but it would also appear to be straightened somewhat. The reason is that 1 unit on the horizontal scale would equal roughly 6 units on the vertical scale, and the average ratio of Y to X is $4.7 : 1$ as X varies from 2 to 8. The scatter plot with this new scaling is shown in Figure 11.10. This plot gives the false impression that there is approximately a linear relationship between Y and X, but we have not transformed either Y or X so the relationship has not changed. If we let $Y^* = \sqrt{Y}$ and $X^* = X$ (i.e., no transformation of X) we will bend the curve down by virtue of shortening the vertical axis. This will produce the data given in Table 11.6 and the scatter plot given in Figure 11.11. Although there is not much difference between the scatter plots in Figure 11.10 and Figure 11.11, there is

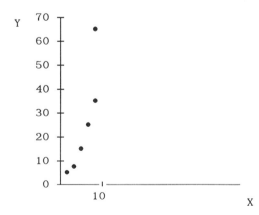

Figure 11.9 Scatter plot of data in Table 11.5.

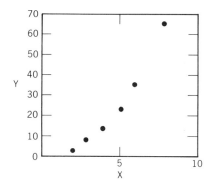

Figure 11.10 Scatter plot with increased horizontal scale.

Table 11.6 Transformed Data

$Y^* = \sqrt{Y}$	$X^* = X$
3	3
3.87	4
4.90	5
1.73	2
6	6
8.06	8

obviously a considerable difference in the values of the variables plotted on the vertical axis. The scale of the vertical axis in Figure 11.11 is appropriate since the values of Y^* are virtually the same as the corresponding values of X, so that if the line were extended to the origin it would form approximately a 45° line, which is what results when two variables have identical values. This, of course, is not to suggest that equal scales should always be

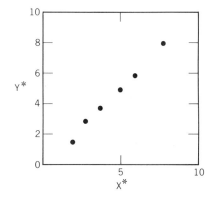

Figure 11.11 Scatter plot with transformed data.

used for the two axes as with many sets of data that will not be possible. Rather, it should be done whenever possible and practical.

The use of transformations to straighten out curves and for other purposes is discussed in detail by Mosteller and Tukey (1977), Velleman and Hoaglin (1981), Box and Cox (1964), Emerson and Stoto (1983), and Emerson (1983).

SUMMARY

Within the past decade or so many new and powerful graphical methods have been developed. Some of these are simple paper-and-pencil techniques, although others essentially require the use of a computer. With the increasing sophistication of computing devices, there is no reason why these superior techniques should not be used.

Old standbys such as histograms and scatter plots still have value, although stem-and-leaf displays are more informative than histograms, and can be used for small-to-moderate amounts of data. Similarly, a conventional scatter plot can be modified in accordance with the suggestions of Tufte (1983) so as to make it more informative. The latter is an excellent treatise on the construction of good graphical displays, including the type of displays often found in newspapers and other types of "nonstatistical" publications. The text by Chambers et al. (1983) is another excellent reference that, on the other hand, emphasizes "statistical graphics" (e.g., probability plotting) rather than general principles in constructing graphical displays. The reader interested in additional reading is referred to these two books, primarily, as well as to the other references cited in this chapter.

REFERENCES

Anderson, E. (1960). A semigraphical method for the analysis of complex problems. *Technometrics* 2(3): 387–391 (August). (Originally published in *Proceedings of the National Academy of Sciences* (1957). *13*: 923–927.)

Boardman, T. J. (1985). The use of simple graphics to study hourly data with several variables. In R. D. Snee, L. B. Hare, and J. R. Trout, eds. *Experiments in Industry: Design, Analysis and Interpretation of Results*. Milwaukee: Quality Press.

Box, G. E. P., and D. R. Cox (1964). An analysis of transformations. *Journal of the Royal Statistical Society, Series B 26*(2): 211–243: Discussion: pp. 244–252.

Box, G. E. P., W. G. Hunter, and J. S. Hunter (1978). *Statistics for Experimenters*. New York: Wiley.

Chambers, J. M., W. S. Cleveland, B. Kleiner, and P. A. Tukey (1983). *Graphical Methods for Data Analysis*. Boston: Duxbury Press.

Chernoff, H. (1973). The use of faces to represent points in K-dimensional space graphically. *Journal of the American Statistical Association 68*(342): 361–368 (June).

Cleveland, W. S., P. Diaconis, and R. McGill (1982). Variables on scatterplots look more highly correlated when the scales are increased. *Science 216*(4550): 1138–1141 (June).

Daniel, C. (1959). Use of half-normal plots in interpreting factorial two-level experiments. *Technometrics 1*(4): 311–341 (November).

Emerson, J. D. (1983). Mathematical aspects of transformation. In D. C. Hoaglin, F. Mosteller, and J. W. Tukey, eds. *Understanding Robust and Exploratory Data Analysis*, Chapter 8. New York: Wiley.

Emerson, J. D., and D. C. Hoaglin (1983). Stem-and-leaf displays. In D. C. Hoaglin, F. Mosteller, and J. W. Tukey, eds. *Understanding Robust and Exploratory Data Analysis*, Chapter 1. New York: Wiley.

Emerson, J. D., and M. A. Stoto (1983). Transforming data. In D. C. Hoaglin, F. Mosteller, and J. W. Tukey, eds. *Understanding Robust and Exploratory Data Analysis*, Chapter 4. New York: Wiley.

Godfrey, A. B. (1985). Training and education in quality and reliability—A modern approach. *Communications in Statistics, Part A (Theory and Methods) 14*(11): 2621–2638.

Heyes, G. B. (1985). The box plot. *Quality Progress 18*(12): 12–17 (December).

Huff, D. (1954). *How to Lie with Statistics*. New York: Norton.

Ishikawa, K. (1976). *Guide to Quality Control*. Hong Kong: Asian Productivity Organization, Nordica International Limited. (Available in the United States from UNIPUB, New York, New York.)

Mosteller, F., and J. W. Tukey (1977). *Data Analysis and Regression*. Reading, MA: Addison-Wesley.

Nelson, L. S. (1976). Constructing normal probability paper. *Journal of Quality Technology 8*(1): 56–57 (January).

Ott, E. R. (1975). *Process Quality Control*. New York: McGraw-Hill.

Seder, L. A. (1950). Diagnosis with diagrams—Part I. *Industrial Quality Control 6*(4): 11–19 (January).

Tufte, E. R. (1983). *The Visual Display of Quantitative Information*. Cheshire, CT: Graphics Press.

Tukey, J. W. (1977). *Exploratory Data Analysis*. Reading, MA: Addison-Wesley.

Tukey, J. W., and P. A. Tukey (1983). Some graphics for studying four-dimensional data. *Computer Science and Statistics: Proceedings of the 14th Symposium on the Interface*, pp. 60–66. New York: Springer-Verlag.

Tukey, P. A., and J. W. Tukey (1981). Graphical display of data sets in three or more dimensions. In V. Barnett, ed. *Interpreting Multivariate Data*, Chapters 10, 11, and 12. Chichester, U.K.: Wiley.

Velleman, P. V., and D. C. Hoaglin (1981). *ABC of EDA*. Boston: Duxbury Press.

Wadsworth, H. M., K. S. Stephens, and A. B. Godfrey (1986). *Modern Methods for Quality Control and Improvement*. New York: Wiley.

Zahn, D. A. (1975a). Modifications of and revised critical values for the half-normal plot. *Technometrics 17*(2): 189–200 (May).

Zahn, D. A. (1975b). An empirical study of the half-normal plot. *Technometrics 17*(2): 201–211 (May).

EXERCISES

1. If 500 numbers are to be grouped into classes, how many classes will be used if the "power of 2" rule is applied?

2. To see how a normal probability plot would look for nonnormal data, consider the following data sets.

(a) Uniform (0, 1) ($n = 20$)	(b) t_{30} ($n = 20$)	(c) χ^2_5 ($n = 20$)
0.2639	−0.0674	8.1278
0.6985	0.2307	1.0846
0.1529	−0.0616	6.2232
0.5760	−0.7760	2.8507
0.2816	−0.5425	2.4717
0.5663	−1.0136	2.7880
0.9196	−0.8606	6.8144
0.7045	−0.2912	18.2239
0.6802	−0.6809	3.6573
0.2446	0.1260	2.4020
0.7704	0.3174	3.1241
0.9092	1.1917	6.6827
0.2409	1.6762	7.3324
0.1398	1.4463	3.5686
0.2363	−2.3747	3.9961
0.3464	0.3117	9.1297
0.2449	0.7305	7.0888
0.1580	−0.7936	3.3413
0.3487	−1.4877	5.4827
0.6722	−0.0027	3.3195

Construct a normal probability plot for each of these distributions, preferably by computer or using normal probability paper. [Note: A uniform $(0, 1)$ distribution is flat and graphs as a unit square, the t distribution was covered in Chapter 3, and a chi-square distribution with five degrees of freedom is skewed (i.e., has a long tail) to the right.]

3. The following 20 numbers were generated from a normal distribution with $\mu = 20$ and $\sigma = 4$.

11.5360	22.0665	16.0396	18.8414
11.4074	16.7529	22.8638	18.3333
18.2744	23.4409	12.9792	17.8925
27.2872	26.7256	20.9274	18.3116
21.1735	18.8092	20.5048	18.1904

   a. Construct a boxplot and identify any outliers.

   b. Estimate σ using the values corresponding to the top and bottom of the box. How does your estimate compare with the known value of σ?

4. Construct a stem-and-leaf display using each of the data sets in Problem #2. Does the general shape of each display conform to what you would expect considering the nature of the distributions in #2? (Use only the integer part of the number and the first decimal place.)

5. Explain the advantages of a range frame over a conventional scatter plot?

6. Would it make any sense to construct a histogram for any of the data sets in Problem #2?

7. Construct a dot diagram for the data in (b) of #2. What does the diagram tell you relative to what you might have expected?

CHAPTER 12

Linear Regression

Regression analysis is one of the two most widely used statistical procedures; the other is analysis of variance, which is covered in Chapter 13.

There are various procedures within the broad area of linear regression that have direct application in quality improvement work, and a regression approach is the standard way of analyzing data from designed experiments.

The word "regression" has a much different meaning outside the realm of statistics than it does within it; literally it means to revert back to a previous state or form. In the field of statistics, the word was coined by Sir Francis Galton (1822–1911) who observed that children's heights regressed toward the average height of the population rather than digressing from it. (This is essentially unrelated to the present-day use of regression, however.)

In this chapter we present regression as a statistical tool that can be used for (1) description, (2) prediction, and (3) estimation. A regression control chart is also illustrated.

12.1 SIMPLE LINEAR REGRESSION

In (univariate) regression there is always a single "dependent" variable, and one or more "independent" variables. For example, we might think of the number of nonconforming units produced within a particular company each month as being dependent upon the amount of time that is devoted to maintaining control charts and using other statistical tools. In this case the amount of time (in minutes, say) would be the single independent variable. *Simple* is used to denote the fact that a single independent variable is being used.

Linear does not have quite the meaning that one would expect. Specifically, it does not necessarily mean that the relationship between the dependent variable and the independent variable is a straight line relationship. The equation

$$Y = \beta_0 + \beta_1 X + \varepsilon \tag{12.1}$$

is a linear regression equation, but so is the equation

$$Y = \beta_0' + \beta_1' X + \beta_{11} X^2 + \varepsilon' \tag{12.2}$$

A regression equation is linear if it is linear in the parameters (the betas), and both of these equations satisfy that condition.

If the ε in Eq. (12.1) was absent, the equation would then be in the general form of the equation for a straight line that is given in algebra books. Its presence indicates that there is not an exact linear relationship between X and Y.

Regression analysis is not used for variables that have an exact linear relationship, as there would be no need for it. For example, the equation

$$F = \frac{9}{5}C + 32 \tag{12.3}$$

expresses temperature in Fahrenheit as a function of temperature measured on the Celsius scale. Thus, F can be determined exactly for any given value of C. This is not the case for Y in Eq. (12.1), however, as β_0 and β_1 are generally unknown and therefore must be estimated. Even if they were known [as is the case with the constants 9/5 and 32 in Eq. (12-3)], the presence of ε in Eq. (12.1) would still prevent Y from being determined exactly for a given value of X.

The ε is generally thought of as an error term. This does not mean that a mistake is being made, however; it is merely a symbol used to indicate the lack of an exact relationship between X and Y.

The first step in any regression analysis with a single X is to plot the data. This would be done to see if there is evidence of a linear relationship between X and Y as well as for other purposes such as checking for outlying observations (outliers).

Assume that Y denotes the number of nonconforming units produced each month and X represents the amount of time, in hours, devoted to using control charts and other statistical procedures each month. Assume that data from a company's records for the preceding 12 months are given in Table 12.1.

We can see from Table 12.1 that there is apparently a moderately strong relationship between X and Y. Specifically, as X increases Y decreases,

Table 12.1 Quality Improvement Data

Month	X Time Devoted to Quality Improvement (Hours)	Y Number of Nonconforming Units
January	56	20
February	58	19
March	55	20
April	62	16
May	63	15
June	68	14
July	66	15
August	68	13
September	70	10
October	67	13
November	72	9
December	74	8

although we can see that the relationship is far from being exact. We can obtain a better idea of the strength of the relationship by simply plotting the data in the form of a scatter plot, which was illustrated in Chapter 11. The scatter plot is given in Figure 12.1.

As noted in Chapter 11, there are a number of ways to make a scatter plot, and some attention needs to be given to the scaling of the axes. If, for

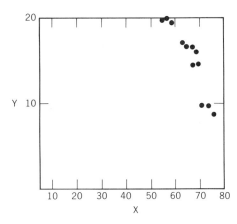

Figure 12.1 Scatter plot of the data in Table 12.1.

example, the months had been numbered and the numbers used in place of the dots, the plot would then show that the amount of time devoted to quality improvement is generally increasing from month to month, and that the number of nonconforming units produced each month is simultaneously declining. The intent with Figure 12.1 is to simply show the strength of the linear relationship, however.

Since there is evidence of a fairly strong relationship between X and Y, we could develop a regression equation for the purpose of predicting Y from X. In essence, we will be fitting a line through the center of the points in Figure 12.1. But then what do we mean by "center"? Minimizing the sum of the (signed) deviations from each point to the line will not uniquely determine the line, but minimizing the sum of the *squared* distances will do so. This is known as the *method of least squares*, which is the most commonly used method for determining a regression equation, although there are several other methods. Thus, $\sum_{i=1}^{n} \varepsilon_i^2$ is to be minimized where $\varepsilon_i = Y_i - \beta_0 - \beta_1 X_i$.

It can be shown using simple methods of calculus that for a sample of size n, minimizing $\sum_{i=1}^{n} \varepsilon_i^2$ produces two equations, which when solved simultaneously provide estimators for β_0 and β_1. These least squares estimators are of the general form

$$\hat{\beta}_1 = \frac{\Sigma XY - (\Sigma X)(\Sigma Y)/n}{\Sigma X^2 - (\Sigma X)^2/n}$$

and

$$\hat{\beta}_0 = \bar{Y} - \hat{\beta}_1 \bar{X}$$

Obviously $\hat{\beta}_1$ would have to be computed first since it is used in computing $\hat{\beta}_0$.

Using the values in Table 12.1 we obtain

$$\hat{\beta}_1 = \frac{10896 - (779)(172)/12}{50991 - (779)^2/12}$$

$$= \frac{-269.67}{420.92}$$

$$= -0.64$$

and

$$\hat{\beta}_0 = 14.33 - (-0.64)(64.92)$$

$$= 55.92$$

(Note: Roundoff error can be a troublesome problem in regression analysis. The calculated values are displayed here using two decimal places, but the intermediate calculations are not rounded off to two places. In general, such rounding should not be performed for any statistical analysis, but particularly not for regression analysis in which serious problems can ensue.)

The *prediction equation* is of the general form

$$\hat{Y} = \hat{\beta}_0 + \hat{\beta}_1 X$$

so that with these data

$$\hat{Y} = 55.92 - 0.64 X$$

This prediction equation could then be used to predict future values of Y (say, for next year) for given values of X. The general idea would be to predict what is impossible or impractical to observe. For example, if an admissions committee is having a difficult time trying to decide whether or not to admit a student to a college, it would be helpful to be able to predict reasonably well what his or her grade point average would be at the end of 4 years. The student's Y would thus not be observable, but it could be predicted by a prediction equation obtained by using the records of previous students. (Many colleges and universities actually use regression analysis for this purpose.)

For the data in Table 12.1, Y could be observed, but that would require 100% inspection. Thus, it would be preferable to predict Y if that could be done with accuracy.

The prediction equation could also be used for descriptive purposes. With $\hat{\beta}_1 = -0.064$ we can state that, on the average, there is approximately a decrease of 0.64 nonconforming units for every additional hour devoted to quality improvement.

We might attempt to interpret $\hat{\beta}_0$ in a similar manner, that is, we could claim that there should be about 56 nonconforming units if no time was devoted to quality improvement. The problem with this assertion is that X ranges from 55 to 74, so the interval does not even come close to containing zero.

In general, a prediction equation with a single X should be used only for values of X that either fall within the interval of values used in producing the equation, or else are only slightly outside the interval. The user who employs a prediction equation for values well outside that interval is guilty of *extrapolation*. See Hahn (1977) for a discussion of the potential hazards of extrapolation.

12.2 WORTH OF THE PREDICTION EQUATION

It is easy to obtain a prediction equation, but its worth needs to be assessed before it is used. If it can be used to predict reasonably well the values of Y used in developing the equation, then it stands to reason that future, unobservable values of Y should also be well predicted.

Using the 12 values of X to obtain the corresponding predicted values of Y, the predicted and observed values are given, along with their difference in Table 12.2.

Remembering that Y must be an integer so that $\hat{Y}$ would be rounded off to the nearest integer, we can see that the predicted values are quite close to the observed values. We can also observe that the prediction is poorest in the middle of the year. This is because there is "pure error" in the middle of the year due to the fact that the X values are the same in June and August, but the Y values are different. This causes the two points to plot vertically on a scatter plot. A regression line cannot be vertical (since the slope would be undefined), so points that plot vertically are said to constitute pure error since they cannot be accommodated by a regression line.

Table 12.2 Predicted Y Values

Y	$\hat{Y}$	$Y - \hat{Y}$
20	20.04	-0.04
19	18.76	0.24
20	20.68	-0.68
16	16.20	-0.20
15	15.56	-0.56
14	12.35	1.65
15	13.64	1.36
13	12.35	0.65
10	11.07	-1.07
13	13.00	0.00
9	9.79	-0.79
8	8.51	-0.51

In spite of the presence of pure error, the predicted values are obviously close to the observed values. A comparison of the two sets of values is, of course, subjective so what is needed is an objective means of assessing the worth of a prediction equation. The most commonly used measure is R^2, which can be written as

$$R^2 = 1 - \frac{\Sigma(Y - \hat{Y})^2}{\Sigma(Y - \overline{Y})^2} \tag{12.4}$$

We want the numerator of the fraction to be as small as possible. If the numerator were zero then R^2 would equal 1.0. This would mean that the observed and predicted values were all the same. This will not happen, of course, but we would like to see R^2 as close to 1.0 as possible. There is no dividing line between good and bad R^2 values, although values in excess of 0.90 will generally indicate that the equation has good predictive ability.

The smallest possible value of R^2 is zero. This can be seen as follows. Since $\hat{\beta}_0 = \overline{Y} - \hat{\beta}_1\overline{X}$, $\hat{Y}$ can be written as

$$\hat{Y} = \overline{Y} - \hat{\beta}_1\overline{X} + \hat{\beta}_1 X$$

$$= \overline{Y} + \hat{\beta}_1(X - \overline{X})$$

If there was no relationship between X and Y, we would expect $\hat{\beta}_1$ to be close to zero. If $\hat{\beta}_1 = 0$ then $\hat{Y} = \overline{Y}$ and substituting $\overline{Y}$ for $\hat{Y}$ in the equation for R^2 produces $R^2 = 0$. Furthermore, substituting $\overline{Y} + \hat{\beta}_1(X - \overline{X})$ for $\hat{Y}$ in Eq. (12.4) and expanding the expression would show that the numerator could never be larger than the denominator.

For the present example

$$R^2 = 1 - \frac{7.90}{180.67} = 0.96$$

This means that 96% of the variation in Y is explained (accounted for) by using X to predict Y.

12.3   ASSUMPTIONS

To this point the only assumption that needed to be made is that the true (unknown) relationship between X and Y can be adequately represented by the model given in Eq. (12.1). That in itself is an important assumption, however, as Box and Newbold (1971) showed what can happen when that model is inappropriately used. Specifically, Coen, Gomme, and Kendall (1969) demonstrated a strong relationship between stock prices and car sales seven quarters earlier. Unfortunately, the $Y - \hat{Y}$ values were correlated over time, and when Box and Newbold fit an appropriate model that accounted for the error structure, they showed that no significant relationship existed between the two variables.

This example is also discussed in Box, Hunter, and Hunter (1978, p. 496).

Plotting the residuals (the $Y - \hat{Y}$ values) is thus an important part of what is referred to as *model criticism*, i.e., checking on whether or not the postulated model is an appropriate model. If the model is appropriate, the residuals should have no discernible pattern when plotted against time, $\hat{Y}$, or any other variable. This applies not just to regression models, but to statistical models in general, including time-series models and analysis of variance models. For example, the use of residual analysis in analyzing data from designed experiments is illustrated in Chapter 13.

The use of an appropriate model thus implies that the errors should be independent. (The residuals are, strictly speaking, not independent since they must sum to zero when β_0 is included in the model, but they are used to check the assumption of independent errors.)

If hypothesis tests and confidence intervals are to be used, it is also necessary to assume that the errors are approximately normally distributed. The mean of the errors should be zero and the variance should be constant so that it does not depend upon X.

These assumptions can be conveniently represented by

$$\varepsilon \sim \text{NID}(0, \sigma^2)$$

This means that the errors are independent (ID) and (approximately) normally (N) distributed with a mean of zero and a constant variance of σ^2.

12.4 CHECKING ASSUMPTIONS THROUGH RESIDUAL PLOTS

In simple linear regression the residuals should be plotted against (1) X or $\hat{Y}$, (2) time (if the time order of the data has been preserved), and (3) any other variable that an experimenter decides might be important. For the first type of plot, the desired configuration is along the lines of what is shown in Figure 12.2. Specifically, we would like to see all of the points close to the midline (which would cause R^2 to be close to 1.0), and form a

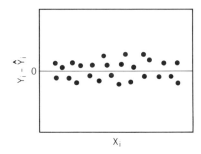

Figure 12.2 Residual plot.

tight cluster that can be enclosed in a rectangle. A rectangular configuration would provide evidence that the error variance is constant.

If there were any points that were far removed from the other points, such points might be labeled (residual) outliers, or they could represent data that were recorded incorrectly.

If Eq. (12.1) is used when a time-series model should have been used, a plot of the residuals against time would reveal a nonrandom pattern such as a sequence of several positive residuals followed by several negative residuals.

If the error variance either increases or decreases as X increases, this could also be detected by plotting the residuals against X. Such a problem can often be remedied by a transformation of X. If transforming X does not solve the problem, then *weighted least squares* would have to be used [see Draper and Smith (1981, p. 111)].

Residual plots can also be used for checking the assumption that the postulated model is an appropriate model. If the plot of the residuals against X was in the form of a parabola, then an X^2 term would probably be needed in the model as in Eq. (12.2). Similarly, if the plot of the residuals against an omitted variable exhibited a linear trend, then a linear term in that variable should be added to the model.

12.5   CONFIDENCE INTERVALS AND HYPOTHESIS TEST

As discussed in Chapter 3, confidence intervals are generally more informative than hypothesis tests. Both can be used in simple linear regression as long as the assumption of approximate normality of the error terms is plausible. If not, an experimenter can choose between, say, robust regression and nonparametric regression. See Draper and Smith (1981) for a discussion of the former and Conover (1980) for a discussion of the latter. Iteratively reweighted least squares is another possibility. It is an alternative to robust regression when the error term has a distribution that is believed to be markedly nonnormal. See Box and Draper (1986).

Confidence intervals on the regression parameters are of the general form

$$\hat{\beta}_i \pm t\, s_{\hat{\beta}_i}$$

A confidence interval for β_0 is of the form

$$\hat{\beta}_0 \pm t\, s\sqrt{\Sigma X^2 / n\Sigma(X - \overline{X})^2}$$

and for β_1 the general form is

$$\hat{\beta}_1 \pm t\,\frac{s}{\sqrt{\Sigma(X - \overline{X})^2}}$$

where, for both expressions, $s = \sqrt{\Sigma(Y - \hat{Y})^2 / (n - 2)}$ and $t = t_{\alpha/2,\,n-2}$.

We certainly want the confidence interval for β_1 to not include zero. If it did include zero, the prediction equation would be of little value, and a test of the hypothesis that $\beta_1 = 0$ would not be rejected.

For the data in Table 12.1 we should be inclined to assume that the interval does not come close to including zero since the prediction equation has high predictive ability. (The reader is asked to show this in Exercise 1.)

A confidence interval for β_0 is sometimes of value even though it is just the constant term. It is generally not desirable to test the hypothesis that $\beta_0 = 0$ and use the outcome of that test to determine whether or not the constant term would be used in the model. Only rarely would we want to use a regression equation that does not have a constant term. If we knew that $Y = 0$ when $X = 0$ *and* we were interested in predicting Y when X is close to zero, then we might omit the constant term and use what is known as *regression through the origin*.

The hypothesis test for $\beta_1 = 0$ is of the form

$$t = \frac{\hat{\beta}_1}{s_{\hat{\beta}_1}}$$

where, as previously stated, $s_{\hat{\beta}_1} = s / \sqrt{\Sigma(X - \overline{X})^2}$.

12.6 PREDICTION INTERVAL FOR Y

In addition to obtaining $\hat{Y}$ for a given value of X (to be denoted in this and the next section as X_0), an experimenter could construct a prediction interval around $\hat{Y}$. The general form is

$$\hat{Y} \pm ts\sqrt{1 + \frac{1}{n} + \frac{(X_0 - \bar{X})^2}{\Sigma(X - \bar{X})^2}}$$

where s is as previously defined, and t is $t_{\alpha/2,\,n-2}$ for a $100(1 - \alpha)\%$ confidence interval.

To illustrate, for the data in Table 12.1, $s = \sqrt{7.90/10} = 0.89$ and for a 95% prediction interval $t_{.025,\,10} = 2.228$. Therefore, for $X_0 = 65$ the interval is obtained as

$$14.28 \pm 2.228(0.89)\sqrt{1 + \frac{1}{12} + \frac{(65 - 64.92)^2}{420.92}}$$

$$= 14.28 \pm 2.06$$

so that the lower limit is 12.22 and the upper limit is 16.34.

It should be noted that this is not a confidence interval since confidence intervals are constructed only for parameters and Y is not a parameter. The general interpretation for a prediction interval is the same as for a confidence interval, however. That is, we are $100(1 - \alpha)\%$ confident that the prediction interval that is to be constructed will contain Y.

A prediction interval for Y is related to a regression control chart, which is discussed in the next section.

12.7   REGRESSION CONTROL CHART

Mandel (1969) presents a regression control chart and provides a number of administrative applications. The general concept differs only slightly from a prediction interval for Y.

In fact, the assumptions for a regression control chart are exactly the same as those for simple linear regression. The general idea is to monitor the dependent variable using a control chart approach.

The centerline on the chart is at $\hat{Y} = \hat{\beta}_0 + \hat{\beta}_1 X$. Mandel (1969) provides an argument for obtaining the control limits from

$$\hat{Y} \pm 2s \tag{12.5}$$

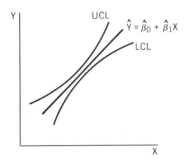

Figure 12.3 Regression control chart with limits obtained from Eq. (12.6).

rather than from

$$\hat{Y} \pm 2s \sqrt{1 + \frac{1}{n} + \frac{(X_0 - \overline{X})^2}{\Sigma(X - \overline{X})^2}} \qquad (12.6)$$

which would seem to be the natural choice for obtaining the control limits.

The argument given is that the use of control limits obtained from $\hat{Y} \pm 2s$ will provide tighter control for extreme values of X_0, which is where tight control is generally desired.

Control lines obtained from Eq. (12.6) will be curved since the value of the expression under the radical depends upon the value of X_0. For values of X_0 that are equidistant from $\overline{X}$, the control lines will be the same distance apart as in Figure 12.3.

The control lines in Figure 12.3 will be the closest when $X_0 = \overline{X}$. Even at that point, however, the lines will be further apart than the lines obtained using Eq. (12.5).

For the data in Table 12.1, the most extreme value of X relative to $\overline{X} = 64.92$ is 55. Using Eq. (12.6) with $X_0 = 55$, the values on the two control lines would be obtained from

$$20.72 \pm 2.04$$

whereas using Eq. (12.5) the values would be

$$20.72 \pm 1.78$$

In addition to the administrative applications described in Mandel (1969), regression control charts have also been used for tool wear, as have acceptance control charts (described in Chapter 5).

12.8   INVERSE REGRESSION

Another important application of simple linear regression for quality improvement is in the area of calibration.

Assume that two measuring tools are available—one is quite accurate but expensive to use and the other is not as expensive but also not as accurate. If the measurements obtained from the two devices are highly correlated (perhaps each pair of measurements differs by almost a constant amount), then the measurement that would have been made using the expensive measuring device could be predicted fairly well from the measurement that is actually obtained using the less expensive device.

Let

$$Y = \text{measurement from the less expensive device}$$

and

$$X = \text{measurement from the accurate device}$$

The general idea is to first regress Y on X in the usual manner to obtain the prediction equation

$$\hat{Y} = \hat{\beta}_0 + \hat{\beta}_1 X$$

If we then "solve'" for X we obtain

$$X = (\hat{Y} - \hat{\beta}_0)/\hat{\beta}_1$$

What is being estimated (predicted) is X instead of Y, however, so for a known value of Y, Y_c, the equation is

$$\hat{X}_c = (Y_c - \hat{\beta}_0)/\hat{\beta}_1$$

Thus, the measurement that would have been obtained using the accurate measuring device is estimated (predicted) using a known measurement from the other device.

This approach has been termed the *classical estimation approach* to calibration. Krutchkoff (1967) reintroduced the concept of "inverse" regression to estimate X where X is regressed on Y. Thus,

$$\hat{X}_c^* = \hat{\beta}_0^* + \hat{\beta}_1^* Y_c$$

where the asterisks are used to signify that the estimated value of X_c and

Table 12.3 Data for Illustrating Inverse Regression

Y	X
2.3	2.4
2.5	2.6
2.4	2.5
2.8	2.9
2.9	3.0
2.6	2.7
2.4	2.5
2.2	2.3
2.1	2.2
2.7	2.7

the parameter estimates will be different from the estimates obtained using the classical approach.

The only way that $\hat{X}_c$ and $\hat{X}_c^*$ could have the same value would be if X and Y were perfectly correlated. Thus, when there is a strong relationship between X and Y, not only will the difference between $\hat{X}_c$ and $\hat{X}_c^*$ be essentially inconsequential, but we should also be able to do a good job of estimating the actual measurement.

To illustrate, assume that we have data as in Table 12.3. We can see that there is almost an exact relationship between X and Y. Specifically, $X = Y + 0.1$ for the first nine values, and $X = Y$ for the tenth value. If the true relationship between X and Y was well represented by these data, and if the measurements given for X differ hardly at all from the actual measurements, then it should be possible to accurately estimate X with Y, and thus accurately estimate the actual measurement.

For the regression of Y on X we obtain

$$\hat{Y} = -0.14375 + 1.021X$$

so that

$$\hat{X}_c = (Y_c + 0.14375)/1.021$$

Regressing X on Y produces

$$\hat{X}_c^* = 0.176 + 0.9655Y_c$$

where the coefficients are obtained by simply reversing the roles of X and Y in the computational formulas. At $Y_c = 2.2$ we obtain $\hat{X}_c = 2.296$ and

$\hat{X}_c^* = 2.300$, so, as expected, there is hardly any difference in the two values. It should also be noted that $X = 2.3$ when $Y = 2.2$ in Table 12.3.

For additional reading on inverse regression and the classical estimation approach to calibration in quality improvement the reader is referred to Crocker (1985).

12.9 MULTIPLE LINEAR REGRESSION

Multiple regression conjures up thoughts of a disease by one author who prefers to discuss "fitting equations to data," which is the title of a well-known text (Daniel and Wood, 1980). *Multiple* is used in this section to mean that there is more than one X, i.e., more than one independent variable.

The model for multiple linear regression is just an extension of the model for simple linear regression. Specifically, the model is

$$Y = \beta_0 + \beta_1 X_1 + \beta_2 X_2 + \cdots + \beta_k X_k + \varepsilon$$

for k independent variables, and the assumptions for the error term are the same as for simple regression.

Whereas the necessary calculations for simple regression can be easily performed by hand calculator, this is not true for multiple regression. For this reason and also because a detailed discussion of multiple regression is beyond the intended scope of this text, the computational formulas will not be illustrated here. Rather, the reader will be referred to other texts for the details as well as to software for handling multiple regression analyses.

12.10 ISSUES IN MULTIPLE REGRESSION

The user of multiple regression must ponder more questions than are faced when using simple regression. How many regressors (i.e., independent variables) should be used and which ones should be used? How does the user know when he is extrapolating beyond the experimental region when the region is multidimensional and cannot be easily pictured? Should alternatives to least squares be used, and, if so, when?

These and other questions will be addressed in this section.

In practice, there is generally more than one regressor that is highly correlated with a particular dependent variable. For example, a student's college grade point average (G.P.A.) could be predicted using his high school G.P.A., but there are other variables such as aptitude test scores which should be considered for inclusion in the prediction equation.

12.10.1 Variable Selection

It might seem as though the objective should be to include as many regressors in the prediction equation as are thought to be related to the dependent variable. In fact, this is the strategy that would be followed if an experimenter wanted to maximize R^2, as R^2 will virtually always increase (and can never decrease) when additional variables are added to a prediction equation.

A price would be paid for such a strategy, however, since $\text{Var}(\hat{Y})$ increases when new regressors are added, as was originally demonstrated by Walls and Weeks (1969).

Thus, the objective should be to essentially identify a point of diminishing returns such that adding additional regressors will create more harm [in terms of increasing $\text{Var}(\hat{Y})$] than good (in terms of increasing R^2).

A commonly used statistic for making this determination is the C_p statistic proposed by Mallows (1973). It is defined as

$$C_p = \frac{SSE_p}{\hat{\sigma}^2_{\text{full}}} - n + 2p$$

where p is the number of parameters in the model, SSE_p is the residual sum of squares [equal to $\Sigma(Y - \hat{Y})^2$], $\hat{\sigma}^2_{\text{full}}$ is the estimate of the error variance using all of the available regressors, and n is the sample size.

With k potential regressors there are $2^k - 1$ possible models (1023 when $k = 10$) and the C_p statistic can be used to allow the experimenter to focus attention on a small number of these possible models. Specifically, the idea is to look hard at those prediction equations for which C_p is small and is close to p. The final choice of a model from this group can then be made using other statistical considerations as well as possibly nonstatistical factors such as the cost of acquiring the data and personal preference.

Other methods that can be used for selecting regressors are discussed in Draper and Smith (1981).

12.10.2 Extrapolation

It is easy to determine whether or not extrapolation has occurred when there is only one regressor. This is not true when there are, say, five or six regressors. Weisberg (1980, p. 216) discusses the problem and presents two methods that can be used to determine if extrapolation has occurred.

12.10.3 Multicollinear Data

Problems occur when at least two of the regressors are related in some manner. For example, two of the regressors may be highly correlated (say, $r = .95$). This has the effect of inflating the variances of the least squares estimators, but it will generally have little effect on $\text{Var}(\hat{Y})$. Therefore, multicollinear data should be of no great concern if prediction is the objective, but it is another matter if the objective is estimation.

Solutions to the problem of multicollinear data include discarding one or more of the variables causing the multicollinearity. Another solution is to use ridge regression, which allows an experimenter to use all of the regressors that he may want to use, but in a manner different from least squares. [See, e.g., Hoerl and Kennard (1981).]

12.10.4 Residual Plots

Residual plots are used extensively in multiple regression, and for the same general purposes as in simple regression; that is, for checking on the model assumptions, and for determining if the model could be improved.

The number of necessary residual plots is, of course, much greater in multiple regression. The residuals should generally be plotted against $\hat{Y}$, each of the regressors, time (if possible), and any potential regressor that might later seem important. [Partial residual plots are often more valuable than regular residual plots, however, for determining appropriate transformations of the regressors. An example of this can be found in Gunst and Mason (1980, p. 251). Partial residuals to be plotted vs. the jth regressor ($j = 1, 2, \ldots, k$) are defined as $\ell_i + \hat{\beta}_j X_{ij}$, where ℓ_i is the ith residual and X_{ij} is the ith observation on regressor X_j.]

Residual plots virtually require the use of a computer, and Henderson and Velleman (1981) illustrate how a user can interact with a computer in developing a regression model.

12.10.5 Regression Diagnostics

It is desirable to be able to detect extreme observations that may represent data that have been recorded incorrectly, and also to detect observations that are much more influential than the other observations. Ideally, we would want each of the n observations to have equal influence in determining the coefficients of the regressors in a prediction equation, but this does not happen in general. Methods for detecting extreme observations and influential observations can be found in Belsley, Kuh, and Welsch (1980) and Cook and Weisberg (1982). See also Hocking (1983).

Invalid points can, of course, be discarded. Points of high influence can either be discarded or given less influence as in Krasker and Welsch (1982).

12.10.6 Transformations

A regression model can often be improved by transforming one or more of the regressors, and possibly the dependent variable as well. Logarithmic and other simple transformations can often improve the value of a prediction equation.

Transformations can also often be used to transform a nonlinear regression model into a linear one. For example, the nonlinear model

$$Y = \beta_0 \beta_1^X \varepsilon$$

can be transformed into a linear model by taking the logarithm of both sides of the equation so as to produce

$$\ln Y = \ln \beta_0 + X \ln \beta_1 + \ln \varepsilon$$

Simple linear regression could then be applied to the latter.

The reader is referred to Chapter 8 of Box and Draper (1986), and to Chapter 16 and the Appendix of Mosteller and Tukey (1977) for detailed information concerning the use of transformations.

12.11 SOFTWARE FOR REGRESSION

As with control charts, the user of regression analysis has a multitude of software from which to choose.

Mainframe packages such as the SAS® System, BMDP®, and Minitab (all of which also run on a PC) have excellent regression capabilities, and the same can be said of a number of other general purpose statistical software packages. The numerical accuracy for regression data of a variety of microcomputer statistical packages is assessed in a study conducted by Lesage and Simon (1985).

SUMMARY

The rudiments of regression analysis have been presented in this chapter, with an emphasis on regression tools that can be used in quality improvement, e.g., a regression control chart.

Multiple regression was treated somewhat briefly. This is because multiple regression analyses are generally performed on a computer, and also because a detailed exposition of multiple regression would be somewhat beyond the intended scope of this text.

There is a wealth of reading matter on multiple regression. Readers seeking a capsuled but more detailed account of multiple regression than what is provided here are referred to Ryan (1989). Readers seeking a complete account of all aspects of multiple regression (including nonlinear regression) are referred to Draper and Smith (1981).

Additional information on the use of multiple regression in quality improvement can be found in Hinchen (1968), Hotard and Jordan (1981), and Crocker (1985).

REFERENCES

Belsley, D. A., E. Kuh, and R. Welsch (1980). *Regression Diagnostics: Identifying Influential Data and Sources of Collinearity*. New York: Wiley.

Box, G. E. P., and N. R. Draper (1986). *Empirical Model Building and Response Surfaces*. New York: Wiley.

Box, G. E. P., W. G. Hunter, and J. S. Hunter (1978). *Statistics for Experimenters*. New York: Wiley.

Box, G. E. P., and P. Newbold (1971). Some comments on a paper by Coen, Gomme, and Kendall. *Journal of the Royal Statistical Society, Series A 134*(2): 229–240.

Coen, P. J., E. E. Gomme, and M. G. Kendall (1969). Lagged relationships in economic forecasting. *Journal of the Royal Statistical Society, Series A 132*(2): 133–152.

Conover, W. S. (1980). *Practical Nonparametric Statistics*, 2nd ed. New York: Wiley.

Cook, R. D., and S. Weisberg (1982). *Residuals and Influence in Regression*. New York: Chapman and Hall.

Crocker, D. C. (1985). How to use regression analysis in quality control. *Basic References in Quality Control: Statistical Techniques*, Vol. 9. Milwaukee: American Society for Quality Control.

Daniel, C., and F. S. Wood (1980). *Fitting Equations to Data*, 2nd ed. New York: Wiley.

Draper, N. R., and H. Smith (1981). *Applied Regression Analysis*, 2nd ed. New York: Wiley.

Gunst, R. F., and R. L. Mason (1980). *Regression Analysis and Its Application*. New York: Marcel Dekker.

Hahn, G. J. (1977). The hazards of extrapolation in regression analysis. *Journal of Quality Technology* 9(4): 159–165 (October).

Henderson, H. V. and P. F. Velleman (1981). Building multiple regression models interactively. *Biometrics* 37(2): 391–411 (June).

Hinchen, J. D. (1968). Multiple regression in process development. *Technometrics* 10(2): 257–269 (May).

Hocking, R. R. (1983). Developments in linear regression methodology: 1959–1982. *Technometrics* 25(3): 219–230; Discussion: pp. 230–244 (August).

Hoerl, A. E., and R. W. Kennard (1981). Ridge regression—1980 advances, algorithms, and applications. *Journal of Mathematical and Management Sciences* 1(1): 5–83.

Hotard, D. G., and J. D. Jordan (1981). Regression analysis is applied to improve product quality. *Industrial Engineering* 13(3): 68–75 (March).

Krasker, W. S., and R. E. Welsch (1982). Efficient bounded influence regression estimation. *Journal of the American Statistical Association* 77(379): 595–604 (September).

Krutchkoff, R. G. (1967). Classical and inverse regression methods of calibration. *Technometrics* 9(3): 425–439 (August).

Lesage, J. P., and S. D. Simon (1985). Numerical accuracy of statistical algorithms for microcomputers. *Computational Statistics and Data Analysis* 3(1): 47–57 (May).

Mallows, C. L. (1973). Some comments on C_p. *Technometrics* 15(4): 661–675 (November).

Mandel, B. J. (1969). The regression control chart. *Journal of Quality Technology* 1(1): 1–9 (January).

Mosteller, F., and J. W. Tukey (1977). *Data Analysis and Regression*. Reading, MA: Addison-Wesley.

Ryan, T. P. (1990). Linear regression. In H. M. Wadsworth, ed. *Handbook of Statistical Methods for Engineers and Physical Scientists*, Chapter 13. New York: McGraw-Hill.

Walls, R. C., and D. L. Weeks (1969). A note on the variance of a predicted response in regression. *American Statistician* 23(3): 24–26 (June).

Weisberg, S. (1980). *Applied Linear Regression*. New York: Wiley.

EXERCISES

1. Obtain a 95% confidence interval for β_1 using the data in Table 12.1. Notice that the interval does not come close to including zero. This means that we would reject the hypothesis that $\beta_1 = 0$, but it does not necessarily mean, in general, that the prediction equation has any value (i.e., R^2 could be small).

2. Regression data are often coded by subtracting the mean of each variable from the values of the respective variables. Consider the following coded data:

X	-3	-2	-1	0	1	2	3
Y	9	4	1	2	1	4	7

a. Construct a scatter plot of the data.

b. Does the scatter plot suggest a linear relationship?

c. Fit a linear regression equation and then plot the residuals against $\hat{Y}$.

d. Why does that plot have a parabolic shape?

e. What does this suggest about how the prediction equation should be modified?

3. Consider the following calibration data in which X represents a measurement made on a measuring instrument that is highly accurate, and Y represents the corresponding measurement (on the same physical unit) made with a less-accurate instrument.

X	3.6	3.5	3.7	3.7	3.4	3.8	3.7	3.5	3.6	3.5
Y	3.3	3.2	3.4	3.3	3.1	3.5	3.4	3.2	3.2	3.2

Obtain the estimates of X using the classical estimation approach to calibration, and comment on the apparent worth of the approach for these data.

4. What assumption(s) does an experimenter need to make if he or she is going to develop a prediction equation solely for the purpose of obtaining predicted values for Y?

5. Consider the data in Table 12.1. What would be wrong with using the prediction equation to predict Y when $X = 45$?

6. For the following data:

X	23	31	26	25	28	30	34	38	29	32	24
Y	41	50	45	46	48	50	58	60	47	52	43

a. Plot the data using a scatter plot.

b. Determine $\hat{\beta}_0$ and $\hat{\beta}_1$ for the model $Y = \beta_0 + \beta_1 X + \varepsilon$.

c. Determine R^2.

d. Construct the 95% confidence interval for β_1.

e. Construct the 95% prediction interval for Y using $X_0 = 25$.

CHAPTER 13

Design of Experiments

When industrial personnel began to apply statistical quality control methods extensively in industry in the United States in the early 1980s, the emphasis was on control charts. This prompted a number of prominent statisticians to recommend the use of "conversational" or active statistical tools to supplement the use of "listening" or passive statistical tools. Specifically, a control chart is a listening tool in that data are obtained from a process but no attempt is made to see what happens when the process is changed.

Assume that our objective is to control the diameter of a machined part within fixed limits. Our chances of successfully doing so will be increased if we can identify the factors that affect the diameter (temperature, humidity, pressure, machine setting, etc.), and the extent to which the diameter is dependent upon each factor.

In this chapter we present experimental design procedures that can be used to identify the factors that affect the quality of products and services. The intent is to present a capsule account of the statistical principles of experimental design. We emphasize the planning of experiments, and the fact that statistical experiments should generally be viewed as being part of a sequence of such experiments, as opposed to a "one-shot-only" approach. Many books have been written on experimental design in which the emphasis is on the analysis of standard designs. Such analysis is deemphasized in this chapter, as are the computational formulas and tables that are inherent in such analyses. Instead, the reader is referred to such books (and journal articles) for additional reading.

13.1 A SIMPLE EXAMPLE OF EXPERIMENTAL DESIGN PRINCIPLES

We begin with a practical design problem that has been discussed in a number of sources including Hahn (1977) and Hicks (1982). The objective

285

	Car			
Wheel Position	1	2	3	4
LF	A	B	A	B
RF	B	A	B	A
LR	D	C	D	C
RR	C	D	C	D

Figure 13.1 Tire brand layout—unacceptable design.

is to compare four different brands of tires for tread wear using 16 tires (four of each brand) and four cars in an experiment. We can often learn more about experimental design by looking at how *not* to design an experiment than we can by reading about the analyses of data from standard designs.

What would be an illogical way to design this experiment? One simple approach would be to assign the tires to the cars in such a way that each car would have all four tires of a given brand. This would be a poor design; even if the cars were identical, the drivers might have different driving habits, and the driving conditions might also be expected to vary.

With such a design, the differences in tire wear among the four brands would be, in statistical terminology, "confounded" (i.e., confused) with differences between cars, drivers, and driving conditions.

A simple way to alleviate this problem would be to assign the tires to the cars in such a way that each car will have one tire of each brand. The design layout might then appear as in Figure 13.1 where the letters A, B, C, and D denote the four brands. This would also be a poor design, however, because brands A and B would be used only on the front of each car, and brands C and D would be used only on the rear positions. Thus, the brand effect would be confounded with the position effect.

The way to remedy this problem would be to construct the design layout in such a way that each brand is used once at each position, as well as once with each car. One possible configuration is given in Figure 13.2. With this design the brand differences would not be confounded with wheel position differences or with differences in cars, drivers or driving conditions. (Of course, there still might be a driver-by-position effect since tires do not wear evenly at each wheel position, and an overly aggressive driver might thus create problems.)

We have thus looked at two unacceptable designs and one acceptable design. (Another unacceptable design would be to randomly assign the 16

| | Car | | | |
Wheel Position	1	2	3	4
LF	A	B	C	D
RF	B	A	D	C
LR	C	D	A	B
RR	D	C	B	A

Figure 13.2 Tire brand layout—acceptable design.

tires to the four cars, as this would likely create an imbalance similar to what was seen for the first two designs.)

The statistical analysis of these types of designs will be discussed later in the chapter; the intent at this point is to introduce the reader to the types of considerations that need to be made in designing an experiment.

13.2   STATISTICAL CONCEPTS IN EXPERIMENTAL DESIGN

Assume that the objective is to determine the effect of two different levels of temperature on process yield, where the current temperature is 250°F and the experimental setting is 300°. We shall also assume for the purpose of illustration that temperature is the only factor that is to be varied. Later, it will be explained why varying one factor at a time is generally not a good strategy. For the moment, however, the emphasis is on simplification.

This experiment might be conducted by recording the process yield at the end of each day for a 2 -week period. (Why 2 weeks? Why not 1 week or 1 day? This issue will be addressed shortly.) One temperature setting could be used for the first 2 weeks, and the other setting for the following 2 weeks. The data might then appear as in Table 13.1. How might we analyze these data to determine if temperature has any effect on yield? It has often been stated that the first step in analyzing any set of data is to plot the data. This point was emphasized in Chapter 11, in which it was also emphasized that a particularly useful plot is to plot the data against time, assuming that the data have been collected over time, and the time order has been preserved.

The time sequence plot in Figure 13.3 is for the data in Table 13.1. What can be gleaned from this plot? First, it is readily apparent that neither temperature setting is uniformly superior to the other over the entire test period since the lines cross several times. This coupled with the fact that the lines are fairly close together would suggest that increasing the temperature

Table 13.1 Process Yield Data (in Tons)

	Day	Temperature		
		250°	300°	
Week #1	M	2.4	2.6	
	Tu	2.7	2.4	
	W	2.2	2.8	Week #3
	Th	2.5	2.5	
	F	2.0	2.2	
Week #2	M	2.5	2.7	
	Tu	2.8	2.3	
	W	2.9	3.1	Week #4
	Th	2.4	2.9	
	F	2.1	2.2	

from 250° to 300° might not have a perceptible effect on the process yield. Before this question is addressed statistically, rather than pictorially, it is important to recognize the other information that is apparent from Figure 13.3. In particular, it can be observed that the yield at each temperature setting is the lowest on Friday of each week. Although this discovery might be viewed as incidental relative to the main objective of determining whether or not the 50° increase in temperature affects the process yield, it would certainly be viewed as important information. For example, some subsequent "detective" work might reveal that the workers were leaving an hour early on Friday afternoons! Or perhaps worker fatigue was a very real

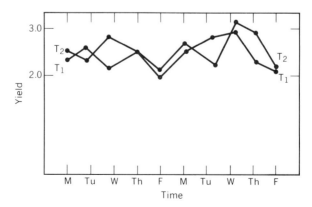

Figure 13.3 Time-sequence plot.

factor at the end of the week. In any event, this is an example of a discovery that might not have been made if a perfunctory statistical analysis had been performed without first plotting the data (although it is also apparent from Table 13.1).

We can also see from Figure 13.3 that there is considerable variability within each temperature setting, particularly relative to the magnitude of the difference between the temperature settings for each day. This coupled with the fact that the lines cross several times would tend to suggest that there is no real difference in the two settings. To elaborate on this somewhat, would this suggest that there would be a real (true) difference in the temperature settings if the lines never crossed? No, it would depend upon the variability within each setting. We have simply obtained a sample of 10 values from a (theoretically infinite) set of yield data for each setting. If there are a number of factors that are operating to cause random variability within each setting, we would logically expect some variability between the two settings, even when there is no difference in the effect of the two settings. On the other hand, if the two lines were both straight and parallel we would conclude that there is indeed a real difference (although perhaps slight) even if the lines were almost touching!

It is extremely important for the reader to understand the reasoning that has been presented in the preceding paragraph, as it essentially forms the foundation for the *t* test that is presented in the next section, as well as for analysis of variance that is generally used in analyzing data from experimental designs.

13.3 *t* TESTS

Although the graphical analysis of the data in Table 13.1 is helpful for gaining insight, it is also desirable to analyze data with numerical analyses. The *t* distribution was covered in Chapter 3, and it was stated that a *t* statistic is of the general form

$$ t = \frac{\hat{\theta} - \theta}{s_{\hat{\theta}}} $$

where θ is the parameter to be estimated, $\hat{\theta}$ is the sample statistic that is the estimator of θ, and $s_{\hat{\theta}}$ is the estimator of the standard deviation of $\hat{\theta}$.

If we let μ_1 represent the true, but unknown, average yield that would be obtained using 250°, and define μ_2 similarly for 300°, our interest would then center upon the difference $\mu_1 - \mu_2$. (It should be noted that we are only approximating reality when we speak of "true" values of μ_1 and μ_2, or for any other parameter. Conditions change, so we might think of μ_1, for example, as representing what the process yield *would be* using 250° if all other relevant factors could be held constant. Since the latter might hold true only for laboratory experiments, it should be noted that inferences made from experimental designs and extended to the future could be seriously undermined if conditions change greatly in the future. Since the future is obviously unknown, there is no statistical adjustment that can be made. It is simply a matter of combining common sense with statistical methods, and recognizing the limitations of the latter.)

If we let θ represent this difference, then $\hat{\theta} = \bar{x}_1 - \bar{x}_2$, where $\bar{x}_1$ and $\bar{x}_2$ are the averages of the first and second columns, respectively, in Table 13.1. It can be shown that

$$\sigma_{\bar{x}_1 - \bar{x}_2} = \sqrt{\frac{\sigma_1^2}{n_1} + \frac{\sigma_2^2}{n_2}} \tag{13.1}$$

(assuming the samples to be independent, which they are here) where σ_1^2 and σ_2^2 are the true (unknown) variances for 250° and 300°, respectively, and n_1 and n_2 are the two sample sizes. (Here, of course, $n_1 = n_2 = 10$.) Of course, σ_1^2 and σ_2^2 are generally unknown and must be estimated. The logical estimators are s_1^2 and s_2^2, the two sample variances.

It would seem reasonable to substitute s_1^2 for σ_1^2 and s_2^2 for σ_2^2 in Eq. (13.1) and proceed from there. This would be logical if (1) n_1 and n_2 were both reasonably large (say, at least 30), or (2) n_1 and n_2 were small and differed considerably (e.g., 5 and 10), and it would be unreasonable to assume $\sigma_1^2 = \sigma_2^2$. The first condition is clearly not satisfied for this example since both sample sizes are equal to 10. The second condition would lead to the use of an approximate t test such as the one discussed in Section 13.3.2.

13.3.1 Exact t Test

The exact t test is of the form

$$t = \frac{(\bar{x}_1 - \bar{x}_2) - 0}{s_p\sqrt{(1/n_1) + (1/n_2)}} \tag{13.2}$$

where $\bar{x}_1$, $\bar{x}_2$, n_1, and n_2 are as previously defined and $s_p (= \sqrt{s_p^2})$ is the square root of the estimate of the (assumed) common variance, $\sigma_1^2 = \sigma_2^2 =$

σ^2, where that estimate is obtained from

$$s_p^2 = \frac{(n_1 - 1)s_1^2 + (n_2 - 1)s_2^2}{n_1 + n_2 - 2}$$

The latter reduces to a simple average of s_1^2 and s_2^2 when $n_1 = n_2$, as in this example. The zero in Eq. (13.2) represents the fact that $\mu_1 - \mu_2 = 0$ if $\mu_1 = \mu_2$. Note that the denominator of Eq. (13.2) is in the general form of Eq. (13.1), with s_p^2 substituted for $\sigma_1^2 = \sigma_2^2 = \sigma^2$.

It is not necessary to always use zero in Eq. (13.2), however. In particular, if a new operating procedure is to be tested against the standard procedure, we might require that the new procedure be considerably better than the standard procedure, particularly if use of the new procedure would lead to an increase in costs (see Deming, 1975, p. 150). Thus, we might require that $\mu_1 - \mu_2 < d$ where the value of d would be determined from monetary factors. That value would then be used in place of zero in Eq. (13.2).

A t statistic always has a certain number of "degrees of freedom" associated with it, specifically the degrees of freedom associated with the denominator of the statistic. For this test statistic μ_1 and μ_2 are estimated by $\bar{x}_1$ and $\bar{x}_2$, respectively, in the process of computing s_1^2 and s_2^2 for estimating σ^2 by s_p^2. Thus, two degrees of freedom (d.f.) are used in estimating μ_1 and μ_2, so there are $20 - 2 = 18$ d.f. left for estimating σ^2, and hence 18 d.f. for the t statistic.

Applying this t test to the data in Table 13.1 produces

$$t = \frac{(2.45 - 2.57) - 0}{0.3005\sqrt{(1/10) + (1/10)}}$$

$$= -0.893$$

It can be shown (by computer) that the probability of observing a value for t that is as small or smaller than -0.893 when $\mu_1 = \mu_2$ is 0.1919. Thus, there is almost a 20% chance of this occurring, so there is not sufficiently strong evidence to lead us to reject the hypothesis that $\mu_1 = \mu_2$ in favor of $\mu_1 < \mu_2$ (less than 5% would constitute strong evidence). Thus, the conclusion is that the difference between the sample averages is due to sampling variation, and does not reflect a true difference (of any magnitude) in the effects of the two temperature settings. Specifically, we are not concluding that $\mu_1 = \mu_2$, as it is highly improbable that two process means would be equal. Rather, we simply conclude that the data do not provide us with sufficiently strong evidence to allow us to claim that $\mu_1 < \mu_2$. This can happen when μ_1 is approximately equal to μ_2, and/or the data in each sample are highly variable.

It should be noted that $\sigma_1^2 = \sigma_2^2$ was assumed, but was not checked. In general, necessary assumptions should be checked, but this one is not crucial as long as $n_1 = n_2$. The (exact) t test is undermined when $\sigma_1^2 \neq \sigma_2^2$ and n_1 and n_2 differ considerably, however, particularly when at least one of the two sample sizes is relatively small. See Cressie and Whitford (1986) for a discussion of the robustness of the t test to violation of the equal variance assumption for equal and unequal sample sizes, and recommendations concerning the use of two-sample t tests. See also Posten, Yeh, and Owen (1982).

One problem in testing for equality of variances is that virtually all of the standard tests are sensitive to nonnormality. Layard (1973) presents a test that is not sensitive, however. (The t test itself is not sensitive to slight-to-moderate departures from normality.) The test is also described in Miller and Wichern (1977, p. 167).

Before leaving this example, we should note the other requisite assumptions for this t test: (1) the two samples are independent, and (2) the observations are independent within each sample. The first requirement is clearly met since the data in each sample were obtained over different weeks, but the fact that the data were collected over time might suggest that the second requirement is not met. In particular, is the process yield on a given day related to the yield on the preceding day? The data in Table 13.1 are fictitious, and no trend is apparent in Figure 13.3 for either temperature setting, but in practice the issue of possible dependent observations should be addressed. If dependency is to be expected, this experiment could have been conducted by randomly assigning the temperature settings to the days (if frequent changes in the temperature could be tolerated).

We can also note that $\sigma_1^2 = \sigma_2^2$ is the requisite assumption that is usually stated for the exact t test, but Nelson (1984) points out that we would still have an exact t test if $\sigma_1^2 = c\sigma_2^2$ where c is a constant that would have to be known.

13.3.2 Approximate t Test

If n_1 and n_2 differ considerably and $c = \sigma_1^2/\sigma_2^2$ is unknown, an approximate t test should be used. The one to be discussed here (a number have been proposed) is due to Welch (1937) and is of the form

$$t^* = \frac{(\bar{x}_1 - \bar{x}_2) - 0}{\sqrt{(s_1^2/n_1) + (s_2^2/n_2)}} \tag{13.3}$$

where the zero represents the fact that $\mu_1 - \mu_2 = 0$ *if* μ_1 and μ_2 are equal, and the asterisk indicates that this is an approximate t test. It can be shown that t^* will have the same value as t for the exact t test when $n_1 = n_2$, but the d.f. will differ if $s_1^2 \neq s_2^2$. In general, the degrees of freedom are calculated as

$$\text{d.f.} = \frac{\left(s_1^2/n_1 + s_2^2/n_2\right)^2}{\left(s_1^2/n_1\right)^2/(n_1 - 1) + \left(s_2^2/n_2\right)^2/(n_2 - 1)}$$

Plugging in the appropriate numbers produces d.f. = 17.98, so that 18 would be used. Thus, for this example the two t tests produce identical results, which is not surprising since $n_1 = n_2$ and s_1^2 and s_2^2 differ only slightly.

13.3.3 Confidence Intervals for Differences

We can also express the outcome of an experiment such as the one given in Section 13.3.1 by constructing a confidence interval for the difference of two means. If we wanted to see if the experimental evidence suggested $\mu_1 < \mu_2$, we could construct a $100(1 - \alpha)\%$ confidence interval (see Chapter 3) of the form $(\overline{X}_1 - \overline{X}_2) + t_{\alpha, \nu} s_{\overline{x}_1 - \overline{x}_2}$ where ν is the degrees of freedom for the t statistic in Eq. (13.2). This would provide an upper bound on $\mu_1 - \mu_2$ that if less than zero would suggest that $\mu_1 < \mu_2$. Similarly, a two-sided interval could be constructed that would be of the form $(\overline{X}_1 - \overline{X}_2) \pm t_{\alpha/2, \nu} s_{\overline{x}_1 - \overline{x}_2}$, which could be used to determine if $\mu_1 \neq \mu_2$. Thus, a decision could be reached using a confidence interval, and the decision would be the same as that reached with the corresponding t test. An interval obviously provides an experimenter with more information than a "yes or no" test, however.

13.4 ANALYSIS OF VARIANCE FOR ONE FACTOR

The data in Table 13.1 could also have been analyzed by a technique known as analysis of variance. Historically, this technique has been used to analyze data obtained from the use of experimental designs. Such data can also be analyzed by regression methods that offer some comparative advantages; these will be discussed later in the chapter.

The expression *analysis of variance* is actually somewhat of a misnomer as it would tend to connote to a statistical neophyte that a "variance" is being analyzed. A variance in statistics is, of course, a single number, and it would be difficult to analyze a single number. What is actually being analyzed is *variation*—variation attributable to different sources.

The variation both within and between the temperature settings for the data in Table 13.1 was discussed in the graphical analysis of those data. This variation is handled more explicitly in analysis of variance, generally abbreviated as ANOVA.

Before embarking upon an analysis of these data using ANOVA, it is necessary to introduce some new terminology. The variable *temperature* would generally be referred to as the experimental variable or *factor*, and the two temperature settings are *levels*. What is being measured is the process yield, and this would be labeled the response variable.

The use of graphical displays for ANOVA will be presented shortly when the current example is modified somewhat. At this point, however, we shall assume that the data have previously been studied with graphical methods and will proceed directly to the ANOVA calculations.

As was discussed previously, there are two types of variation in the data —variation between the temperature settings and variation within each temperature setting. Accordingly, these sources are often designated in ANOVA tables as "between" and "within."

A measure of the "between" variability would be the difference between the average value at each temperature setting and the overall average. Numerically we obtain $\bar{x}_{250°} - \bar{x}_{all} = 2.45 - 2.51 = -0.06$ and $\bar{x}_{300°} - \bar{x}_{all} = 2.57 - 2.51 = 0.06$. With two levels these two numbers must be the same, except for the signs that must be opposite, since the numbers must sum to zero. The extent to which these two numbers differ from zero is a measure of the temperature "effect" (another new term). Since the sum must always equal zero (even when there are more than two levels), the sum of the numbers will not provide any useful information. We can, however, add the squares of the numbers together, and this sum is then multiplied by n ($= 10$ here) and the product used in ANOVA tables. [The n results from summing the squares over the observations within each group. See Neter, Wasserman, and Kutner (1985, p. 535) for the algebraic details.] Numerically, we obtain $0.0072 \times 10 = 0.072$ and we will let this be represented by SS_{temp}, which represents the *sum of squares* (SS) due to the temperature effect. A measure of variability for all of the data (20 numbers in this example) is obtained by squaring the difference between each number and $\bar{x}_{all}$, and then adding all of the squared differences. (The reader may recall from Exercise 1 in Chapter 3 that this is also how the numerator of the sample variance is obtained, and should recall that an equivalent formula was given for obtaining the numerator. That equivalent formula can be used in ANOVA.) For these data we obtain 1.698, and this will be represented by SS_{total}. The difference between SS_{total} and SS_{temp} can be

Table 13.2 ANOVA Table for Temperature Data

Source of Variation	d.f.	SS	MS	F
Temperature	1	0.072	0.072	0.797
Within	18	1.626	0.090	
Total	19	1.698		

represented by SS_{within}, so that $SS_{within} = SS_{total} - SS_{temp}$, and for these data we obtain $1.698 - 0.072 = 1.626$. It could be shown that SS_{within} is the same as the numerator of the expression that was given for s_p^2 in the preceding section for the exact t test. Thus, the (equivalent) relationship between the exact t test and ANOVA for a single factor with two levels will now begin to take shape.

An ANOVA table can be constructed using these sums of squares and other quantities. The ANOVA table is given in Table 13.2.

An explanation of the entries in this table is as follows. The degrees of freedom for "Total" will always be equal to the total number of data values minus one. (This is true for *any* ANOVA table and for any type of design.) One is subtracted from the total number of values because there is one linear constraint on these values, namely, the sum of their deviations from the overall average must equal zero. The d.f. for the factor (temperature, in this case) will always be equal to the number of levels of the factor minus one. The "one" results from the fact that the sum of the differences of each factor level average from the overall average must equal zero. The d.f. for within will always be equal to one less than the number of observations per level multiplied by the number of levels. The entries in the MS column (where MS is an abbreviation for *mean square*) are obtained by taking the values in the SS column and dividing them by the corresponding values in the d.f. column (e.g., $0.090 = 1.626/18$). The F value is obtained by taking the top mean square and dividing it by the bottom one. The ratio of these mean squares is (before the numbers are plugged in) a random variable that has an F distribution (discussed in Chapter 3) with 1 d.f. for the numerator and 18 d.f. for the denominator. Thus, the analysis of these data could be carried out using the F Table contained in Table D of the Appendix of Statistical Tables. We might then ask what is the probability of obtaining a value of the F statistic that is as large or larger than 0.797 when there is no true difference in the effects of the temperature settings? The probability is .3838, which is exactly double the probability obtained using the exact t test. Is this a coincidence? No, this will always happen. This is due in part to the fact that the square of any value in the t Table (Table C in the

Appendix of Statistical Tables) with "ν" d.f. and a tail area of a will equal the value in the F Table (Table D at the end of the book) with 1 d.f. for the numerator and ν d.f. for the denominator, and a tail area of $2a$. It can also be shown that the square of the t statistic given by Eq. (13.3) is equivalent to the F statistic. [It is easy to see this with numbers, such as the numbers in this example, as $(-0.893)^2 = 0.797$.] The reason that the tail area is doubled is because the F statistic cannot be negative (sums of *squares* and mean *squares* must obviously be nonnegative), whereas the t statistic could be either positive or negative. Thus, the tail areas for the negative and positive portions of the t distribution are added together to form the tail area for the F distribution.

Since the use of ANOVA for a single factor with two levels will produce results identical to the use of an exact t test, it would seem reasonable to assume that the ANOVA approach would be based upon the same assumptions as the exact t test. This is indeed the case. Thus, ANOVA is based upon the assumptions of normality of the populations and equality of the variances. As with the exact t test, it is relatively insensitive to slight-to-moderate departures from the first assumption, and is also relatively insensitive to the assumption of equal variances, provided that the sample sizes are at least approximately equal. Unlike the t test, however, ANOVA can be used when a factor has more than two levels.

13.4.1 ANOVA for a Single Factor with More Than Two Levels

Let us assume now that the experiment to compare the effect of different temperature settings on process yield actually had three different settings, and the data for the third setting, 350°, were temporarily mislaid. The full data set appears in Table 13.3.

For simplicity we will assume that these data have been collected over a period of 6 weeks, with 2 weeks at each temperature setting. This is the way the experiment would have to be designed if a company had only one plant that could be used in the experiment. If a company had three plants, however, one temperature setting could be used at each plant, and the experiment could then be conducted in 2 rather than 6 weeks. That would certainly seem desirable, but one possible drawback is that the plants might not be identical (and probably would not be) in terms of productive capability. Differences in process yield for the three temperature settings might actually be due to plant differences, and with this design it would be impossible to separate the temperature effect from the plant effect. This illustrates why the design of an experiment is so important—much more so than the analysis of the data.

**Table 13.3 Process Yield Data for All Three
Temperature Settings (in Tons, 6-Week Period)**

	Temperature		
Day	250°	300°	350°
M	2.4	2.6	3.2
Tu	2.7	2.4	3.0
W	2.2	2.8	3.1
Th	2.5	2.5	2.8
F	2.0	2.2	2.5
M	2.5	2.7	2.9
Tu	2.8	2.3	3.1
W	2.9	3.1	3.4
Th	2.4	2.9	3.2
F	2.1	2.2	2.6

What about variation between the 2 weeks, as well as day-to-day variation? It might seem as though we should be particularly concerned about the latter since it was previously determined in the analysis of the first two settings that the process yield drops off on Fridays.

Remember, however, that our objective is to determine whether or not these three temperature settings affect process yield, not to isolate every possible cause of variation in process yield. If the objective had been to identify factors that may influence process yield, then the experimental design should have been constructed with that objective in mind, and the design would likely have been different from the current design. Designs for the identification of such factors are called *screening designs*, and they will be discussed later in the chapter.

It would seem unlikely that there would be significant week-to-week variation, particularly if normal operating conditions existed in each of the 6 weeks. It can also be seen that the 2-week totals within each temperature setting do not differ greatly. Even if the totals did differ considerably, it would be a question of how the totals differed. For example, if the differences between the totals for weeks 1 and 2, 3 and 4, and 5 and 6 were virtually the same, the analysis to be presented would not be seriously affected unless the differences were large. (Large differences would cause the within mean square to be considerably inflated.) On the other hand, if weeks 1 and 6 differed considerably (and the difference was due to external factors), but the totals for the other weeks were virtually the same, the analysis would be of no value.

Day-to-day variation would not be a problem as long as the variation was essentially the same for each week and for each temperature setting. If not, this type of variation could also contaminate the analysis.

In general, much thought must go into the design of an experiment. The analysis of data from an experiment that has been designed properly is generally straightforward; the analysis of data from an experiment that is poorly designed is either difficult or impossible.

We will assume that the data in Table 13.3 are being analyzed for the first time, ignoring the fact that the data for the first two temperature settings were analyzed previously.

It has been stated that the first step in analyzing any set of data (regardless of the analysis that is to be performed) is to plot the data—usually in more than one way. The present use of graphical methods to analyze data from designed experiments is largely attributable to the teachings of Horace P. Andrews and Ellis R. Ott, and the subsequent teachings of their students. The influence of the former is especially evident in *Experiments in Industry—Design, Analysis, and Interpretation of Results* (1985), a collection of papers written by Andrews' former students and dedicated to his memory. Dr. Ott's text *Process Quality Control* (1975) also emphasizes graphical procedures, particularly analysis of means. (The latter is discussed in detail in Chapter 16.)

A box-and-whisker plot was introduced in Chapter 11 as a simple way of providing a useful graphical summary of data. A first step in analyzing the

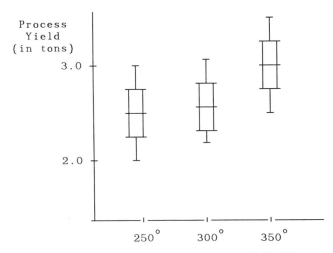

Figure 13.4 Box-and-whisker plot of the data in Table 13.3.

data in Table 13.3 might well be to construct such a plot for each temperature setting.

Figure 13.4 shows the yield for the third temperature setting to be considerably higher than for the first two. The fact that the boxes appear to be of roughly the same height coupled with the absence of any outlying values (none was labeled on the plot) would tend to suggest that the variability within each setting probably does not differ very much from setting to setting. (Of course, we have already seen that this was true for the first two settings.) This is important since, as noted in the preceding section, equality of variances is a prerequisite for the use of ANOVA, and the analysis is undermined somewhat when the requirement is not met, particularly when the sample sizes differ considerably.

How might we determine whether or not the requirement is met in a more precise manner than is provided by graphs? One approach would be to use the test given by Layard (1973), which was mentioned previously. Another test that does not require an assumption of normality is given by Conover (1980, p. 241), and there are various other tests which are sensitive to nonnormality.

There does not appear to be a need to use such a test for the present example, however, as the (sample) variances for each temperature setting appear to be roughly equal.

As with the data in Table 13.1, there is a need to compute the sum of squares for between (temperature), within, and total. The approach to obtaining the first sum of squares was motivated somewhat heuristically in the preceding section. The sum of squares for temperature can also be computed as

$$SS_{temp} = \sum_{i=1}^{3} \frac{T_i^2}{n_i} - \frac{\left(\sum_{i=1}^{3} T_i\right)^2}{N} \tag{13.4}$$

where T_i represents the total of the observations for the ith level of temperature, and n_i represents the number of observations for the ith level. Similarly, $\sum_{i=1}^{3} T_i$ denotes the grand total of all of the observations, and N is the number of such observations. For ANOVA formulas in general, whenever a number is squared, it is always divided by the number of observations that were summed to produce that number.

For the current data we obtain

$$SS_{temp} = \frac{(24.5)^2 + (25.7)^2 + (29.8)^2}{10} - \frac{(24.5 + 25.7 + 29.8)^2}{30}$$

$$= 214.878 - 213.333$$

$$= 1.545$$

We should note, however, that such "sums of squares" formulas should not always be routinely used for computations, as they can sometimes produce results that are very much in error due to roundoff errors. This can happen in particular when a sum of squares value is close to zero and the two terms in the formula are both large. [See Chan, Golub, and Leveque (1983) for further details.] Computer software with good numerical properties should generally be used for computations, rather than performing hand computations with the usual "cookbook" formulas. The latter are being used here simply for illustrative purposes, although their use with this data set is not going to cause any problems.

It was noted previously that the "total sum of squares" is always computed the same way. This can be expressed as

$$SS_{total} = \sum_{i=1}^{N} y_i^2 - \frac{\left(\sum_{i=1}^{N} y_i \right)^2}{N}$$

where y_i denotes the ith observation, and, as before, N denotes the total number of such observations. For these data we obtain

$$SS_{total} = 217.220 - \frac{(80)^2}{30}$$

$$= 217.220 - 213.333$$

$$= 3.887$$

It then follows that the "within" sum of squares is $3.887 - 1.545 = 2.342$. These numbers can then be used to produce the ANOVA table that is given in Table 13.4. The probability of obtaining a value for F that is greater than or equal to 8.91 when there is no true difference in the effects of the temperature settings is .001. Since this is a very small probability, we would thus conclude that there is a difference in the effects of the temperature settings, and it is apparent from the boxplot given previously that the difference is due to the third setting. Thus, based on this and previous

Table 13.4 ANOVA Table for the Data in Table 13.3

Source of Variation	d.f.	SS	MS	F
Temperature	2	1.545	0.7725	8.91
Within	27	2.342	0.0867	
Total	29	3.887		

analyses, it would seem reasonable to conclude that the effect of the third setting differs significantly from the effect of the first two settings, but the latter do not differ significantly from each other.

13.4.2 Multiple Comparison Procedures

The formal assessment of such differences is generally made through the use of multiple comparison procedures. The problem in using such procedures is that a sizable number of them have been proposed, and there is no one procedure that can be deemed superior to all the others. Some procedures are conservative in that they produce few significant differences, some can only be used if the F test is significant, some can be used only to construct comparisons before the data are collected, and so on. As a result of this one might successfully argue that graphical procedures, although approximate, might be a better choice for practitioners. The boxplot is one such approach. A slightly more refined graphical procedure is the reference distribution approach suggested by Box, Hunter, and Hunter (1978, p. 190). Another graphical approach for detecting differences is analysis of means, which is discussed in Chapter 16. Readers interested in formal multiple comparison procedures are referred to Chapter 17 of Neter, Wasserman, and Kutner (1985) and Chapter 2 of Miller (1981).

13.4.3 Sample Size Determination

The question of how many days or weeks to run the temperature experiment was alluded to at the beginning of the discussion. There is no one correct answer to this question, so we might lead into a discussion by determining the shortest length of time that the experiment can be run. The answer is 6 days—two at each setting. Why 6 days? Recall that we are actually pooling the variances for the different levels of the factor, and at least two numbers must be present before a variance can be calculated. So it would be possible to run the experiment using 2 days for each temperature setting, but would it be desirable? The answer is no. The variance of a sample variance is a function of both the population variance and the sample size, and for a sample of size two from a normal population that variance will be double the *square* of the population variance. Thus, judging whether or not the temperature effect is significant could depend on a poorly estimated common population variance.

In general, the determination of sample size in ANOVA can be done explicitly if the experimenter has in mind the minimum difference in the effects of (at least) two factor levels that he wants to detect with a given probability. He can then use tables for sample size determination such as those found in Nelson (1985). The reader is referred to Chapter 18 of Neter, Wasserman, and Kutner (1985) for additional reading, as well as Odeh and Fox (1975).

13.4.4 Additional Terms and Concepts in One-Factor ANOVA

In this section we introduce some new terms, and briefly discuss some common experimental designs.

An *experimental unit* is the unit (of material perhaps) to which a treatment is applied. The days are the experimental units in the experiment just analyzed.

If the temperature settings had been randomly assigned to the days, we would have had a *completely randomized design*. Would such a design have been advisable for the temperature experiment? Only if it was believed that production might be correlated over the days and weeks involved in the experiment, independent of the particular temperature setting. It has often been stated that one should *block* on factors that could be expected to influence the response variable (i.e., what is being measured) and randomize over factors that might be influential, but that could not be "blocked."

In the configuration for the tire experiment given in Figure 13.1, the cars were the blocks and the variation due to cars (blocks) would be isolated when the data were analyzed. If the tire brands had been randomly assigned to the wheel positions within each block (car) we would have had a *randomized block design*. As we saw at the time, however, this would be a poor design because it would (likely) result in an imbalance relative to wheel positions. The design settled upon and illustrated in Figure 13.2 is called a *Latin square design*.

It should not be inferred that the latter design is "good" and a randomized block design is "bad." Their appropriate use depends on how many extraneous factors are to be adjusted for—one in the case of a randomized block design (e.g., cars) and two in the case of a Latin square design (e.g., cars and wheel position).

Factors are generally classified as *fixed* or *random*. When there is only one factor, the classification does not have any effect on how the data are analyzed, but it does make a difference when there are two or more factors. A factor is fixed if the levels of a factor are predetermined, and the experimenter is interested only in those particular levels (e.g., 250°, 300°, 350°). A factor is classified as random if the levels are selected at random from a population of levels (e.g., 254°, 287°, 326°), and the inference is to apply to this population of levels rather than to the particular levels used in the experiment, as is the case with fixed factors.

A completely randomized design is sometimes (erroneously) equated with one-factor ANOVA, but the two are really not the same. The latter is simply a way to classify the general layout of an experiment (which is why it is sometimes termed a one-way layout), whereas the former refers to how the treatments are assigned to the experimental units.

Regression models were discussed in the preceding chapter. Similarly, analysis of variance models can also be presented and discussed. The model for one-factor ANOVA can be written as

$$Y_{ij} = \mu + \tau_j + \varepsilon_{ij} \tag{13.5}$$

where j denotes the jth level of the single factor, and i denotes the ith observation. Thus, Y_{ij} represents the ith observation for the jth level. Further, τ_j represents the effect of the jth level, μ is a constant that is the value that we would expect for each Y_{ij} if the effects of each level were the same, and ε_{ij} represents the error term (with the errors assumed to be random), analogous to the error term in a regression model. If the effects were all the same, there would be no need for a τ_j term in the model, so the model could then be written as

$$Y_{ij} = \mu + \varepsilon_{ij} \tag{13.6}$$

The F test illustrated previously determines whether the appropriate model is Eq. (13.5) or Eq. (13.6).

As stated previously, the data in one-factor ANOVA are analyzed in the same way regardless of whether the single factor is fixed or random, but the interpretation of the components of Eq. (13.5) does differ. Specifically, τ_j is a constant if the factor is fixed, and a random variable if the factor is random. The error term, ε_{ij}, is NID$(0, \sigma^2)$ in both cases, and the Y_{ij} are assumed to be normally distributed in both cases. In the random-factor case, however, the Y_{ij} are not independent as the observations for the jth factor level are correlated since τ_j is a random variable and each observation is commonly influenced by the jth level. (It might seem that the same could be said of the fixed-factor case since each observation within the jth factor level shares the effect of the jth factor level, but these effects are constants, and variables are not correlated just because they have a constant in common.)

The data in the temperature experiment were "balanced" in that there was the same number of observations (10) for each level of the factor. When there is just a single factor, there is no difficulty in analyzing the data for an unequal number of observations. Specifically, the total sum of squares would be calculated in the same way, and Eq. (13.4) would be used to compute the "between" sum of squares, with the n_i not all equal.

13.5 REGRESSION ANALYSIS OF DATA
FROM DESIGNED EXPERIMENTS

The material in the preceding sections of this chapter was intended to introduce the reader to ANOVA, and, in general, to the analysis of data from designed experiments. ANOVA for a single factor is intuitive, and, if necessary, could be easily performed with a hand calculator. Regression could also be used as the method of analysis, however, and it has greater utility than ANOVA, particularly for complex designs. Regression provides the user with the tools for residual analysis, whereas the latter is not generally regarded as being part of ANOVA. The value of residual analyses in regression was discussed in Chapter 12; residual analyses are also important in analyzing data obtained through the use of experimental designs.

The essential differences between regression and ANOVA will be noted. With the former, parameters are estimated, which is not always the case when the latter is used. The general form of an ANOVA table results from the implicit assumption of an underlying model, but the model is not always used explicitly. When the model is not used explicitly, diagnostic checking (through the use of residual analysis) cannot be performed. ANOVA is straightforward but mechanical, and for fixed factors should either be supplemented or supplanted by regression analysis.

The least squares estimators in regression analysis resulted from minimizing the sum of squared errors. From Eq. (13.5) we obtain

$$\varepsilon_{ij} = Y_{ij} - \mu - \tau_j$$

so that

$$\sum_j \sum_i \varepsilon_{ij}^2 = \sum_j \sum_i \left(Y_{ij} - \mu - \tau_j \right)^2 \tag{13.7}$$

At this point we will make the assumption that the levels of the factor are fixed. (When this is the case it is logical to estimate τ_j; when the factor is random we would want to estimate σ_τ^2, the variance of the effects of the different possible levels, as there would be no point in estimating the effect when interest centers upon an entire range of possible levels.) We will also make the assumption that we are working with balanced data, as this results in some simplification in notation.

It is customary to think of the τ_j effect as a deviation from the overall mean μ. Specifically, $\tau_j = \mu_j - \mu$, where μ_j is the expected value of the response variable for the jth level of the factor. If we define μ to be the average of the μ_j components, it follows that $\Sigma_j(\mu_j - \mu) = 0$ so that $\Sigma_j \tau_j = 0$.

This restriction on the τ_j components, which is implied by the definitions of τ_j, μ_j, and μ, allows μ and each τ_j to be estimated using least squares. Specifically, the minimization of Eq. (13.7) produces

$$\hat{\mu} = \overline{Y}..$$

and

$$\hat{\tau}_j = \overline{Y}_{.j} - \overline{Y}..$$

where $\overline{Y}..$ denotes the average of all of the observations, and $\overline{Y}_{.j}$ denotes the average of the observations for the jth factor level. It then follows that

$$\hat{Y}_{ij} = \hat{\mu} + \hat{\tau}_j$$
$$= \overline{Y}.. + \left(\overline{Y}_{.j} - \overline{Y}..\right)$$
$$= \overline{Y}_{.j}$$

This is quite intuitive, as we would logically estimate a particular Y_{ij} by using the average of the values for that particular j. It then follows that, analogous to the regression methodology presented in Chapter 12, the residuals are defined as

$$e_{ij} = Y_{ij} - \overline{Y}_{.j}$$

The data in Table 13.3 were previously analyzed using ANOVA. We will now see how those data can be analyzed using regression.

Since we wish to emphasize residual analysis, as well as to provide additional insight, we will obtain the residual sum of squares from the residuals. The value obtained should, of course, be equal to 2.342, which is what was obtained using ANOVA. The residuals are given in Table 13.5.

These residuals uncover some facts that may not have been apparent when the data were analyzed using ANOVA. First, the production is higher for the second week at each temperature setting (since the sums are positive). What could this mean? Does it take some time for the process to adjust to the new temperature setting? Second, not only is the production high during the second week, but it is especially high (relatively speaking) during Wednesday of that week since the residuals are considerably larger than any of the other residuals.

Table 13.5 Residuals for the Temperature Setting Data

			Temperature		
		Day	250°	300°	350°
Weeks			1	3	5
			2	4	6
		M	−0.05	0.03	0.22
		Tu	0.25	−0.17	0.02
		W	−0.25	0.23	0.12
		Th	0.05	−0.07	−0.18
		F	−0.45	−0.37	−0.48
	Sum		−0.45	−0.35	−0.30
		M	0.05	0.13	−0.08
		Tu	0.35	−0.27	0.12
		W	0.45	0.53	0.42
		Th	−0.05	0.33	0.22
		F	−0.35	−0.37	−0.38
	Sum		0.45	0.35	0.30
$\overline{Y}_{.j}$			2.45	2.57	2.98

This illustrates one very important premise of data analysis—the more ways you look at data, the more you are apt to discover. It would take a person with a fairly sharp eye to detect this "peak day" by looking at the data in Table 13.3, whereas the comparatively large positive residuals stand out since about half of the residuals should be negative.

If the residuals in Table 13.5 are squared and the squares are summed, the sum is 2.342, which agrees with the result obtained previously using ANOVA.

The assumption of normality of the residuals could be checked by constructing a *dot diagram* of the residuals (covered in Chapter 11). (Note that a histogram could also be constructed, but a histogram is not likely to be very informative when there is a small number of observations, as there will necessarily be a small number of classes using any of the methods for determining the number of classes given in Chapter 11.) The dot diagram for the residuals in Table 13.5 is given in Figure 13.5. There is no strong evidence from Figure 13.5 of a serious departure from a normal distribution. The estimated standard deviation of the error term is, from Table 13.4, equal to $\sqrt{0.0867}$, which is 0.2944. With 32 residuals we would expect all of them to be within ± 3 standard deviations, which is the case. We would theoretically expect 1 or 2 to be outside of ± 2 standard deviations; there is

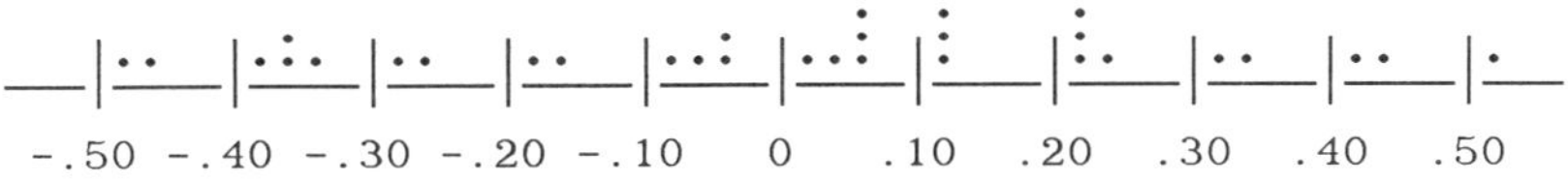

Figure 13.5 Dot diagram of the residuals in Table 13.5.

actually none, although one, 0.53, is close to the upper boundary. We would also expect approximately 10 to be outside ± 1 standard deviation, and there are actually 11 that are outside. (These expectations were obtained by multiplying the probabilities in the standard normal table, Table B, times 32.) Thus, there appears to be at least approximate normality.

The residuals for each temperature setting and for each week should also be examined. Since there are 2 weeks for each temperature setting, a diagram could be constructed for each temperature setting in which "F" would denote a residual for the first week, and "S" would denote a residual for the second week.

The diagrams for each of the three temperature settings are given in Figure 13.6. It is clear from Figure 13.6 that the largest residuals occur in the second week, and that the range of the residuals is roughly the same for each temperature setting. (The latter is reasonably important as it relates to the prerequisite assumption of equal variances.)

As was indicated in the chapter on linear regression, the residuals should also be plotted against time and against the predicted values of the response variable. The plot against time is given in Figure 13.7, and the plot against the predicted values in Figure 13.8. As can be seen from Figure 13.8, the spread of the residuals is virtually the same for each temperature setting,

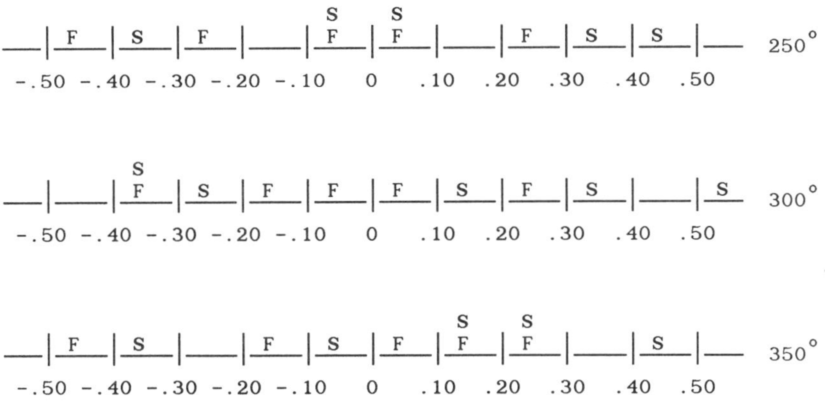

Figure 13.6 Residuals from Table 13.5 by week and by temperature.

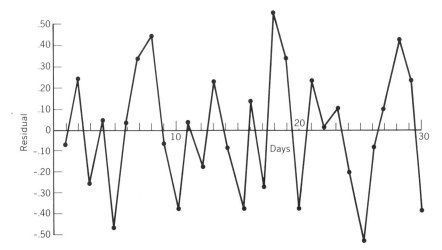

Figure 13.7 Plot of the residuals from Table 13.5 against time.

which is also part of the information provided by Figure 13.6. The points in residual plots are not generally connected, although it does make sense to connect points when "time" is the label of the horizontal axis (as with a control chart). Here, connecting the points provides fairly strong evidence of a cyclical pattern relative to the peaks. Subsequent analysis would then likely lead to the same discovery that was made when the data in Table 13.5

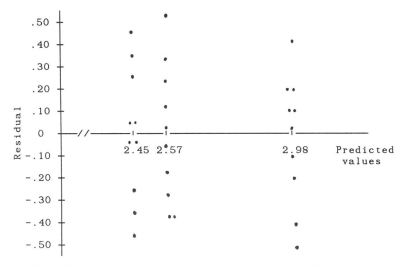

Figure 13.8 Plot of the residuals from Table 13.5 against the predicted values.

were analyzed, namely, an increase in production during the second week for each temperature setting.

It has been previously determined that there is a "week effect," that is, the production clearly differs for the 2 weeks at each temperature setting. This effect may or may not be significant, however. Could an experimenter at this point reanalyze the data to determine if the week effect is significant? The answer is "yes," and this brings up an important point. Data from a designed experiment do not have to be analyzed in accordance with what the experimenter had in mind when the experiment was designed. Fewer factors can be examined than what the experimenter had originally intended to look at, and, occasionally, more factors can be examined. The latter will often be impossible, however, as it can be difficult to isolate factors if an experiment has not been designed in such a way as to permit this isolation.

13.6 ANOVA FOR TWO FACTORS

We will introduce this new topic by using "weeks" and "temperature" as the two factors. This might be called a *factorial design* or a *cross-classified design*, but some care needs to be exercised, as for the data in Table 13.3 it is really more complicated than that. Specifically, in a factorial design each level of every factor is "crossed" with each level of every other factor. Thus, if there are a levels of one factor and b levels of a second factor, there are then ab combinations of factor levels. Since there are actually 6 weeks involved in the temperature-setting experiment, there would have to be $6 \times 3 = 18$ combinations for it to be a cross-classified design. Since, there are obviously only six combinations of weeks and temperatures, it clearly cannot be a cross-classified design. (An actual cross-classified design will be presented later in this section.) What type of design is this then?

It is actually a *nested factor design* as weeks are "nested" within temperature. The corresponding model is

$$Y_{ijk} = \mu + \tau_i + \beta_{j(i)} + \varepsilon_{k(ij)}$$

where $i = 1, 2, 3$
$\quad\quad j = 1, 2$
$\quad\quad k = 1, 2, 3, 4, 5$
where, as before, i designates the temperature, j the week, and k the replicate factor (days in this case). Further, $j(i)$ indicates that weeks are nested within temperature, and $k(ij)$ indicates that the replicate factor is nested within each i, j combination. The use of nested designs in process

control and process variation studies has been discussed by Sinibaldi (1983), Snee (1983), and Bainbridge (1965), among others. These designs are also called *hierarchical designs*, and are generally used for estimating *components of variance*.

The reader is referred to these and other references for the analysis of nested designs. The intent here is to alert the reader that a design with two factors could be a nested factor design or a crossed (classification) design, and it is desirable to be able to distinguish between them.

13.6.1   ANOVA with Two Factors: Factorial Designs

As we extend the discussion of designed experiments and consider more than one factor, it seems logical to pose the following question: "Why not study each factor separately rather than simultaneously?" Figure 13.9 provides an answer to that question. Assume that a company's engineering department is asked to investigate how to maximize process yield, where it is generally accepted that temperature and pressure have a profound effect upon yield. Three of the engineers are given this assignment, and these will be represented by A, B, and C, respectively. Each engineer conducts his own experiment. Assume that A and B each investigates only one factor at a time, whereas C decides to look at both factors simultaneously. Assume further that Figure 13.9 depicts what can be expected to result when both factors are studied together.

If A had used the low temperature (T_1) and varied the pressure from low to high, he would conclude that the best way to increase the yield is to increase the pressure, whereas he would have reached the opposite conclusion if he had used the high temperature. Similarly, if engineer B had set the pressure at the high level (P_2), he would have concluded that the best way to increase yield is to reduce the temperature, whereas he would have reached the opposite conclusion if he had used the low pressure level.

Engineer C, on the other hand, would be in the proper position to conclude that interpreting the effects of the two factors would be somewhat difficult because of the *interaction effect* of the two factors. Interaction effects are depicted graphically by the lack of parallelism of lines as in Figure 13.9.

This type of feedback is not available when factors are studied separately rather than together. These "one-at-a-time" plans have, unfortunately, been used extensively in industry. They are considered to have very little value, in general, although Daniel (1973, 1976, p. 25) discusses their value when examining three factors.

The presence of interaction, particularly extreme interaction, can easily result in completely erroneous conclusions being drawn if an experimenter

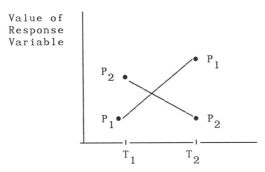

Figure 13.9 Interaction profile. P_1, low pressure; P_2, high pressure; T_1, low temperature; T_2, high temperature.

is not careful. Consider the configuration in Figure 13.10, which is a slight modification of Figure 13.9. It is clear that the value of the response variable varies by 10 units when either temperature or pressure is set at one of the two levels, and the other factor is varied between its two levels. Yet when the data are analyzed we would find that the sum of squares for each of the two factors is exactly zero. Thus, a "blind" analysis of computer output or a hand-constructed ANOVA table would lead an experimenter to conclude that there is neither a temperature nor a pressure effect, although each clearly has an effect on the response variable.

This falls in line with what has been stressed throughout this book, namely, there is much more to analyzing statistical data than just looking at numbers. Graphical displays are extremely important, and should be used with virtually every statistical procedure.

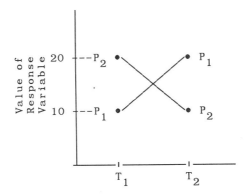

Figure 13.10 Extreme interaction. Abbreviations as in Figure 13.9.

Figure 13.9 and Figure 13.10 are examples of *interaction profiles*, and it is important that these and other graphical displays be used in analyzing data from multifactor designs.

Although the configuration in Figure 13.10 is an extreme example, and not likely to occur exactly in practice, we should not be surprised to find significant interactions and nonsignificant factor effects. (Factor effects are generally called *main effects*.) Daniel (1976, p. 21) stresses that data from a designed experiment should not be reported in terms of main effects and interactions if an interaction is more than one-third of a main effect.

To this point in our discussion of multifactor experiments, the terms *main effects* and *factor effects* have been used rather generally, with implied reference to an ANOVA table. An effect of a factor can be defined more specifically as the change in the response variable that results from a change in the level of that factor.

13.6.2   Effect Estimates

Referring to Figure 13.10, if the pressure is set at P_1 and the temperature is increased from T_1 to T_2, the value of the response variable increases by 10 units. On the other hand, if the pressure is set at P_2 and the temperature is increased from T_1 to T_2, the value of the response variable decreases by 10 units. It would seem logical to define the *temperature effect* as the average of these two changes (which of course is zero in this case). That is

$$T = \frac{1}{2}(T_2P_1 - T_1P_1 + T_2P_2 - T_1P_2) \tag{13.8}$$

Similar reasoning for the *pressure effect* would lead us to define that effect, P, as

$$P = \frac{1}{2}(T_1P_2 - T_1P_1 + T_2P_2 - T_2P_1) \tag{13.9}$$

which is also zero for this example. The way in which the *interaction effect* would be defined might not be quite so intuitive, but another diagram may help. Although Figure 13.11 looks quite different from Figure 13.10, only one change has been made, namely, T_2P_2 was changed from 10 to 30. However, this now causes the lines to be parallel. It was stated previously that interaction results from nonparallelism of the two lines. It is clear from Figure 13.11 that the two lines are parallel because $T_2P_2 - T_2P_1 = T_1P_2 - T_1P_1$. Thus, the extent of the interaction will depend upon the difference of these two expressions, that is, $T_2P_2 - T_2P_1 - (T_1P_2 - T_1P_1)$. Accordingly,

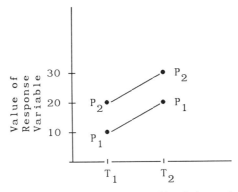

Figure 13.11 Profile showing no interaction. Abbreviations as in Figure 13.9.

we could (and do) define the interaction effect, TP, as

$$TP = \frac{1}{2} \left[T_2 P_2 - T_2 P_1 - (T_1 P_2 - T_1 P_1) \right]$$

$$= \frac{1}{2} (T_2 P_2 - T_2 P_1 - T_1 P_2 + T_1 P_1) \qquad (13.10)$$

For Figure 13.11 this value is, of course, zero, but for the original interaction profile in Figure 13.10 the value is -10. Since we now know that for the data in Figure 13.10 $T = 0$, $P = 0$, and $TP = -10$, we could obtain the sum of squares for these three effects by squaring the effect estimates, where the effect estimates are given by Eqs. (13.8), (13.9), and (13.10). We thus have $SS_t = 0^2 = 0$, $SS_p = 0^2 = 0$, and $SS_{tp} = (-10)^2 = 100$. In general, for a 2^k design with r observations per treatment combination, $SS_{effect} = r(2^{k-2})(\text{effect estimate})^2$. Here $k = 2$ and $r = 1$ so the result is simply (effect estimate)^2.

13.6.3 ANOVA Table for Unreplicated Two-Factor Design

Since we now have these sums of squares, we might attempt to construct an ANOVA table. Remembering that the degrees of freedom (d.f.) for Total is always the total number of observations minus one, and that the d.f. for a factor is always the number of factor levels minus one, we thus have d.f.(Total) = 3, d.f.(T) = 1, and d.f.(P) = 1. The d.f. for any interaction effect is always obtained as the product of the separate d.f. of each factor

Table 13.6 ANOVA for the Data in Figure 13.10

Source of variation	d.f.	SS	MS	F
T	1	0	0	
P	1	0	0	
TP (residual)	1	100	100	
Total	3	100		

that comprises the interaction. Thus, in this case we have d.f.$(TP) = (1)(1) = 1$.

If we add the d.f. for T, P, and TP, we recognize immediately that we have a problem. Specifically, there is no d.f. left for estimating σ^2. Thus, unless we have an estimate of σ^2 from a previous experiment (remember that experimentation should be thought of as being sequential) we have a case in which the interaction is said to be "confounded" (i.e., confused or entangled) with the "residual," where the latter might be used in estimating σ^2. We can summarize what we know to this point in the ANOVA table given in Table 13.6.

Notice that the F values are not filled in. It is "clear" that there is no temperature effect and no pressure effect since the sum of squares for each is zero. (Remember, however, we recently saw that each does have an effect on the response variable; their effect is simply masked by the interaction effect.)

It was stated in the section on one-factor ANOVA that the analysis is not influenced by whether the factor is fixed or random. This is not true when there is more than one factor, however. In general, when both factors are fixed, the main effects and the interaction (if separable from the residual) are tested against the residual. When both factors are random, the main effects are tested against the interaction effect, which, in turn, is tested against the residual. When one factor is fixed and the other one random, the fixed factor is tested against the interaction, the random factor is tested against the residual, and the interaction is tested against the residual. (By "tested against" we mean that the mean square for what follows these words is used in producing the F statistic.)

In this example the interaction is not separable from the residual because the experiment has not been "replicated," that is, the entire experiment has not been repeated so as to produce more than one observation ($r > 1$) per treatment combination. This should be distinguished from *multiple readings* obtained within a *single* experiment which does *not* constitute a replicated experiment (i.e., the entire experiment is not being replicated). This may seem like a subtle difference, but it is an important distinction. For additional reading the reader is referred to Box, Hunter, and Hunter (1978, p. 319).

If a prior estimate of σ^2 is available, possibly from a previous replicated experiment with perhaps slightly different factor levels, that estimate could be used in testing for significance of the main effects. [This idea of using an estimate of σ^2 from a previous experiment forms part of the foundation of evolutionary operation (EVOP), which is covered in Chapter 15.] If a prior estimate is not available, we might still be able to obtain an estimate of σ^2.

Tukey (1949) proposed a test for detecting interaction of a specific functional form for an unreplicated factorial. The test is described in detail in various sources, including Neter, Wasserman, and Kutner (1985, p. 779). The general idea is to decompose the residual into an interaction component and an experimental error component, and perform an F test on the interaction. If the test is not significant then σ^2 might be estimated using the residual. It should be recognized, however, that this test will only detect an interaction that can be expressed as a product of main effects times a constant.

It should be noted, however, that there is a difference, conceptually, between "experimental error" and "residual," and the latter cannot be used, in general, as a substitute for the former. Experimental error should be thought of as the variability that results for a given combination of factor levels in a replicated experiment, and is comprised of variability due to factors not included in the experiment, sampling variability, and perhaps variability due to measurement error. A residual (as in residual sum of squares) may consist of various interaction terms that are thought to be not significant, in addition to experimental error. Specifically, it would be logical to estimate σ^2 by 0.0867 from Table 13.4, but it would be totally illogical to estimate σ^2 by 100 from Table 13.6. With the latter σ^2 would be estimated using an interaction that from Figure 13.10 is obviously large.

It is interesting to note that Tukey's test would not detect this interaction. In fact, the test would indicate that the interaction is zero because the main effects are zero. We should remember that the test is not a general test for detecting the presence of interaction, nor can there be such a test for an unreplicated experiment.

This idea of experimental error vs. residual is a very important one, and we will see later in the chapter how we can go wrong by using an interaction to estimate σ^2 for a set of real data.

Can the analysis begun in Table 13.6 be completed? The analysis was actually completed *before* the (attempted) construction of the ANOVA table, as the data are not appropriate for analysis by an ANOVA table. We have seen that there is indeed a temperature effect and a pressure effect, and the interaction profile in Figure 13.10 clearly shows the strong interaction.

In the absence of a prior estimate of σ^2, the only course of action that would allow completion of the ANOVA table would be to use the interaction as the residual, and to test the two main effects against it. This, of course, would be sheer folly for these data as it would lead to the conclusion that nothing is significant, whereas in actuality all three effects are of significance.

This example was given for the purpose of illustrating how a routine analysis of data could easily lead to the wrong conclusions. This message can also be found in other sources such as Box, Hunter, and Hunter (1978, p. 329) and Daniel (1976). In fact, the reader is referred to p. 20 of Daniel for additional reading on the interpretation of data from a design of this type when a significant interaction effect exists.

It might appear that one solution to the problem of not being able to separate an interaction from the residual is simply to replicate the experiment. Although this is generally desirable, it is not always practical. One possible impediment is, of course, money, and as Ziegel (1984) points out, the data may be so expensive to collect as to preclude replication.

There are, however, some methods for assessing the possible significance of main effects and interactions in unreplicated experiments. One of these methods is due to Daniel (1959), and consists of plotting effect estimates on normal probability paper. This is illustrated in a later example.

13.6.4 Yates' Algorithm

For any 2^k design, where k is the number of factors and 2 is the number of levels of each factor, any treatment combination can be represented by the presence or absence of each of k lower-case letters, where "presence" would denote the high level, and "absence" the low level. For example, if $k = 2$, ab would designate the treatment combination with factors A and B set at their high levels, a would represent A at its high level and B at its low level, b would represent just the opposite, and (1) would be used for each factor at its low level.

Yates (1937) presented a simple method for the analysis of 2^k designs, and the methodology has since been extended for use with other types of designs [see Daniel (1976, p. 38)]. We shall illustrate the procedure for a replicated 2^2 design with 3 observations per treatment combination. The data are given in Table 13.7.

The procedure is initiated by writing down the treatment combinations in *standard order*, by which we mean the following. The treatment combination (1) is always written first. The other combinations are listed relative to

Table 13.7 Data for Illustrating Yates' Algorithm

		A	
		Low	High
B	Low	10, 12, 16	8, 10, 13
	High	14, 12, 15	12, 15, 16

the natural alphabetic ordering, including combinations of letters. Thus, (1) would be followed by a, b, and ab, in that order, and if there were three factors, ab would precede c and ac would follow c.

The procedure can be employed using either the totals or averages for each treatment combination. Since totals are simpler to compute, we shall use those. (Of course, for an unreplicated experiment the two would be the same.) The computations are illustrated in Table 13.8.

The columns designated by (1) and (2) are columns in which addition and subtraction are performed for each ordered pair of numbers. (In general, there will be k such columns for k factors.) Specifically, the numbers in each pair are first added, and then the first number in each pair is subtracted from the second number. Thus, $38 + 31 = 69$, $41 + 43 = 84$, $31 - 38 = -7$, and $43 - 41 = 2$. This process is continued on each new column that is created until the number of such columns is equal to the number of factors. The last column that is created by these operations is used to compute the sum of squares for each effect. Specifically, each number except the first is squared and divided by the number of replicates times 2^k. When this operation is carried out, it produces the sum of squares of the effect for the corresponding treatment combination. For example, $(-5)^2/(3 \cdot 2^2) = 2.08$, which is the sum of squares for the main effect of factor A.

Notice that the first entry in the SS column is blank, and that this corresponds to (1). The number could be filled in, but it is left blank here so

Table 13.8 Illustration of Yates' Algorithm

Treatment Combination	Total	(1)	(2)	SS
(1)	38	69	153	
a	31	84	-5	2.08 (A)
b	41	-7	15	18.75 (B)
ab	43	2	9	6.75 (AB)

Table 13.9 ANOVA for Data in Table 13.7

Source	d.f.	SS	MS	F^a
A	1	2.08	2.08	< 1
B	1	18.75	18.75	3.36
AB	1	6.75	6.75	1.21
Residual	8	44.67	5.58	
Total	11	72.25		

[a] The F values are computed on the assumption that A and B are fixed factors.

as to emphasize the fact that the corresponding number in column (2) cannot be squared and divided by $3 \cdot 2^2$ to produce the sum of squares for any effect. Specifically, neither SS_{total} nor $SS_{residual}$ can be obtained directly by using Yates' algorithm. The squares of the individual observations are, of course, used in obtaining SS_{total}, but they are not used in Yates' algorithm. The first number in column (2) is used in calculating SS_{total}, however, since it is the sum of all of the observations.

Thus, $SS_{total} = 10^2 + 12^2 + 16^2 + \cdots + 15^2 + 16^2 - (153)^2/12 = 72.25$. $SS_{residual}$ would then be obtained by adding the sum of squares for A, B, and AB, and subtracting the sum of those three from SS_{total}. This produces $SS_{residual} = 44.67$. It can be shown that this is equivalent to computing the sum of the squared deviations from the average in each cell, and adding those sums over the cells. An ANOVA table could then be constructed, and the results are displayed in Table 13.9. Since $F_{1, 8, .95} = 5.32$ it appears as though neither A nor B nor its interaction has a significant effect upon the response variable. (Here a $1 - 0.95 = 0.05$ "significance level" is being assumed.) Of course, the ANOVA table would generally be supplemented by other analyses, both graphical and nongraphical, but that will not be done with these data for two reasons: (1) the intent here was simply to introduce Yates' algorithm, and (2) we do not wish to give undue emphasis to a 2^2 design, as it is not a commonly used design.

Gupta (1981) provides a procedure for checking the calculations for Yates' algorithm and refers to other checks that have been proposed.

13.7 THE 2^3 DESIGN

It was mentioned previously that the analysis of an unreplicated factorial can be performed if there is an external estimate of σ^2 that is available, presumably from a prior experiment. (Another method of analyzing unreplicated factorials will be presented shortly that is not dependent upon such an external estimate.)

One approach that is often followed, but which is not easily defensible, is to estimate σ^2 using the mean square of pooled high-order interactions— either assuming that they are not significant, or performing F tests on them and subsequently pooling those that are not significant. Daniel (1976, p. 72) takes a rather dim view of F tests resulting from the somewhat arbitrary pooling of high-order interactions (those involving three or more factors) when he states:

> This method, recommended in most textbooks, is frequently violated as soon as the data are in, first of all by the use of several levels of significance to indicate which effects are more and which less "significant." The lack of seriousness of the whole enterprise is revealed by the fact that no statistician has thought to investigate the operating characteristic (frequency of missing real effects) of the combined multilevel test. Examples will be given later of entirely jejune conclusions drawn in this way.*

The point is that significance levels for F tests are somewhat arbitrary, and the practice of pooling interaction terms based upon the outcome of F tests with arbitrary significance levels creates a fair amount of arbitrariness. This is compounded somewhat by the fact that if enough F tests are constructed, even if they are independent, we are apt to find some that are significant due to chance alone.

Daniel (1976, p. 54) provides data from an actual experiment in which a 2^3 design was used. The factors were time of stirring (A), temperature (B), and pressure (C), and the objective was to investigate their effect on the thickening time of a certain type of cement. The data are given in Table 13.10.

The two levels of each factor were not given by Daniel, but the question of which levels to use had to be answered before the experiment was conducted. Box, Hunter, and Hunter (1978, p. 298) address this issue:

> The basic problem of experimental design is deciding what pattern of design points will best reveal aspects of the situation of interest.... The question of where the points should be placed is a circular one in the sense that, if we knew what the response function was like, we could decide where the points should be. But to find out what the response function is like is precisely the object of the investigation. Fortunately this circularity is not crippling, particularly when

---

*From *Applications of Statistics to Industrial Experimentation* by C. Daniel. Copyright © 1976 John Wiley & Sons, Inc. Reprinted by permission.

Table 13.10 Data from an Example in Daniel (1976)

Treatment Combination	Response
(1)	297
a	300
b	106
ab	131
c	177
ac	178
bc	76
abc	109

experiments may be conducted sequentially so that information gained in one set directly influences the choice of experiments in the next.*

We can eyeball the data in Table 13.10 and easily gain some insight into what effects are likely to be significant before beginning a formal analysis of the data.

Specifically, we can compare the value of the response variable at the high level of each factor with the value at the low level of that factor. With the way that the treatment combinations are ordered in Table 13.10, it is easy to compare high C with low C since the first four are at low C and the last four are at high C. (It should be understood, however, that the ordering in Table 13.10 is what would be used for implementation of Yates' algorithm. When the experiment is actually carried out the treatment combinations should be run in some random order, if possible.) It should be apparent without even adding the two sets of numbers that low C differs considerably from high C. Thus, factor C appears to be important.

For factor B, the levels alternate in pairs (i.e., two lows, two highs, two lows, two highs), and it should be clear from a cursory inspection that the sums for low B and high B differ greatly, as all four responses at low B are considerably greater than any of the responses at high B. Thus, there appears to be a very strong B effect. Conversely, there appears to be virtually no A effect, as the levels alternate starting with low, and the responses in each pair obviously differ very little. (It should be noted that

*Reprinted from *Statistics for Experimenters* by G. E. P. Box, W. G. Hunter, and J. S. Hunter. Copyright © 1978 John Wiley & Sons, Inc. Reprinted by permission.

these conclusions are specifically for the factor levels used in the experiment. Other levels might produce different conclusions.)

The identification of interaction effects can be done somewhat similarly, but not quite as easily. Therefore, we shall not discuss how to identify interactions that are likely to be significant simply from eyeballing the data.

Where do we go from here in continuing the analysis? One possibility would be to use Yates' algorithm to obtain the appropriate sums of squares, and then proceed to an ANOVA table. That approach will not be used for this example, however, because (1) it was illustrated previously, and (2) we do not wish to give undue emphasis to ANOVA tables. Although such tables have been used extensively in practice and are an integral part of computer output, they should be supplemented with other types of analyses, as was stated previously.

Yates' algorithm can be used for producing more than just sums of squares, however, so even if an ANOVA table is not to be the focal point of the analysis, the algorithm can still be used to good advantage.

It is left for the reader to verify that the last column of additions and subtractions, which would be denoted by (3) because there are three factors, would be as follows: 1374, 62, $-530, 54, -294, 6, 190, 10$.

These numbers by themselves have ready interpretations. As indicated previously, the first number will always be the total (regardless of the number of factors), so that number divided by 8 is the average response value for the 8 treatment combinations. Similarly, the fifth number (-294), which when aligned vertically would be across from treatment combination c, represents the difference between the sum at high C and the sum at low C. Thus, when the number is divided by 4 it will be the difference between the two averages (at high C and low C), and will thus be the estimate of the "C effect." Dividing each of the other six numbers by 4 will produce estimates of the other main effects as well as the interaction effects.

Performing this division produces the effect estimates given in Table 13.11.

The figures in Table 13.11 reveal what we had discovered earlier from the simple calculations, namely, that the main effects of B and C seem to be important, although the fact that the BC interaction is also of some magnitude may complicate the analysis somewhat. To determine the statistical significance of these effects, we need to know (or estimate) the standard deviation of each effect.

Recognizing that we have an unreplicated factorial, we know that we cannot obtain a clean estimate of σ. Remembering that interactions of third order (those containing three factors) and higher are generally not significant, we might "create" a residual term by using the ABC interaction as the

Table 13.11 Effect Estimates for the Data in Table 13.10

Effect	Estimate
Average	171.75
Main effects	
A	15.5
B	−132.5
C	−73.5
Interaction effects	
AB	13.5
AC	1.5
BC	47.5
ABC	2.5

residual. We could then use that to estimate σ and subsequently test for the significance of the various effects.

Of course, such an approach would be shaky at best, as *interaction* and *experimental error* are totally different concepts, as was previously discussed. For these data the estimate of σ using the ABC interaction would be $\sqrt{(10)^2/2^3} = 3.54$, where the 10 is from Yates' algorithm. Daniel (1976, p. 54) reports that σ was known to be about 12, however, so our estimate from this "ad hoc" approach is quite poor.

Earlier in this chapter the exact t test for two independent samples was illustrated. This can be used to test for the significance of the main effects and interactions, since each effect estimate is simply the difference of two averages. Since the variance of the difference of two (independent) averages is equal to the variance of the first average plus the variance of the second, we have that the (estimated) $\mathrm{Var}(\bar{y}_{\text{high}} - \bar{y}_{\text{low}}) = (s^2/n) + (s^2/n) = 2s^2/n$, where s^2 is the estimate of σ^2 and n is the number of observations from which each average is calculated. (Here the two numbers are assumed equal.) Using $(12)^2 = 144$ for s^2 and 4 for n, we obtain 72 as our estimate of the variance for each effect estimate, so that $\sqrt{72} = 8.49$ is our estimate of the standard deviation.

Dividing each effect estimate in Table 13.11 by 8.49 produces quotients that are less than 2 in absolute value for every effect except B, C, and BC. (Here 2 is used as a rough cutoff for the significance of a t statistic.)

Recalling Daniel's admonition that main effects should not be reported and interpreted separately when the interaction effect of those factors is more than one-third of the main effects, we need to look at the BC

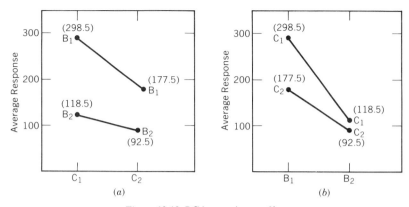

Figure 13.12 BC interaction profiles.

interaction profile to get a better handle on what is happening. The profiles are given in Figure 13.12.

These profiles illustrate why graphical displays should be used to supplement results such as those given in Table 13.11 and in ANOVA tables. The interaction effect is apparent from either Figure 13.12a or 13.12b, and it is this BC interaction that makes the B effect considerably different for the two levels of C, and the C effect considerably different for the two levels of B. Specifically, Table 13.11 indicates that the estimate of the B effect is -132.5. Using Figure 13.12a, the B effect is the average of $118.5 - 298.5 = -180$ and $92.5 - 177.5 = -85$. There is obviously a considerable difference between -180 and -85, and this difference results from the significant BC interaction. Thus, reporting that the estimate of the B effect is -132.5 is really not sufficient, since the effect is considerably greater than that (-180) at low C, and considerably less than that (-85) at high C.

Although interaction profiles are generally constructed in such a way that the factor letter that comes second in the alphabet is on the horizontal axis, there is no compelling reason for always following such a procedure. Figure 13.12b also illustrates the BC interaction, and allows us to view the C effect for the different levels of B. Specifically, the estimate of the C effect must be equal to the average of $177.5 - 298.5 = -121$ and $92.5 - 118.5 = -26$. The average of these two numbers is, of course, equal to -73.5, which is the estimate of the C effect that is given in Table 13.11. Again, these two estimates differ greatly, so simply reporting the estimate to be -73.5 does not give the full story.

If the two lines in Figure 13.12a are not parallel, then the lines in Figure 13.12b are not going to be parallel either (and similarly when the lines are parallel), so the two interaction profiles simply provide a different view of the interaction.

13.8 ASSESSMENT OF EFFECTS WITHOUT A RESIDUAL TERM

In this example it was possible to assess the significance of the main effects and interaction effects because there was an estimate of the experimental error standard deviation that was available as prior information.

We cannot always expect prior information to be available, however, so we need a method of assessing the possible significance of main effects and interactions without having to use a residual term, or, for that matter, having to arbitrarily pool high-order interactions to create a residual term. Daniel (1959) developed a method for making this assessment that entails the plotting of the effect estimates on normal probability paper, and seeing if they form roughly a straight line. If they do, none of the effects is likely to be significant. Conversely, points that lie some distance from a line that links the other points likely represent significant effects.

We would like to have a computer available for constructing such plots, but it is not difficult to construct them by hand. The construction of normal probability paper for making such plots was mentioned briefly in Chapter 11, and the procedure has been presented in Nelson (1976) and other sources.

The plot for these data is given in Figure 13.13. The plot gives the same message as was given by the other analyses that have been presented, namely, that the B, C, and BC effects appear to be significant.

The plot is interpreted by looking for effect estimates that are considerably off the line that will almost connect most of the effect estimates. When effects are not significant, their estimates should be reasonably close to zero, and a straight line through (0,0) will virtually connect the points. We should always have enough points to form such a line, as it would be somewhat rare to encounter a factorial design with three or more factors in which most of the effects are significant. [Daniel (1976, p. 75) roughly estimates that about 4 significant effects is average for a 2^4 design, and 7 for a 2^5.]

It should be noted that this plotting procedure does not incorporate an estimate of σ, and the magnitude of that standard deviation will essentially determine how far a point should be from the line before the effect that it represents could be judged a real (significant) effect. Therefore, this is not a precise method for determining real effects, but it is a very useful method.

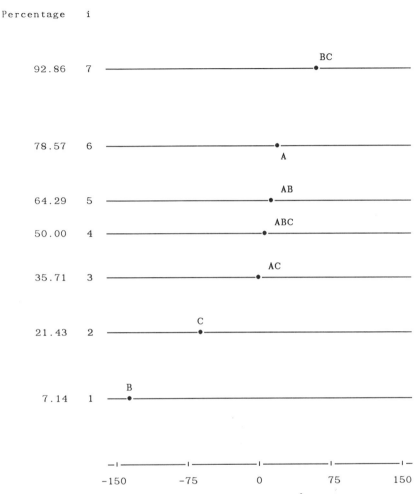

Figure 13.13 Normal probability plot for effects in 2^3 example.

We should not expect virtually all of the points to fall on a line even when there are no real effects, however, since, assuming normality, we would expect the effect estimates to vary as would a normally distributed random variable with a mean of zero. Daniel (1976) provides a set of 40 normal probability plots, in which each plot contains 16 points, and each point is generated from a standard normal distribution. Not one of the 40 plots is a straight line plot, and many are not even close, and this is due to the fact that 16 values generated from a standard normal distribution simply will not form an empirical standard normal distribution.

Box and Meyer (1986) presented a statistical procedure for unreplicated fractional factorials that can be used to supplement the graphical procedure of Daniel.

13.9 RESIDUAL PLOT

Another use of a normal probability plot in analyzing data from a designed experiment is in analyzing the residuals. For this type of plot we would expect the points (residuals) to come reasonably close to forming a straight line.

Residual plots and the calculation of residuals were discussed earlier in Section 13.5, in which a residual was presented as the difference between the observed value and the predicted value. Thus, in this section "residual" will not represent the residual sum of squares. Rather, it will represent $Y - \hat{Y}$, which when squared and summed over the design points equals the residual sum of squares.

Predicted values for experimental design data can be obtained by using the *reverse Yates' algorithm* (see Daniel, 1976), in which the predicted values are obtained from a prediction equation that contains only those effects that are judged to be real.

The reverse Yates' algorithm begins where the (forward) Yates' algorithm leaves off. That is, the starting point is the last column of numbers obtained from the various sums and differences. The numbers are written in reverse order, however, with zeros substituted for those numbers that correspond to effects that are judged to be not significant. From that point on the additions and subtractions are performed in the same way, and when the numbers in column (3) are divided by the number of design points, the result is the column of predicted values for each of the treatment combinations. The residuals are then obtained by subtracting each of the predicted values from the corresponding observed values. The results are shown in Table 13.12.

The fact that the $\hat{Y}$ values repeat in pairs is due to the fact that every other number in the first column of numbers is a zero. The reader will observe that the numbers that repeat are the averages of the corresponding Y values. Again, this is due to the pattern of zeros in the first column, and is not a general result.

The plot of the residuals, $Y - \hat{Y}$, is given in Figure 13.14. It can be observed that the points come reasonably close to forming a straight line and exhibit no gross abnormalities, although assessing normality is difficult with such a small number of points.

Table 13.12 Reverse Yates' Algorithm for 2^3 Data

Effect	Column (3) from Forward Yates with Zeros Inserted	(1)	(2)	(3)	Divisor	$\hat{Y}$	Y	$Y - \hat{Y}$
ABC	0	190	−104	740	8	92.5	109	16.5
BC	190	−294	844	740	8	92.5	76	−16.5
AC	0	−530	−104	1420	8	177.5	178	0.5
C	−294	1374	844	1420	8	177.5	177	−0.5
AB	0	190	−484	948	8	118.5	131	12.5
B	−530	−294	1904	948	8	118.5	106	−12.5
A	0	−530	−484	2388	8	298.5	300	1.5
Average	1374	1374	1904	2388	8	298.5	297	−1.5

The predicted values could also be obtained from the prediction equation

$$\hat{Y} = 171.75 - 66.25X_1 - 36.75X_2 + 23.75X_1X_2$$

where the coefficients for X_1, X_2, and X_1X_2 are obtained by dividing by two the estimates of the B, C, and BC effects. The values for X_1 are -1 for the low level of B, and $+1$ for the high level of B, and similarly for X_2 as it represents factor C. The values for X_1X_2 are simply the product of the individual values for X_1 and X_2. A measure of the adequacy of the prediction equation is R^2, which, the reader may recall, can be calculated as

$$R^2 = 1 - \frac{\Sigma(Y - \hat{Y})^2}{\Sigma(Y - \overline{Y})^2}$$

Using the appropriate values from Table 13.12, we obtain

$$R^2 = 1 - \frac{862}{51,291.5}$$
$$= 0.983$$

so that the use of B, C, and BC explains almost all of the variability in the data.

Are we now finished with the analysis? It would appear so, but Daniel (1976, p. 59) reports that the experimenter believed strongly that factor A

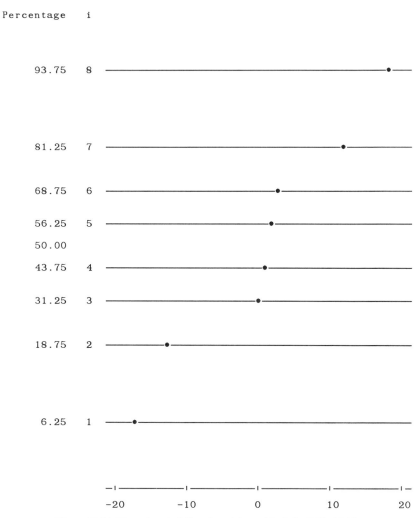

Percentage   i

Figure 13.14 Normal probability plot of the residuals in Table 13.12.

did indeed have some effect. Our analysis, however, revealed otherwise, so should we conclude that the experimenter must have been wrong? Not without taking a closer look at the data.

We saw previously in Table 13.11 that the estimate of the A effect is 15.5. This effect can be viewed as the average of four differences, in which each difference is obtained by subtracting the response with A at the low level from the response with A at the high level, and the levels of B and C held constant in each pair. Thus, the differences are $[a - (1)]$, $(ab - b)$, $(ac - c)$, and $(abc - bc)$. The first and third differences are obviously at low B, and the second and fourth differences are at high B. It can be seen from Table 13.10 that the average of the first and third differences is 2.0, whereas the average of the second and fourth differences is 29.0. The estimated standard deviation of this second average is 12 (obtained from $\text{Var}(\bar{y}_{\text{high}} - \bar{y}_{\text{low}})$ with $n = 2$) so that the value of the t statistic for testing the significance of the A effect at high B would thus be $29/12$, which is greater than the previously mentioned cutoff value of 2.0. Thus, there does appear to be a significant A effect at high B but obviously not at low B.

Again, the important point is that a routine analysis does not suffice, and even when it appears as though a thorough analysis has been conducted, it is quite possible that something may have been overlooked. In fact, it is not uncommon for a data set to be analyzed by a number of people (including prominent statisticians) and then someone would discover an important bit of information that had previously been undetected. [See Box et al. (1978, p. 496) for such an example.]

This concludes our discussion of the example for the 2^3 design. Although the design is favored by some, Daniel (1976, p. 53) indicates that 16-point designs are much more valuable, and gives conditions under which a 2^3 might be used.

13.10 TWO-LEVEL DESIGNS WITH MORE THAN THREE FACTORS

The analysis of designs such as the 2^4 and 2^5 can be carried out by following essentially the same steps that were illustrated for the 2^3. There is, of course, more computation that has to be performed (either by hand or by computer), and more "detective work" will generally be required as the number of factors increases. Extensive discussion and analysis of some actual experiments conducted using 2^4 and 2^5 designs (including some classic experiments) can be found in Chapters 6 and 7 of Daniel (1976), and the reader is urged to study that material carefully.

At this point the reader might wonder how one goes about determining the number of factors to study in an experiment. In some instances an experimenter may have a reasonably good idea as to the number of factors that seem to be worth investigating, and this number might be fairly small. In other applications, however, there might be a large number of potentially significant factors. If there were 10 such factors, a 2^{10} design would require 1024 treatment combinations. An experiment with this many design points would not only be virtually impossible to carry out, but the cost would likely be prohibitive. Accordingly, a fractional factorial design would be a logical alternative, in which a small fraction of the 1024 design points would actually be used. Once influential factors have been identified from the use of such a design, a two- or three-level design might then be used to study the k influential factors further, assuming that k is small. Fractional factorial designs are discussed in Section 13.13.

13.11 THREE-LEVEL FACTORIAL DESIGNS

Often there will be three levels of two or more factors that are logical to study, rather than just two levels. If a full factorial is to be used, however, the use of three levels imposes a practical limitation on the number of factors that can be investigated since the number of design points increases rapidly as k increases. Consequently, 3^2 and 3^3 designs are those that are of practical interest. They can be analyzed using the *extended Yates' algorithm* [Davies (1954)].

When a factor has three levels, it will have two degrees of freedom, and the associated sum of squares can be decomposed into two components— one that represents the linear effect of the factor, and the other that represents the quadratic effect. Assuming that the factor is continuous and has equally spaced levels, a linear effect is where the value of the response variable changes at (almost) a constant rate over the different levels. Conversely, a quadratic effect is where the value of the response variable changes along the lines of a quadratic relationship between the variable and the factor (i.e., a quadratic relationship would be of the general form $y = ax^2 + bx + c$ where y would be the response variable, and x the factor).

If there was only one factor, the relationship between the response variable and the factor could be displayed as a two-dimensional graph. With two factors, however, a three-dimensional display is needed and this is generally termed a surface, more specifically, a response surface. Thus, a 3^2 design enables the experimenter to gain insight into the response region (surface), although response surface designs (discussed briefly at the end of this chapter) are better suited for that purpose. (The same general conclusion can be drawn for a 3^3 design.)

Thus, although three-level factorial designs have been used to some extent, their usefulness is somewhat limited.

13.12 MIXED FACTORIALS

To this point there has been an implicit assumption that the number of levels of interest is the same for each of the factors to be studied. This will not always be the case, however. A mixed factorial (also called an asymmetrical factorial) in two factors is of the general form $a^{k_1}b^{k_2}$ where k_1 and k_2 are greater than or equal to 1, and $a \neq b$. Data from such designs can be analyzed using the extended Yates' algorithm provided that $a = 2$ and $b = 3$ (Margolin, 1967). Mixed factorial designs have been discussed, in particular, by Addelman (1962) and in Chapter 18 of Kempthorne (1973), although the treatment in these sources is somewhat mathematical.

13.13   FRACTIONAL FACTORIALS

As was previously mentioned, the number of design points can be rather large when there are more than just a few factors of interest. As Steinberg and Hunter (1984) indicate, there might be as many as 50 or 100 potentially important factors in some applications. (A 2^{50} design might take a few lifetimes to run.)

We shall focus attention upon two-level fractional factorial designs as this type of fractional factorial has been used extensively in practice. Fractional factorials were first presented by Finney (1945) and popularized in the landmark papers of Box and Hunter (1961a, b), and we shall adopt the notation of the latter throughout this section.

13.13.1 2^{k-1} Designs

A two-level fractional factorial can be written in the general form 2^{k-p}, where, as before, k denotes the number of factors, and the fraction of the full 2^k factorial that is to be run is $1/2^p$. Thus, a 2^{3-1} design would be a $1/2$ fraction of a 2^3. Sixteen point designs (so that $k - p = 4$) are the ones that have been used the most often in industry.

For simplicity, however, we shall first illustrate a 2^{3-1}, which, although of limited usefulness, does have value for illustrative purposes. We should first recognize that with only four design points (here we are assuming that the design is not replicated), we will have only 3 d.f. so we can estimate only 3 effects. Which three effects do we choose to estimate? Although in rare instances a two-factor interaction might be of more interest to an experimenter than a main effect, we would generally choose to estimate main effects over interactions, if we had to select one over the other. Thus, the logical choice would be to estimate the three main effects: A, B, and C. Before we can undertake that task, however, we must determine what four design points to use. We cannot randomly select four treatment combinations from the eight that are available. For example, we obviously could not estimate the main effect of A if we happened to select four treatment combinations in which A was at the high level, and none in which A was at

Figure 13.15 Two 1/2 fractions of 2^3.

the low level; similarly for B and C. Thus, we would clearly want to have two treatment combinations in which A is at the high level and two in which A is at the low level, and the same for B and C.

With a little trial and error we could obtain four treatment combinations that satisfy this property without too much difficulty, but it would obviously be preferable to use some systematic approach. Whenever a 1/2 fraction is used, we have to select one effect to "confound" with the difference between the two fractions, that is, that particular effect would be estimated by the difference of the averages of the treatment combinations in each fraction (which of course is the way that we would logically estimate the difference between the two fractions). If we have to "give up" the estimate of one effect in this way (which is obviously what we are doing since we will run only one of the two fractions), it would be logical to select the highest order interaction to relinquish. For a 2^3 that is the ABC interaction.

One simple way to construct the two 1/2 fractions (from which one would be randomly selected) would be to assign those treatment combinations with an even number of letters in common with ABC to one fraction, and those with an odd number of letters in common with ABC to the other fraction. This produces the two fractions given in Figure 13.15.

For illustration, we shall use the data in Table 13.10, which were used previously to illustrate the full 2^3. It was suggested earlier that the reader use Yates' algorithm on that data. If that were done, the numbers in Table 13.13 should look familiar. It can be observed that the 10, which is the last number in column (3), is obtained by adding the response values of the treatment combinations in the first fraction in Figure 13.15 and subtracting off the response values of the treatment combinations in the second fraction.

Before proceeding any further, we should think about what we are giving up in addition to an estimate of the ABC interaction when we run one of the fractions in Figure 13.15. We assume that we are relinquishing information on the three two-factor interactions by using one of the fractions in Figure 13.15 (since we have only 3 degrees of freedom), but we also assume that we will be able to estimate the three main effects.

Table 13.13 Yates' Algorithm Calculations Using the Data in Table 13.10

Treatment Combination	Response	(1)	(2)	(3)	Column (3) Representation
(1)	297	597	834	1374	(Sum of all responses)
a	300	237	540	62	$a + ab + ac + abc$ $- b - c - bc - (1)$
b	106	355	28	-530	$b + ab + bc + abc$ $- a - c - ac - (1)$
ab	131	185	34	54	$c + ab + abc + (1)$ $- a - b - ac - bc$
c	177	3	-360	-294	$c + ac + bc + abc$ $- a - b - ab - (1)$
ac	178	25	-170	6	$b + ac + abc + (1)$ $- a - c - ab - bc$
bc	76	1	22	190	$a + bc + abc + (1)$ $- b - c - ac - ab$
abc	109	33	32	10	$a + b + c + abc - ac$ $- ab - bc - (1)$

Let's verify this by looking at some of the other parenthetical expressions in Table 13.13. Assume that we have randomly selected the first fraction in Figure 13.15 to run. The sum and difference of the various treatment combinations beside the number -294 indicate that we would estimate the main effect of C by $(abc + c - a - b)/2 = (109 + 177 - 300 - 106)/2 = -60$, which does not differ greatly from the -73.5 that was obtained using all eight treatment combinations. Further, we can see from Table 13.13 that, using the first fraction, we would also estimate AB by $(abc + c - a - b)/2$. What this means is that the estimate of the C effect is *confounded* (i.e., confused) with the AB effect.

Similarly, it could be shown that A is confounded with BC and B is confounded with AC, as can be verified from Table 13.13. Fortunately, there are easier ways to determine what effects are confounded. One way is to write out how each effect is estimated using plus and minus signs, and then identify those effects that have the same configuration of signs. The other method is even easier and is simply a matter of multiplying each effect times the effect that was confounded with the difference of the two fractions (ABC in this example), and removing any letter whose exponent is a 2. (This applies to any two-level fractional factorial.) Thus, $A(ABC) = A^2BC = BC$, $B(ABC) = AB^2C = AC$, and $C(ABC) = ABC^2 = AB$. The effects that are confounded with each other are said to be *aliases* of each other, and the set of such aliases is said to be the *alias structure*.

Another way to view the alias structure is to use Yates' algorithm after filling in zeros for the treatment combinations that are in the fraction that is not used. Factors that are aliased will then have the same totals in column (3), as the reader is asked to demonstrate for these data in Exercise 1.

This is not a recommended approach for determining the alias structure, however, as effect estimates [and, hence, numbers in column (3)] can be the same without the effects being confounded. It is also far more time consuming than the multiplication approach just illustrated. It is simply another way of viewing the alias structure.

We saw from the analysis of the full factorial that the AB interaction was not significant, and we can also see from Table 13.11 that the estimate of C plus the estimate of AB equals the -60 that we just obtained using the four treatment combinations in the first fraction. Thus, we are actually estimating C + AB rather than just C, and the extent to which our estimate of C is contaminated depends upon the size of the AB interaction. Here there is no serious problem because the AB interaction is not large.

What if we had randomly selected the other fraction? A little arithmetic would reveal that our estimate of C would be -87, and that we would really be estimating C $-$ AB.

We saw previously that the BC interaction was significant, and we know now that BC is aliased with A. Therefore, we can see to what extent the estimate of the A effect is contaminated by the presence of a strong BC interaction. Again assuming that we had used the first fraction, our estimate of the A effect would be obtained from $(abc + a - b - c)/2 = (109 + 300 - 106 - 177)/2 = 63$, which differs dramatically from our estimate of 15.5 obtained from the full factorial. As the reader might suspect, we are actually estimating A + BC (A $-$ BC with the other fraction), so that, in this example, we would erroneously conclude that there is a strong A effect when in fact there is not. (We remember, however, that our detective work did reveal that A was somewhat influential when B was at its high level.)

The upshot of all of this is that when we run a fractional factorial we do take a risk, and the severity of the risk depends upon the order of the interactions that are lost. Second-order interactions (i.e., involving two factors) and the third-order interaction were lost in the 2^{3-1} example, so that design should be considered only if there is a strong prior belief that none of the interactions will be significant. Even then, the advantage of the fractional factorial would be minimal, as four design points would be run instead of eight—not much of a saving.

The picture changes considerably, however, when there are more than three factors. What about a 2^{4-1}? The alias structure would certainly be more palatable in that the fractions could be constructed in such a way that the main effects would be aliased with third-order interactions, but, unfortunately, the second-order interactions are aliased in pairs. The ABCD interaction would be confounded with the difference between the two fractions, and we would then have A = BCD, B = ACD...AB = CD, AC = BD, etc.

Snee (1985) considers the 2^{5-1}, 2^{6-2}, 2^{7-3}, and 2^{8-4} designs for the study of 5, 6, 7, and 8 factors, respectively, to be the most useful fractional factorial designs, and provides an example of a 2^{5-1} and a 2^{7-3}. We will briefly discuss the former.

In the 2^{5-1} experiment the objective was to identify the process variables that affect the color of a product produced by a chemical process, so that a process control procedure could be implemented for controlling the variation in the color. Five process variables that were thought to be potentially important were (1) solvent/reactant ratio, (2) catalyst/reactant ratio, (3) temperature, (4) reactant purity, and (5) pH of reactant.

If we were to proceed as before, we would select ABCDE to confound with the difference between fractions. This is generally called the *defining contrast*. ABCDE is the best choice because it would produce the most palatable alias structure. Specifically, main effects will be aliased with four-factor interactions, and two-factor interactions will be aliased with three-factor interactions. Thus, we can estimate main effects and all two-factor interactions provided that third-order and higher order interactions are negligible (which will usually be the case).

What is estimable for a particular fractional factorial design can be expressed compactly by indicating the *resolution* of the design. Coined by Box and Hunter (1961a), a design of Resolution III is one in which only the main effects are estimable, and they are estimable only if the two-factor interactions are negligible, since main effects and two-factor interactions are confounded. We recall that this was the alias structure for the 2^{3-1} design. Thus, that design is a Resolution III design. A Resolution IV design is one in which no main effects are confounded with two-factor interactions, but two-factor interactions are confounded with each other. An example was the 2^{4-1} design. The 2^{5-1} design is an example of a Resolution V design in which both main effects and two-factor interactions are estimable in the absence of third and higher order interactions.

It should be emphasized, however, that a 2^{5-1} design is not automatically a Resolution V design. It is such a design only when the best choice is made for the defining contrast (ABCDE), and it should be observed that the number of letters in the defining contrast determines the resolution of the design for any one-half fraction. (Determining the resolution for smaller fractions is slightly more involved and will be discussed later.)

To construct the two fractions of the 2^{5-1} design we could proceed as before and allocate those treatment combinations with an even number of letters in common with ABCDE to one fraction, and those with an odd number of letters in common to the other fraction. This would require enumerating all $2^5 = 32$ treatment combinations, however, so that when there are more than four factors such an approach is somewhat laborious.

An alternative procedure, following Box et al. (1978, p. 386), is to enumerate a full 2^4 factorial using plus and minus signs (to designate the high and low levels, respectively) and then use the product of those signs for each treatment combination to form the signs for the fifth factor.

Specifically, for the full 2^4 factorial there are 16 treatment combinations, and these can be expressed by alternating plus and minus signs in a certain way as is shown in Table 13.4. (I = ABCDE means that ABCDE is the defining contrast.) The pattern that is exhibited by the various columns should be apparent. The last column in the full factorial part (column D in this case) will always have 2^{k-1} minus signs followed by 2^{k-1} plus signs for a 2^k factorial, so that all of the columns begin with a consecutive number of minus signs which are each a power of 2 (i.e., $2^0, 2^1, 2^2, 2^3$). (If we were constructing a 2^{6-1} fractional factorial, the last column in the full factorial part would have 16 consecutive minus signs followed by 16 consecutive plus signs.) Notice that the sign for the E factor in the first fraction is simply the product of the signs for the other four factors, and the negative of that product in the second fraction. Notice also that each of the treatment

Table 13.14 The Two Half Fractions of a 2^5

Treatment Combination	Fraction #1 (I = ABCDE)					Treatment Combination	Fraction #2 (I = −ABCDE)				
	A	B	C	D	E		A	B	C	D	E
e	−	−	−	−	+	(1)	−	−	−	−	−
a	+	−	−	−	−	ae	+	−	−	−	+
b	−	+	−	−	−	be	−	+	−	−	+
abe	+	+	−	−	+	ab	+	+	−	−	−
c	−	−	+	−	−	ce	−	−	+	−	+
ace	+	−	+	−	+	ac	+	−	+	−	−
bce	−	+	+	−	+	bc	−	+	+	−	−
abc	+	+	+	−	−	abce	+	+	+	−	+
d	−	−	−	+	−	de	−	−	−	+	+
ade	+	−	−	+	+	ad	+	−	−	+	−
bde	−	+	−	+	+	bd	−	+	−	+	−
abd	+	+	−	+	−	abde	+	+	−	+	+
cde	−	−	+	+	+	cd	−	−	+	+	−
acd	+	−	+	+	−	acde	+	−	+	+	+
bcd	−	+	+	+	−	bcde	−	+	+	+	+
abcde	+	+	+	+	+	abcd	+	+	+	+	−

combinations in the first fraction has an even number of letters in common with ABCDE, and an odd number of letters in common in the second fraction. Thus, this new approach gives us the same fractions that we would have obtained using the previously described approach. As Box et al. point out (p. 386) this approach will always produce a 2^{k-1} design with the highest possible resolution.

The first fraction is the one that was used in the experiment described by Snee (1985). The values of the response variable (color) were (in coded units) in order: -0.63, 2.51, -2.68, -1.66, 2.06, 1.22, -2.09, 1.93, 6.79, 6.47, 3.45, 5.68, 5.22, 9.38, 4.30, and 4.05.

How would we proceed to analyze these data? We *could* use the same approach as was illustrated for the 2^{3-1} example, that is, use Yates' algorithm to obtain the plus and minus signs of each treatment combination for the full 2^5 factorial, and then use just the treatment combinations that actually occurred in the fraction. This would be quite laborious for 5 factors, however.

Another approach is to use a modification of Yates' algorithm for 2^{k-p} designs, in which the algorithm is applied to a full factorial in $k - p$ factors. This approach is discussed by Box, Hunter, and Hunter (1978, p. 407) and illustrated in Cochran and Cox (1957, p. 254). Berger (1972) shows how to generate the 2^{k-p} treatment combinations in the proper order so that Yates' algorithm can be applied, and McLean and Anderson (1984, p. 263) illustrate the approach.

A third approach would be to produce the column of plus and minus signs for each interaction that is estimable (the two-factor interactions in this case since this is a Resolution V design) and use those columns and the columns for A, B, C, D, and E in Table 13.14 in obtaining estimates of the two-factor interactions and main effects, respectively. The interaction columns would be obtained by multiplying together the columns of the factors that comprise each interaction. For example, the AB interaction column would be obtained by multiplying the A column times the B column, thus starting with the pattern $+ - - +$, with the pattern repeated three more times. The estimate of each effect would then be obtained by taking the average of the eight response values that are associated with a treatment combination that has a plus sign, and subtracting off the average of the eight response values that are associated with a treatment combination that has a minus sign. The reader can use the A column to verify that the estimate of the A effect is 1.645 and the estimate of the AB effect is 0.11.

Since this is a Resolution V design we know that the main effects and two-factor interactions are estimable, and since we have 15 of them, altogether, we have no d.f. for estimating σ with 16 design points. Therefore, there is a need to assess the possible significance of each effect by plotting the estimates of the effects on normal probability paper (or using some other method). Snee (1985) portrayed these estimates in a half-normal plot (recall that this differs from a normal plot only by dropping the sign on negative estimates and plotting the positive value). It was shown that D, B, E, and A have a significant effect, especially D.

It was stated previously that the procedure given by Box and Meyer (1986) can also be used to identify significant effects in unreplicated fractional factorials. A description of the procedure would be beyond the level of this text, however, as the procedure requires the use of posterior probabilities and numerical integration. Readers with a strong foundation in statistics are referred to their paper for details.

13.13.2 2^{k-2} Designs

It was observed that the 2^{5-1} design with 16 points allowed for the estimation of the main effects and two-factor interactions. What would be sacrificed if the experimenter had decided that 16 design points would be too expensive (or otherwise impractical) and chose to run a 2^{5-2} design instead?

In general, when the fraction is of the form $1/2^p$, there will be 2^{p-1} effects that must be confounded with the difference between the fractions, and their product(s) will also be confounded. Thus, for the 2^{5-2} we must select two effects to confound, and their product will also be confounded. This set of effects (i.e., defining contrasts) forms what is termed the *defining relation*. Since the resolution of a two-level fractional factorial is defined as the number of letters in the shortest defining contrast, it might seem as though we should select ABCDE and one of the four factor interactions. This would be disastrous, however, as their product would contain only a single letter, and we would consequently lose a main effect. Similarly, a little reflection should indicate that any pair of four-factor interactions will have three factors in common, and will thus produce a two-factor interaction when multiplied together. We can, however, choose a pair of three factor interactions in such a way that the product is a four-factor interaction. For example, ABC and BDE would produce ACDE when multiplied together. (There is no advantage in selecting any particular pair, as only main effects are estimable, anyway.)

The alias structure is then obtained by multiplying each of the effects by the three defining contrasts. For example, A = BC = ABDE = CDE. The four 1/4 fractions could be constructed by determining (1) the treatment combinations that have an even number of letters in common with both ABC and BDE, (2) those combinations with an even number in common with ABC and an odd number in common with BDE, (3) those combina-

Table 13.15 Treatment Combinations of Four 1 / 4 Fractions of a 2^5
(I = ABC = BDE = ACDE)

(1)	(2)	(3)	(4)
(1)	ab	a	b
ac	acd	c	cd
de	ace	abcd	ce
acde	d	abce	bde
abd	e	bd	abc
abe	bc	be	ae
bcd	bcde	ade	ad
bce	abde	cde	abcde

tions with an odd number in common with ABC and an even number in common with BDE [i.e., the reverse of (2)], and (4) those combinations with an odd number in common with both ABC and BDE.

Although theoretically desirable, it is not absolutely essential to write out all four fractions and then randomly select one. This is generally not done in practice. The four fractions are given in Table 13.15, however, for the sake of clarity.

The five main effects would then be estimated in the usual way—the average of the four values in which the factor is at the high level minus the average of the four values in which the factor is at the low level. For example, if the first fraction was used, the main effect of A would be estimated by $(ac + abe + abd + acde)/4 - [bcd + bce + de + (1)]/4$.

It should be noted that with this fractional factorial there will be two d.f. for the residual, so the plotting of effect estimates on normal probability paper would not be absolutely essential, although probably desirable since the two d.f. correspond to two-factor interactions that are not being estimated.

It was stated previously that obtaining the design configuration by enumerating the treatment combinations is somewhat laborious when there are more than just a few factors. For 1/4 fractions, however, that is the most straightforward approach. Another approach is described by Box, Hunter, and Hunter (1978, p. 397) who show how to obtain a 2^{5-2} from a 2^{7-4}.

For detailed information on the construction of two-level fractional factorials, the reader is referred to Chapter 12 of Box, Hunter, and Hunter (1978) and Chapters 11 and 12 of Daniel (1976), in particular, as well as Box and Hunter (1961a, b). Additional examples of these designs can be found in Daniel (1976) and Chapter 13 of Box, Hunter, and Hunter (1978).

13.13.3 Fractions of Three-Level Factorials

In general, three-level factorials are not used as extensively as two-level factorials, and the same can be said for fractional factorials. The 3^{k-p} designs have the shortcoming that quite a few design points are required for such a design to be Resolution V. Response surface designs, to be discussed briefly in a later section, require fewer design points and are considered to be superior to the 3^{k-p} designs (as well as the 3^k designs).

For readers who may have an interest in 3^{k-p} designs, we mention the catalog of such designs in Connor and Zelen (1959). Although this publication is now out of print, it has been reproduced as Appendix 2 in McLean and Anderson (1984).

13.13.4 Incomplete Mixed Factorials

The term *incomplete* is used here instead of *fractional*, as the number of design points is not generally a common fraction of the full mixed factorial. These designs are summarized in Chapter 13 of Daniel (1976), and the interested reader is referred to that material.

13.14 OTHER TOPICS IN EXPERIMENTAL DESIGN AND THEIR APPLICATIONS

13.14.1 Mixture Designs

An important application of experimental design techniques is in the area of mixture models. The general idea is to determine the best mixture of ingredients (factors) to optimize the response variable. A classic example is determining the best composition of gasoline to maximize miles per gallon. The proportions of the ingredients must add to 100%, which induces a type of restriction not generally found in other experimental design applications. Consequently, it requires the use of design procedures that were not discussed in this chapter. The development of such procedures dates from around 1970, although the initial impetus was provided by the pioneering paper of Scheffé (1958). For an introduction to mixture designs the reader is referred to Snee (1971, 1973, 1981), and Cornell (1979, 1983). A comprehensive treatment is given in the text by Cornell (1981).

13.14.2 Response Surface Designs

The emphasis in this chapter has been on designs for factors with two levels because those are the designs used most frequently in practice. There is a need to use more than two levels to detect curvature, however, and, in general, to determine the shape of the "response surface." That is, how does the response vary over different combinations of values of the process variables? In what region(s) is the change approximately linear? Are there humps, and valleys, and saddle points, and, if so, where do they occur? These are the type of questions that response surface methodology (oftentimes abbreviated as RSM) attempts to answer.

The work on RSM dates from the pioneering paper of Box and Wilson (1951). Other important papers include Box and Hunter (1957) and Box and Behnken (1960). A review of the early work on RSM is given by Hill and Hunter (1966). Cornell (1985) is another of the ASQC-published instructional booklets that are recommended for initial reading. Until recently, the only text ever written on RSM was Myers (1971). An extensive treatment of RSM is now available in Box and Draper (1986) and Khuri and Cornell (1987).

13.14.3 Computer-Aided Design and Expert Systems

The statistical design of experiments is not an easy task. There are literally hundreds of designs, and for a particular objective and physical setting there might be several designs that could be used. Consequently, the choice of a particular design can be difficult. Some type of guidance is necessary, not only for the experienced user who may be aware of some of his or her options, but especially for the experimenter whose knowledge of experimental designs is limited.

The assistance that is provided could be of several forms: (1) advice from a statistical consultant, (2) software for computer-aided design of experiments, and (3) software for expert systems.

Both (2) and (3) are recent innovations. The difference between them is that with the latter there is minimal user input; the decision making is essentially performed by the software. The question naturally arises as to whether or not this is desirable. This and other issues are addressed by Hahn (1985) and the discussants of that paper.

Experimental design software that additionally guides users is a necessity, so it is really a matter of degree. A totally automated system would preclude the infusion of common sense and real-world experience, so some balance must be reached. Computer-aided design of fractional factorial experiments is discussed by Knight and Neuhardt (1983).

13.14.4 Sequential Experimentation

Experimentation does not end, of course, when a design has been selected and the data subsequently collected and analyzed. A physical system will generally change over time, and even if it did not, follow-up experiments should still be used to gain better insight into the nature of the system. Such experiments can often be used to resolve ambiguities from the previous experiment.

Consequently, the construction of subsequent designs should be performed using knowledge of how the previous design was constructed, and the results of the analysis. This also requires, of course, that financial resources be allocated judiciously. Box, Hunter, and Hunter (1978) recommend that at most 25% of the resources be used for the first experiment.

SUMMARY

The statistical design of experiments is a very broad area, and dozens of books have been written on the subject. The focus for most of these, however, has been the analysis of data from standard designs. The first step must be the design of the experiment, and that is the hard part. Much thought needs to be given to the design, and the experimenter must also realize that a routine "cookbook" analysis of the data will generally be insufficient.

Since design of experiments is important, and much thought needs to be given to it, how can experimenters acquire the necessary expertise without having to spend a large amount of company funds, and then possibly drawing erroneous conclusions?

The author has found the ideas and sample experiments presented in Hunter (1977) to be quite helpful in enabling students in a statistics course to "get their feet wet" in designing experiments and analyzing resultant data. Such ideas can be incorporated into corporate training programs to enable personnel to acquire the necessary expertise without committing the labor and materials that would be required for an actual company experiment.

REFERENCES

Addelman, S. (1962). Orthogonal main-effect plans for asymmetrical factorial experiments. *Technometrics* 4(1): 21–46 (February).

Bainbridge, T. R. (1965). Staggered, nested designs for estimating variance components. *Industrial Quality Control* 22(1): 12–20 (July).

Berger, P. D. (1972). On Yates' order in fractional factorial designs. *Technometrics* 14(4): 971–972 (November).

Box, G. E. P., and D. Behnken (1960). Some new three level designs for the study of quantitative variables. *Technometrics* 2(4): 455–475 (November).

Box, G. E. P., and N. R. Draper (1986). *Empirical Model Building and Response Surfaces*. New York: Wiley.

Box, G. E. P., and J. S. Hunter (1957). Multifactor designs for exploring response surfaces. *Annals of Mathematical Statistics 28*: 195–241.

Box, G. E. P., and J. S. Hunter (1961a). The 2^{k-p} fractional factorial designs Part I. *Technometrics 3*(3): 311–351 (August).

Box, G. E. P., and J. S. Hunter (1961b). The 2^{k-p} fractional factorial designs Part II. *Technometrics 3*(4): 449–458 (November).

Box, G. E. P., and R. D. Meyer (1986). An analysis for unreplicated fractional factorials. *Technometrics 28*(1): 11–18 (February).

Box, G. E. P., and K. B. Wilson (1951). On the experimental attainment of optimum conditions. *Journal of the Royal Statistical Society, Series B 13*(1): 1–45 (with discussion).

Box, G. E. P., W. G. Hunter, and J. S. Hunter (1978). *Statistics for Experimenters*. New York: Wiley.

Chan, T. F., G. H. Golub, and R. J. Leveque (1983). Algorithms for computing the sample variance: Analysis and recommendations. *The American Statistician 37*(3): 242–247 (August).

Cochran, W. G., and G. M. Cox (1957). *Experimental Designs*, 2nd ed. New York: Wiley.

Connor, W. S., and M. Zelen (1959). *Fractional Factorial Experiment Designs for Factors at Three Levels*. National Bureau of Standards, Applied Mathematics Series, No. 54.

Conover, W. J. (1980). *Practical Nonparametric Statistics*, 2nd ed. New York: Wiley.

Cornell, J. A. (1979). Experiments with mixtures: An update and bibliography. *Technometrics 21*(1): 95–106 (February).

Cornell, J. A. (1981). *Experiments with Mixtures: Designs, Models, and the Analysis of Mixture Data*. New York: Wiley.

Cornell, J. A. (1983). How to run mixture experiments for product quality. *Basic References in Quality Control: Statistical Techniques*, Vol. 5. Milwaukee: American Society for Quality Control.

Cornell, J. A. (1985). How to apply response surface methodology. *Basic References in Quality Control: Statistical Techniques*, Vol. 8. Milwaukee: American Society for Quality Control.

Cressie, N. A. C., and H. J. Whitford (1986). How to use the two sample T-test. *Biometrical Journal 28*(2): 131–148.

Daniel, C. (1959). Use of half-normal plots in interpreting factorial two-level experiments. *Technometrics 1*(4): 311–341 (November).

Daniel, C. (1973). One-at-a-time plans. *Journal of the American Statistical Association 68*(342): 353–360 (June).

Daniel, C. (1976). *Applications of Statistics to Industrial Experimentation*. New York: Wiley.

Davies, O. L. (ed.) (1954). *Design and Analysis of Industrial Experiments*. New York: Hafner Press (Macmillan).

Deming, W. E. (1975). On probability as a basis for action. *American Statistician* 29(4): 146–152 (November).

Finney, D. J. (1945). Fractional replication of factorial arrangements. *Annals of Eugenics 12*: 291–301.

Gupta, B. C. (1981). Checks on Yates' algorithm for a 2^m factorial experiment. *Australian Journal of Statistics 23*(2): 256–258 (August).

Hahn, G. J. (1977). Some things engineers should know about experimental design. *Journal of Quality Technology 9*(1): 13–20 (January).

Hahn, G. J. (1985). More intelligent statistical software and statistical expert systems: Future directions. *The American Statistician 39*(1): 1–8; Discussion: pp. 8–16 (February).

Hicks, C. R. (1982). *Fundamental Concepts in the Design of Experiments*, 3rd ed. New York: Holt, Rinehart, and Winston.

Hill, W. J., and W. G. Hunter (1966). A review of response surface methodology. *Technometrics 8*(4): 571–590 (November).

Hunter, W. G. (1977). Some ideas about teaching design of experiments with 2^5 examples of experiments conducted by students. *The American Statistician 31*(1): 12–17 (February).

Hunter, W. G., and M. E. Hoff (1967). Planning experiments to increase research efficiency. *Industrial and Engineering Chemistry 59*(3): 43–48 (March).

Kempthorne, O. (1973). *Design and Analysis of Experiments*. New York: Robert E. Krieger Publishing Co. (copyright held by John Wiley & Sons, Inc.).

Khuri, A., and J. Cornell (1987). *Response Surfaces: Designs and Analyses*. New York: Marcel Dekker.

Knight, J. W., and J. B. Neuhardt (1983). Computer-aided design of fractional factorial experiments given a list of feasible observations. *IIE Transactions 15*: 142–149.

Layard, M. W. J. (1973). Robust large-sample tests for homogeneity of variances. *Journal of the American Statistical Association 68*(341): 195–198 (March).

Margolin, B. H. (1967). Systematic methods for analyzing $2^N 3^M$ factorial experiments. *Technometrics 9*(2): 245–260 (May).

McLean, R. A., and V. L. Anderson (1984). *Applied Factorial and Fractional Designs*. New York: Marcel Dekker.

Miller, R. B., and D. W. Wichern (1977). *Intermediate Business Statistics*. New York: Holt, Rinehart, & Winston.

Miller, R. G. (1981). *Simultaneous Statistical Inference*, 2nd ed. New York: Springer-Verlag.

Myers, R. H. (1971). *Response Surface Methodology*. Boston: Allyn and Bacon.

Nelson, L. S. (1976). Constructing normal probability paper. *Journal of Quality Technology 8*(1): 56–57 (January).

Nelson, L. S. (1984). Some notes on Student's t. *Journal of Quality Technology* *16*(1): 64–65 (January).

Nelson, L. S. (1985). Sample size tables for analysis of variance. *Journal of Quality Technology* *17*(3): 167–169 (July).

Neter, J., W. Wasserman, and M. H. Kutner (1985). *Applied Linear Statistical Models*, 2nd ed. Homewood, IL: Irwin.

Odeh, R. E., and M. Fox (1975). *Sample Size Choice: Charts for Experiments with Linear Models*. New York: Marcel Dekker.

Ott, E. R. (1975). *Process Quality Control*. New York: McGraw-Hill.

Posten, H. O., H. C. Yeh, and D. B. Owen (1982). Robustness of the two sample t-test under violations of the homogeneity of variance assumption. *Communications in Statistics, Part A — Theory and Methods* *11*(2): 109–126.

Scheffé, H. (1958). Experiments with mixtures. *Journal of the Royal Statistical Society, Series B* *20*(2): 344–360.

Sinibaldi, F. J. (1983). Nested designs in process variation studies. *ASQC Annual Quality Congress Transactions*, pp. 503–508.

Snee, R. D. (1971). Design and analysis of mixture experiments. *Journal of Quality Technology* *3*(4): 159–169 (October).

Snee, R. D. (1973). Techniques for the analysis of mixture data. *Technometrics* *15*(3): 517–528 (August).

Snee, R. D. (1981). Developing blending models for gasoline and other mixtures. *Technometrics* *23*(2): 119–130 (May).

Snee, R. D. (1983). Graphical analysis of process variation studies. *Journal of Quality Technology* *15*(2): 76–88 (April).

Snee, R. D. (1985). Experimenting with a large number of variables. In R. D. Snee, L. B. Hare, and J. R. Trout, eds. *Experiments in Industry — Design, Analysis and Interpretation of Results*. Milwaukee: Quality Press.

Steinberg, D. M., and W. G. Hunter (1984). Experimental design: Review and comment. *Technometrics* *26*(2): 71–97; Discussion: pp. 98–130 (May).

Tukey, J. W. (1949). One degree of freedom for non-additivity. *Biometrics* *5*(3): 232–242 (September).

Welch, B. L. (1937). The significance of the difference between two means when the population variances are equal. *Biometrika* *29*: 350–362.

Yates, F. (1937). *Design and Analysis of Factorial Experiments*. London: Imperial Bureau of Soil Sciences.

Ziegel, E. R. (1984). Discussion (of an invited paper by Steinberg and Hunter). *Technometrics* *26*(2): 98–104 (May).

EXERCISES

1. Assume that a 2^{3-1} design has been run using the treatment combinations (1), ab, ac, and bc, and the response values are 12, 16, 14, and 20,

respectively. Use Yates' algorithm to show that the defining contrast is
$I = -ABC$ by pairing the totals for column (3) that are the same.

2. It was stated at the beginning of the chapter that a plot of the values
from two groups (as in Figure 13.3) in which the lines are straight and
almost touching would indicate that $\mu_1 \neq \mu_2$. Assume that the values
from the two groups are 13.00, 13.00, 13.00, 13.00, 13.001 from the first
group, and 13.01, 13.01, 13.01, 13.01, 13.011 from the second group.
What would be the result if we use an exact or approximate t test to
test whether $\mu_1 = \mu_2$? Do you think the difference is of any practical
significance if this is yield data? What does this imply that we should
keep in mind when using tests such as this?

3. Explain why the value of t^* is the same as the value for t using the data
in Problem #2.

4. An experimenter decides to use a 2^{6-2} design and elects to confound
ABD and CEF in constructing the fraction.

   a. Determine what effect(s) would be aliased with the two-factor interaction AB.

   b. Is there a better choice for the two defining contrasts?

5. A 2^2 design with 2 replicates is run and the following results are
obtained. The response totals are 20 when both factors are at the low
level, 30 when both factors are at the high level, 15 when A is high and
B is low, and 20 when A is low and B is high. Assume both factors to
be fixed and use $SS_{total} = 70$ to test for the significance of the A, B, and
AB effects.

6. Explain why residual plots should be used with data from designed
experiments.

7. How many degrees of freedom will be available for estimating σ^2 if a
2^3 design is run with 3 replicates?

8. Four factors, each at two levels, are studied with the design points given
by the following treatment combinations: (1), ab, bc, abd, acd, bcd, d,
and ac.

   a. What is the defining contrast?

   b. Could the design be improved upon using the same number of
   design points?

   c. In particular, which three main effects are confounded with two-factor interactions?

9. Construct a sample of six observations from each of two populations in
which the exact t test for testing $\mu_1 = \mu_2$ produces a t value of zero.

10. Six similar (but not identical) machines are used in a production process. Each machine has a head that is not interchangeable between machines, although there are three different types of heads that can be used on a given machine. A study is to be performed to analyze process variability by studying the 6 machines and 3 heads. Could the data be analyzed as a 3 × 6 factorial design? Why or why not?

11. Assume that ANOVA is applied to three groups and the F test is significant. What graphical aid could be used to determine which groups differ in terms of their means?

12. Assume that data from a 2^3 design have been analyzed, and one or more of the interactions are significant. What action should be taken in investigating main effects for factors that comprise those interactions?

13. Analyze the following data for two groups using both an exact t test and an F test. Show that $F = t^2$. Do the samples seem to be independent? Comment. Then construct a confidence interval for the difference between the two means.

1	2
14.3	14.8
16.2	16.6
13.5	13.6
14.6	14.9
14.9	15.3
15.4	15.8
16.0	16.4
15.7	16.2

14. Name one disadvantage in using a highly fractionated fractional factorial.

15. The following interaction profile shows the results of an unreplicated 2^2 design.

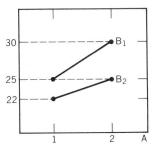

Estimate the A effect.

CHAPTER 14

Taguchi Methods and Related Procedures

In this chapter we shall examine the methods that have been proposed by the Japanese engineer, Genichi Taguchi. His quality engineering ideas and statistical procedures have been used in Japan for decades, but it was the mid-1980s when the Western world became aware of his views toward process control and quality improvement in general, and the set of tools that he advocates.

This eventual awareness led to the creation of the American Supplier Institute, Inc., which is situated in a suburb of Detroit. The objective has been to educate engineers, in particular, in statistical process control (SPC) and Taguchi methods. Shin Taguchi, a nephew of Dr. Genichi Taguchi, and Professor Yuin Wu have taught Taguchi methods as well as standard control-charting procedures to American industrial personnel.

In this chapter we introduce the reader to Taguchi's quality engineering ideas, which for the most part have been enthusiastically received. We then discuss his statistical procedures, which are somewhat controversial.

14.1 QUALITY ENGINEERING

Specification limits (when they are, in fact, true tolerance limits) have generally been regarded as providing a range for the values of a process characteristic such that values within this range are acceptable. Implicit in this view is the idea that all values within this range are equally good.

Common sense should tell us, however, that if we have a complicated piece of machinery that consists of a large number of moving parts, the machinery is likely to perform better if the dimensions of the individual

348

parts were made to conform to certain "optimal" values, than if the dimensions were merely within tolerance limits.

This type of thinking is at the heart of the loss-function approach advocated by Taguchi, who contends that the "loss to society'" increases as the value of a quality characteristic departs from its optimal value, regardless of whether or not a tolerance limit has been exceeded.

The "loss to society" idea of Taguchi has been replaced by "long-term loss to the firm" by those in the Western world, but the general idea is the same. That is, individual firms and society as a whole suffer a loss when products do not function as they could if they were made properly.

14.2 LOSS FUNCTIONS

The simplest type of loss function is *squared error*, which is also referred to as *quadratic loss*. Specifically, if we let t denote a *target value* (i.e., optimal value) of a quality characteristic, Y the actual value of that characteristic, and L the loss that is incurred when $Y \neq t$, then

$$L = (Y - t)^2 \tag{14.1}$$

would be a simple (quadratic) loss function. To illustrate, if $t = 5$ and $Y = 8$, then $L = 9$ (dollars, say). If the tolerance limits on Y are $(1, 9)$, there is thus a "loss" even though the value of Y is within the tolerance limits.

This should not be construed to mean that the loss will actually be 9 when $Y = 8$. Rather, a quadratic loss is simply being used as a model for the true loss function (which will generally be unknown). Quadratic loss will have the general shape shown in Figure 14.1 so that, for example, at Y_1 the (predicted) loss would be L_1.

If the loss was actually known for various values of Y, a more precise graph might be as in Figure 14.2. It would not be practical to try to determine a loss function that would generate these actual losses. Rather,

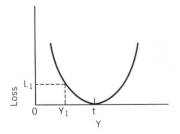

Figure 14.1 Quadratic loss.

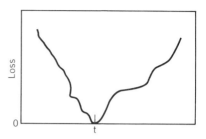

Figure 14.2 Actual loss.

quadratic loss would be a (useful in this case) approximation to the actual loss function.

A more general type of quadratic loss function is

$$L = k(Y - t)^2 \tag{14.2}$$

where k is a constant that would have to be determined. A value for k can be easily determined if the actual loss is known for a particular value of Y. Specifically, if we solve Eq. (14.2) for k, we obtain

$$k = L/(Y - t)^2$$

so that if $L = 50$ when $Y = 10$ and $t = 5$, then k should be set equal to 2. Thus, the loss function would be

$$L = 2(Y - 5)^2 \tag{14.3}$$

Although the predicted loss at various values of Y is of interest [and could be obtained using Eq. (14.3)], a practitioner may be more interested in the average squared error, which is generally referred to as the *mean squared error* (MSE).

For quadratic loss given by Eq. (14.1), MSE(Y) is given by

$$E(L) = E(Y - t)^2$$

where, as discussed in Chapter 3, E represents "expected value" (i.e., average). If we had $E(Y) = t$, then $E(L)$ would equal σ_y^2 and $E(L)$ could then be thought of as the (theoretical) average of the squared deviations, $(Y - t)^2$.

If $E(Y) \neq t$, then with μ substituted for $E(Y)$ we have

$$
\begin{aligned}
E(L) &= E(Y - t)^2 \\
&= E\left[(Y - \mu) + (\mu - t)\right]^2 \\
&= E\left[(Y - \mu)^2 + 2(Y - \mu)(\mu - t) + (\mu - t)^2\right] \\
&= E(Y - \mu)^2 + 0 + E(\mu - t)^2 \\
&= \sigma_y^2 + \left[E(Y) - t\right]^2
\end{aligned}
$$

The last two lines follow from the fact that $E(Y - \mu) = E(Y) - \mu = 0$, $E(Y - \mu)^2$ is, by definition, σ_y^2, $E(\mu - t)^2 = (\mu - t)^2$, and $\mu = E(Y)$. The quantity $[E(Y) - t]^2$ is generally called the *squared bias*.

It should be noted that if $L = k(Y - t)^2$, then $E(L) = k\{\sigma_y^2 + [(E(Y) - t]^2\}$.

We shall use a few simple examples to illustrate the use of loss functions. Assume that a loss function is given by

$$
L = (Y - t)^2
$$

where $t = 5$ and $Y \sim N(\mu = 5, \sigma^2 = 1)$. Then $E(Y) = t$ so that $E(L) = \sigma_y^2 = 1$. How can this expected loss be reduced? Since the distribution of Y is already centered at the target value (as shown in Figure 14.3), the only way to reduce the expected loss is to reduce σ_y^2. If σ_y^2 is reduced to 0.5, then $E(L) = 0.5$, assuming that the distribution remains centered at t. This is, of course, intuitive because the loss depends upon the distance that Y is from t, and by reducing σ_y^2 we increase the proportion of values of Y that is a given distance from t. *This reduction in expected loss resulting from a*

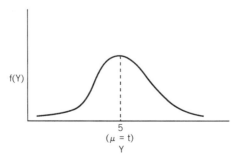

Figure 14.3 $Y \sim N(\mu = t = 5, \sigma^2 = 1)$.

reduction of the variance is one reason why firms should continually strive to reduce the variance for all of their processes.

14.3   DISTRIBUTION NOT CENTERED AT THE TARGET

If, on the other hand, the distribution of Y is not centered so that $E(Y) = t$, the expected loss can be reduced simply by shifting the center of the distribution closer to t, even if previous attempts at reducing the variance had failed. Centering the distribution will often cause a greater reduction in the expected loss than a reduction in the variance. For example, if $\sigma^2 = 1$, $\mu = 7$, and $t = 5$, there is no reduction in σ^2 that could cause a reduction in the expected loss equal to the reduction caused by shifting μ from 7 to 5.

As pointed out by Kackar (1985), in many engineering applications the sample average and sample variance are independent, so reducing one will not necessarily have any effect on the other. (Theoretically, this is true only for a normal distribution.)

14.4   LOSS FUNCTIONS AND SPECIFICATION LIMITS

To this point in the chapter there has been no mention of loss functions used in conjunction with specification limits. Under conventional thinking there has been the implicit assumption that the expected loss is zero as long as the value of a quality characteristic is within the specification limits. If, however, we accept the notion that a loss occurs whenever the target value is not met, the expected loss could be virtually independent of the specifications. For example, consider Figure 14.4a and 14.4b. The expected losses will differ considerably, but the differences will not depend to any extent upon the upper and lower specification limits, which are denoted by USL and LSL, respectively.

14.5   ASYMMETRIC LOSS FUNCTIONS

An asymmetric loss function would be appropriate if the loss differs for values of Y that are equidistant from the target. For example, a value that exceeds the target might be more detrimental than a value that is below the

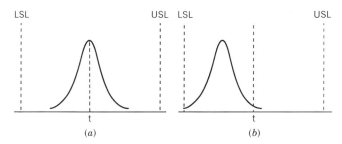

Figure 14.4 Normal distributions: centered about the target in (a), not centered in (b). Both within specifications.

target. In that case, one could use a loss function of the form

$$L = k_1(Y - t)^2 \quad \text{if } Y \leq t$$
$$= k_2(Y - t)^2 \quad \text{if } Y > t$$

where $k_2 > k_1$.

The appropriate values for k_1 and k_2 can be easily determined if the actual loss is known for one value of Y above t, and for one value of Y below t. These might be at the specification limits or at some other values. (It would be impractical to use the specification limits, however, if the distribution of Y was well inside the limits as in Figure 14.4a.)

Consider the following example: $Y \sim N(\mu = 5, \sigma^2 = 4)$, $E(Y) = t$, and $L(7) = 8$ and $L(3) = 2$. We are thus assuming that the losses are known at points that are one standard deviation above and below the mean. These would likely have to be estimated, but, assuming that reasonably good estimates could be obtained, it would be better to use these estimates than to use losses at the specification limits, which would likely be easier to obtain. This is particularly true when the specification limits are well beyond the spread of the distribution of Y. This can be explained as follows. Assume that the USL is 6 standard deviations above the mean (and assume $\mu = t$). When the loss at the USL is used to determine k_2, it then provides an estimate of the loss for every other value of Y between t and the USL. Thus, the loss in a region that Y is not likely to reach is being used in estimating the loss for a region $(\mu, \mu + 3\sigma)$ that values of Y will fall in with probability of roughly 0.5. Granted, one value of k for the region (μ, USL) may not be completely satisfactory, but if a sizable error is to be made in estimating $L(Y)$ for various values of Y, such errors in the region $(\mu + 3\sigma, \text{USL})$ can be tolerated much easier than errors in the region $(\mu, \mu + 3\sigma)$.

For the present example we would estimate k_2 as

$$k_2 = \frac{L(Y)}{(Y - t)^2} \qquad Y > t$$

$$= \frac{L(7)}{(7 - 5)^2}$$

$$= \frac{\$8}{4} = \$2$$

Similarly, k_1 would be estimated as

$$k_1 = \frac{L(Y)}{(Y - t)^2} \qquad Y \le t$$

$$= \frac{L(3)}{(3 - 5)^2}$$

$$= \frac{\$2}{4} = \$0.50$$

Thus, the loss function would be

$$L = \$0.50(Y - 5)^2 \qquad \text{if } Y \le 5$$

$$= \$2(Y - 5)^2 \qquad \text{if } Y > 5$$

How can the expected loss for this function be obtained? The formal approach to obtaining the expected loss utilizes the truncated normal distribution, which was covered in Chapter 3. Specifically,

$$E(L) = \$0.50 E\left[(Y - 5)^2 \middle| Y \le 5\right] \cdot P(Y \le 5)$$

$$+ \$2 E\left[(Y - 5)^2 \middle| Y > 5\right] \cdot P(Y > 5)$$

$$= \$0.50\left\{\sigma^2_{y|y \le 5} + \left[E(Y|Y \le 5) - 5\right]^2\right\} \cdot (0.5)$$

$$+ \$2\left\{\sigma^2_{y|y > 5} + \left[E(Y|Y > 5) - 5\right]^2\right\} \cdot (0.5)$$

where we would seemingly need to obtain values for the four components inside the two bracketed expressions—two expected values and two variances. (Each vertical line is read as "given.")

Actually, however, we only need one of each. Because the normal distribution is being split in half (since $\mu = t$), it follows that $\sigma^2_{y|y \leq 5}$ must equal $\sigma^2_{y|y > 5}$. Furthermore, it also follows that the distance that $E(Y|Y \leq 5)$ is from μ must be the same as the distance that $E(Y|Y > 5)$ is from μ. Thus, the values of the two bracketed expressions are the same.

Accordingly, we need to utilize the general expression for either a left truncated or right truncated normal distribution, and the single expression for the variance of a truncated normal. For a left truncated normal distribution,

$$E(Y|Y > c) = \mu + \sigma f(u)[1 - \Phi(u)]^{-1}$$

where c is the truncation point, $u = (c - \mu)/\sigma$, $f(u)$ is the ordinate of the standard normal distribution, and $\Phi(u)$ is the cumulative area under the standard normal curve at the point u.

Using the numbers in this example,

$$E(Y|Y > 5) = 5 + 2f(0)[1 - \Phi(0)]^{-1}$$

$$= 5 + 2(.3989)[1 - 0.5]^{-1}$$

$$= 5 + 1.5956$$

$$= 6.5956$$

where $u = (c - \mu)/\sigma = 0$ since $c = \mu$. It then follows that $E(Y|Y \leq 5) = 5 - 1.5956 = 3.4044$.

The variance of a left truncated normal distribution is

$$\text{Var}(Y|Y > c) = \sigma^2\{1 + uf(u)[1 - \Phi(u)]^{-1} - [f(u)]^2[1 - \Phi(u)]^{-2}\}$$

so we thus have

$$\text{Var}(Y|Y > 5) = 4\{1 + 0f(0)[1 - \Phi(0)]^{-1} - [f(0)]^2[1 - \Phi(0)]^{-2}\}$$

$$= 4[1 - (.3989)^2(0.5)^{-2}]$$

$$= 1.454$$

Using these numbers for the expected value and the variance, we then obtain

$$E(L) = \$0.50\left[1.454 + (3.4044 - 5)^2\right] \cdot (0.5)$$

$$+ \$2\left[1.454 + (6.5956 - 5)^2\right] \cdot (0.5)$$

$$= \$0.50(4)(0.5) + \$2(4)(0.5)$$

$$= \$5$$

The reader may observe that when the general expressions for $\sigma^2_{y|y>5}$ and $[E(Y|Y>5) - 5]^2$ are added together, the result is σ^2_y when $u = 0$, and similarly for $Y \leq 5$. Consequently, a shorter approach would have been to take the average of \$0.50 and \$2.00 and multiply that by σ^2_y.

If $\mu \neq t$ the formal approach would have to be used, and more work would also be involved. Specifically, both $E(Y|Y \leq t)$ and $E(Y|Y > t)$ would have to be evaluated. Also, both variances would likewise have to be calculated, but $\text{Var}(Y|Y \leq t)$ can be obtained using the expression for $\text{Var}(Y|Y > t)$ by using the fact that the normal distribution is symmetric and using a value for t, say t', such that the area under the curve to the right of t' is the same as the area under the curve to the left of t. Then $\text{Var}(Y|Y \leq t) = \text{Var}(Y|Y > t')$.

[It should be noted that most of the material presented to this point in the chapter has been motivated by Jessup (1986).]

14.6   SIGNAL-TO-NOISE RATIOS AND ALTERNATIVES

The Taguchi approach to experimental design utilizes what are termed *signal-to-noise ratios*. As discussed by Kackar (1985), Taguchi has defined more than 60 signal-to-noise ratios (S/N) for various engineering applications. The general idea is to use an S/N that is appropriate for a particular situation. This S/N, which is to be maximized, is presumed to be a logical estimator of some performance measure.

For example, if a target value is to be used (as in the preceding section), squared error would be a logical loss function, and the expected loss will be equal to the variance plus $[E(Y) - t]^2$. If the sample average and sample variance are independent, factors that are thought to affect the value of a particular quality characteristic might be separated into two categories— those that affect the variance and those that affect the mean, but would have little, if any, effect on the variance.

The objective would then be to vary the levels of the first set of factors (those that are assumed to affect the variance) in an experimental design for the purpose of determining the levels of those factors that will minimize the variability of the values of a particular quality characteristic. In general, the objective is to use the results of such designed experiments to design products in which the product quality is relatively insensitive to "noise" (uncontrollable factors both during and after the time the product is manufactured).

Once the levels of the first set of factors have been determined, the second set of factors (called adjustment parameters by other authors) are used to drive the quality characteristic to its target value by using the appropriate levels of the factors.

Thus, it is a two-stage procedure. For the first stage it would seem logical to use some function of σ^2 as the performance measure, or perhaps σ^2 itself. The latter could be used if it were not for the fact that performance measures are generally defined in such a way that their estimates are to be maximized. Accordingly, $-\log(\sigma^2)$ would be one such performance measure, which would logically be estimated by $-\log(s^2)$. The latter could not be called an S/N, however, as there is no "signal" since s^2 is a measure of the noise. Kackar (1985) calls this a performance statistic, and we shall also adopt this terminology for the remainder of the chapter.

Other performance statistics discussed by Kackar (1985) include $10\log(\bar{y}^2/s^2)$, which could be used when the average and variance are not independent. (In general, $\bar{y}$ and s^2 would be computed for each design point from replicates at each point. This is discussed further in the next section.) Hunter (1985) points out that a simple way to maximize the function $10\log(\bar{y}^2/s^2)$ would be to take the logarithm of all of the y values and then identify the factor-level settings (i.e., the design point) that produce the minimum value of s^2. Box (1986) demonstrates that this loss function can be rationalized if (and only if) a log transformation is needed to make the average and variance independent, and to satisfy the other assumptions (normality, constant error variance). If we are using σ^2 as a performance measure, we certainly do not want σ^2 to be a function of μ, as μ would be "adjusted" in the second stage, after the attempted minimization of σ^2 in the first stage.

The use of signal-to-noise ratios has received considerable stated or implied criticism. Pignatiello and Ramberg (1985) point out that the use of the S/N discussed in the preceding paragraph implies the somewhat bold assumption that a unit increase in $\log(\bar{y}^2)$ is of equal importance as a unit decrease in $\log(s^2)$. They conclude that it would be better to simply study the variability by itself. A general criticism of performance statistics has been voiced by Lucas (1985).

León, Shoemaker, and Kackar (1987) have proposed an alternative to the use of an S/N. They point out weaknesses in the latter, and suggest that a performance measure independent of adjustment (PERMIA) be used instead. The general approach when a PERMIA is used is essentially the same as when an S/N is used. That is, a two-stage procedure is used where appropriate levels of the nonadjustment factors are determined using a PERMIA (rather than an S/N) as the response variable. The second stage entails using appropriate levels of the adjustment factors to drive the quality characteristic toward its target value, just as is done with the Taguchi approach.

A detailed explanation of their paper would be at a level somewhat beyond that intended for this book. Nevertheless, some general comments can be made. The use of loss functions in quality improvement work was illustrated earlier in this chapter. León et al. show that for certain models and appropriate loss functions, the use of a suggested S/N will not minimize expected loss. Furthermore, León et al. give an example of a measuring instrument problem in which the suggested S/N is not independent of an adjustment factor. This is obviously undesirable since the settings of the adjustment factors are considered to be arbitrary during the first stage when appropriate levels of the nonadjustment factors are determined.

The point is that some thought must be given to the selection of the response variable (e.g., PERMIA) that is to be used in determining the levels of the nonadjustment factors that are to be used for future production. It should be chosen after determining the model and an appropriate loss function, and its value should not depend on the values of any adjustment factors. The metric in which the analysis is to be performed is also of paramount importance.

In the next section we examine the experimental designs that Taguchi has indicated can be used in the first stage, and compare them to the designs presented in Chapter 13, as well as examine recent developments.

14.7 EXPERIMENTAL DESIGNS FOR STAGE ONE

For some of the models considered by León et al. the logical PERMIA was σ^2, where σ^2 was a function of the nonadjustment factors. Therefore, the experimental design(s) used in the first stage should first be used for determining the factors that affect process variability (if such information is not already available), and then appropriate levels of those factors should be selected. The Taguchi experimental design approach is not fashioned in this manner, however, nor is standard experimental design methodology.

The former incorporates "noise factors" (uncontrollable factors) that are varied over levels likely to occur in practice, thus providing replicates for each design point. The variance, s^2, is then computed at each design point, and then used in estimating σ^2 if σ^2 is part of an S/N. (Alternatively, it could be used in estimating σ^2 in a PERMIA if a PERMIA is to be used.)

Using enough replicates to be able to obtain a reasonable estimate of σ^2 *at each design point* offsets, to some extent, one of the purported advantages of the designs advocated by Taguchi; namely, the ability to investigate the main effects of a moderate-to-large number of factors without having to use an inordinate number of design points.

Recognizing this, Box and Meyer (1986) have provided a method for estimating the effects on variability of factors in an unreplicated fractional factorial design, in addition to the location effects of those factors. The intent here is somewhat different, however, from the intent of the Taguchi approach (or with a similar approach that utilizes a PERMIA). There the intent is to determine the levels of factors that have already been selected. It should be apparent, however, that the factors have to be selected first, and those selected should have a significant effect on variability (or, in general, upon the S/N or PERMIA that is used).

It should be noted that in the Taguchi terminology, the designs discussed in the next section would be used during the *parameter design* stage, during which the experimenter seeks to determine the optimum levels of the controllable factors. (Engineers use the term *parameter* in place of *factor*.) This is preceded by the *system design* stage in which attempts are made to reduce noise by using subject matter knowledge (only), and followed by the *allowance (tolerance) design* stage in which improvements are sought beyond what was realized during the parameter design stage. In the latter stage further quality improvement is sought by taking actions such as switching to higher quality (and more expensive) raw materials, and using narrower tolerances. The Japanese will use tolerance design only when the desired quality level has not been achieved through parameter design (Byrne and Taguchi, 1986).

14.8 TAGUCHI METHODS OF DESIGN

One of the striking developments in the field of experimental design during the 1980s has been the gravitation of engineers and other industrial personnel in the United States toward what is generally referred to as "Taguchi methods of design." Taguchi and Wu (1979) contains the essentials of the Taguchi approach. That approach incorporates orthogonal arrays and linear graphs, as well as a number of other tools that are not a part of classical experimental design methodology.

The term *orthogonal array* has not been used in any of the preceding sections although each design that was illustrated in Chapter 13 was indeed an orthogonal array. A complete definition of an orthogonal array can be found in Raktoe, Hedayat, and Federer (1981, p. 169), which also contains rules for constructing such arrays, but a simpler definition will suffice for our purposes. For two-level factorial designs we have used the presence of a letter to indicate the high level of that factor, and absence to indicate the low level. If we now substitute " $+1$ " and " -1 ", respectively, we can think of an orthogonal array as a design in which all products of pairs of columns representing estimable effects are zero.

To illustrate, for a 2^3 design we would have the following.

Treatment combination	Estimable effects						
	A	**B**	**C**	**AB**	**AC**	**BC**	**ABC**
(1)	-1	-1	-1	1	1	1	-1
a	1	-1	-1	-1	-1	1	1
b	-1	1	-1	-1	1	-1	1
ab	1	1	-1	1	-1	-1	-1
c	-1	-1	1	1	-1	-1	1
ac	1	-1	1	-1	1	-1	-1
bc	-1	1	1	-1	-1	1	-1
abc	1	1	1	1	1	1	1

The reader who has the time and patience can easily verify that each of the 21 pairs of columns has a "dot product" of zero; each dot product is obtained by multiplying the corresponding numbers together and summing the eight products. For example, multiplying the A column by the AB column would produce $(-1)(1) + (1)(-1) + (-1)(-1) + (1)(1) + (-1)(1) + (1)(-1) + (-1)(-1) + (1)(1) = 0$.

Similarly, a 2^{4-1} design can be constructed by forming the full 2^3 factorial with the fourth column equal to the product of the first three columns. Thus, verifying that the 2^3 is an orthogonal array also verifies that the 2^{4-1} design is an orthogonal array since the latter would consist of the columns A, B, C, and ABC ($= D$).

The reader should thus realize that the full and fractional factorials discussed in this chapter are orthogonal arrays. Not every fractional factorial can be viewed as an orthogonal array, however (see Raktoe, Hedayat, and Federer (1981, p. 174)).

Table 14.1 L_8 **Orthogonal Array Given in Taguchi and Wu**[a]

Treatment Combination	B	C	BC	D	BD	A	e
(1)	1	1	1	1	1	1	1
ad	1	1	1	2	2	2	2
ac	1	2	2	1	1	2	2
cd	1	2	2	2	2	1	1
b	2	1	2	1	2	1	2
abd	2	1	2	2	1	2	1
abc	2	2	1	1	2	2	1
bcd	2	2	1	2	1	1	2

[a] Table 14.1 is from G. Taguchi and Y. Wu (1979), Introduction to Off-Line Quality Control (p. 66). Central Japan Quality Control Association. © 1979 Central Japan Quality Control Association. Reprinted by permission.

14.8.1 Orthogonal Arrays as Fractional Factorials

We shall begin our discussion of the relationship between the orthogonal arrays presented in Taguchi and Wu (1979) and fractional factorial designs by considering their 8-point orthogonal array on p. 66. (Their notation for such a design is L_8.) They use a "1" to indicate the low level and "2" the high level of a two-level orthogonal array with four factors, with the design configuration given in Table 14.1. There is no compelling reason for preferring one notational system over another. Other authors have used "0" and "1" to denote the two different levels. The advantage of using "+1" and "−1" is that it allows the orthogonality of the orthogonal array to be very apparent.

Accordingly, Table 14.1 becomes Table 14.2 when this substitution is made. The orthogonality could now be easily verified by taking products of columns, as was previously discussed.

Even with the "+1" and "−1" notation, however, we notice some new wrinkles in Table 14.2. In particular, the "e" as the heading for the last column simply indicates that not every degree of freedom will be used for estimating effects; one will be used for estimating σ. (We should question the worth of that estimate based on only 1 d.f. We would likely be better off not even attempting to estimate σ and, instead, simply construct a normal probability plot of the effect estimates.) We also notice that the BC column is the *negative* of the product of the B and C columns. Therefore, we would actually be estimating − BC rather than BC (which is of no real consequence); similarly, we would be actually estimating − BD.

In our discussion of the resolution of a design in Chapter 13 we did not discuss the possibility that some (but not all) of the effects of a particular

Table 14.2 The L_8 Orthogonal Array of Table 14.1 Using "$+1$" and "-1" for the Two Levels

Treatment Combination	B	C	$(-)$BC	D	$(-)$BD	A	e
(1)	-1	-1	-1	-1	-1	-1	-1
ad	-1	-1	-1	1	1	1	1
ac	-1	1	1	-1	-1	1	1
cd	-1	1	1	1	1	-1	-1
b	1	-1	1	-1	1	-1	1
abd	1	-1	1	1	-1	1	-1
abc	1	1	-1	-1	1	1	-1
bcd	1	1	-1	1	-1	-1	1

order could be estimable. With this particular orthogonal array we can do more than just estimate the main effects A, B, C, and D since we have 7 d.f. for estimating effects (provided that we are willing to forego an estimate of σ and settle for plotting the effects).

What is not clear from Table 14.2, however, is the alias structure. We know that none of the six effects that are to be estimated could be aliased among themselves since the columns are obviously pairwise orthogonal. It would be helpful, however, to know the alias structure, and the structure is not readily apparent from the array.

This is a potential weakness of the orthogonal array approach, as the equivalent fractional factorial design (if one exists) needs to be identified for the alias structure to be clear. [Actually, the resolution of a fractional factorial that is an orthogonal array can be determined from the "strength" of the array in which strength 2 corresponds to Resolution III and strength 3 to Resolution IV. For details see Raktoe, Hedayat, and Federer (1981, p. 172).] It can be determined that this is actually a 2^{4-1} design with $-ACD$ as the defining contrast. (The reader can easily verify this by multiplying the C and D columns together and recognizing that the product is the negative of the A column. Thus, $CD = -A$, which is what one obtains when multiplying CD by $-ACD$ to find the alias of CD.) Therefore, the alias structure can now be determined, which is as follows:

$$A = -CD \qquad AB = -BCD$$
$$B = -ABCD \qquad -BC = ABD$$
$$C = -AD \qquad -BD = ABC$$
$$D = -AC \qquad I = -ACD$$

We can see that the BC and BD interactions that are to be estimated are confounded with three-factor interactions. Thus, if the BC and BD interactions were deemed as likely to be significant before the experiment is carried out (as was true for this experiment), there is no problem in estimating them provided that the three-factor interactions are not significant. What could be quite risky, however, is the fact that three of the four main effects are aliased with two-factor interactions. The experimenter had better have a strong belief that those three interactions are not likely to be important. In other words, in using this design he would be assuming that two of the two-factor interactions are likely to be important (i.e., statistically significant), but not the others. That would be a rather bold assumption in the absence of data from a previous experiment.

Could this design be improved? Most definitely! There is no need to confound main effects with two-factor interactions. We can always construct a 2^{4-1} design in such a way that main effects are confounded with three-factor interactions (i.e., the design is Resolution IV). (This could be designated as 2^{4-1}_{IV}.) We simply use ABCD as the defining contrast so that the alias structure is as follows.

$$A = BCD \qquad BC = AD$$
$$B = ACD \qquad BD = AC$$
$$C = ABD \qquad AB = CD$$
$$D = ABC$$

Of course, we now have the two-factor interactions that are anticipated as being important aliased with other two-factor interactions. This is a lesser evil, however, than having main effects aliased with two-factor interactions.

Table 14.3 2^{4-1} Design with I = ABCD

Treatment Combination	A	B	C	D	BC	BD	e
(1)	−1	−1	−1	−1	1	1	1
ad	1	−1	−1	1	1	−1	−1
bd	−1	1	−1	1	−1	1	−1
ab	1	1	−1	−1	−1	−1	1
cd	−1	−1	1	1	−1	−1	1
ac	1	−1	1	−1	−1	1	−1
bc	−1	1	1	−1	1	−1	−1
abcd	1	1	1	1	1	1	1

If the estimates of the BC and BD effects were determined to be significant, additional design points could be used (if feasible) to disentangle BC from AD and BD from AC. [See Appendix 12B of Box Hunter, and Hunter (1978) for general information concerning the selection of such additional points.]

The treatment combinations to be used in the 2^{4-1} design are given in Table 14.3. The column headings in Table 14.3 are the same as those in Table 14.2, so the same effects would be estimable. The e in Table 14.3 represents AB − CD, whereas the e in Table 14.2 represents BCD + AB.

14.8.2   Other Orthogonal Arrays versus Fractional Factorials

Taguchi and Wu (1979, p. 68) also present an L_{16} orthogonal array for the purpose of studying nine factors (each at two levels), with four two-factor interactions deemed to be important. The same objective could be met by constructing a 2^{9-5}_{III} design following the directions of Box et al. (1978, p. 410).

In the experiment for which the L_{16} was used, the objective was to estimate the nine main effects and four of the two-factor interactions: AC, AG, AH, and GH. In the preceding example we saw that the L_8 array was of lower resolution than the corresponding 2^{4-1} design that allowed for estimation of the same effects. That will not be the case for the L_{16} versus the 2^{9-5}_{III}, however, as the L_{16} is also of Resolution III. The L_{16} array given by Taguchi and Wu is given in Table 14.4. (Again, we use −1 and 1 in place of their 1 and 2, respectively. The fact that the design is Resolution III can be verified by simply observing that $A = -DE$.) The negative signs are placed in front of the two-factor interactions to indicate that the array actually estimates the negative of the interaction.

The reader can easily verify that each lower case letter occurs exactly 8 times (as it must) over the 16 treatment combinations. As with the L_8 array, the "e" designates a column that will be used not for estimating any effect, but rather for estimating σ.

Tables of orthogonal arrays are needed to construct these designs, but a design configuration using the Box and Hunter approach can be constructed that will provide for estimation of the same effects that are estimable in Table 14.4. The general idea is to construct a full 2^4 factorial ("4" because $9 - 5 = 4$) and then obtain the columns for estimating the other five main effects by taking all possible combinations of three of the four columns, and then the product of all four columns. Desired interactions can then be estimated by forming products of the appropriate columns. There is really no need to designate columns for estimating σ (i.e., the "e" columns) as d.f. that are not used for estimating effects are automatically used for this purpose anyway.

Table 14.4 L_{16} Array from Taguchi and Wu[a] (p. 68)

Treatment Combination	A	G	(−)AG	H	(−)AH	(−)GH	B	D	E	F	I	e	e	(−)AC	C
(1)	−1	−1	−1	−1	−1	−1	−1	−1	−1	−1	−1	−1	−1	−1	−1
cdefi	−1	−1	−1	−1	−1	−1	−1	1	1	1	1	1	1	1	1
bch	−1	−1	−1	1	1	1	1	−1	−1	−1	−1	1	1	1	1
bdefhi	−1	−1	−1	1	1	1	1	1	1	1	1	−1	−1	−1	−1
bcfgi	−1	1	1	−1	−1	1	1	−1	−1	1	1	−1	−1	1	1
bdeg	−1	1	1	−1	−1	1	1	1	1	−1	−1	1	1	−1	−1
fghi	−1	1	1	1	1	−1	−1	−1	−1	1	1	1	1	−1	−1
cdegh	−1	1	1	1	1	−1	−1	1	1	−1	−1	−1	−1	1	1
abcei	1	−1	1	−1	1	−1	1	−1	1	−1	1	−1	1	−1	1
abdf	1	−1	1	−1	1	−1	1	1	−1	1	−1	1	−1	1	−1
aehi	1	−1	1	1	−1	1	−1	−1	1	−1	1	1	−1	1	−1
acdfh	1	−1	1	1	−1	1	−1	1	−1	1	−1	−1	1	−1	1
aefg	1	1	−1	−1	1	1	−1	−1	1	1	−1	−1	1	1	−1
acdgi	1	1	−1	−1	1	1	−1	1	−1	−1	1	1	−1	−1	1
abcefgh	1	1	−1	1	−1	−1	1	−1	1	1	−1	1	−1	−1	1
abdghi	1	1	−1	1	−1	−1	1	1	−1	−1	1	−1	1	1	−1

[a]The fourth number in the "I" column is corrected from the error in G. Taguchi and Y. Wu, Introduction to Off-Line Quality Control (1979), Central Japan Quality Control Association. © 1979 Central Japan Quality Control Association. Reprinted by permission.

The 2_{III}^{9-5} design is given in Table 14.5. The effect in parentheses above each column label indicates the effect in the L_{16} array to which each column label corresponds. The representation of the e columns is also given for completeness, although, as indicated, such columns really are not necessary. The reader will observe that the treatment combinations in Table 14.5 are totally different from the treatment combinations in Table 14.4. That does not make any difference; what is important is that the columns be orthogonal (which they are), and that each factor occurs eight times at its high level and eight times at its low level (which they do).

We can observe that none of the estimable effects in Table 14.5 corresponds to either E or F in Table 14.4. This is because E = $-$AD and F = $-$DG in Table 14.4, with $-$AD in Table 14.4 = $-$AD in Table 14.5 and $-$DG = $-$AC in Table 14.5, and the columns for the five additional main effects in Table 14.5 are not formed by taking the product of any *pair* of columns (such as A and D).

We do observe one serious problem with the 2^{9-5} design, however. Specifically, the DI column is the same as the E column. Thus, the two are confounded. This is undesirable since DI in Table 14.5 corresponds to $-$AC in Table 14.4, and AC is one of the effects to be estimated. Therefore, by following the Box–Hunter approach directly we run into a problem, and this is due to the fact that this approach forces specific two-factor interactions (2 f.i.) to be nonestimable, and it happens that we need to estimate one of those interactions. Does this mean that we have to forsake the Box–Hunter approach for the orthogonal array approach? Not really. The Box–Hunter approach will guarantee that the resultant design will have maximum resolution, but the procedure can often be modified; the modified approach produces a design with the same resolution.

There are two obvious solutions to the problem. Since the problem results from the way in which E and I are defined in terms of the factors in the full factorial, we could solve the problem by redefining either of these. For example, we could let E = AC (as mentioned previously, E = $-$AD in the L_{16} array; that would also work here). Just so we do not let it equal one of the two-factor interactions that we are trying to estimate (CD, BD, and BC in the Table 14.5 notation). (Notice that E = AC would not work if we wanted to estimate DG, for example, since DG = AC.)

Thus, we can still use the Box–Hunter approach, although sometimes a slight modification will be necessary.

The "final" 2^{9-5} design with the appropriate modification is given in Table 14.6.

To this point we have seen one example in which the fractional factorial was superior to the orthogonal array, and one in which the fractional factorial approach had to be modified slightly.

Table 14.5 2_{III}^{9-5} Design

Estimable Effects[a]

Treatment Combination	(D) A	(H) B	(G) C	(A) D	(−AC) E(=ABC)	(B) F(=BCD)	(I) G(=ACD)	(e − 13) H(=ABD)	(−C) I(=ABCD)	(AG) CD	(AH) BD	(GH) BC	(−AC) DI	(−DH) e	(e − 13) e
i	−1	−1	−1	−1	−1	−1	−1	−1	1	1	1	1	−1	−1	1
aegh	1	−1	−1	−1	1	−1	1	1	−1	1	1	1	1	1	−1
befh	−1	1	−1	−1	1	1	−1	1	−1	1	−1	−1	−1	1	1
abfgi	1	1	−1	−1	−1	1	1	−1	1	1	−1	−1	1	−1	−1
cefg	−1	−1	1	−1	1	1	1	−1	−1	−1	1	−1	1	−1	1
acfhi	1	−1	1	−1	−1	1	−1	1	1	−1	1	−1	−1	1	−1
bcghi	−1	1	1	−1	−1	−1	1	1	1	−1	−1	1	1	1	1
abce	1	1	1	−1	1	−1	−1	−1	−1	−1	−1	1	−1	−1	−1
dfgh	−1	−1	−1	1	−1	1	1	1	−1	−1	−1	1	−1	−1	−1
adefi	1	−1	−1	1	1	1	−1	−1	1	−1	−1	1	1	1	1
bdegi	−1	1	−1	1	1	−1	1	−1	1	−1	1	−1	−1	1	−1
abdh	1	1	−1	1	−1	−1	−1	1	−1	−1	1	−1	1	−1	1
cdehi	−1	−1	1	1	1	−1	−1	1	1	1	−1	−1	1	−1	−1
acdg	1	−1	1	1	−1	−1	1	−1	−1	1	−1	−1	−1	1	1
bcdf	−1	1	1	1	−1	1	−1	−1	−1	1	1	1	1	1	−1
abcdefghi	1	1	1	1	1	1	1	1	1	1	1	1	−1	−1	1

[a] The column designations in Table 14.4 are given above each effect, with e − 13 designating column 13.

Table 14.6 2_{III}^{9-5} Design Analogous to the L_{16} Array

Estimable Effects[a]

Treatment Combination	(D) A	(H) B	(G) C	(A) D	(-F) E(=AC)	(B) F(=BCD)	(I) G(=ACD)	(e-13) H(=ABD)	(-C) I(=ABCD)	(AG) CD	(AH) BD	(GH) BC	(-AC) DI	(-DH) e	(e-13) e
ei	-1	-1	-1	-1	1	-1	-1	-1	1	1	1	1	-1	-1	1
agh	1	-1	-1	-1	-1	-1	1	1	-1	1	1	1	1	1	-1
befh	-1	1	-1	-1	1	1	-1	1	-1	1	-1	-1	1	1	1
abfgi	1	1	-1	-1	-1	1	1	-1	1	1	-1	-1	-1	-1	-1
cfg	-1	-1	1	-1	-1	1	1	-1	-1	-1	1	-1	1	-1	1
acefhi	1	-1	1	-1	1	1	-1	1	1	-1	1	-1	-1	1	-1
bcghi	-1	1	1	-1	-1	-1	1	1	1	-1	-1	1	-1	1	1
abce	1	1	1	-1	1	-1	-1	-1	-1	-1	-1	1	1	-1	-1
defgh	-1	-1	-1	1	1	1	1	1	-1	-1	-1	1	-1	-1	-1
adfi	1	-1	-1	1	-1	1	-1	-1	1	-1	-1	1	1	1	1
bdegi	-1	1	-1	1	1	-1	1	-1	1	-1	1	-1	1	1	-1
abdh	1	1	-1	1	-1	-1	-1	1	-1	-1	1	-1	-1	-1	1
cdhi	-1	-1	1	1	-1	-1	-1	1	1	1	-1	-1	1	-1	-1
acdeg	1	-1	1	1	1	-1	1	-1	-1	1	-1	-1	-1	1	1
bcdf	-1	1	1	1	-1	1	-1	-1	-1	1	1	1	-1	1	-1
abcdefghi	1	1	1	1	1	1	1	1	1	1	1	1	1	-1	1

[a] The column designations in Table 14.4 are given above each effect, with e – 13 designating column 13.

Taguchi and Wu present an L_{16} array on p. 75 for the purpose of investigating eight factors and three of the 2 f.i., AB, AD, and BD. (The column labels are in error, however, as two of them are labeled D when one of them should obviously be labeled C.) One of the columns created for a main effect (H) is formed by taking the negative of the product of two of the factors in the full factorial part ($-DF$). Thus, the design cannot be higher than Resolution III since H = $-DF$.

If we follow the Box and Hunter approach, however, we can construct a 2_{IV}^{8-4} design for the same purpose, with the desired interactions simply appended to the basic 2_{IV}^{8-4} as additional columns.

Accordingly, the Box and Hunter approach produces a superior design since the user would not have to worry about the possible significance of any of the 2 f.i. involving any pair of factors D, F, and H.

As Taguchi and Wu report in their Foreward (sic), the L_8 and L_{16} were the most frequently used arrays for two-level factors employed by NEC (a Japanese company), as indicated in their 1959 report.

This is not to suggest that all two-level orthogonal arrays should be discarded in favor of 2^{k-p} designs. Some of these orthogonal arrays do not correspond to an equivalent 2^{k-p} because the number of design points is not a power of two. We should, however, strive to select the best design for a given number of design points.

Orthogonal arrays for 3-level factors are also given by Taguchi and Wu as well as for mixed factorials. In particular, a nine-point array for examining four factors, each at three levels, is given by Taguchi and Wu (1979, p. 65) who indicate that this is a frequently-used design. This design, which is obtained from a Graeco-Latin square, is also used for illustration by Kackar (1985). Such designs are criticized by Hunter (1985), however, on the grounds that all two-factor interactions must be assumed equal to zero.

Equivalences can also be demonstrated between 3-level orthogonal arrays and 3^{k-p} designs. Taguchi and Wu (1979, p. 109) provide an L_{27} array which could be used for examining the main effect of 13 factors, each at 3 levels. The same design could be obtained by constructing a 3^{13-10} design in a prescribed manner. Addelman (1962, p. 38) gives a 3^{13-10} design which can be seen to differ only slightly from the L_{27} array. The criticism of 3^{k-p} designs mentioned in Chapter 13 would thus also apply to these 3-level arrays. Consequently, the potential user of such designs might wish to consider other (superior) designs (e.g., response surface designs).

14.9 DETERMINING OPTIMUM CONDITIONS

For whichever type of design is used, it is desirable to use the resultant data to determine the best combination of levels of the process variables ("best"

Table 14.7 Data from an Unreplicated 3^2 Design—Small AB Interaction

		A		
		1	2	3
	1	8	8	10
B	2	6	8	11
	3	5	9	10

in terms of optimizing some function such as a PERMIA). This determination is not easily made, however.

Taguchi and Wu (1979, p. 37) and other writers have used graphs of marginal averages in attempting to arrive at the optimal levels of the process variables (factors). Marginal averages are obtained by computing the average of the response variable at each level of each process variable, while ignoring the other process variables. Unfortunately, this method will not identify optimum conditions, in general, but might identify conditions that are close to the optimum.

To illustrate, we shall assume that we have data from an unreplicated 3^2 design as in Table 14.7. The marginal averages for A and B are given in Figure 14.5. Following Taguchi and Wu, if we were to use marginal averages in determining the levels of A and B so as to maximize the response variable, we would use the third level of A and the first level of B, as can be seen from Figure 14.5. It is apparent from Table 14.7, however, that the maximum occurs with the second level of B, not the first. Notice,

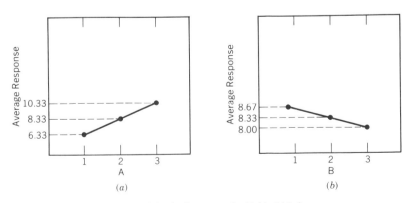

Figure 14.5 Marginal averages for Table 14.7 data.

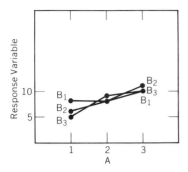

Figure 14.6 Interaction profile for Table 14.7 data.

however, that we do not miss the maximum by very much—for this example.

Of course, we can *see* in Table 14.7 the combination of A and B that produces the highest number; we do not need to construct marginal averages to determine that. All possible combinations of factor levels are not used in orthogonal arrays, however, so the user of marginal averages would be trying to infer what the best combination would be *if* all possible combinations had been used. This is what is done in Taguchi and Wu (1979, p. 37) and in Barker (1986, p. 41). It should be clear, however, that since the marginal averages approach will frequently not work when we *do* have all combinations of factor levels, then obviously it will not work, in general, when we do not have all possible combinations.

Even when the marginal averages form straight lines, as in Figure 14.5a and 14.5b, the interactions will not necessarily be zero, so the optimum combination might not be selected.

For this example the interaction profile is given in Figure 14.6. We can see that the interaction is not extreme, and this is why the marginal averages approach closely approximates the maximum.

Consider, however, the data given in Table 14.8. For these data the marginal averages approach would lead to the selection of A_3B_3 as the best

Table 14.8 Data from an Unreplicated 3^2 Design—Moderate AB Interaction

		A		
		1	2	3
	1	10	17	24
B	2	17	20	23
	3	24	23	22

Table 14.9 Data from a 3^2 Design in Terms of c and d

		$X_1(A)$			
		-1	0	1	Totals
	-1	$-2c - d$	$-c$	d	$-3c$
$X_2(B)$	0	$-c$	0	c	0
	1	d	c	$2c - d$	$3c$
Totals		$-3c$	0	$3c$	

combination, but we can see from Table 14.8 that this is only the fifth best combination. The reason is that the AB interaction is more pronounced for these data than for the data in Table 14.7.

We can see how the marginal averages approach will be undermined by varying degrees of interaction by letting Y, the response variable that we are trying to maximize, have the functional form

$$Y = cX_1 + cX_2 - dX_1X_2$$

where X_1 (and X_2) = -1, 0, or 1, corresponding to the three levels of A and B. (This is analogous to what was discussed in Section 13.9 for the 2^2 design, where the values used there were -1 and $+1$ for the two levels.) Notice that we are assuming a model without an error term for the purpose of simplification.

By using c as the coefficient for both X_1 and X_2, we are assuming that the main effects of A and B are equal, and the magnitude of d relative to c will determine the magnitude of the AB interaction relative to the two main effects. Table 14.9 contains the nine values of Y that result from using the nine combinations of X_1 and X_2. We can observe that the marginal totals (and thus the marginal averages) are not a function of d, and the use of the marginal averages approach would lead to the selection of A_3B_3 (equivalently, $X_1 = 1$ and $X_2 = 1$) as the best combination. That selection would be correct, however, only if $d < c$. If $d = c$ there are five combinations that are "equally best," but the combination that is only the fifth best would be selected when $c < d < 2c$.

The interaction profiles for values of d that correspond to these three cases are given in Figure 14.7. We can see that large interactions will seriously undermine the marginal averages approach, but it might work moderately well, *as an approximation*, when the interactions are quite small.

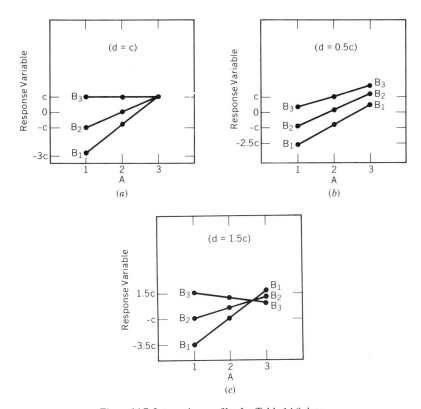

Figure 14.7 Interaction profiles for Table 14.9 data.

In general, this use of marginal averages is analogous to the one-factor-at-a-time approach that was discussed in Chapter 13, and is thus fallible in the same way. In essence, the user of marginal averages is implicitly imputing values for the factor-level combinations that are not included in an orthogonal array, and the implied imputation forces the interactions to be (approximately) zero. It is difficult to estimate what the response variable would be for factor-level combinations that are missing without knowledge of the response surface.

We should also keep in mind that we should not expect to be able to identify the true optimum combination of factor levels from a single experiment. We looked at what was the best combination of A and B for *one set* of nine combinations of factor levels in *one* experiment. In general, some optimization technique should be used in trying to determine optimum conditions.

14.10   TAGUCHI OR NOT?

Genichi Taguchi and his co-workers have taught us some valuable lessons concerning product quality. No one could dispute the idea of focusing attention on a target value rather than just operating within specification limits (which might be arbitrarily defined). Similarly, it certainly makes sense to try to design a product that will be relatively insensitive to manufacturing variations.

The extent to which it is important to operate at or very close to a target value will depend greatly upon the steepness of the actual loss function in the vicinity of the target value. A quadratic loss function will probably be a reasonable approximation in most cases, but losses within, say, two standard deviations of the target value would still have to be obtained or estimated to determine the steepness of the curve. The amount of money that is being saved could then be approximated as the variability is reduced and the mean of the process characteristic is brought closer to the target value.

Determining the values of design parameters is accomplished by Taguchi's methods through the use of orthogonal arrays. In using experimental designs we should not lose sight of the fact that we first need to determine the factors (variables) that affect the quality of the product. It would be unwise to initially select a moderate number of factors to use in a fractional factorial or orthogonal array design and then select the design point that minimizes or maximizes an S/N or PERMIA, acting as if these are the only factors that could be important.

It would be judicious to first use a screening design of some type with a large number of factors for the purpose of screening out factors that seem not to be important. A confirmatory experiment could then be conducted using a design that is similar to or identical to the design used in the first stage, for the purpose of corroborating the factor selection performed after the first experiment.

These selected factors could then be used in an experiment to determine the values of the factors that minimize (maximize) an S/N or PERMIA.

The reader should recognize, however, that with this approach an S/N or PERMIA is not being minimized in a strict mathematical sense. Rather, the minimization is only over the design points used in the design. It would be only by sheer coincidence that the minimum for the design points would minimize the function over all plausible values of the factors that are being used.

Viewed with a broader perspective, the problem is actually one of trying to optimize a function subject to constraints on the possible values of the factors. A function such as $-\log(s^2)$ is clearly a nonlinear (objective) function, so the problem is logically a nonlinear programming problem.

Box and Fung (1986) discuss this approach in detail, using an example from Taguchi and Wu (1979) for illustration. The former show that the 36-point array used by the latter for studying five factors does not maximize the chosen S/N, even when only the three levels of each factor are considered.

To summarize what we have learned, we have seen that the orthogonal arrays illustrated by Taguchi and Wu are often inferior to the better known and understood fractional factorials, and if we wish to maximize or minimize an S/N or PERMIA, it is logical to attempt to do so using known mathematical optimization procedures such as nonlinear programming, rather than trying to rely upon graphs of marginal averages.

Taguchi's main contribution appears to be in focusing our attention on new objectives in achieving quality improvement. The statistical tools for accomplishing these objectives will likely continue to be developed.

REFERENCES

Addelman, S. (1962). Orthogonal main-effect plans for asymmetrical factorial experiments. *Technometrics* *4*(1): 21–46 (February).

Barker, T. R. (1986). Quality engineering by design: Taguchi's philosophy. *Quality Progress 19*(12): 32–42 (December).

Box, G. E. P. (1986). *Studies in Quality Improvement: Signal to Noise Ratios, Performance Criteria and Statistical Analysis: Part I*. Report No. 11, Center for Quality and Productivity Improvement, University of Wisconsin.

Box, G. E. P., and C. A. Fung (1986). *Studies in Quality Improvement: Minimizing Transmitted Variation by Parameter Design*. Report No. 8, Center for Quality and Productivity Improvement, University of Wisconsin.

Box, G. E. P., and R. D. Meyer (1986). Dispersion effects from fractional designs. *Technometrics 28*(1): 19–27 (February).

Box, G. E. P., W. G. Hunter, and J. S. Hunter (1978). *Statistics for Experimenters*. New York: Wiley.

Byrne, D. M., and S. Taguchi (1986). The Taguchi approach to parameter design. *Annual Quality Congress Transactions*, pp. 168–177. Milwaukee: American Society for Quality Control.

Hunter, J. S. (1985). Statistical design applied to product design. *Journal of Quality Technology 17*(4): 210–221 (October).

Jessup, P. (1986). The value of continuing improvement. *ASQC Automotive Division Newsletter*, pp. 5–10 (March).

Kackar, R. N. (1985). Off-line quality control, parameter design, and the Taguchi method. *Journal of Quality Technology 17*(4): 176–188; Discussion: pp. 189–209 (November).

León, R. V., A. C. Shoemaker, and R. N. Kackar (1987). Performance measures independent of adjustment. *Technometrics 29*(3): 253–265; Discussion: pp. 266–285 (August).

Lucas, J. M. (1985). Discussion (of Kackar, 1985). *Journal of Quality Technology 17*(4): 195–197 (November).

Pignatiello, J. J., and J. S. Ramberg (1985). Discussion (of Kackar, 1985). *Journal of Quality Technology 17*(4): 198–206 (November).

Raktoe, B. L., A. Hedayat, and W. T. Federer (1981). *Factorial Designs*. New York: Wiley.

Taguchi, G., and Y. Wu (1979). Introduction to off-line quality control. Central Japan Quality Control Association, (available from American Supplier Institute, 32100 Detroit Industrial Expressway, Romulus, MI 48174).

EXERCISES

1. Consider the following orthogonal array (called a Plackett–Burman design) for 11 factors:

A	B	C	D	E	F	G	H	J	K	L
1	1	−1	1	1	1	−1	−1	−1	1	−1
−1	1	1	−1	1	1	1	−1	−1	−1	1
1	−1	1	1	−1	1	1	1	−1	−1	−1
−1	1	−1	1	1	−1	1	1	1	−1	−1
−1	−1	1	−1	1	1	−1	1	1	1	−1
−1	−1	−1	1	−1	1	1	−1	1	1	1
1	−1	−1	−1	1	−1	1	1	−1	1	1
1	1	−1	−1	−1	1	−1	1	1	−1	1
1	1	1	−1	−1	−1	1	−1	1	1	−1
−1	1	1	1	−1	−1	−1	1	−1	1	1
1	−1	1	1	1	−1	−1	−1	1	−1	1
−1	−1	−1	−1	−1	−1	−1	−1	−1	−1	−1

   a. Could this design be equivalent to a 2^{k-p} design?
   b. What effects are estimable with this design? (Hint: how many design points are there?)

2. For the loss function $L = (X - \mu)^2$, what is the expected loss for a process that is on target, and has a standard deviation of 2.5?

3. Assume that an experimenter wishes to study the effects of four factors, and recognizes that the cost for each design point will be sizable. For this reason he rules out a 2^4 design. Additionally, he believes that interactions above second order are not likely to be significant. He decides to use the first four columns of the design given in Problem #1, as he believes that he can afford 12 design points.

   a. He would like to be able to estimate the 2 f.i. involving factor A. Consider, for example, the AB interaction. Is that estimable with this design? Specifically, would the AB column be orthogonal to the four columns for A, B, C, and D?

   b. What would this suggest about modifying Plackett–Burman designs to meet specific objectives?

   c. Could the experimenter obtain the AB interaction with a 2^{4-1} design, as well as the AC and AD interactions if the other 2 f.i. are negligible?

4. Notice that the distribution of Y is not used explicitly in computing the expected loss unless an asymmetric loss function is used. Assume that a process is on target so that $E(L) = E(Y - t)^2 = \sigma^2$. To illustrate that $E(Y - t)^2$ is just the average of the $(Y - t)^2$ values, we do need to assume a distribution, however. Assume that $f(y) = 1/5$, $y = 1, 2, 3, 4, 5$. Compute $E(Y - 3)^2 = \sum_{i=1}^{5}(y_i - 3)^2/5$ and show that the result is 2 which is what σ_y^2 can be shown to equal. [Note that an "unweighted" average is produced here because of the form of $f(y)$.]

5. Assume that a company has two production processes in which the first process is on target with a variance of 6, whereas the second process has a variance of 4 but is off target such that $E(Y) = 6$ but $t = 5$. With the loss function $L = \$2(Y - t)^2$, which process is costing the company the most money?

6. Explain how a company can have a "loss" if all of its processes are operating within specification limits.

7. Construct the interaction profile for the data in Table 14.8 and use this to explain why the marginal averages approach does not work for these data.

CHAPTER 15

Evolutionary Operation

Evolutionary operation (EVOP) was introduced by G. E. P. Box (1957) as a technique that can be used to facilitate continuous process improvement. It is based upon experimental design concepts, but is used much differently than the experimental designs presented in Chapter 13. With those designs the objective is to determine the relationship between a response variable and a number of process variables, and this determination is made by varying the process variables over a reasonable range. Doing so, however, will generally disrupt the normal production process. With EVOP only very small changes are made in the settings of the process variables so that the process is not disrupted, and, in particular, there is (hopefully) no increase in the percentage of nonconforming units.

EVOP is intended to be used by plant personnel, and thus does not require the participation of someone with statistical expertise. The formation of an EVOP committee is generally recommended, however, and the committee is charged with periodically reviewing the results and determining what progress has been made.

EVOP also does not require the use of special equipment, although as Hunter and Chacko (1971) point out: "The results from the work sheet should be posted on an information board...which is, in general, a large board prominently displayed near the process being studied." The work sheet that the authors refer to is used for performing the statistical calculations. Alternatively, computer software could be used for this purpose, although there does not appear to be any EVOP software that is generally available.

The (apparent) absence of software reflects the state of disuse into which EVOP has fallen. Indeed, Hahn (1984) asks "Whatever happened to EVOP?" There is general agreement (among statisticians) that EVOP is being underutilized in industry, and that this condition has existed for some

378

time. A study conducted by Hahn and Dershowitz in 1972 revealed that many industrial personnel are well aware of the value of EVOP, however, and how it could be used to improve the production lines of their respective companies.

Why then, is EVOP not being used? The primary reason seems to be a general reluctance to perturb a production process that is viewed as running smoothly. Other reasons cited by Hahn and Dershowitz (1974) include political reasons, lack of knowledge about EVOP, and lack of proper personnel. Only a small percentage of the respondents indicated that EVOP was not being used at their respective companies because of poor past experience.

The general admonition that is often heard—"If it isn't broke, don't fix it"—seems to have been adopted by many potential users of EVOP, and thus serves as an impediment to its general usage. As Hahn (1984) points out: "One might even argue that the concept of EVOP runs contrary to the desire to maintain a process in statistical control." This could not be a valid argument against the use of EVOP, however, as the objective should be process *improvement*, not process control.

The real problem is perhaps captured in an important point made by Joiner (1985); namely, that the proper managerial climate must exist before statistical procedures can be effectively applied on a wide scale.

15.1 EVOP ILLUSTRATIONS

We shall illustrate the EVOP methodology developed by Box, and a variation of that approach which has been used to some extent. Other variations will be mentioned briefly but not illustrated, as there is no evidence that they have ever been used.

The Box–EVOP procedure is generally performed using either a 2^2 or 2^3 design when EVOP is used on a full-scale manufacturing process. The general idea is to keep the design as simple as possible since the data will be analyzed by plant personnel. When EVOP is used in a laboratory or pilot plant, more factors can be analyzed, and a fractional factorial might be used.

The form of the worksheets used in EVOP and the necessary calculations that are performed on them are illustrated in Box and Hunter (1959), and are reproduced in Box and Draper (1969).

We shall begin with a hypothetical example in which there are two process variables to be studied, temperature and pressure, and process yield is the response variable. These two variables might have been identified through the use of a screening design as apparently having a significant

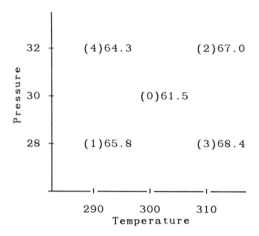

Figure 15.1 Experimental data on process yield.

effect upon yield, or it simply might be the case that they were selected because they were believed to be important, with such a belief unsupported by data from prior experimentation.

In Chapter 13 an example was given in which the different levels of the factor "temperature" were 250°, 300°, and 350°. Using such widely varying levels in an EVOP program could be disastrous, however, as the percentage of bad product might increase considerably. If the temperature used in the current plant operation is 300°, a safer strategy would be to use 290° and 310° in the first phase of the EVOP program. Similarly, if 30 pounds per square inch (p.s.i.) of pressure is currently being used, we might use 28 and 32 in the EVOP program.

A 2^2 design in an EVOP program is generally used with a center point, which denotes the *reference condition*. This is assumed to be the current best known operating conditions (i.e., values of the process variables). Assume that process yield is the response variable and that data have been collected for the previously mentioned levels of temperature and pressure, with the data given in Figure 15.1. The design points in Figure 15.1 are numbered using the same numbering system employed by Box and Draper (1969); namely, zero denotes the current operating values, and 1, 2, 3, and 4 specify the order in which the four combinations are run. (The order is not "randomized" as is the usual case when experimental designs are used because several cycles are typically used, and changing the order each time a new cycle is run could easily confuse the plant personnel.)

With data as in Figure 15.1, it appears as though the current operating values are not the optimal values. How might we determine this statistically? In Chapter 13 we said that for an unreplicated factorial we need either a prior estimate of the residual variance, or to plot the effect estimates on normal probability paper, or use an approach suggested by Box and Meyer (1986). We need not do one of these in an EVOP program, however, as new data should be as easy to obtain as the initial data since there is no interference with the operation of the plant process.

Consequently, a new cycle should be run to obtain another set of five values. Of course, *if* a prior estimate of the residual standard deviation was available from plant records, that estimate could be used in assessing the possible significance of the two main effects and the single interaction. Remembering how to estimate such effects from Chapter 13, it should be clear that the estimate of the temperature effect is 2.65 [1/2(68.4 − 65.8 + 67.0 − 64.3)], −1.45 is the estimate of the pressure effect, and the estimate of the temperature × pressure interaction is 0.05 [1/2(67.0 + 65.8 − 64.3 − 68.4)].

Then, if we had a prior estimate of the residual standard deviation, we could construct 2 standard error limits (i.e., approximately 95% confidence limits) for each effect, where *standard error* is the standard deviation of the estimator of the effect. Assume that we have such an estimate of the residual standard deviation (σ), and the estimate is 0.5. It can be shown that for a 2^2 design with one observation per design point, the standard deviation of the estimators of the two main effects and interaction effect is σ for each of the three effects.

For the main effects and interaction effect the limits are thus 2.65 ± 1.0 for T, −1.45 ± 1.0 for P, and 0.05 ± 1.0 for TP. Since the first two intervals do not cover zero, we would conclude there is likely a temperature effect and a pressure effect.

It should be noted that 2 standard error limits in EVOP will not, in general, simplify to 2σ. The expression will be different, for example, when more than one cycle has been completed. This is discussed further later in the chapter.

The use of the center point (point zero) to represent the current operating values allows us to estimate another effect—the "change in mean" effect. Specifically, has the process suffered as a result of altering the current operating conditions, or has there been an improvement? Using response surface terminology, Figure 15.1 provides evidence of a "valley" in the general region of the current operating values, with the yield increasing as movement is made in any one of the four directions. To determine whether or not this increase is statistically significant, we need to estimate the standard deviation of $[(0) + (1) + (2) + (3) + (4)]/5 - (0)$, which we will denote by the square root of

$$\mathrm{Var}\left(\frac{y_0 + y_1 + y_2 + y_3 + y_4}{5} - y_0\right)$$

$$= \mathrm{Var}\left(\frac{y_1 + y_2 + y_3 + y_4 - 4y_0}{5}\right)$$

$$= \mathrm{Var}\left[\left(\frac{1}{5}\right)(y_1 + y_2 + y_3 + y_4)\right] + \mathrm{Var}\left[\left(\frac{1}{5}\right)(4)y_0\right]$$

$$= \frac{1}{25}(4\sigma^2) + \frac{16}{25}\sigma^2$$

$$= \frac{20}{25}\sigma^2$$

The end result follows from the fact that the variance of the sum and/or difference of independent random variables is equal to the sum of the variances, and the variance of a constant times a random variable is equal to the constant squared times the variance of the random variable.

Our estimate of the standard deviation of the "change in mean" effect would then be $\sqrt{(20/25)}\sigma^2 = 0.894\sigma = 0.447$ using our prior estimate of 0.50 for σ. The estimate of the "change in mean' effect is obviously $[(y_0 + y_1 + y_2 + y_3 + y_4)/5] - y_0 = 65.4 - 61.5 = 3.9$, so the confidence limits are 3.9 ± 0.894, which clearly do not contain zero. Therefore, the change in mean is significant, which tells us that the current operating values should be changed.

If a prior estimate of σ is unobtainable, the standard approach is to repeat the same combination of factor levels and thus obtain a second set of five values. Assume that this new set of five values is as follows: (0) 62.3, (1) 66.0, (2) 66.8, (3) 68.2, and (4) 64.8.

At this point we could estimate σ by using one of the methods suggested in Chapter 13 (e.g., pooling the s^2 values at each design point or using Yates' algorithm). We should remember, however, that EVOP is meant to be used by plant personnel who generally should not be expected to produce variances or to use Yates' algorithm without appropriate computer software. Therefore, σ is estimated (in the literature on EVOP) the same way as it has historically been estimated for an $\overline{X}$ chart—by using the range.

Using the range method, the first step is to obtain the set of differences between the values in the second *cycle* (as it is called) and the corresponding values in the first cycle. The range of these differences is then divided by the appropriate value of d_2 (from Table E with $n = 5$ since there are five design points) and then multiplied by $[(k - 1)/k]^{1/2}$ where k is the number of cycles that has been carried out. Thus, for $k = 2$, our estimate of σ would be $(R/d_2)(\sqrt{0.5})$, and, in general, the estimate would be $(R/d_2)[(k - 1)/k]^{1/2}$. [The derivation of the constant $(k - 1)/k$ is given in the Appendix to this chapter, and can also be found in Appendix 1 of Box and Draper (1969).]

The necessary calculations for this example are given in Table 15.1. The estimate of sigma is thus 0.304. The effect estimates are obtained at the end of the second cycle analogous to the way they are obtained for the first cycle. When the calculations are performed, the effect estimates are as given in Table 15.2 along with the 2 standard error limits. It should be noted that the standard errors differ somewhat from those that were used at the end of the first cycle. This is due to the fact that the latter were based upon a prior estimate of sigma, but it is also true that the standard errors will generally differ from one cycle to the next, even when the estimate of sigma does not change. This is because the standard errors are a function of the number of cycles, k. Specifically, for a 2^2 design with one additional point (such as a center point), the standard error for the main effects and interaction effect is $\hat{\sigma}/\sqrt{k}$ where $\hat{\sigma}$ is the estimate of σ obtained from $(R/d_2)[(k - 1)/k]^{1/2}$, and the standard error for the change in mean is $0.894\hat{\sigma}/\sqrt{k}$. The numerical values of these two different standard errors are then $(0.304)/\sqrt{2} = 0.215$ and $0.894(0.304)/\sqrt{2} = 0.192$. If we used the prior estimate ($\sigma = 0.5$), the two standard errors would be 0.354 and 0.316, respectively.

Table 15.1 Estimating Sigma after the Second Cycle in an EVOP Program

	Operating Conditions				
	(0)	(1)	(2)	(3)	(4)
Response values					
Cycle I	61.5	65.8	67.0	68.4	64.3
Cycle II	62.3	66.0	66.8	68.2	64.8
Differences					
Cycle II minus cycle I	0.8	0.2	−0.2	−0.2	0.5
Range of differences = R = 1.0					
Estimate of sigma = $(R/d_2)(\sqrt{0.5})$					
= $(1.0/2.326)(\sqrt{0.5}) = 0.304$					

Table 15.2 Process Averages and Effect Estimates with Confidence Limits after Two Cycles

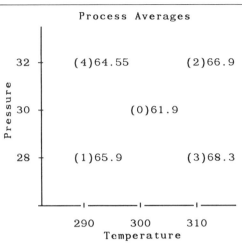

Process Averages

Effects with 2 Standard Error Limits

	A. Using $\sigma = 0.50$ (prior estimate)	B. Using $\hat{\sigma} = 0.286$
Pressure	-1.375 ± 0.707	-1.375 ± 0.43
Temperature	2.375 ± 0.707	2.375 ± 0.43
Temperature $\times$ Pressure	-0.025 ± 0.707	-0.025 ± 0.43
Change in mean	3.61 ± 0.632	3.61 ± 0.384

Box and Hunter (1959, p. 85) and Box and Draper (1969, p. 108) suggest that the prior estimate of sigma (assuming that one is available) be used in calculating the standard errors for the first two cycles, with the data being first used to estimate σ upon completion of the third cycle. This is based upon the tacit assumption that a reliable estimate of σ will be obtainable from plant records, and the recognition that such an estimate should be more reliable than an estimate obtained from the small amount of data that will be available after only two cycles have been completed. Of course, if no prior estimate is available, or if such an estimate is not based upon factual information, it would be preferable to use the estimate obtained from the first two cycles.

The 2 standard error limits are given in Table 15.2 using both the prior estimate of sigma and the estimate obtained from the first two cycles.

The question naturally arises as to how many cycles should be performed. Critics of the Box–EVOP approach argue that this is one of the weaknesses of the method in that there is no obvious stopping point. Box

Table 15.3 Calculations for Four Cycles

Response values	Operating Conditions				
	(0)	(1)	(2)	(3)	(4)
Cycle I	61.5	65.8	67.0	68.4	64.3
Average (one cycle)	61.5	65.8	67.0	68.4	64.3
Cycle II	62.3	66.0	66.8	68.2	64.8
Cycle II minus average	0.8	0.2	−0.2	−0.2	0.5
Range of differences = 1.0	$(1.0/2.326)(\sqrt{0.5}) = 0.304 = \hat{\sigma}$				
Average (two cycles)	61.9	65.9	66.9	68.3	64.55
Cycle III	62.5	66.2	67.0	68.2	64.6
Cycle III minus average	0.6	0.3	0.1	−0.1	0.05
Range of differences = 0.7	$(0.7/2.326)(\sqrt{2/3}) = 0.246 = \hat{\sigma}$				
Average (three cycles)	62.1	66.0	66.93	68.27	64.57
Cycle IV	62.2	65.9	66.8	68.2	64.8
Cycle IV minus average	0.1	−0.1	−0.13	−0.07	0.23
Range of differences = 0.36	$(0.36/2.326)(\sqrt{3/4}) = 0.134 = \hat{\sigma}$				
Average (four cycles)	62.125	65.975	66.9	68.25	64.625
Combined estimate of sigma =	$\dfrac{0.304 + 0.246 + 0.134}{3} = 0.228$				

and Draper (1969, p. 212) do provide a table that can serve as a guideline, however. Their table gives the number of cycles required to detect main effects, with a given probability, which increases the process standard deviation from σ to $k\sigma$. For example, if a 30% increase in σ could be tolerated without causing any serious problems, either four or five cycles would be appropriate when a 2^2 design is used (as in the present example). If only a 20% increase could be tolerated, then seven or eight cycles would be appropriate.

Assume that two additional cycles are carried out (for a total of four) and the results are summarized in Tables 15.3 and 15.4.

It is worth noting that four cycles are sufficient to allow a sample variance, s^2, to be computed at each design point. These s^2 values could then be pooled to provide s^2_{pooled} (as discussed in Chapter 13), which would be used in estimating σ. This would produce a better estimate of σ than would be obtained using the range of the differences (for reasons similar to

**Table 15.4 Process Averages and Effect Estimates with Confidence
Limits after Four Cycles ($k = 4$)**

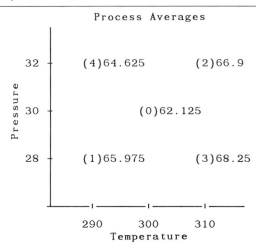

Process Averages

$$\text{Effects with 2 Standard Error Limits}$$

Pressure	$\frac{1}{2}[(4) + (2) - (1) - (3)] \pm 2\dfrac{\hat{\sigma}}{\sqrt{k}} = -1.35 \pm 0.228$
Temperature	$\frac{1}{2}[(2) + (3) - (1) - (4)] \pm 2\dfrac{\hat{\sigma}}{\sqrt{k}} = 2.275 \pm 0.228$
Temperature × Pressure	$\frac{1}{2}[(1) + (2) - (3) - (4)] \pm 2\dfrac{\hat{\sigma}}{\sqrt{k}} = 0 \pm 0.228$
Change in mean	$\frac{1}{5}[(0) + (1) + (2) + (3) + (4)] - (0)$
	$\pm 1.79\dfrac{\hat{\sigma}}{\sqrt{k}} = 3.45 \pm 0.204$

those given in Chapter 5). For the data in Table 15.3 it could be shown that
$\hat{\sigma} = \sqrt{s^2_{\text{pooled}}} = 0.244$, where s^2_{pooled} is the average of the s^2 values for the
five design points. This estimate does not differ greatly from the estimate of
0.228 obtained using the range method, however, and would lead to the
same conclusions regarding the significance of the four effects. (It should
also be noted that the constant c_4, used in Chapter 5, would not be used
here. For control charts s is divided by c_4 in estimating σ, but s is used in
place of σ in other statistical procedures.)

The results shown in Table 15.4 suggest that there is a pressure effect and
a temperature effect as well as a "change in mean" effect, since each of the
three intervals does not cover zero. Furthermore, the fact that the tempera-

Table 15.5 Process Averages and Effect Estimates with Confidence Limits after Four Cycles of the Second Phase

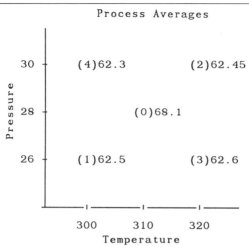

Process Averages

Effects with 2 Standard Error Limits

Pressure
$$\tfrac{1}{2}[(4) + (2) - (1) - (3)] \pm 2\frac{\hat{\sigma}}{\sqrt{k}} = -0.175 \pm 0.225$$

Temperature
$$\tfrac{1}{2}[(2) + (3) - (1) - (4)] \pm 2\frac{\hat{\sigma}}{\sqrt{k}} = 0.125 \pm 0.225$$

Temperature × Pressure
$$\tfrac{1}{2}[(1) + (2) - (3) - (4)] \pm 2\frac{\hat{\sigma}}{\sqrt{k}} = 0.025 \pm 0.225$$

Change in mean
$$\tfrac{1}{5}[(0) + (1) + (2) + (3) + (4)] - (0)$$
$$\pm 1.79\frac{\hat{\sigma}}{\sqrt{k}} = -4.51 \pm 0.201$$

ture × pressure interval does cover zero makes the interpretation straightforward.

The results suggest that temperature should be increased and pressure should be lowered. Following this suggestion would produce a new set of operating conditions for the next *phase*. Thus, we might use pressure set at 26, 28, and 30, and temperature set at 300, 310, and 320. Assume that four cycles are carried out in this phase, with the results given in Table 15.5, with sigma estimated at 0.225 from these four cycles. (Note: Whenever a new phase is entered, the estimate of sigma from the previous phase would generally be used for the first two cycles of the new phase, with the data from that phase being used to produce an estimate of sigma starting with the third cycle.) It is obvious from Table 15.5 that increasing the temperature to 320 and decreasing the pressure to 26 have a deleterious effect on the process yield. A three-dimensional display of these data would indicate a "peak" at operating condition (0), with the process yield dropping off rather sharply as changes are made in any of the indicated directions.

Thus, it would appear as though the optimum operating condition is in the general vicinity of 310 and 28 for these two process variables. We should not stop here, however, because the "peak" might actually occur at a slightly different combination of values. Therefore, in the next phase the pressure might be set at 27.5, 28, and 28.5, and the temperature might be set at 308, 310, and 312.

As indicated previously, the use of new operating conditions should be almost a nonending process, with an EVOP program being continued as long as the cost of running the program is less than the savings that are being realized. [See p. 21 of Box and Draper (1969) for a detailed explanation of cost vs. savings for an EVOP program.]

15.2   THREE VARIABLES

Box and Draper (1969, p. 99) indicate that no more than three variables could be considered practical for an EVOP program. Why? Remembering that an EVOP program is to be a permanent part of the normal operating procedure, it would be too much to expect plant operators to make changes in a half dozen or so process variables on a continuing basis. [See Box and Draper (1969, p. 176) for a similar view.]

A logical strategy would be to first use a fractional factorial design as a screening design to identify the process variables and two-factor interactions that seem to be important. If this initial study indicates that there are more than two or three process variables that seem to be important, and that some of the two-factor interactions are significant, two or more EVOP programs could be set up, with process variables involved in significant two-factor interactions being assigned to the same EVOP program.

Assume that the use of a screening design has led to the identification of six process variables that seem to be significantly related to the response variable, and that the few pairwise interactions that were significant have led to the assignment of the involved variables to the same EVOP program. How do we use three variables in an EVOP program? We could run all three variables simultaneously, with or without a reference condition. If a reference condition is used, a logical place for it would be the center of the cube as shown in Figure 15.2.

Other possible approaches to the handling of three variables in an EVOP program include (1) using only two of the three variables in each phase, and (2) running the different operating conditions in two blocks.

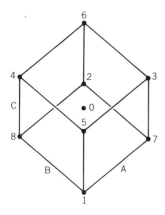

Figure 15.2 A 2^3 design with a center point, for use in a three-variable EVOP program.

The former is illustrated in Hunter and Chacko (1971), which describes how a company that manufactures a polymer latex used an EVOP program for the initial objective of minimizing the optical density of the latex. [This study is also described in Box et al. (1978, p. 365).] The three process variables were temperature, stirring rate, and addition time. A total of five phases were used. Stirring rate and addition time were studied in the first two phases, with temperature and stirring rate studied in the fourth phase, and temperature and addition time studied in the other two phases. (The decision to use only two variables in each phase was made for the sake of simplicity.)

The analysis of the data resulting from an EVOP program conducted in this manner would be the same as that illustrated earlier in this chapter (assuming that two levels were used with a center point, which was the case).

One of the most significant results of this particular study was that it led to the discovery that addition time could be reduced by 45 minutes, which subsequently resulted in approximately a 25% increase in production, with beneficial results also being realized from changes in the other two variables.

The second alternative entails running a $1/2$ fraction of a 2^3 design in each block (with or without a reference condition), with the ABC interaction confounded with the difference between blocks. This approach is illustrated by Box and Draper (1969), and its advantage (over a regular 2^3 design) is also simplicity in that the plant worker would be working with the same number of observations within each block as he would have with an EVOP program that utilized a 2^2 design.

In each cycle (starting with the third), the standard deviation would be estimated by pooling the estimates obtained from each of the two blocks, and the data from the two blocks would be combined and analyzed using

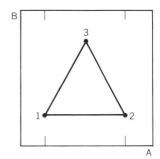

Figure 15.3 Simplex for studying two variables in an EVOP program.

some method of analysis such as Yates' algorithm. [See Box and Draper (1969) for additional details.]

15.3 SIMPLEX EVOP

As was mentioned at the beginning of this chapter, several alternatives to Box–EVOP have been proposed, but Simplex EVOP seems to be the only alternative procedure that has actually been used. The procedure is very easy to use, but it draws its name from the fact that it is based upon a geometrical figure termed a (regular) simplex. In two dimensions this is an equilateral triangle, as illustrated in Figure 15.3, which would be used for studying two variables. In general, the number of design points is always one more than the number of variables.

Simplex EVOP was originally proposed by Spendley, Hext, and Himsworth (1962), and it is discussed favorably by Lowe (1974), in particular, and Hahn (1976b). We shall illustrate the methodology using the same data that were utilized in introducing Box–EVOP, namely, the data in Figure 15.1.

We shall now assume, however, that the current operating conditions are 290° for temperature and 28 p.s.i. for pressure, rather than 300° and 30 p.s.i., respectively, which were originally assumed. Also, since we need only two more points, we will select those points that were labeled (0) and (3) in Figure 15.1 to form our simplex. In general, the other two points are chosen by determining what changes in the two process variables might lead to improvement in the response variable that is being studied, without simultaneously running a substantial risk of causing a deterioration in the process (i.e., changes that are relatively small, but at the same time large enough to possibly cause some process improvement). The initial setup is given in Figure 15.4. Point #2 obviously represents the least favorable operating condition. Since we are trying to maximize the response variable (yield), the

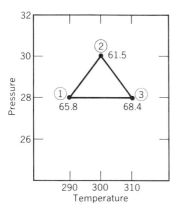

Figure 15.4 Starting simplex for Simplex EVOP.

next step is to create a new simplex by adding a new point that is as far from point #2 as possible. This requires that the new point be at 26 p.s.i. for pressure and 300° for temperature. The reader will recall that this combination was used in the second phase of the Box–EVOP illustration, and that the average yield after four cycles was 62.5. With Simplex EVOP, however, there are no cycles; rather, only a single run is made at each operating condition. Assume that this run produces a value of 62.3. Now, if we create a new simplex by "reflecting" this second simplex about its least desirable operating condition, we would return to the original simplex. Therefore, we must introduce a new rule [termed rule 3 by Spendley et al. (1962)], which states that the second least favorable point is used in constructing the next simplex, whenever the basic rule of using the worst point would return us to the same simplex that we just left.

Thus, the third simplex would be created by reflecting the second simplex about point #1. This new simplex and subsequent simplexes that would result from assumed observations are shown in Figure 15.5.

The values displayed for points 4, 5, and 7 are in general agreement with the averages at those operating conditions that were given in Table 15.5, whereas point #6 was not part of the Box–EVOP illustration.

What can be said for Simplex EVOP vs. Box–EVOP? First, the former is clearly much easier than the latter. With the simplex approach there are no statistical calculations to perform, and new operating conditions are obtained by following simple, well-defined rules. If the optimum value of the response variable drifts over time, the simplex approach could be expected to track such a drift much faster than the Box–EVOP approach. The simplex approach can also be applied when there are more than just a few process variables to be varied, whereas Box–EVOP should generally not be used with more than three process variables.

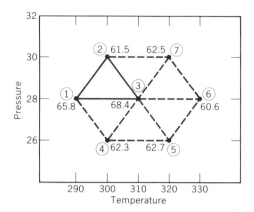

Figure 15.5 Starting simplex and subsequent simplexes.

Spendley, Hext, and Himsworth (1962) presented simplex EVOP as an approach that would be appropriate for "Automated EVOP"; that is, movement to new operating conditions would be performed automatically by computer. The desirability of using some automated or inflexible procedure is questionable, however. As G. E. P. Box has repeatedly emphasized, an experimenter learns about a process by perturbing it and seeing what happens, and, in general, communicating with the process. With Simplex EVOP, in its general form, there is really no explicit provision for flexibility, and the resultant "communication" is thus likely to be suboptimal.

Clearly, as the optimum value of the response variable is approached, smaller simplexes would need to be created [as Hahn (1976b) suggests]. Otherwise, we would be using simplexes that would just keep circling the optimum operating condition, and producing values of the response variable that could differ considerably from the optimum value. This would put Simplex EVOP more in line with Box–EVOP, where changes in the process variables are generally not constant amounts, and the changes result from decisions coming from the EVOP committee, not from a computer.

A wholly automated, inflexible procedure is undesirable. For processes that drift over time and then temporarily stabilize, the use of Simplex EVOP followed by Box–EVOP would probably be the best approach.

Why not just modify the general simplex approach to allow for the construction of smaller simplexes rather than resorting to Box–EVOP? The answer is that it is generally easier to analyze data from a rectangular region than from a triangular region. Although the analysis of data from a simplex design is generally known, one could not expect the analysis to be performed by plant personnel, and the (statistical) analysis would be necessary in determining the sizes of the simplexes.

One of the main problems with Simplex EVOP is that changes in the operating conditions are based, at each stage, on a single number; specifically the number at the operating condition that is reflected to form the next simplex. This could easily result in a move in a bad direction, especially for a process that has considerable variability. Proponents of Simplex EVOP contend that a move into a bad area should be immediately followed by a move out of that area, but the fact remains that a sizable number of bad moves could result over a period of time. (Here a "bad area" is one that is somewhat removed from the optimum operating region, and where nonconforming units might be produced.)

Everything considered, Box–EVOP seems to be preferable to Simplex EVOP when a process is relatively stable. Readers seeking more details about Simplex EVOP are referred to the paper by Spendley, Hext, and Himsworth (1962), which contains information concerning how the coordinates of each process variable in each simplex would be obtained, for any number of variables, as well as additional information. Papers that describe industrial applications of Simplex EVOP include Kenworthy (1967). Lowe (1974) provides a comparison of Simplex EVOP vs. Box–EVOP.

15.4 OTHER EVOP PROCEDURES

Other modifications of Box–EVOP that have been proposed include REVOP (random evolutionary operation) and ROVOP (rotating square evolutionary operation). Operating conditions in an EVOP program are generated randomly under REVOP, whereas under ROVOP successively larger (square) operating regions are generated that include the previous square, with the orientation of each square alternating between a regular square and a square oriented as a diamond. The reader is referred to Lowe (1964) for additional details of these two procedures, as well as to Box and Draper (1969).

Recommended reading on EVOP would include Box (1957) and the review paper by Hunter and Kittrell (1966). The latter contains some discussion regarding companies that have used EVOP, and the amount of money that some companies have saved. The paper contains a considerable number of references [as does Box and Draper (1969)].

More recent papers on EVOP include Draper and Box (1970), and Hahn (1976a), both of which are very general. The fundamental concepts of EVOP are given in Barnett (1974), and Himmelblau (1970) is a text that emphasizes the mathematics of some of the proposed variations of Box–EVOP.

SUMMARY

Evolutionary operation (EVOP) is a program based upon statistical concepts which is meant to be a permanent part of normal plant operation. It is intended for use by regular plant personnel, and the necessary calculations can be easily performed by hand computation or by computer. Box–EVOP has been used much more extensively than Simplex EVOP, although there are conditions under which Simplex EVOP might be used in tandem with Box–EVOP (e.g., process drift).

As was indicated in the summary of Chapter 13, one learns about experimental design by designing experiments. Similar in spirit to Hunter (1977), Russell and Stephens (1970) present an EVOP teaching game which utilizes a simulated process. (It is obviously preferable to learn statistical principles of experimentation using something other than actual production processes that are critical to the quality of manufactured products.)

APPENDIX TO CHAPTER 15

Derivation of Formula for Estimating σ

The process standard deviation is estimated using differences between values at the same design point, and then determining the range of those differences.

The first time that the differences can be computed is after the second cycle. If we let y_{1i} and y_{2i} denote the value observed at the ith design point for the first and second cycle, respectively, then

$$\text{Var}(y_{2i} - y_{1i}) = 2\sigma^2$$

since the values are assumed to be independent between cycles. If we let $\text{Var}(y_{2i} - y_{1i})$ be denoted by σ_{diff}^2, it follows that we would estimate σ after the second cycle as

$$\hat{\sigma} = \hat{\sigma}_{\text{diff}}\left(\sqrt{1/2}\right)$$

where $\sqrt{1/2}$ follows the form $\sqrt{(K-1)/k}$ for $k = 2$ cycles.

In general, after k cycles the differences would be obtained as

$$y_{ki} - \bar{y}_{(k-1)i}$$

where $\bar{y}_{(k-1)i}$ denotes the average at the ith design point for the first $k - 1$ cycles. It follows that

$$\mathrm{Var}\left(y_{ki} - \bar{y}_{(k-1)i}\right)$$

$$= \sigma_{\mathrm{diff}}^2$$

$$= \sigma^2 + \frac{\sigma^2}{k - 1} = \frac{k\sigma^2}{k - 1} = \frac{k}{k - 1}\sigma^2$$

Therefore, $\sigma_{\mathrm{diff}}^2 = [k/(k - 1)]\sigma^2$ so that

$$\hat{\sigma} = \sqrt{\frac{k - 1}{k}}\,\hat{\sigma}_{\mathrm{diff}}$$

The standard deviation of the differences, σ_{diff}, is then estimated using the range of the differences.

REFERENCES

Barnett, E. H. (1974). Evolutionary operation. In J. M. Juran, F. M. Gryna, and R. S. Bingham, eds. *Quality Control Handbook*, 3rd ed., Section 27A. New York: McGraw-Hill.

Box, G. E. P. (1957). Evolutionary operation: A method for increasing industrial productivity. *Applied Statistics* 6(2): 81–101 (June).

Box, G. E. P., and N. R. Draper (1969). *Evolutionary Operation*. New York: Wiley.

Box, G. E. P., and J. S. Hunter (1959). Condensed calculations for evolutionary operation programs. *Technometrics* 1(1): 77–95 (February).

Box, G. E. P., and R. D. Meyer (1986). An analysis for unreplicated fractional factorials. *Technometrics* 28(1): 11–18 (February).

Box, G. E. P., W. G. Hunter, and J. S. Hunter (1978). *Statistics for Experimenters*. New York: Wiley.

Draper, N. R., and G. E. P. Box (1970). EVOP—makes a plant grow better. *Industrial Engineering*, 31–33 (April).

Hahn, G. J. (1976a). Process improvement using evolutionary operation. *Chemtech* 6: 204–206 (March).

Hahn, G. J. (1976b). Process improvement through Simplex EVOP. *Chemtech 6*: 343–345 (May).

Hahn, G. J. (1984). Discussion (of an invited paper by Steinberg and Hunter). *Technometrics 26*(2): 110–115 (May).

Hahn, G. J., and A. F. Dershowitz (1974). Evolutionary operation today—some survey results and observations. *Applied Statistics 23*(2): 214–218.

Himmelblau, D. M. (1970). *Process Analysis by Statistical Methods.* New York: Wiley.

Hunter, W. G. (1977). Some ideas about teaching design of experiments with 2^5 examples of experiments conducted by students. *The American Statistician 31*(1): 12–17 (February).

Hunter, W. G., and E. Chacko (1971). Increasing industrial productivity in developing countries. *International Development Review 13*: 311–316.

Hunter, W. G., and J. R. Kittrell (1966). Evolutionary operation: A review. *Technometrics 8*(3): 389–397 (August).

Joiner, B. L. (1985). The key role of statisticians in the transformation of North American industry. *The American Statistician 39*(3): 224–227; Discussion: pp. 228–234 (August).

Kenworthy, I. C. (1967). Some examples of simplex evolutionary operation in the paper industry. *Applied Statistics 16*(3): 211–224.

Lowe, C. W. (1964). Some techniques of evolutionary operation. *Transactions of the Institution of Chemical Engineers 42*: T332–344.

Lowe, C. W. (1974). Evolutionary operation in action. *Applied Statistics 23*(2): 218–226.

Russell, E. R., and K. S. Stephens (1970). An EVOP teaching game using a simulated process. *Journal of Quality Technology 2*(2): 61–66 (April).

Spendley, W., G. R. Hext, and F. R. Himsworth (1962). Sequential applications of simplex designs in optimization and EVOP. *Technometrics 4*(4): 441–461 (November).

EXERCISES

1. Explain the conditions under which an experimenter might decide to use (1) Box–EVOP instead of Simplex EVOP, (2) the latter instead of the former, and (3) a combination of the two.

2. Explain why an estimate of sigma is unnecessary when Simplex EVOP is used.

3. Assume that a Box–EVOP program is being initiated using two factors. How should sigma be estimated for the first couple of cycles of the first phase?

4. If an experimenter is ready to progress from the first phase to the second phase of a Box–EVOP program, how should he adjust the levels of his two factors if the 2 standard error limits are both below zero for his first factor, and also below zero for the second factor. (Assume that the limits for the interaction include zero.)

5. Referring to Exercise #4, what would you recommend to the experimenter if the limits for the interaction effect did not include zero?

6. Consider the data given below, which represent averages after five cycles in the second phase of a Box–EVOP program.

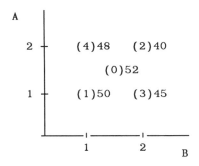

If $\hat{\sigma} = 5.14$, what are the two standard error limits for A, B, and AB?

7. An experimenter runs a Box–EVOP program using a 2^2 design with a center point. The average response values after two cycles are (0) 32.6, (1) 36.4, (2) 35.2, (3) 38.0, and (4) 34.2. Thinking of the two factors as A and B for the vertical and horizontal axes, respectively, and using 1.0 as a prior estimate of sigma,

   a. Determine what effects, if any, appear to be significant.

   b. What do these results suggest about how the values for A and B should be altered in the next phase?

8. Which of the two procedures, Box–EVOP or Simplex EVOP, would you choose if you believed that the optimum operating region could possibly be far removed from the initial conditions?

9. Using a 2^2 design with a center point, what is the estimate of sigma if the range of differences after the second, third, and fourth cycles of the first phase are 0.82, 0.64, and 0.29, respectively?

CHAPTER 16

Analysis of Means

To some people the term *analysis of means* conjures up notions of *analysis of variance* (ANOVA), which is also concerned with the analysis of means, and which is much better known and more widely used than the statistical technique known as *analysis of means* (ANOM). (The relative obscurity of ANOM is indicated by the fact that it is not included in the hundreds of statistical methods and topics that are included in the *Encyclopedia of Statistical Sciences*.) It is apt to have more appeal to engineers and other industrial personnel than does ANOVA, however, since ANOM is inherently a graphical procedure and is somewhat similar to a control chart. Consequently, it is to be expected that the increasing interest in control charts should lead to an increased interest in ANOM.

ANOM was developed by E. R. Ott and presented in Ott (1958). It was introduced into the literature in Ott (1967), and Ott's text (1975) contains many illustrative examples. The original concept has been extended by Schilling (1973a, b) and L. S. Nelson (1983) provides values of the necessary mathematical constants.

Ott's 1967 paper appeared in the Walter Shewhart Memorial issue of *Industrial Quality Control*, and it is fitting that the January 1983 issue of the *Journal of Quality Technology* (which was previously named *Industrial Quality Control*) contains articles only on ANOM, with the purpose of serving as a tribute to Ellis Ott upon his passing. That issue also serves as a definitive work on the state of the art of ANOM, and, in particular, the article by P. F. Ramig contains the step-by-step procedures for variables and attribute data, as well as several illustrative examples. (Ott's original paper on ANOM is also reprinted in that issue.)

Our first illustration of ANOM will be made using the temperature data in Table 13.3 that were analyzed in Chapter 13 using ANOVA. When the latter was used as the method of analysis it was concluded that there was at least one mean that was different from the other means. It was mentioned that a multiple comparison procedure could be used to identify means that differ, although the box-and-whisker plot provided evidence that the mean at the highest temperature level was different from the means at the other two levels.

The reader will recall that with ANOVA the experimenter concludes either that all of the means are equal, or that at least one of the means differs from the others. With ANOM, however, the user will see whether or not one or more means differ from the average of all of the means. Thus, what is being tested is different for the two procedures, so the results will not necessarily agree. In particular, when $k - 1$ sample averages are bunched tightly together but the kth sample average (i.e., the other one) differs considerably from the $k - 1$ averages, the F value in ANOVA would likely be relatively small (thus indicating that the population means are equal), whereas the difference would probably be detected using ANOM. Conversely, if the differences between adjacent sample averages are both sizable and similar, the (likely) difference in the population means is more apt to be detected with ANOVA than with ANOM.

One procedure need not be used to the exclusion of the other, however. As Ott (1967) indicates, ANOM can be used either alone or as a supplement to ANOVA.

16.1   ANOM FOR ONE-WAY CLASSIFICATIONS

It was stated previously that with ANOM one compares $\bar{x}_i$ against the average of the $\bar{x}_i$, which will be denoted by $\bar{\bar{x}}$, analogous to the notation used for an $\bar{X}$ chart. The original ANOM methodology given by Ott (1967) was based upon the multiple significance test for a group of means given by Halperin, Greenhouse, Cornfield, and Zalokar (1955), which was based upon the studentized maximum absolute deviate. That approach provided an upper bound for the unknown critical value, but will not be discussed here since it is no longer used. The interested reader is referred to Schilling (1973a) for more details, including the theoretical development.

The current approach is based upon the exact critical value, h, and is described in P. R. Nelson (1983, p. 35).

If we were testing for the significance of a single deviation, $\bar{x}_i - \bar{\bar{x}}$, it would stand to reason that we would want to look at some test statistic of the form

$$\frac{\bar{x}_i - \bar{\bar{x}} - E\left(\bar{x}_i - \bar{\bar{x}}\right)}{s_{\bar{x}_i - \bar{\bar{x}}}} \tag{16.1}$$

where E stands for expected value. If $\mu_i = (\mu_1 + \mu_2 + \cdots + \mu_k)/k$ then $E(\bar{x}_i - \bar{\bar{x}}) = 0$, and since the former is what would be tested, we take $E(\bar{x}_i - \bar{\bar{x}})$ to be zero.

It can be observed that Eq. (16.1) becomes a t test when $k = 2$ since $\bar{x}_i - \bar{\bar{x}}$ is then $\bar{x}_1 - (\bar{x}_1 + \bar{x}_2)/2 = (\bar{x}_1 - \bar{x}_2)/2$ for $i = 1$ [and $(\bar{x}_2 - \bar{x}_1)/2$ for $i = 2$] so that

$$t = \frac{(\bar{x}_1 - \bar{x}_2)/2 - 0}{s_{(\bar{x}_1 - \bar{x}_2)/2}} = \frac{\bar{x}_1 - \bar{x}_2}{s_{\bar{x}_1 - \bar{x}_2}}$$

since the twos cancel.

The two deviations $\bar{x}_1 - \bar{\bar{x}}$ and $\bar{x}_2 - \bar{\bar{x}}$ are thus equal, so we would conclude that the two means differ if

$$t = \frac{|\bar{x}_1 - \bar{x}_2|}{s_{\bar{x}_1 - \bar{x}_2}} > t_\alpha$$

for a selected value of α.

When $k > 2$ the t distribution cannot be used, however, so another procedure is needed. It can be shown that, assuming equal sample sizes, the deviations $\bar{x}_i - \bar{\bar{x}}$ are equally correlated with correlation coefficient $\rho = -1/(k - 1)$. If we let $T_i = (\bar{x}_i - \bar{\bar{x}})/s_{\bar{x}_i - \bar{\bar{x}}}$, the joint distribution of $T_1, T_2, \ldots, T_k$ is an equicorrelated multivariate noncentral t distribution, assuming that the sample averages are independent and normally distributed with a common variance. (See Nelson 1982, p. 701.)

Exact critical values for $k > 2$ were first generated by Nelson (1982), with a few tabular values subsequently corrected, and the corrected tables published in L. S. Nelson (1983).

The general idea is to plot the averages against *decision lines* obtained from

$$\bar{\bar{x}} \pm h_{\alpha, k, \nu} s\sqrt{(k - 1)/(kn)} \tag{16.2}$$

where n is the number of observations from which each average is computed, ν is the degrees of freedom associated with s, the estimate of σ, k is the number of averages, and $h_{\alpha, k, \nu}$ is obtained from the tables in L. S. Nelson (1983) for a selected value of α. It is demonstrated in the appendix to this chapter that $s\sqrt{(k - 1)/(kn)}$ is the estimate of $\sigma_{\bar{x}_i - \bar{\bar{x}}}$.

The value of α is the probability of (wrongly) rejecting the hypothesis that is being tested when, in fact, the hypothesis is true. (Here we are testing that each mean is equal to the average of all the k means.)

The first step is to compute the overall average, $\bar{\bar{x}}$. For the data in Table 13.3 this value is 2.67. The next step is to compute the estimate of σ using s. This can be obtained from Table 13.4 as $\sqrt{0.0867}$. (Ott originally presented ANOM where σ was estimated from the range, but the current tables that are used require the use of s, which might be obtained from an ANOVA table.)

The appropriate value for $h_{\alpha,k,\nu}$ is obtained from Table G. If we use $\alpha = .05$, $h_{.05,3,27} = 2.485$, approximately, so the decision lines are obtained from

$$2.67 \pm 2.485\sqrt{0.0867}\sqrt{(3-1)/(3)(10)} = 2.67 \pm 0.19$$

(2.485 is obtained as the average of 2.47 and 2.50 since 27 d.f. is halfway between 24 and 30.) Thus, we have the two "limits" 2.48 and 2.86, which are termed decision lines rather than control limits, as they are used in reaching a decision about the k means instead of for controlling a process. Accordingly, with UDL representing the upper decision line and LDL representing the lower decision line, we have

$$LDL = 2.48$$

$$UDL = 2.86$$

The results can then be displayed graphically as in Figure 16.1. We would thus conclude that the true effects of 250° and 350° differ from the average process yield averaged over all three temperatures.

There is nothing sacrosanct about $\alpha = .05$, however. Ott (1967) suggests that .01 might be used in addition to or in place of .05, and in Ott (1975) one finds numerous displays in which both are used, and one display (p. 115) in which three sets of lines (for .01, .05, and .10) are shown.

For this example $h_{.01,3,27}$ is obtained as 3.18 (the average of 3.15 and 3.21), which would produce LDL(.01) = 2.43 and UDL(.01) = 2.91. If these lines had been displayed in Figure 16.1, only the average at 350° would have been outside these decision lines. Therefore, since the choice of α will often lead to different conclusions, the use of multiple decision lines is desirable.

The assumptions that need to be made when ANOM is applied to one-way classification data are the same as those needed for one-way ANOVA; namely, the k averages must be independent and normally distributed with a common variance. (We must make the additional assumption that the single classification factor is fixed, however, since ANOM is not for random effects.) Schilling (1973b) has extended ANOM to apply to nonnormal distributions.

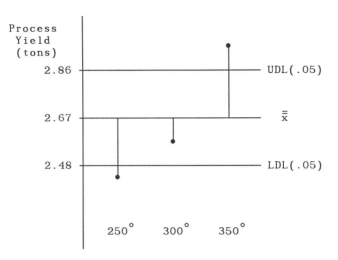

Figure 16.1 ANOM for the data in Table 13.3.

In the previous example the sample sizes for each level of the factor (temperature) were equal. This, of course, is not a requirement for ANOVA, nor is it a requirement for ANOM. L. S. Nelson (1983) gives approximate values of $h_{\alpha, k, \nu}$ to be used for unequal sample sizes.

16.2 ANOM FOR ATTRIBUTE DATA

16.2.1 Proportions

ANOM can be applied just as easily to attribute data as to measurement data. The following example is drawn from the author's consulting experience, and although the data are fictitious, it is the type of problem faced by many industrial managers.

A company in the agricultural industry employs a number of (human) harvesters, and is interested in assessing the relative performance of each harvester. Specifically, the percentage of crops that do not meet specifications is to be recorded for each harvester, and the company is interested in identifying harvesters who perform significantly better than the overall average (for the purpose of meritorious recognition), as well as to identify those who are significantly below the overall average so that they might be retrained or reassigned.

Assume that the company has 20 harvesters and that the data for a particular month are given in Table 16.1. The steps that are followed in

Table 16.1 Percentage of Nonconforming Crops for Each Harvester (March 1987)

Harvester Number	Nonconforming Crops (%) ($n = 1000$)
1	1.4
2	2.6
3	1.0
4	3.1
5	2.9
6	5.1
7	2.4
8	4.1
9	1.1
10	2.1
11	2.0
12	2.6
13	3.1
14	2.7
15	3.7
16	4.0
17	4.4
18	3.2
19	2.2
20	1.8

producing the ANOM display for attribute data are similar to the steps that are followed for measurement data. Specifically, for proportions data the decision lines are obtained from

$$\bar{p} \pm h_{\alpha, k, \infty} s_p \sqrt{\frac{k-1}{k}} \qquad (16.3)$$

where $\bar{p}$ is the average of all the proportions (20 in this example), $s_p = \sqrt{\bar{p}(1 - \bar{p})/n}$ is the estimate of σ_p, and k is the number of proportions.

For this example we have

$$\bar{p} = 2.775\% = 0.02775,$$

$$s_p = \sqrt{(0.02775)(0.97225)/1000} = 0.0052, \quad \text{and} \quad k = 20.$$

The value of $h_{\alpha, k}$ is obtained from Table G using infinity for the number of degrees of freedom. Thus, we have $h_{.05} = 3.02$ and $h_{.01} = 3.48$. Following Tomlinson and Lavigna (1983) we shall use $h_{.01}$ rather than $h_{.05}$ so as to pick the smaller of the two risks of telling a worker that he is worse than the average of the group when he really is not, and, in general, in recognition of the sensitivity of workers to being identified in this manner, even if they are, in fact, below par.

The decision lines are thus obtained from

$$0.02775 \pm 3.48(0.0052)\sqrt{\tfrac{19}{20}} = 0.02775 \pm 0.01764$$

so that the decision lines are LDL = 0.0101 and UDL = 0.0454. The display is given in Figure 16.2. It can be observed that 11 of the values are below the midline and 9 are above. Should the 11 that are below the midline be reprimanded? This is reminiscent of the story frequently told by W. Edwards Deming about the company that notified its workers who were below average, apparently not realizing that roughly half of them will always be below average regardless of how well or how poorly they are performing their job tasks.

In ANOM it is a question of how far each point is from the midline. In Figure 16.2 it is apparent that the proportion nonconforming for worker #6 is well above the UDL. Therefore, retraining or reassignment would seem to be called for. At the other extreme, we can see that worker #3 is virtually at the LDL, and worker #9 is slightly above it. Thus, their respective performances seem to be especially meritorious.

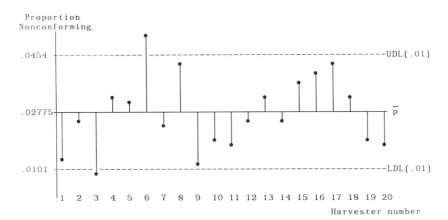

Figure 16.2 ANOM display for Table 16.1 data.

Students of statistics will recognize that this use of ANOM for data in the form of proportions serves as an alternative to a chi-square test, in which equality of the 20 proportions would be tested using the chi-square distribution. ANOM is more sensitive than a chi-square test in detecting a few extreme deviations from the average, however (vis-à-vis ANOM vs. ANOVA for measurement data), and the ability to detect extreme observations is what is really needed for this problem.

The requisite assumption for the application of ANOM to proportions data is the adequacy of the normal approximation to the binomial distribution. [Recall from Chapter 8 the rough rule of thumb that both np and $n(1 - p)$ exceed 5 for the approximation to be of any value.] If the adequacy of the approximation is in doubt, then one of the transformations discussed in Chapter 8 for binomial (proportions) data should be used.

16.2.2 Count Data

ANOM can also be applied to count data (e.g., nonconformities) in which the Poisson distribution is an appropriate model for the data. The decision lines are obtained from

$$\bar{c} \pm h_{\alpha, k, \infty} \sqrt{\bar{c}} \sqrt{\frac{k - 1}{k}}$$

where $\bar{c}$ is the average of k "counts" (e.g., nonconformities), and, for a given value of α, $h_{\alpha, k, \infty}$ is the same value as is used for proportions data. The use of ANOM with count data is based upon the assumed adequacy of the normal approximation to the Poisson distribution. (Recall from Chapter 8 that the approximation is generally assumed to be adequate when the mean of the Poisson distribution, estimated by $\bar{c}$, is at least 5.) When the adequacy is questionable, the counts should be transformed using one of the transformations for Poisson data given in Chapter 8, with ANOM then applied to the transformed data.

16.3 ANOM WHEN STANDARDS ARE GIVEN

16.3.1 Nonconforming Units

Ott (1958, 1975) also presented the methodology for ANOM when standards are given. In the example used to illustrate ANOM for proportions data, $\bar{p}$ was obtained as the overall proportion of nonconforming crops for the 20 harvesters. That value was 0.02775. How would the ANOM have been performed if the company had established a "standard" of 2% nonconforming? (Here the word *standard* is used analogously to *target value* in Chapter 14.)

If we denote the standard value by p, the decision lines are obtained from

$$p \pm h_{\alpha, k, \infty} \sqrt{\frac{p(1 - p)}{n}} \qquad (16.4)$$

where, as before, n is the number of items inspected by each harvester, and $h_{\alpha, k, \infty}$ is the value obtained from Table G for specified values of α and k, with infinity for the degrees of freedom.

If we compare Eq. (16.4) with Eq. (16.3), the main difference is that the former does not contain the factor $\sqrt{(k - 1)/k}$ that is used in the latter. In general, this factor will be a part of the decision line calculations only when the midline is estimated from data. The other difference, of course, is that p is used in place of $\bar{p}$.

What would an ANOM display with decision lines obtained from Eq. (16.4) actually show? It would indicate whether or not any of the workers' true ability appears to differ from that of the standard. If the decision lines in Figure 16.2 had been obtained using Eq. (16.4) rather than Eq. (16.3), the values for UDL and LDL would have been 0.03541 and 0.00459, respectively. Comparing these values with the data in Table 16.1 would lead to the identification of five workers as being worse than the standard, and none being better than the standard.

The use of these decision lines would have to be given careful consideration, however, as the harvesters' performance might be affected by factors outside of their control (e.g., growing conditions), and the company standard thus might not be easily attainable. In general, this is comparable to determining whether or not a process is in a state of statistical control (with, say an $\bar{X}$ chart) with the control limits determined by the current process capability vs. determined from a target value.

16.3.2 Nonconformities

When ANOM is applied to count data and a standard is to be used, the decision lines are obtained from

$$c \pm h_{\alpha, k, \infty} \sqrt{c}$$

where c is the standard acceptable count (e.g., the number of surface imperfections per 50 square yards of sheet metal), and $h_{\alpha, k, \infty}$ is as designated in the preceding section.

16.3.3 Measurement Data

The decision lines in Figure 16.1 were obtained under the assumption that μ and σ are unknown, so they were estimated by $\bar{\bar{x}}$ and s, respectively. If μ and σ were both known, the decision lines would be obtained from $\mu \pm h_{\alpha, k, \infty}(\sigma/\sqrt{n})$; if σ was known but μ unknown the lines would be obtained from $\bar{\bar{x}} \pm h_{\alpha, k, \infty}(\sigma/\sqrt{n})\sqrt{(k-1)/k}$; and if μ was known but σ unknown the lines would be obtained from $\mu \pm h_{\alpha, k, \nu}(s/\sqrt{n})$ where ν is the degrees of freedom upon which s is based. These special cases have been listed by Schilling (1973a).

16.4 ANOM FOR FACTORIAL DESIGNS

ANOM can also be used when there is more than one factor provided that at least one factor is fixed. (Remember that ANOM is used only for fixed factors.)

We begin with a simple example by using the data in Table 13.7 (for a 2^2 design) which were used in Chapter 13 to introduce the analysis of 2^k designs using Yates' algorithm. When that data set was analyzed using ANOVA it was found that neither the two main effects nor the interaction effect were significant. The analysis of that data by ANOM could proceed as follows.

The decision lines for the main effects A and B could be computed from

$$\bar{\bar{x}} \pm h_{\alpha, k, \nu} \frac{s}{\sqrt{n}} \sqrt{\frac{k-1}{k}} \qquad (16.5)$$

where, as previously defined, s is the estimate of σ based on ν degrees of freedom, k is the number of averages (i.e., factor levels) for each of the two factors, $\bar{\bar{x}}$ is the overall average, and $h_{\alpha, k, \nu}$ is obtained from Table G for specified values of α, k, and ν.

Note that k is being used differently in this chapter from the way that it was used in the material on design of experiments (Chapter 13). In the latter it was used to denote the number of factors; in ANOM it denotes the number of plotted points (e.g., averages) that are compared per test. Thus, references to 2^k or 2^{k-p} designs in this section are for k = number of factors; all other uses of k in this section are for k = number of averages.

This creates a slight inconsistency of notation, but the notation has been retained since it is the accepted notation in each of the two subject areas.

There are two ways in which the decision lines for the AB interaction can be generated, depending upon what is to be graphed in illustrating the interaction. The approach used by Ott (1975) will be discussed first.

It was shown in Chapter 13 that for factors T and P the TP interaction could be written as

$$TP = \tfrac{1}{2}(T_2 P_2 - T_2 P_1 - T_1 P_2 + T_1 P_1)$$

where the subscript 1 denotes the "low" level, and 2 the "high" level. This can obviously be rewritten as

$$TP = \tfrac{1}{2}(T_1 P_1 + T_2 P_2) - \tfrac{1}{2}(T_1 P_2 + T_2 P_1)$$

If we replace T and P by A and B, respectively, we thus have

$$AB = \tfrac{1}{2}(A_1 B_1 + A_2 B_2) - \tfrac{1}{2}(A_1 B_2 + A_2 B_1)$$

In Ott's notation this would be $AB = \overline{L} - \overline{U}$ where $\overline{L} = (1/2)(\overline{A_1 B_1} + \overline{A_2 B_2})$ and $\overline{U} = (1/2)(\overline{A_1 B_2} + \overline{A_2 B_1})$, with the bar above the treatment combination denoting the average response for that treatment combination. The choice of notation results from the fact that the first component is obtained from treatment combinations that have like subscripts, and the second component is obtained from treatment combinations that have unlike subscripts.

Therefore, since $AB = \overline{L} - \overline{U}$, one way to portray the magnitude of the interaction effect is to plot $\overline{L}$ and $\overline{U}$ as "averages," with the vertical distance between them equal to the interaction effect. The decision lines for $\overline{L}$ and $\overline{U}$ are also obtained from Eq. (16.5).

Whenever ANOM is applied to data from any 2^k or 2^{k-p} design, each main effect and each interaction effect will have two components (i.e., two "averages"), and, as Ott (1975, p. 215) has pointed out, ANOM is then a "graphical t-test," and the decision lines can be obtained from use of a t table. Specifically, for a 2^2 design $h_{\alpha, k, \nu}$ becomes $t_{\alpha/2, \nu}$, $\sqrt{(k-1)/k}$ is then $\sqrt{2}/2$, and $n = 2r$ where r is the number of replicates. Thus, for a 2^2 design with r replicates the decision lines are obtained from

$$\overline{\overline{x}} \pm \tfrac{1}{2} t_{\alpha/2, \nu} \frac{s}{\sqrt{r}} \tag{16.6}$$

From the data in Table 13.7 we have $\bar{\bar{x}} = 153/12 = 12.75$, and from Table 13.9 we have that $s^2 = 5.58$ (based upon 8 degrees of freedom) so that $s = \sqrt{5.58} = 2.36$. For $\alpha = .01$, $t_{\alpha/2,8} = t_{.005,8} = 3.355$, and for $\alpha = .05$, $t_{\alpha/2,8} = t_{.025,8} = 2.306$. Therefore, with $r = 3$ the 0.01 decision lines are obtained from

$$12.75 \pm \frac{1}{2}(3.355)\frac{2.36}{\sqrt{3}} = 12.75 \pm 2.29$$

Thus, UDL(.01) = 15.04 and LDL(.01) = 10.46. Using $t_{.025,8} = 2.306$, the corresponding .05 decision lines are UDL(.05) = 14.32 and LDL(.05) = 11.18.

The interaction components that are to be plotted have been previously defined. The main effect components that are to be plotted are $\bar{A}_{\text{low}}$ and $\bar{A}_{\text{high}}$ for the A effect, and $\bar{B}_{\text{low}}$ and $\bar{B}_{\text{high}}$ for the B effect. Letting 1 represent "low" and 2 represent "high," we then find from Table 13.7 that $\bar{A}_1 = 13.17$, $\bar{A}_2 = 12.33$, $\bar{B}_1 = 11.50$, and $\bar{B}_2 = 14.00$. Plotting these together with $\bar{L} = 13.5$ and $\bar{U} = 12.0$ produces the ANOM display given in Figure 16.3.

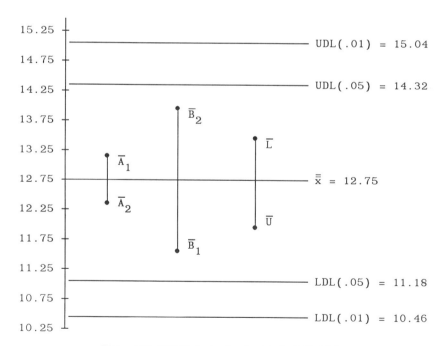

Figure 16.3 ANOM display for the data in Table 13.7.

This ANOM display shows what was seen numerically in the ANOVA table that was given in Table 13.9; namely, that the B effect is the largest of the three effects, but none of the effects is significant since all of the points are inside both the .01 and .05 decision lines.

It was stated at the beginning of this chapter that ANOM and ANOVA are similar but will not necessarily give the same results since what is being tested is slightly different for the two procedures. Although that is true in general, the two procedures will give identical results when each effect is represented by two means (as in the present example).

This can be demonstrated as follows. For a 2^2 design with r replicates, it can be shown, using ANOVA terminology, that the sum of squares due to the A effect, SS_A, can be represented by $r(\overline{A}_1 - \overline{A}_2)^2$. (The reader is asked to demonstrate this in Exercise 1.) With $r = 3$ we then have

$$3(\overline{A}_1 - \overline{A}_2)^2 = SS_A$$

so that

$$\overline{A}_1 - \overline{A}_2 = \frac{\sqrt{SS_A}}{\sqrt{3}}$$

Since the F statistic for testing the significance of the A effect can be written as $F = SS_A/s^2$, we then have

$$\overline{A}_1 - \overline{A}_2 = s\sqrt{F}/\sqrt{3}$$

$$= st/\sqrt{3}$$

since $t^2_{\alpha/2,\,\nu} = F_{\alpha,1,\nu}$. The length of the (equal) line segments above and below $\overline{x}$ is $(\overline{A}_1 - \overline{A}_2)/2$ and

$$\frac{\overline{A}_1 - \overline{A}_2}{2} = \frac{1}{2}t\frac{s}{\sqrt{3}} \tag{16.7}$$

Notice that the right-hand side of Eq. (16.7) is of the same general form as the right-hand side of Eq. (16.6). Therefore, if the F test (or, equivalently a t test) for the A effect results in $F_{\text{calculated}} = F_{\alpha,1,\nu}$, then

$$\frac{\overline{A}_1 - \overline{A}_2}{2} = \frac{1}{2}t_{\alpha/2,\,\nu}\frac{s}{\sqrt{3}}$$

so that the line segment connecting $\overline{A}_1$ and $\overline{A}_2$ will extend from one of the

α decision lines to the other with $\overline{A}_1$ and $\overline{A}_2$ lying directly on the lines. It follows that if $F_{\text{calculated}} < F_{\alpha, 1, \nu}$ then

$$\frac{\overline{A}_1 - \overline{A}_2}{2} < \frac{1}{2} t_{\alpha/2, \nu} \frac{s}{\sqrt{3}}$$

and the line segment will lie entirely within the decision lines. Conversely, if $F_{\text{calculated}} > F_{\alpha, 1, \nu}$ then

$$\frac{\overline{A}_1 - \overline{A}_2}{2} > \frac{1}{2} t_{\alpha/2, \nu} \frac{s}{\sqrt{3}}$$

and the ends of the line segment will fall outside the decision lines.

Companion results could be easily obtained for the B and AB effects that would show the same type of relationship.

16.4.1 Assumptions

The assumptions upon which ANOM for factorial designs is based are the same as for ANOVA for factorial designs. In particular, we must assume (approximate) normality (since a t table is being used) and equality of variances for every treatment combination.

Ott (1975) suggests using an R chart for verifying the second assumption. The four ranges are 6, 5, 3, and 4 so that $\overline{R} = 4.5$. For $r = 3$ we have $D_4 \overline{R} = 2.57(4.5) = 11.565$. Since all of the ranges are below 11.565 we would thus conclude that there is no evidence of inequality of variances.

The assumption of normality is not crucial since the appropriate t values are relatively insensitive to slight-to-moderate departures from normality. This is fortunate because it is difficult to check normality with only 12 numbers.

16.4.2 An Alternative Way of Displaying Interaction Effects

Schilling (1973a) and Ramig (1983) illustrate ANOM for interaction effects by plotting interaction components that are different from those plotted in the preceding examples [although Schilling (1973b) does give an example of such a display]. For a two-factor design they display interaction components (say, AB_{ij}) where

$$AB_{ij} = \overline{AB}_{ij} - \overline{A}_i - \overline{B}_j + \overline{\overline{x}}$$

where $\overline{AB}_{ij}$, $\overline{A}_i$, and $\overline{B}_j$ are essentially the same as used in the preceding section with i and j denoting the factor levels. (Note that the symbols that these and other writers have used for factor level combinations are slightly different from what was used earlier in this chapter and in Chapter 13. Specifically, they use AB_{ij} instead of A_iB_j.)

There are some problems inherent in this approach, however. First, the AB_{ij} values would be plotted on a display with a centerline of zero, which means that the interaction components would be plotted on a display different from the display used for the main effects. (This could be avoided, however, by adding $\overline{\overline{x}}$ to each AB_{ij} value.) More importantly, the interaction components do not have engineering significance when defined in this way, which is why some people believe that the interaction components should not be displayed. We should remember that ANOM was designed to show engineering significance, so we should determine what is to be plotted with that in mind.

Another major problem with this approach is that the h_α values are not known or determinable as of this writing. Ramig (1983) suggests that an approximation approach given by L. S. Nelson (1983) be used to give approximate h_α values, but this approach was devised for unequal sample sizes and the worth of the procedure for displaying interaction components with equal sample sizes is unknown. Furthermore, the approximation produces upper bounds on the h_α values, so the approach could be too conservative.

Nothing would be gained by displaying these components for any two-level factorial design, anyway, as the four components will be the same except for the sign. There is a potential benefit when used with designs other than two-level designs, however, as they can be used to pinpoint the cell or cells that cause an interaction to be significant. When used for this purpose there is hardly any need for decision lines, as it would already be known that the overall interaction is significant. This use of the interaction components will be illustrated later in the chapter.

16.5 ANOM WHEN AT LEAST ONE FACTOR HAS MORE THAN TWO LEVELS

16.5.1 Main Effects

The analysis is somewhat more involved when at least one of the factors has more than two levels. Ott (1975, p. 253) applied ANOM to data from a $2 \times 3 \times 4$ design with $r = 4$, and P. R. Nelson (1983) used these data as one of his examples for illustrating output from his ANOM computer

Table 16.2 Length of Steel Bars (Coded Data)[a]

	Heat Treatment							
	W				L			
	Machine				Machine			
Time	A	B	C	D	A	B	C	D
1	6	7	1	6	4	6	−1	4
	9	9	2	6	6	5	0	5
	1	5	0	7	0	3	0	5
	3	5	4	3	1	4	1	4
2	6	8	3	7	3	6	2	9
	3	7	2	9	1	4	0	4
	1	4	1	11	1	1	−1	6
	−1	8	0	6	−2	3	1	3
3	5	10	−1	10	6	8	0	4
	4	11	2	5	0	7	−2	3
	9	6	6	4	3	10	4	7
	6	4	1	8	7	0	−4	0

[a] These data originally appeared in Baten (1956). © 1956 American Society for Quality Control. Reprinted by permission.

program for which he listed the FORTRAN code. The data are given in Table 16.2. That output showed the main effects as deviations from $\bar{\bar{x}}$; alternatively, the means could be plotted with a center line of $\bar{\bar{x}}$, as in the previous examples in this chapter. Interactions are another matter, however, since only one of the factors has two levels.

When there is a sizable number of effects to be shown, it is preferable to use more than one ANOM display. Thus, we could show the main effects on one display, and the interaction effects on one or more additional displays.

We begin by computing the average value (length) at each level of each factor. For time we have $\bar{T}_1 = 3.78$, $\bar{T}_2 = 3.625$, and $\bar{T}_3 = 4.47$. For heat treatment we have $\bar{W} = 4.98$ and $\bar{L} = 2.94$. The averages for each machine are $\bar{A} = 3.42$, $\bar{B} = 5.875$, $\bar{C} = 0.875$, and $\bar{D} = 5.67$. The overall average is $\bar{\bar{x}} = 3.96$.

Since heat treatment has only two levels, its decision lines can be obtained from Eq. (16.5) with $h_{\alpha, k, \nu}$ replaced by $t_{\alpha/2, \nu}$. From the computer output given by P. R. Nelson (1983, p. 48), we have $s = \sqrt{6.2153} = 2.493$. (The use of computer software is almost essential for obtaining s with designs that have several factors. If such software was not available, we could, for these data, compute s^2 for each of the 24 cells, and then take the average of the 24 values to obtain the 6.2153.) With 72 degrees of freedom for error we have $t_{.025, 72} = 1.994$, so the decision lines are obtained from

$$\bar{\bar{x}} \pm t_{\alpha/2, \nu} \frac{s}{\sqrt{n}} \sqrt{\frac{1}{2}}$$

$$= \bar{\bar{x}} \pm t_{\alpha/2, \nu} \frac{s}{\sqrt{2n}} \qquad (16.8)$$

$$= 3.96 \pm 1.994 \frac{2.493}{\sqrt{96}}$$

$$= 3.96 \pm 0.51$$

Thus, the .05 decision lines are UDL(.05) = 4.47 and LDL(.05) = 3.45. Since $\bar{W} = 4.98$ and $\bar{L} = 2.94$, these two averages obviously lie outside the .05 decision lines, so it would be desirable to compute the .01 decision lines and see whether or not the averages also lie outside these lines.

With $t_{.005, 72} = 2.646$ we obtain UDL(.01) = 4.63 and LDL(.01) = 3.29, so the averages also lie outside the .01 decision lines. Thus, there is apparently a difference in the effects of the two heat treatments.

It should be noted that these decision lines differ slightly from those obtained by Ott (1975, p. 256). This is due in part to rounding, but primarily to the fact that Ott estimated σ by $\bar{R}/d_2^*$ whereas here we are using s (in accordance with the current methodology), with d_2^* slightly different from d_2. When the cell ranges are used, $(0.9)k(r - 1)$ should be used for the degrees of freedom (before rounding to the nearest integer) in obtaining the value of $t_{\alpha/2, \nu}$, where r and k are as previously defined and $r > 1$.

It should also be noted that Eq. (16.8) is the general formula that should be used in producing the decision lines for the main effects and interaction effects for any two-level factorial design (full or fractional) as well as for other designs that have two-level factors (as in the current example).

The time factor has three levels so the decision lines will not be obtained using a t value. Instead, $h_{\alpha, k, \nu}$ can be obtained from the approximation formula given by L. S. Nelson (1983, p. 43), which generates the exact (to two decimal places) tabular values also given in L. S. Nelson (1983). Alternatively, since the latter does not provide, for a given α, the exact value for 72 degrees of freedom, this could be approximated using linear interpolation in the appropriate table.

The approximation formula is

$$h_{\alpha, k, \nu} = B_1 + B_2 K_1^{B_3} + \left(B_4 + B_5 K_1 \right) V_1 + \left(B_6 + B_7 K_2 + B_8 K_2^2 \right) V_1^2$$

$$(16.9)$$

where

$$k = \text{number of averages}$$

$$K_1 = \ln(k) \qquad (\text{"ln" represents } \log_e)$$

$$K_2 = \ln(k - 2)$$

$$\nu = \text{degrees of freedom for error}$$

and

$$V_1 = 1/(\nu - 1)$$

The values for $B_1, B_2, \ldots, B_8$ are given in Table 16.3.

The use of Eq. (16.9) produces $h_{.05, 3, 72} = 2.398$ where the third decimal place could be off by at most one digit. With Eq. (16.5) we then have the .05 decision lines determined from

$$3.96 \pm 2.398 \frac{2.493}{\sqrt{32}} \sqrt{\frac{2}{3}} = 3.96 \pm 0.86$$

Table 16.3 Constants for Eq. (16.9)[a]

	α			
	0.1	0.05	0.01	0.001
B_1	1.2092	1.7011	2.3539	3.1981
B_2	0.7992	0.6047	0.5176	0.3619
B_3	0.6238	0.7102	0.7107	0.7886
B_4	0.4797	1.4605	4.3161	8.3489
B_5	1.6819	1.9102	2.3629	3.1003
B_6	−0.2155	0.2250	4.6400	27.7005
B_7	0.4529	0.6300	1.8640	5.1277
B_8	−0.6095	−0.2202	0.3204	0.7271

[a] Table 16.3 is from L. S. Nelson (1983), exact critical values for use with the analysis of means. Journal of Quality Technology 15(1) 40–44. © 1983 American Society for Quality Control. Reprinted by permission.

so that UDL(.05) = 4.82 and LDL(.05) = 3.10. Since the three averages for the time factor are all between these numbers, they would also fall between the .01 decision lines, so the time factor appears not to be significant.

The decision lines for the machine factor would be obtained essentially the same way as for the time factor, the only difference being that the machine factor has four levels. The computations reveal that UDL(.05) = 5.07 and LDL(.05) = 2.85. Three of the four averages lie outside of these lines, so it is desirable to compute the .01 decision lines. Doing so produces UDL(.01) = 5.33 and LDL(.01) = 2.59. Since the three averages are also well beyond these decision lines, there is strong evidence of a machine effect.

Although conclusions about each factor can obviously be reached without producing the graphical display, the magnitude of each main effect and the comparison of the effects for the different factors can be seen much better with the display, which is shown in Figure 16.4.

With this display we can clearly see how much larger the machine effect is when compared with the other two main effects, although some comparability is lost due to the fact that the three factors all have different decision lines. In particular, even though the machine effect is obviously greater than

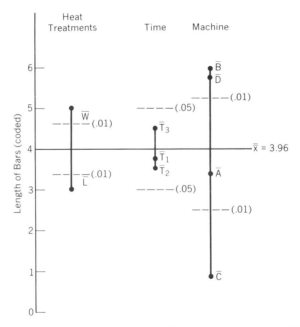

Figure 16.4 ANOM display for main effects for the data in Table 16.2.

the heat treatments effect, the 0.01 decision lines for the machines are noticeably farther apart than those for the heat treatments.

Nevertheless, such an ANOM display can be used effectively.

The display given in Figure 16.4 is somewhat different from the ANOM displays given in other sources. Ott (1975, p. 256) uses lines that are slanted rather than vertical in providing a display of the main effects for these same data. Such a display requires more space than the one in Figure 16.4, however, and space saving can be important when there are several factors. As stated previously, other writers have plotted the distance of each average from $\bar{\bar{x}}$ rather than the averages themselves, using zero for the centerline. This tends to obscure the "engineering significance" of the averages, however, and ANOM was developed for the purpose of providing experimenters with a better "picture" of the results than can be obtained through the use of ANOVA.

16.5.2 Interaction Effects

Just as there are different ways in which the main effects can be displayed, there are also a couple of options for the interaction effects when one factor involved in the interaction has exactly two levels.

Keeping in mind that we want to construct ANOM displays in such a way as to show the practical significance of the values that are charted, we recall that interactions were displayed in Chapter 13 by using interaction profiles.

We start with the heat treatments × machines interaction since the former has exactly two levels. The profile is given in Figure 16.5.

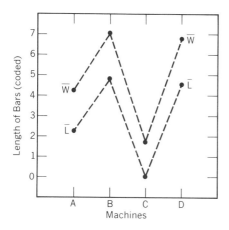

Figure 16.5 Heat treatments × machines interaction profile for the data in Table 16.2.

We can see that there is apparently no interaction effect due to the fact that the lines for $\overline{W}$ and $\overline{L}$ are almost parallel, meaning that the extra length of the steel bars for heat treatment W relative to the length for heat treatment L is virtually the same for each of the four machines.

What is needed in addition to Figure 16.5, however, is an objective way of assessing the interaction effect, preferably within the context of ANOM.

Since the extent to which the differences $\overline{W} - \overline{L}$ differ (over the four machines) provides evidence as to the presence or absence of an interaction effect, it is logical to plot those differences against an appropriate midline and decision lines. This is the approach followed by Ott (1975, p. 259).

Since $\overline{W}$ and $\overline{L}$ are independent, it follows that $\text{Var}(\overline{W} - \overline{L}) = 2\sigma^2/n$, where n is the number of observations from which each average is computed. If we let $\overline{D}_i = \overline{W}_i - \overline{L}_i$ ($i = A, B, C, D$), the midline will be $\overline{\overline{D}}$, and the decision lines computed from

$$\overline{\overline{D}} \pm h_{\alpha,k,\nu} \frac{s\sqrt{2}}{\sqrt{n}} \sqrt{\frac{k-1}{k}}$$

It can be shown that the four differences $\overline{W}_i - \overline{L}_i$ have pairwise correlations of $-1/3$, which is of the general form $-1/(k-1)$ for k means ($\overline{D}_i$) to be plotted. Consequently, the tables contained in L. S. Nelson (1983) can be used to obtain $h_{\alpha,k,\nu}$.

The values for $\overline{D}_i$ and $\overline{\overline{D}}$ are $\overline{D}_A = 1.83$, $\overline{D}_B = 2.25$, $\overline{D}_C = 1.75$, $\overline{D}_D = 2.33$, and $\overline{\overline{D}} = 2.04$. The 0.05 decision lines are then obtained from

$$2.04 \pm 2.52 \frac{2.493\sqrt{2}}{\sqrt{12}} \sqrt{\frac{3}{4}} = 2.04 \pm 2.22$$

so that UDL(.05) = 4.26 and LDL(.05) = -0.18. [These values differ slightly from those given by Ott (1975, p. 258) due primarily to the fact that Ott uses the range method for estimating sigma.] We can see that the $\overline{D}$ values are well within the values for the decision lines, which we would naturally expect since the $\overline{D}$ values differ very little. The ANOM display is given in Figure 16.6.

The other way to construct an ANOM display for this interaction is to compute

$$HM_{ij} = \overline{HM}_{ij} - \overline{H}_i - \overline{M}_j + \overline{\overline{x}}$$

for each of the eight combinations of i and j, where i denotes the ith heat treatment and j denotes the jth machine. These eight combinations would

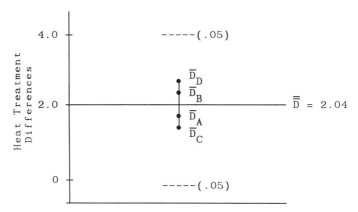

Figure 16.6 ANOM display for heat treatments × machines interaction.

be plotted against decision lines obtained from

$$0 \pm h^*_{\alpha, k, \nu} s \sqrt{\frac{q}{N}}$$

where q is the number of degrees of freedom for the interaction effect, N is the total number of observations, s is as previously defined, and $h^*_{\alpha, k, \nu}$ is an upper bound on the true (unknown) value for $h_{\alpha, k, \nu}$. [An approximation is needed because the deviations $HM_{ij} - \bar{\bar{x}}$ are not equally correlated with $\rho = -1/(k - 1)$ for k deviations.] Using the approach for obtaining an upper bound suggested by L. S. Nelson (1983), we obtain

$$0 \pm 2.554(2.493) \sqrt{\frac{3}{96}} = 0 \pm 1.13$$

The eight values of HM_{ij} are ± 0.104 and ± 0.146, with each of these four values repeated once. The eight values are obviously well within the decision lines where UDL(.05) = 1.13 and LDL(.05) = −1.13.

This approach has two shortcomings—one major and one minor. The main problem is that the HM_{ij} values do not have engineering significance, and the other problem is that the exact value of $h_{\alpha, k, \nu}$ is unknown since the HM_{ij} do not have the requisite correlation structure. In particular, $HM_{ij} = -HM_{i'j}$ for each value of j, where i and i' denote the two heat treatments.

For fixed i, however, HM_{ij} and $HM_{ij'}$ are equally correlated with $\rho = -1/(k - 1)$ for each j and j', so an exact value of $h_{\alpha, k, \nu}$ could be obtained if either of the four HM_{ij} or $HM_{i'j}$ values is plotted.

For the first heat treatment, W, we have $HM_{WA} = -0.104$, $HM_{WB} = 0.104$, $HM_{WC} = -0.146$, and $HM_{WD} = 0.146$. These four values could then be plotted against decision lines obtained from

$$0 \pm h_{\alpha, k, \nu} s \sqrt{\frac{q}{N}}$$

$$= 0 \pm 2.52(2.493) \sqrt{\frac{3}{96}}$$

$$= 0 \pm 1.11$$

where, as before, $\alpha = .05$ and s and N are as previously defined. It should be noted that 1.11 is exactly half of the value (2.22) that was used to produce the decision lines in the approach suggested by Ott. This is due to the fact that, for example, $\overline{D}_A - \overline{\overline{D}}$ equals twice the absolute value of HM_{WA}, and similarly for the other three machines.

Accordingly, either approach could be used to identify the one or more cells that are causing an interaction to be significant. Daniel (1976, p. 41) asserts that, in his experience, a "one-cell" interaction is the type that occurs most frequently, and that for factors with quantitative levels the cell is usually a corner cell.

A simple example should suffice. Consider the set of cell averages given in Table 16.4.

If the "13" in the first cell was changed to a 5, the interaction profile would exhibit two parallel lines, and there would be no interaction effect. Since only one cell is causing an interaction effect [either $(1, 1)$ or $(2, 1)$, where the first number designates the row and the second the column], the overall interaction might not be deemed statistically significant, but the AB_{ij} values can detect the discrepant cell (or cells), which won't always be

Table 16.4 Cell Averages for Illustrative Example

			B			Average
		13	6	5	4	7
	A					
		3	4	3	2	3
Average		8	5	4	3	5

as obvious as in this example. For the discrepant cell we have

$$AB_{11} = \overline{AB}_{11} - \overline{A}_1 - \overline{B}_1 + \overline{\overline{x}}$$

$$= 13 - 7 - 8 + 5$$

$$= 3$$

whereas $AB_{12} = AB_{13} = AB_{14} = -1$, and $AB_{2j} = -AB_{1j}$ for $j = 1, 2, 3, 4$. Thus, a plot of the AB_{2j} or AB_{1j} values with a midline of zero would detect the corner cell (or the cell below it if the AB_{2j} values were plotted), and whether or not AB_{11} (or AB_{21}) is outside the decision lines would depend upon the values of s and the other components that determine the decision lines.

The same message would be received if the $\overline{D}$ values were calculated, where $\overline{D}_1 = 10$, $\overline{D}_2 = 2$, $\overline{D}_3 = 2$, and $\overline{D}_4 = 2$. The values for $(\overline{D}_i - \overline{\overline{D}})$ are 6, -2, -2, and -2, respectively, which, of course, are twice the AB_{1j} values.

The heat treatments $\times$ time interaction could also be analyzed using either of these two methods. For the three different times the $\overline{D}$ values are $\overline{D}_1 = 1.6875$, $\overline{D}_2 = 2.125$, and $\overline{D}_3 = 2.3125$. The .05 decision lines are UDL(.05) = 3.767 and LDL(.05) = 0.316, so the $\overline{D}$ values are well within the decision lines and there is thus no evidence of an interaction effect.

The time $\times$ machines interaction presents a problem since neither of the factors has two levels. The approach using $h^*_{\alpha, k, \nu}$ as an approximation for $h_{\alpha, k, \nu}$ leads to the conclusion that the interaction is not significant for $\alpha = .05$. Ott (1975, p. 259) creates two sets of $\overline{D}$ values after pairing what seem to be the most similar and most dissimilar machines relative to the time factor, with this assessment made after viewing the overall time $\times$ machines interaction profile. This is an ad hoc procedure, but one that can provide important information. In particular, if the differences formed from the most similar machines are judged to be different, then the overall interaction will likely be significant. Conversely, if the differences formed from the least similar machines are not significant then the overall interaction is probably not significant. On the other hand, when the results differ at these two extremes, then no conclusion can be drawn.

This approach suggested by Ott is essentially analogous to the use of a multiple comparison procedure for means; the difference is that there is no exact ANOM procedure for determining whether or not the overall interaction is significant before testing components of that interaction.

P. R. Nelson (1988) has provided a procedure for approximating $h_{\alpha, k, \nu}$ for two-factor interactions where each factor has more than two levels, and for three-factor interactions where at least two of the factors have exactly two levels. That approach could be applied to the time × machines interaction, but it could not be applied to the three-factor interaction since only one of the three factors has two levels.

SUMMARY

Analysis of means (ANOM) is a viable alternative or supplement to analysis of variance. It can be used with either measurement data or attribute data. When used with two-level designs it becomes essentially a graphical t test. The use of ANOM with other designs was also illustrated. Two types of ANOM displays were discussed—one that has engineering significance and one that does not.

APPENDIX TO CHAPTER 16

We stated in Section 16.1 that $s\sqrt{(k-1)/(kn)}$ is the estimated standard deviation of $\overline{X}_i - \overline{\overline{X}}$. This can be demonstrated as follows:

$$\mathrm{Var}\!\left(\overline{X}_i - \overline{\overline{X}}\right)$$

$$= \mathrm{Var}\!\left(\overline{X}_i - \frac{\overline{X}_1 + \cdots + \overline{X}_i + \cdots + \overline{X}_k}{k}\right)$$

$$= \mathrm{Var}(\overline{X}_i) - 2\,\mathrm{Cov}\!\left(\overline{X}_i, \frac{\overline{X}_i}{k}\right) + \mathrm{Var}(\overline{\overline{X}})$$

$$= \frac{\sigma^2}{n} - \frac{2}{k}\left(\frac{\sigma^2}{n}\right) + \frac{\sigma^2}{kn}$$

$$= \frac{\sigma^2(k-1)}{kn}$$

The result then follows after the square root of the last expression is taken, and s is substituted for σ.

REFERENCES

Baten, W. D. (1956). An analysis of variance applied to screw machines. *Industrial Quality Control 12*(10): 8–9 (April).

Daniel, C. (1976). *Applications of Statistics to Industrial Experimentation.* New York: Wiley.

Halperin, M., S. W. Greenhouse, J. Cornfield, and J. Zalokar (1955). Tables of percentage points for the studentized maximum absolute deviate in normal samples. *Journal of the American Statistical Association 50*(269): 185–195 (March).

Nelson, L. S. (1983). Exact critical values for use with the analysis of means. *Journal of Quality Technology 15*(1): 40–44 (January).

Nelson, P. R. (1982). Exact critical points for the analysis of means. *Communications in Statistics—Part A, Theory and Methods 11*(6): 699–709.

Nelson, P. R. (1983). The analysis of means for balanced experimental designs (computer program). *Journal of Quality Technology 15*(1): 45–54 (January).

Nelson, P. R. (1988). Testing for interactions using the analysis of means. *Technometrics 30*(1): 53–61 (February).

Ott, E. R. (1958). *Analysis of Means.* Technical Report #1, Rutgers University.

Ott, E. R. (1967). Analysis of means—a graphical procedure. *Industrial Quality Control 24*(2): 101–109 (August).

Ott, E. R. (1975). *Process Quality Control.* New York: McGraw-Hill.

Ramig, P. F. (1983). Applications of the analysis of means. *Journal of Quality Technology 15*(1): 19–25 (January).

Schilling, E. G. (1973a). A systematic approach to the analysis of means, Part I. Analysis of treatment effects. *Journal of Quality Technology 5*(3): 93–108 (July).

Schilling, E. G. (1973b). A systematic approach to the analysis of means, Part II. Analysis of contrasts; Part III. Analysis of non-normal data. *Journal of Quality Technology 5*(4): 147–159 (October).

Tomlinson, L. H., and R. J. Lavigna (1983). Silicon crystal termination—an application of ANOM for percent defective data. *Journal of Quality Technology 15*(1): 26–32 (January).

EXERCISES

1. Show that for a 2^2 design with r replicates, SS_A can be written as $r(\bar{A}_1 - \bar{A}_2)^2$.

2. Consider the data in Table 13.10. Use 12 as an estimate of sigma and analyze the data using analysis of means, displaying both the .05 and .01 decision lines. Use the "column (3) representation" in Table 13.13 to

compute the two averages (i.e., use the four plus signs to compute one average and the four minus signs to compute the other, for each effect). Compare your results with the results obtained in Chapter 13. Will the conclusions have to be the same? Why or why not?

3. When analysis of variance is applied to a one-way classification with k levels, what is being tested is $\mu_1 = \mu_2 = \cdots = \mu_k$. Write what is being tested, as a function of $\mu_1, \mu_2, \ldots, \mu_k$, when analysis of means is used.

4. Assume that ANOM is being used to analyze proportions data with 10 proportions. If $n = 900$ and $\bar{p} = .02$, what is the numerical value of UDL(.01)?

5. Consider the following data for a one-way classification:

1	2	3	4
11	10	10	13.6
12	14	13	12.6
9	11	8	15.6
13	12	12	11.6
7	8	8	16.6

Analyze the data using both ANOVA and ANOM (use $\alpha = 0.05$). Explain why the two procedures produce different results.

6. A company has five plants that produce automobile headlights. Given below are the number of surface scratches recorded at each plant for 1 month.

Plant Number	Number of Scratches
1	121
2	163
3	148
4	152
5	182

Should any plant(s) be singled out as being either particularly good or bad relative to the others?

Answers to Selected Exercises

Chapter 3

1. $S^2 = 7.3$. Adding a constant to every number in a sample does not change the value of S^2.

5. (a) 0.95053; (d) 0.9545; (e) $z_0 = 1.96$.

7. $1/12$.

9. 0.06681. The probability is approximate since the particular probability distribution was not stated.

15. 2. We would have 3% as the estimate of the proportion nonconforming, and conclude that the process needs improving.

17. 0.9727.

Chapter 5

6. (a) 5.75 assuming a basic CUSUM scheme. (b) 15.

7. When doubt exists as to whether or not an assignable cause was removed.

Chapter 6

3. 13, 2.

4. The moving ranges and moving averages are correlated, so interpreting the charts can be difficult, and the control limits are not strictly valid.

6. An $\overline{X}$ chart is more sensitive in detecting a shift in the process mean (as the answers to exercise #3 indicate).

Chapter 7

1. (a) $2/3$; (c) decrease, 0.02278 (before) 0.0027 (after).
3. 1.475, no.

Chapter 8

1. 0.0462 and 0.2583.
3. Because the lower control limit will be zero.
6. The midline is 0.095 and all of the points are well within the (variable) limits.

Chapter 9

1. (a) 11.58.

Chapter 11

1. 9.
3. (a) No outliers are identified; (b) the estimate of sigma is 3.21.
5. A range frame shows the largest and smallest values for the two variables, and quartiles can also be displayed.

Chapter 12

2. (c) $\hat{Y} = 4.0 - 0.214X$; (d) the plot is parabolic because the relationship between Y and X is parabolic, as can be seen from the scatter plot.
6. (b) $\hat{\beta}_0 = 12.69$; $\hat{\beta}_1 = 1.25$; (c) $R^2 = 0.945$; (d) $(1.02, 1.48)$; (e) $(40.39, 47.49)$.

Chapter 13

3. t will have the same value as t^* since $s_1^2 = s_2^2$.
5. The B effect and the AB interaction seem to be significant ($F = 10.59$).
7. 16.
11. Boxplot.

Chapter 14

1. (a) No, 12 is not a multiple of 2; (b) only main effects.

2. 6.25.

3. No, AB would not be independent of the C and D effects.

5. The first process.

Chapter 15

2. No standard error limits are computed with Simplex EVOP.

8. Simplex EVOP.

Chapter 16

3. k hypotheses are tested: $\mu_i = \dfrac{\mu_1 + \mu_2 + \ldots \mu_k}{k}$ $i = 1, 2, \ldots k.$

4. LDL = 0.0054, UDL = 0.0346.

Appendix: Statistical Tables

Table A Random Numbers[a]

1559	9068	9290	8303	8508	8954	1051	6677	6415	0342
5550	6245	7313	0117	7652	5069	6354	7668	1096	5780
4735	6214	8037	1385	1882	0828	2957	0530	9210	0177
5333	1313	3063	1134	8676	6241	9960	5304	1582	6198
8495	2956	1121	8484	2920	7934	0670	5263	0968	0069
1947	3353	1197	7363	9003	9313	3434	4261	0066	2714
4785	6325	1868	5020	9100	0823	7379	7391	1250	5501
9972	9163	5833	0100	5758	3696	6496	6297	5653	7782
0472	4629	2007	4464	3312	8728	1193	2497	4219	5339
4727	6994	1175	5622	2341	8562	5192	1471	7206	2027
3658	3226	5981	9025	1080	1437	6721	7331	0792	5383
6906	9758	0244	0259	4609	1269	5957	7556	1975	7898
3793	6916	0132	8873	8987	4975	4814	2098	6683	0901
3376	5966	1614	4025	0721	1537	6695	6090	8083	5450
6126	0224	7169	3596	1593	5097	7286	2686	1796	1150
0466	7566	1320	8777	8470	5448	9575	4669	1402	3905
9908	9832	8185	8835	0384	3699	1272	1181	8627	1968
7594	3636	1224	6808	1184	3404	6752	4391	2016	6167
5715	9301	5847	3524	0077	6674	8061	5438	6508	9673
7932	4739	4567	6797	4540	8488	3639	9777	1621	7244
6311	2025	5250	6099	6718	7539	9681	3204	9637	1091
0476	1624	3470	1600	0675	3261	7749	4195	2660	2150
5317	3903	6098	9438	3482	5505	5167	9993	8191	8488
7474	8876	1918	9828	2061	6664	0391	9170	2776	4025
7460	6800	1987	2758	0737	6880	1500	5763	2061	9373
1002	1494	9972	3877	6104	4006	0477	0669	8557	0513
5449	6891	9047	6297	1075	7762	8091	7153	8881	3367
9453	0809	7151	9982	0411	1120	6129	5090	2053	7570
0471	2725	7588	6573	0546	0110	6132	1224	3124	6563
5469	2668	1996	2249	3857	6637	8010	1701	3141	6147
2782	9603	1877	4159	9809	2570	4544	0544	2660	6737
3129	7217	5020	3788	0853	9465	2186	3945	1696	2286
7092	9885	3714	8557	7804	9524	6228	7774	6674	2775
9566	0501	8352	1062	0634	2401	0379	1697	7153	6208
5863	7000	1714	9276	7218	6922	1032	4838	1954	1680

Table A (*Continued*)

5881	9151	2321	3147	6755	2510	5759	6947	7102	0097
6416	9939	9569	0439	1705	4860	9881	7071	9596	8758
9568	3012	6316	9065	0710	2158	1639	9149	4848	8634
0452	9538	5730	1893	1186	9245	6558	9562	8534	9321
8762	5920	8989	4777	2169	7073	7082	9495	1594	8600
0194	0270	7601	0342	3897	4133	7650	9228	5558	3597
3306	5478	2797	1605	4996	0023	9780	9429	3937	7573
7198	3079	2171	6972	0928	6599	9328	0597	5948	5753
8350	4846	1309	0612	4584	4988	4642	4430	9481	9048
7449	4279	4224	1018	2496	2091	9750	6086	1955	9860
6126	5399	0852	5491	6557	4946	9918	1541	7894	1843
1851	7940	9908	3860	1536	8011	4314	7269	7047	0382
7698	4218	2726	5130	3132	1722	8592	9662	4795	7718
0810	0118	4979	0458	1059	5739	7919	4557	0245	4861
6647	7149	1409	6809	3313	0082	9024	7477	7320	5822
3867	7111	5549	9439	3427	9793	3071	6651	4267	8099
1172	7278	7527	2492	6211	9457	5120	4903	1023	5745
6701	1668	5067	0413	7961	7825	9261	8572	0634	1140
8244	0620	8736	2649	1429	6253	4181	8120	6500	8127
8009	4031	7884	2215	2382	1931	1252	8088	2490	9122
1947	8315	9755	7187	4074	4743	6669	6060	2319	0635
9562	4821	8050	0106	2782	4665	9436	4973	4879	8900
0729	9026	9631	8096	8906	5713	3212	8854	3435	4206
6904	2569	3251	0079	8838	8738	8503	6333	0952	1641

[a]Table A was produced using MINITAB, which is a registered trademark of Minitab, Inc., 3081 Enterprise Drive, State College, PA 16801, (814) 238-3280, Telex: 881612.

Table B Normal Distribution[a] **[$P(0 \leq Z \leq z)$ where $Z \sim N(0, 1)$]**

z	0.00	0.01	0.02	0.03	0.04	0.05	0.06	0.07	0.08	0.09
0.0	0.00000	0.00399	0.00798	0.01197	0.01595	0.01994	0.02392	0.02790	0.03188	0.03586
0.1	0.03983	0.04380	0.04776	0.05172	0.05567	0.05962	0.06356	0.06749	0.07142	0.07535
0.2	0.07926	0.08317	0.08706	0.09095	0.09483	0.09871	0.10257	0.10642	0.11026	0.11409
0.3	0.11791	0.12172	0.12552	0.12930	0.13307	0.13683	0.14058	0.14431	0.14803	0.15173
0.4	0.15542	0.15910	0.16276	0.16640	0.17003	0.17364	0.17724	0.18082	0.18439	0.18793
0.5	0.19146	0.19497	0.19847	0.20194	0.20540	0.20884	0.21226	0.21566	0.21904	0.22240
0.6	0.22575	0.22907	0.23237	0.23565	0.23891	0.24215	0.24537	0.24857	0.25175	0.25490
0.7	0.25804	0.26115	0.26424	0.26730	0.27035	0.27337	0.27637	0.27935	0.28230	0.28524
0.8	0.28814	0.29103	0.29389	0.29673	0.29955	0.30234	0.30511	0.30785	0.31057	0.31327
0.9	0.31594	0.31859	0.32121	0.32381	0.32639	0.32894	0.33147	0.33398	0.33646	0.33891
1.0	0.34134	0.34375	0.34614	0.34849	0.35083	0.35314	0.35543	0.35769	0.35993	0.36214
1.1	0.36433	0.36650	0.36864	0.37076	0.37286	0.37493	0.37698	0.37900	0.38100	0.38298
1.2	0.38493	0.38686	0.38877	0.39065	0.39251	0.39435	0.39617	0.39796	0.39973	0.40147
1.3	0.40320	0.40490	0.40658	0.40824	0.40988	0.41149	0.41308	0.41466	0.41621	0.41774
1.4	0.41924	0.42073	0.42220	0.42364	0.42507	0.42647	0.42785	0.42922	0.43056	0.43189
1.5	0.43319	0.43448	0.43574	0.43699	0.43822	0.43943	0.44062	0.44179	0.44295	0.44408
1.6	0.44520	0.44630	0.44738	0.44845	0.44950	0.45053	0.45154	0.45254	0.45352	0.45449
1.7	0.45543	0.45637	0.45728	0.45818	0.45907	0.45994	0.46080	0.46164	0.46246	0.46327
1.8	0.46407	0.46485	0.46562	0.46638	0.46712	0.46784	0.46856	0.46926	0.46995	0.47062
1.9	0.47128	0.47193	0.47257	0.47320	0.47381	0.47441	0.47500	0.47558	0.47615	0.47670
2.0	0.47725	0.47778	0.47831	0.47882	0.47932	0.47982	0.48030	0.48077	0.48124	0.48169
2.1	0.48214	0.48257	0.48300	0.48341	0.48382	0.48422	0.48461	0.48500	0.48537	0.48574
2.2	0.48610	0.48645	0.48679	0.48713	0.48745	0.48778	0.48809	0.48840	0.48870	0.48899
2.3	0.48928	0.48956	0.48983	0.49010	0.49036	0.49061	0.49086	0.49111	0.49134	0.49158
2.4	0.49180	0.49202	0.49224	0.49245	0.49266	0.49286	0.49305	0.49324	0.49343	0.49361
2.5	0.49379	0.49396	0.49413	0.49430	0.49446	0.49461	0.49477	0.49492	0.49506	0.49520
2.6	0.49534	0.49547	0.49560	0.49573	0.49585	0.49598	0.49609	0.49621	0.49632	0.49643
2.7	0.49653	0.49664	0.49674	0.49683	0.49693	0.49702	0.49711	0.49720	0.49728	0.49736
2.8	0.49744	0.49752	0.49760	0.49767	0.49774	0.49781	0.49788	0.49795	0.49801	0.49807
2.9	0.49813	0.49819	0.49825	0.49831	0.49836	0.49841	0.49846	0.49851	0.49856	0.49861
3.0	0.49865	0.49869	0.49874	0.49878	0.49882	0.49886	0.49889	0.49893	0.49896	0.49900
3.1	0.49903	0.49906	0.49910	0.49913	0.49916	0.49918	0.49921	0.49924	0.49926	0.49929
3.2	0.49931	0.49934	0.49936	0.49938	0.49940	0.49942	0.49944	0.49946	0.49948	0.49950
3.3	0.49952	0.49953	0.49955	0.49957	0.49958	0.49960	0.49961	0.49962	0.49964	0.49965
3.4	0.49966	0.49968	0.49969	0.49970	0.49971	0.49972	0.49973	0.49974	0.49975	0.49976
3.5	0.49977	0.49978	0.49978	0.49979	0.49980	0.49981	0.49981	0.49982	0.49983	0.49983
3.6	0.49984	0.49985	0.49985	0.49986	0.49986	0.49987	0.49987	0.49988	0.49988	0.49989
3.7	0.49989	0.49990	0.49990	0.49990	0.49991	0.49991	0.49992	0.49992	0.49992	0.49992
3.8	0.49993	0.49993	0.49993	0.49994	0.49994	0.49994	0.49994	0.49995	0.49995	0.49995
3.9	0.49995	0.49995	0.49996	0.49996	0.49996	0.49996	0.49996	0.49996	0.49997	0.49997

[a] These values were generated using MINITAB.

Table C *t* Distribution[a]

d.f. (ν)/α	0.40	0.25	0.10	0.05	0.01	0.005	0.0025	0.001	0.0005
1	0.325	1.000	3.078	6.314	31.820	63.655	127.315	318.275	636.438
2	0.289	0.816	1.886	2.920	6.965	9.925	14.089	22.327	31.596
3	0.277	0.765	1.638	2.353	4.541	5.841	7.453	10.214	12.923
4	0.271	0.741	1.533	2.132	3.747	4.604	5.597	7.173	8.610
5	0.267	0.727	1.476	2.015	3.365	4.032	4.773	5.893	6.869
6	0.265	0.718	1.440	1.943	3.143	3.707	4.317	5.208	5.959
7	0.263	0.711	1.415	1.895	2.998	3.499	4.029	4.785	5.408
8	0.262	0.706	1.397	1.860	2.896	3.355	3.833	4.501	5.041
9	0.261	0.703	1.383	1.833	2.821	3.250	3.690	4.297	4.781
10	0.260	0.700	1.372	1.812	2.764	3.169	3.581	4.144	4.587
11	0.260	0.697	1.363	1.796	2.718	3.106	3.497	4.025	4.437
12	0.259	0.695	1.356	1.782	2.681	3.055	3.428	3.930	4.318
13	0.259	0.694	1.350	1.771	2.650	3.012	3.372	3.852	4.221
14	0.258	0.692	1.345	1.761	2.624	2.977	3.326	3.787	4.140
15	0.258	0.691	1.341	1.753	2.602	2.947	3.286	3.733	4.073
16	0.258	0.690	1.337	1.746	2.583	2.921	3.252	3.686	4.015
17	0.257	0.689	1.333	1.740	2.567	2.898	3.222	3.646	3.965
18	0.257	0.688	1.330	1.734	2.552	2.878	3.197	3.610	3.922
19	0.257	0.688	1.328	1.729	2.539	2.861	3.174	3.579	3.883
20	0.257	0.687	1.325	1.725	2.528	2.845	3.153	3.552	3.849
21	0.257	0.686	1.323	1.721	2.518	2.831	3.135	3.527	3.819
22	0.256	0.686	1.321	1.717	2.508	2.819	3.119	3.505	3.792
23	0.256	0.685	1.319	1.714	2.500	2.807	3.104	3.485	3.768
24	0.256	0.685	1.318	1.711	2.492	2.797	3.091	3.467	3.745
25	0.256	0.684	1.316	1.708	2.485	2.787	3.078	3.450	3.725
26	0.256	0.684	1.315	1.706	2.479	2.779	3.067	3.435	3.707
27	0.256	0.684	1.314	1.703	2.473	2.771	3.057	3.421	3.690
28	0.256	0.683	1.313	1.701	2.467	2.763	3.047	3.408	3.674
29	0.256	0.683	1.311	1.699	2.462	2.756	3.038	3.396	3.659
30	0.256	0.683	1.310	1.697	2.457	2.750	3.030	3.385	3.646
40	0.255	0.681	1.303	1.684	2.423	2.704	2.971	3.307	3.551
60	0.254	0.679	1.296	1.671	2.390	2.660	2.915	3.232	3.460
100	0.254	0.677	1.290	1.660	2.364	2.626	2.871	3.174	3.391
Infinity	0.253	0.674	1.282	1.645	2.326	2.576	2.807	3.090	3.290

[a] These values were generated using MINITAB.

Table D F Distribution[a, b]

$.05$

$0 \quad F_{\nu_1, \nu_2, .05}$

ν_1	1	2	3	4	5	6	7	8	9	10	11	12	13	14	15

$a.\ F_{\nu_1, \nu_2, .05}$

ν_2	1	2	3	4	5	6	7	8	9	10	11	12	13	14	15
1	161.44	199.50	215.69	224.57	230.16	233.98	236.78	238.89	240.55	241.89	242.97	243.91	244.67	245.35	245.97
2	18.51	19.00	19.16	19.25	19.30	19.33	19.35	19.37	19.39	19.40	19.40	19.41	19.42	19.42	19.43
3	10.13	9.55	9.28	9.12	9.01	8.94	8.89	8.85	8.81	8.79	8.76	8.74	8.73	8.71	8.70
4	7.71	6.94	6.59	6.39	6.26	6.16	6.09	6.04	6.00	5.96	5.94	5.91	5.89	5.87	5.86
5	6.61	5.79	5.41	5.19	5.05	4.95	4.88	4.82	4.77	4.74	4.70	4.68	4.66	4.64	4.62
6	5.99	5.14	4.76	4.53	4.39	4.28	4.21	4.15	4.10	4.06	4.03	4.00	3.98	3.96	3.94
7	5.59	4.74	4.35	4.12	3.97	3.87	3.79	3.73	3.68	3.64	3.60	3.57	3.55	3.53	3.51
8	5.32	4.46	4.07	3.84	3.69	3.58	3.50	3.44	3.39	3.35	3.31	3.28	3.26	3.24	3.22
9	5.12	4.26	3.86	3.63	3.48	3.37	3.29	3.23	3.18	3.14	3.10	3.07	3.05	3.03	3.01
10	4.96	4.10	3.71	3.48	3.33	3.22	3.14	3.07	3.02	2.98	2.94	2.91	2.89	2.86	2.85
11	4.84	3.98	3.59	3.36	3.20	3.09	3.01	2.95	2.90	2.85	2.82	2.79	2.76	2.74	2.72
12	4.75	3.89	3.49	3.26	3.11	3.00	2.91	2.85	2.80	2.75	2.72	2.69	2.66	2.64	2.62
13	4.67	3.81	3.41	3.18	3.03	2.92	2.83	2.77	2.71	2.67	2.63	2.60	2.58	2.55	2.53
14	4.60	3.74	3.34	3.11	2.96	2.85	2.76	2.70	2.65	2.60	2.57	2.53	2.51	2.48	2.46
15	4.54	3.68	3.29	3.06	2.90	2.79	2.71	2.64	2.59	2.54	2.51	2.48	2.45	2.42	2.40
16	4.49	3.63	3.24	3.01	2.85	2.74	2.66	2.59	2.54	2.49	2.46	2.42	2.40	2.37	2.35
17	4.45	3.59	3.20	2.96	2.81	2.70	2.61	2.55	2.49	2.45	2.41	2.38	2.35	2.33	2.31
18	4.41	3.55	3.16	2.93	2.77	2.66	2.58	2.51	2.46	2.41	2.37	2.34	2.31	2.29	2.27
19	4.38	3.52	3.13	2.90	2.74	2.63	2.54	2.48	2.42	2.38	2.34	2.31	2.28	2.26	2.23
20	4.35	3.49	3.10	2.87	2.71	2.60	2.51	2.45	2.39	2.35	2.31	2.28	2.25	2.22	2.20
21	4.32	3.47	3.07	2.84	2.68	2.57	2.49	2.42	2.37	2.32	2.28	2.25	2.22	2.20	2.18
22	4.30	3.44	3.05	2.82	2.66	2.55	2.46	2.40	2.34	2.30	2.26	2.23	2.20	2.17	2.15
23	4.28	3.42	3.03	2.80	2.64	2.53	2.44	2.37	2.32	2.27	2.24	2.20	2.18	2.15	2.13
24	4.26	3.40	3.01	2.78	2.62	2.51	2.42	2.36	2.30	2.25	2.22	2.18	2.15	2.13	2.11
25	4.24	3.39	2.99	2.76	2.60	2.49	2.40	2.34	2.28	2.24	2.20	2.16	2.14	2.11	2.09
26	4.23	3.37	2.98	2.74	2.59	2.47	2.39	2.32	2.27	2.22	2.18	2.15	2.12	2.09	2.07
27	4.21	3.35	2.96	2.73	2.57	2.46	2.37	2.31	2.25	2.20	2.17	2.13	2.10	2.08	2.06
28	4.20	3.34	2.95	2.71	2.56	2.45	2.36	2.29	2.24	2.19	2.15	2.12	2.09	2.06	2.04
29	4.18	3.33	2.93	2.70	2.55	2.43	2.35	2.28	2.22	2.18	2.14	2.10	2.08	2.05	2.03
30	4.17	3.32	2.92	2.69	2.53	2.42	2.33	2.27	2.21	2.16	2.13	2.09	2.06	2.04	2.01
40	4.08	3.23	2.84	2.61	2.45	2.34	2.25	2.18	2.12	2.08	2.04	2.00	1.97	1.95	1.92

Table D (*Continued*)

$$b.\ F_{\nu_1, \nu_2, 0.01}$$

ν_1	1	2	3	4	5	6	7	8	9	10	11	12	13	14	15
ν_2															
1	4052.45	4999.42	5402.96	5624.03	5763.93	5858.82	5928.73	5981.06	6021.73	6055.29	6083.22	6106.00	6125.37	6142.48	6157.06
2	98.51	99.00	99.17	99.25	99.30	99.33	99.35	99.38	99.39	99.40	99.41	99.41	99.42	99.42	99.43
3	34.12	30.82	29.46	28.71	28.24	27.91	27.67	27.49	27.35	27.23	27.13	27.05	26.98	26.92	26.87
4	21.20	18.00	16.69	15.98	15.52	15.21	14.98	14.80	14.66	14.55	14.45	14.37	14.31	14.25	14.20
5	16.26	13.27	12.06	11.39	10.97	10.67	10.46	10.29	10.16	10.05	9.96	9.89	9.82	9.77	9.72
6	13.74	10.92	9.78	9.15	8.75	8.47	8.26	8.10	7.98	7.87	7.79	7.72	7.66	7.60	7.56
7	12.25	9.55	8.45	7.85	7.46	7.19	6.99	6.84	6.72	6.62	6.54	6.47	6.41	6.36	6.31
8	11.26	8.65	7.59	7.01	6.63	6.37	6.18	6.03	5.91	5.81	5.73	5.67	5.61	5.56	5.52
9	10.56	8.02	6.99	6.42	6.06	5.80	5.61	5.47	5.35	5.26	5.18	5.11	5.05	5.01	4.96
10	10.04	7.56	6.55	5.99	5.64	5.39	5.20	5.06	4.94	4.85	4.77	4.71	4.65	4.60	4.56
11	9.65	7.21	6.22	5.67	5.32	5.07	4.89	4.74	4.63	4.54	4.46	4.40	4.34	4.29	4.25
12	9.33	6.93	5.95	5.41	5.06	4.82	4.64	4.50	4.39	4.30	4.22	4.16	4.10	4.05	4.01
13	9.07	6.70	5.74	5.21	4.86	4.62	4.44	4.30	4.19	4.10	4.02	3.96	3.91	3.86	3.82
14	8.86	6.51	5.56	5.04	4.69	4.46	4.28	4.14	4.03	3.94	3.86	3.80	3.75	3.70	3.66
15	8.68	6.36	5.42	4.89	4.56	4.32	4.14	4.00	3.89	3.80	3.73	3.67	3.61	3.56	3.52
16	8.53	6.23	5.29	4.77	4.44	4.20	4.03	3.89	3.78	3.69	3.62	3.55	3.50	3.45	3.41
17	8.40	6.11	5.18	4.67	4.34	4.10	3.93	3.79	3.68	3.59	3.52	3.46	3.40	3.35	3.31
18	8.29	6.01	5.09	4.58	4.25	4.01	3.84	3.71	3.60	3.51	3.43	3.37	3.32	3.27	3.23
19	8.18	5.93	5.01	4.50	4.17	3.94	3.77	3.63	3.52	3.43	3.36	3.30	3.24	3.19	3.15
20	8.10	5.85	4.94	4.43	4.10	3.87	3.70	3.56	3.46	3.37	3.29	3.23	3.18	3.13	3.09
21	8.02	5.78	4.87	4.37	4.04	3.81	3.64	3.51	3.40	3.31	3.24	3.17	3.12	3.07	3.03
22	7.95	5.72	4.82	4.31	3.99	3.76	3.59	3.45	3.35	3.26	3.18	3.12	3.07	3.02	2.98
23	7.88	5.66	4.76	4.26	3.94	3.71	3.54	3.41	3.30	3.21	3.14	3.07	3.02	2.97	2.93
24	7.82	5.61	4.72	4.22	3.90	3.67	3.50	3.36	3.26	3.17	3.09	3.03	2.98	2.93	2.89
25	7.77	5.57	4.68	4.18	3.85	3.63	3.46	3.32	3.22	3.13	3.06	2.99	2.94	2.89	2.85
26	7.72	5.53	4.64	4.14	3.82	3.59	3.42	3.29	3.18	3.09	3.02	2.96	2.90	2.86	2.81
27	7.68	5.49	4.60	4.11	3.78	3.56	3.39	3.26	3.15	3.06	2.99	2.93	2.87	2.82	2.78
28	7.64	5.45	4.57	4.07	3.75	3.53	3.36	3.23	3.12	3.03	2.96	2.90	2.84	2.79	2.75
29	7.60	5.42	4.54	4.04	3.73	3.50	3.33	3.20	3.09	3.00	2.93	2.87	2.81	2.77	2.73
30	7.56	5.39	4.51	4.02	3.70	3.47	3.30	3.17	3.07	2.98	2.91	2.84	2.79	2.74	2.70
40	7.31	5.18	4.31	3.83	3.51	3.29	3.12	2.99	2.89	2.80	2.73	2.66	2.61	2.56	2.52

[a] These values were generated using MINITAB.

[b] ν_2 = degrees of freedom for the denominator; ν_1 = degrees of freedom for the numerator.

Table E Control Chart Constants

n	For Estimating Sigma		For $\bar{X}$ Chart		For $\bar{X}$ Chart (Standard Given)	For R Chart		For R Chart (Standard Given)		For s chart (Standard Given)			
	c_4^*	d_2	A_2	A_3	A	D_3	D_4	D_1	D_2	B_3	B_4	B_5^*	B_6^*
2	0.7979	1.128	1.880	2.659	2.121	0	3.267	0	3.686	0	3.267	0	2.606
3	0.8862	1.693	1.023	1.954	1.732	0	2.575	0	4.358	0	2.568	0	2.276
4	0.9213	2.059	0.729	1.628	1.500	0	2.282	0	4.698	0	2.266	0	2.088
5	0.9400	2.326	0.577	1.427	1.342	0	2.115	0	4.918	0	2.089	0	1.964
6	0.9515	2.534	0.483	1.287	1.225	0	2.004	0	5.078	0.030	1.970	0.029	1.874
7	0.9594	2.704	0.419	1.182	1.134	0.076	1.924	0.205	5.203	0.118	1.882	0.113	1.806
8	0.9650	2.847	0.373	1.099	1.061	0.136	1.864	0.387	5.307	0.185	1.815	0.179	1.751
9	0.9693	2.970	0.337	1.032	1.000	0.184	1.816	0.546	5.394	0.239	1.761	0.232	1.707
10	0.9727	3.078	0.308	0.975	0.949	0.223	1.777	0.687	5.469	0.284	1.716	0.276	1.669
15	0.9823	3.472	0.223	0.789	0.775	0.348	1.652	1.207	5.737	0.428	1.572	0.421	1.544
20	0.9869	3.735	0.180	0.680	0.671	0.414	1.586	1.548	5.922	0.510	1.490	0.504	1.470
25	0.9896	3.931	0.153	0.606	0.600	0.459	1.541	1.804	6.058	0.565	1.435	0.559	1.420

*Columns marked with an asterisk are from The American Society for Quality Control Standard A1, Table 1, 1987. Reprinted with permission of the American Society for Quality Control. The balance of the table is from Table B2 of the *A.S.T.M. Manual of Quality Control of Materials*. Copyright American Society for Testing Materials. Reprinted with permission.

Table F Percentage Points of the Sample Range for Producing Probability Limits for R Charts[a]

D/n	4	5	6	7	8	9	10
0.0005	0.158	0.308	0.464	0.613	0.751	0.878	0.995
0.0010	0.199	0.367	0.535	0.691	0.835	0.966	1.085
0.0050	0.343	0.555	0.749	0.922	1.075	1.212	1.335
0.0100	0.434	0.665	0.870	1.048	1.205	1.343	1.467
0.9900	4.403	4.603	4.757	4.882	4.987	5.078	5.157
0.9950	4.694	4.886	5.033	5.154	5.255	5.341	5.418
0.9990	5.309	5.484	5.619	5.730	5.823	5.903	5.973
0.9995	5.553	5.722	5.853	5.960	6.050	6.127	6.196

[a] These values have been adapted from Table 1 of H. L. Harter, Tables of range and studentized range. *The Annals of Mathematical Statistics 31* (4), December 1960. Reprinted with permission of The Institute of Mathematical Statistics.

Table G Analysis of Means Constants[a]

									Number of Means, k									
d.f.[b] (ν)	3	4	5	6	7	8	9	10	11	12	13	14	15	16	17	18	19	20

a. $h_{0.05}$

d.f.[b] (ν)	3	4	5	6	7	8	9	10	11	12	13	14	15	16	17	18	19	20
3	4.18																	
4	3.56	3.89																
5	3.25	3.53	3.72															
6	3.07	3.31	3.49	3.62														
7	2.94	3.17	3.33	3.45	3.56													
8	2.86	3.07	3.21	3.33	3.43	3.51												
9	2.79	2.99	3.13	3.24	3.33	3.41	3.48											
10	2.74	2.93	3.07	3.17	3.26	3.33	3.40	3.45										
11	2.70	2.88	3.01	3.12	3.20	3.27	3.33	3.39	3.44									
12	2.67	2.85	2.97	3.07	3.15	3.22	3.28	3.33	3.38	3.42								
13	2.64	2.81	2.94	3.03	3.11	3.18	3.24	3.29	3.34	3.38	3.42							
14	2.62	2.79	2.91	3.00	3.08	3.14	3.20	3.25	3.30	3.34	3.37	3.41						
15	2.60	2.76	2.88	2.97	3.05	3.11	3.17	3.22	3.26	3.30	3.34	3.37	3.40					
16	2.58	2.74	2.86	2.95	3.02	3.09	3.14	3.19	3.23	3.27	3.31	3.34	3.37	3.40				
17	2.57	2.73	2.84	2.93	3.00	3.06	3.12	3.16	3.21	3.25	3.28	3.31	3.34	3.37	3.40			
18	2.55	2.71	2.82	2.91	2.98	3.04	3.10	3.14	3.18	3.22	3.26	3.29	3.32	3.35	3.37	3.40		
19	2.54	2.70	2.81	2.89	2.96	3.02	3.08	3.12	3.16	3.20	3.24	3.27	3.30	3.32	3.35	3.37	3.40	
20	2.53	2.68	2.79	2.88	2.95	3.01	3.06	3.11	3.15	3.18	3.22	3.25	3.28	3.30	3.33	3.35	3.37	3.40
24	2.50	2.65	2.75	2.83	2.90	2.96	3.01	3.05	3.09	3.13	3.16	3.19	3.22	3.24	3.27	3.29	3.31	3.33
30	2.47	2.61	2.71	2.79	2.85	2.91	2.96	3.00	3.04	3.07	3.10	3.13	3.16	3.18	3.20	3.22	3.25	3.27
40	2.43	2.57	2.67	2.75	2.81	2.86	2.91	2.95	2.98	3.01	3.04	3.07	3.10	3.12	3.14	3.16	3.18	3.20
60	2.40	2.54	2.63	2.70	2.76	2.81	2.86	2.90	2.93	2.96	2.99	3.02	3.04	3.06	3.08	3.10	3.12	3.14
120	2.37	2.50	2.59	2.66	2.72	2.77	2.81	2.84	2.88	2.91	2.93	2.96	2.98	3.00	3.02	3.04	3.06	3.08
Infinity	2.34	2.47	2.56	2.62	2.68	2.72	2.76	2.80	2.83	2.86	2.88	2.90	2.93	2.95	2.97	2.98	3.00	3.02

Table G (*Continued*)

[a]From Tables 2 and 3 of L. S. Nelson, Exact critical values for use with the analysis of means. *Journal of Quality Technology 15*(1), January 1983. Reprinted with permission of the American Society for Quality Control.
[b]Degrees of freedom for *s*.

b. $h_{0.01}$

d.f.[b] (v)	3	4	5	6	7	8	9	10	11	12	13	14	15	16	17	18	19	20
3	7.51																	
4	5.74	6.21																
5	4.93	5.29	5.55															
6	4.48	4.77	4.98	5.16														
7	4.18	4.44	4.63	4.78	4.90													
8	3.98	4.21	4.38	4.52	4.63	4.72												
9	3.84	4.05	4.20	4.33	4.43	4.51	4.59											
10	3.73	3.92	4.07	4.18	4.28	4.36	4.43	4.49										
11	3.64	3.82	3.96	4.07	4.16	4.23	4.30	4.36	4.41									
12	3.57	3.74	3.87	3.98	4.06	4.13	4.20	4.25	4.31	4.35								
13	3.51	3.68	3.80	3.90	3.98	4.05	4.11	4.17	4.22	4.26	4.30							
14	3.46	3.63	3.74	3.84	3.92	3.98	4.04	4.09	4.14	4.18	4.22	4.26						
15	3.42	3.58	3.69	3.79	3.86	3.92	3.98	4.03	4.08	4.12	4.16	4.19	4.22					
16	3.38	3.54	3.65	3.74	3.81	3.87	3.93	3.98	4.02	4.06	4.10	4.14	4.17	4.20				
17	3.35	3.50	3.61	3.70	3.77	3.83	3.89	3.93	3.98	4.02	4.05	4.09	4.12	4.14	4.17			
18	3.33	3.47	3.58	3.66	3.73	3.79	3.85	3.89	3.94	3.97	4.01	4.04	4.07	4.10	4.12	4.15		
19	3.30	3.45	3.55	3.63	3.70	3.76	3.81	3.86	3.90	3.94	3.97	4.00	4.03	4.06	4.08	4.11	4.13	
20	3.28	3.42	3.53	3.61	3.67	3.73	3.78	3.83	3.87	3.90	3.94	3.97	4.00	4.02	4.05	4.07	4.09	4.12
24	3.21	3.35	3.45	3.52	3.58	3.64	3.69	3.73	3.77	3.80	3.83	3.86	3.89	3.91	3.94	3.96	3.98	4.00
30	3.15	3.28	3.37	3.44	3.50	3.55	3.59	3.63	3.67	3.70	3.73	3.76	3.78	3.81	3.83	3.85	3.87	3.89
40	3.09	3.21	3.29	3.36	3.42	3.46	3.50	3.54	3.58	3.60	3.63	3.66	3.68	3.70	3.72	3.74	3.76	3.78
60	3.03	3.14	3.22	3.29	3.34	3.38	3.42	3.46	3.49	3.51	3.54	3.56	3.59	3.61	3.63	3.64	3.66	3.68
120	2.97	3.07	3.15	3.21	3.26	3.30	3.34	3.37	3.40	3.42	3.45	3.47	3.49	3.51	3.55	3.55	3.56	3.58
Infinity	2.91	3.01	3.08	3.14	3.18	3.22	3.26	3.29	3.32	3.34	3.36	3.38	3.40	3.42	3.44	3.45	3.47	3.48

Index